The State and the Private Sector in Latin America

The State and the Private Sector in Latin America

The Shift to Partnership

Mauricio Font

palgrave
macmillan

THE STATE AND THE PRIVATE SECTOR IN LATIN AMERICA

First published in 2015 by
PALGRAVE MACMILLAN®
in the United States—a division of St. Martin's Press LLC,
175 Fifth Avenue, New York, NY 10010.

Where this book is distributed in the UK, Europe and the rest of the world, this is by Palgrave Macmillan, a division of Macmillan Publishers Limited, registered in England, company number 785998, of Houndmills, Basingstoke, Hampshire RG21 6XS.

Palgrave Macmillan is the global academic imprint of the above companies and has companies and representatives throughout the world.

ISBN: 978–0–230–11140–0

Library of Congress Cataloging-in-Publication Data is available from the Library of Congress.

A catalogue record of the book is available from the British Library.

Design by Newgen Knowledge Works (P) Ltd., Chennai, India.

First edition: June 2015

10 9 8 7 6 5 4 3 2 1

CONTENTS

FIGURES

TABLES

ABBREVIATIONS

ADB	Asian Development Bank
ALL	Latin American Logistics (America Latina Logística)
ALLMN	Latin American Logistics, Northern Network (América Latina Logística Malha Norte S.A)
ANAC	National Civil Aviation Agency (Agência Nacional de Aviação Civil)
ANI	National Infrastructure Agency (Agencia Nacional de Infraestructura)
ANTT	National Ground Transport Agency (Agência Nacional de Transportes Terrestres)
BDP	Bureau for Development Policy
BNDES	Brazilian National Development Bank (Banco Nacional de Desenvolvimento Economico e Social)
BOT	Build-Operate-Transfer
CEF	Federal Savings Bank (Caixa Econômica Federal)
CEPAL	Economic Commission for Latin America and the Caribbean (Comisión Económica para América Latina y el Caribe)
CONAIE	Confederation of Indigenous Nationalities of Ecuador (La Confederación de Nacionalidades Indígenas del Ecuador)
CONAMA	National Environmental Commission (Comisión Nacional del Medio Ambiente)
COREMA	Regional Environmental Commission (Comisión Regional del Medio Ambiente)
CVRD	Brazilian Mining Company (Companhia Vale do Rio Doce)
DNIT	National Department of Transport Infrastructure (Departamento Nacional de Infraestrutura de Transportes)

DNP	National Planning Department (Departamento Nacional de Planeación)
DTPM	Metropolitan Public Transportation Board (Directorio de Transporte Público Metropolitano)
ECLAC	Economic Commission for Latin America and the Caribbean (Also known as CEPAL)
EFC	Estrada de Ferro Carajás
EMBRAPA	Brazilian Agricultural Research Corporation (Empresa-Brasileira de Pesquisa Agropecuaria)
EPL	Brazilian Logistics and Planning Company (Empresa de Planejamento e Logística)
FARAC	Mexican Toll Road Bailout Fund (Fideicomiso de Apoyo para el Rescate de Autopistas Concesionadas)
FCA	Ferrovia Centro Atlântica
FEPASA	Paulista Railways (Ferrovia Paulista S.A.)
Ferroanel	Metropolitan São Paulo Rail Bypass
Ferroban	Ferrovias Bandeirantes S.A.
Ferronorte	Ferronorte Railroad (Ferrovia Ferronorte)
FNS	North-South Railway (Ferrovia Norte-Sul)
IBGE	Brazilian Institute of Geography and Statistics (Instituto Brasileiro de Geografia e Estatística)
IDB	Inter-American Development Bank
IFC	International Finance Corporation
IIRSA	Regional South American Infrastructure (Iniciativa para la Integración de la Infraestructura Regional Suramericana)
IMF	International Monetary Fund
INCO	National Institute of Concessions (Instituto Nacional de Concesiones)
Infraero	Brazilian Airport Infrastructure Company (Empresa Brasileira de Infraestrutura Aeroportuária)
ISI	Import Substitution Industrialization
MAS	Movement toward Socialism (Movimiento al Socialismo)
NAFTA	North American Free Trade Agreement
OECD	Organization for Economic Co-operation and Development
PAC	Growth Acceleration Program (Programa de Aceleração do Crescimento)
PAN	National Action Party (Partido Acción Nacional)
PEMEX	Mexican Petroleums (Petróleo Mexicanos)

PIAPPEM	Program to Promote Public-Private Partnerships in Mexican States (Programa para el Impulso de Asociaciones Público-Privadas en Estados Mexicanos)
PIL	Logistics Investment Plan (Programa de Investimentos em Logística)
PPA	Pluriannual Plan (Plano Plurianual)
PPI	Private Participation in Infrastructure
PPP	Public-Private Partnerships
PPS	Projects for the Provision of Services (Proyectos para Prestación de Servicios)
PRD	Party of the Democratic Revolution (Partido de la Revolución Democrática)
PRI	Institutional Revolutionary Party (Partido Revolucionario Institucional)
PSDB	Brazilian Social Democratic Party (Partido da Social Democracia Brasileira)
PSP	Private Sector Participation
PTUS	Plan for Santiago's Urban Transportation (Plan de Transporte Urbano para Santiago)
RFFSA	Federal Railroad Network (Rede Ferroviária Federal S. A)
RMSP	São Paulo's Metropolitan Region (Regiao Metropolitana de São Paulo)
SAC	Civil Aviation Secretariat (Secretaría de Aviación Civil)
SCT	Ministry of Communications and Transport (Secretaría de Comunicaciones y Transportes)
SEP	Ports Secretariat (Secretaria Especial de Portos)
TCU	Federal Auditing Court (Tribunal de Contas da União)
VALE	Brazilian Mining Company (Companhia Vale do Rio Doce, formally known as CVRD)
Valec	Construction, Engineering and Railways S. A
WB	World Bank
WEF	World Economic Forum
WTO	World Trade Organization
YPF	Treasury Petroleum Fields (Yacimientos Petrolíferos Fiscales)

PREFACE

The idea of a book on public-private collaboration in Latin America seemed straightforward when I first conceived it in the early 2000s. Key countries in this region were praising its role in addressing huge infrastructure gaps and bottlenecks. New programs and projects were designed in Mexico, Chile, and Argentina, while Brazil nodded its approval to concessions and public-private partnerships. The regional debate revolved around identifying policy approaches, the conditions shaping outcomes, and promising or best practices. The main challenge, I thought, was to clarify the mix of institutions, skills, and resources required by emergent state roles. Three years seemed enough to produce such a volume.

Soon new phenomena would challenge my optimism: political shifts in several South American societies now questioned liberalizing premises underlying public-private collaboration; global financial crises and other shocks altered fiscal dynamics; corruption scandals fueled doubt; seemingly robust booms in minerals, hydrocarbons, and other commodities eventually sputtered. Public-private cooperation in Latin America was not quite as open-and-shut a case as I had imagined. Inevitably, updating case studies and adjusting my thinking on the subject prolonged research and analysis.

Responding to these complications, my approach also evolved toward an even stronger emphasis on the embeddedness of public-private collaboration in the reforms of the last part of the twentieth century. Thus, this study explores the liberalization policies embraced or resisted over a few decades. The political economy analysis focuses on political and institutional contexts as well as on external shocks shaping broad processes of state reform. This study relies on literature review, compilation of data from various sources, interviews with experts and practitioners, and site visits to Brazil and Chile.

My first task here is to thank my supporters, associates, sources, and Palgrave MacMillan for their ideas and patience. Hopefully, they will understand why this project called for a more complex analysis that extended for a decade. The Tinker Foundation provided a generous grant that enabled the first-hand interviews, data collection, fieldwork, and writing an early first draft. Colleagues and policymakers from various institutions and agencies provided major insights. In Chile I thank former president Ricardo Lagos and the well-trained reformers that brought fresh thinking and policies to transportation and other urban infrastructure needs. In Brazil I gained insights from past planning minister Martus Tavares and federal planners and policymakers as well as counterparts in the innovative states of São Paulo and Minas Gerais. Needless, I alone am responsible for the conclusions reached in this volume.

At the Bildner Center for Western Hemisphere Studies and the Graduate Center, I am happy to acknowledge the thorough research, editorial, and technical assistance provided by David Jancsics and Rosalina López, as well as by Natalia Sofyina, Janaina Saad, Miguel Barbosa, Whitney Bren, Sophia Balis, Jonathan Aguirre, and Loren Peabody. Jackie Slater, María Paris, Alejandra Kubitscheck Bujones, Jennifer Sugg, and Letizzia Wastavino worked in earlier phases of this undertaking. The Graduate Center and Queens College, City University of New York, offered essential support and superb home for research. To the above and many others I am deeply grateful.

March 30, 2015

Mauricio Font

CHAPTER ONE

State and Market in Global Development

The state has been implicated in major transformations since the last third of the twentieth century, though there is hardly full agreement on this role. In the study of globalization, the nation-state remains a major point of contention; while globalists link globalization to lesser roles for national governments, skeptics posit the latter's enduring centrality (Held and McGrew, 2007; Fritz and Menocal, 2006; Hollingsworth and Boyer, 1997; Baccaro and Howell, 2011).[1] Similarly, the fields of development and post-socialism contrast the dynamics and relative merits of state-centered and market-driven models of social transformation (Evans, 1995). Studies focusing on "varieties of capitalism" in Europe distinguish between state-coordinated regimes and the liberal polities in which markets are presumed as central (Hall and Soskice, 2001; Thelen, 2012). In turn, policymakers working within alternative approaches to governance hold in high esteem the specific impact and policy issues associated with them.

Informed by these broad debates, this book focuses on an area of state action where government and the private sector actually work together—forms of public-private collaboration to enhance infrastructure and development. Such initiatives are found in all major world regions. Their impact, current or prospective, is increasingly salient throughout Latin America, the main focus in this book. Against warnings about its demise, the state retains a major involvement in a broad range of activities central to development.

Openness to increased private participation in infrastructure is embedded in the evolving liberalizing drives initiated in the 1980s and 1990s. In that light, policies promoting it are embedded in broader processes that redefine state action and expand the role of private actors and markets. In transitional and other emergent economies, reforms have transferred state assets or their control to the private sector. As part of this movement, policymakers downgrade direct economic intervention to concentrate on strengthening institutional capabilities in a reduced number of functions: beyond national defense and public security, the list often includes economic stability, improving the collection and allocation of tax revenues, reorganizing national finances, better overall administration, more effective provision of social needs (health, education, welfare), and overall coordination of infrastructure development. The rethinking of relations between government, the private sector, and civil society remains a contested issue. In a growing list of cases, it has resulted in hybrid public-private solutions with a pragmatic rather than ideological orientation.

This volume explores shifts in theory and practice in the relative roles of public and market actors, with special attention to the provision of infrastructure and related public goods. Concessions, public-private partnerships (PPP), and other hybrid business models have spread and persisted despite lingering opposition to reforms from critics. However, anti-liberalization movements, stoked by financial downturns and political shifts, have in some cases succeeded in blocking or reversing some processes of reform. As it explores specific instances of public-private collaboration, this book assesses the broader debate about the role of government and the conditions fostering collaboration.

Modern concessions and partnerships are a distinctive new phenomenon. As privatization via divestiture seemed to reach its limits in the 1990s (see table 2.1), policymakers started to invite the private sector to join new ways for meeting growing demands for better infrastructure and public services. Unlike traditional public procurement and state-owned enterprises, public-private collaboration brings together the two sectors to share risks and resources in the constructing of major projects or delivery of a service for an extended period of time (table A.1). They are often part of a distinctive entrepreneurial model between the traditional private-public dichotomy. Concessions and partnerships have expanded, often quite fast. By 2007, over 60 countries—industrialized, emergent, transitional, and developing alike—were making increasing use of them to provide infrastructure. The global economic recession of 2008 brought down the rate of adoption, but the trend away from insulated states resumed by 2010.

This phenomenon is puzzling. During much of the twentieth century, government generally expanded, insisting on its monopoly over a wide range of areas. In liberal democracies, a simple dichotomy governed the debate about the relative roles of state and market in providing infrastructure. Defined as goods that could not be denied to anyone once they were provided, the costs of public goods could not easily be recovered nor profits generated. The absence of incentives for the private sector to provide them meant that government would need to do so.[2] Policymakers were also driven by the assumption that infrastructure and related areas of state action were natural monopolies that only government could supply. Government was thus responsible for public transportation, streets and highways, ports and airports, water, electricity, and other forms of basic infrastructure. State-centered paradigms added ideological and political defense for this position. Meanwhile, various studies have shown that adequate levels of infrastructure are essential for economic growth, job creation, competitiveness, equity, and the overall quality of life (Andrés, Diop, and Guasch, 2008; Carranza et al., 2011; Calderón and Servén, 2010b; Delmon, 2009; Straub, 2008; World Bank, 1994).

After increasing in periods of modernization, infrastructure expenditures settled at the level of 3–6 percent of GDP (Delmon, 2009). Together with defense and welfare, infrastructure was one of the reasons for state expansion in the twentieth century. In key European countries and the United States, government expenditures grew from an average of less than 13 percent of GDP in 1913 to 44.1 percent in 2005 and 47.7 percent in 2009 (table 1.1). Public spending in the Latin American cases discussed in this volume expanded from a mean of 26.4 in the 1995–1999 period to 33 percent in 2013 (table 1.2).

Against the background of twentieth-century state expansion, recurrent fiscal crises after the 1980s made the limits of state action a major

Table 1.1 Expansion of the state, government spending as percent of GDP

	1870	*1913*	*1920*	*1937*	*1960*	*1980*	*1990*	*2000*	*2005*	*2009*
United States	7.3	7.5	12.1	19.7	27.0	31.4	33.3	32.8	36.1	42.2
Canada	na	na	16.7	25.0	28.6	38.8	46.0	40.6	39.2	43.8
Britain	9.4	12.7	26.2	30.0	32.2	43.0	39.9	36.6	40.6	47.2
France	12.6	17.0	27.6	29.0	34.6	46.1	49.8	51.6	53.4	56.0
Germany	10.0	14.8	25.0	34.1	32.4	47.9	45.1	45.1	46.8	47.6
Sweden	5.7	10.4	10.9	16.5	31.0	60.1	59.1	52.7	51.8	52.7
Spain	na	11.0	8.3	13.2	18.8	32.2	42.0	39.1	38.4	45.8
Average of 13 industrial countries	10.4	12.7	18.4	23.8	28.4	43.8	44.7	43.2	44.1	47.7

Source: Adapted from "Taming Leviathan," *The Economist*, March 17, 2011; based on Tanzi and Schuknecht, 2000, IMF, 2014; OECD, 2009.

Table 1.2 Government spending in Latin America, as percent of GDP

	1990–1994	*1995–1999*	*2000–2004*	*2005–2009*	*2010*	*2011*	*2012*	*2013*	*2014–2019**
Mexico	20.4	22.9	21.4	24.0	26.7	26.3	27.3	27.2	26.2
Brazil	–	40.4	37.1	38.1	39.8	39.1	40.4	40.5	40.0
Chile	21.3	21.4	22.6	20.9	23.8	23.2	23.7	23.6	23.1
Argentina	–	26.1	31.8	33.5	38.5	40.8	44.3	46.0*	46.6
Uruguay	–	32.4	32.6	31.8	34.1	32.9	34.1	35.2*	35.8
Paraguay	13.5	19.4	18.2	17.9	18.9	20.0	24.6	22.7*	22.6
Colombia	18.9	25.7	27.2	27.6	29.4	28.6	28.3	28.7*	27.6
Peru	–	–	19.4	18.9	20.2	19.3	19.6	21.0*	21.7
Ecuador	–	21.1	21.0	26.7	34.6	38.8	40.4	43.1*	39.0
Bolivia	25.2	27.9	31.8	33.3	31.5	35.3	36.1	40.0	37.4

Note: * = Estimates.

Source: IMF, 2014; World Economic Outlook Database, May 20, 2014.

issue worldwide.[3] Analysts and policymakers began to converge on the idea that they were perhaps too large and inefficient. Adjustments, structural or state reforms, transitions and other transformations converged on the goal of reducing the scope of state action. At the same time, the costs of providing a new generation of infrastructure also emerged as a major issue toward the end of the twentieth century. Against the background of deterioration of existing infrastructure, the costs of improved roads and rails transportation, telecommunications, energy, water and sanitation grew dramatically due to several factors—higher standards, complexity and technological content, limited competition, inflation, and labor costs. Governments that had seen themselves as responsible for footing the bill for much of the infrastructure, now found themselves unable to sustain this level of investment.[4]

Fiscal or debt crises and large deficits finally drove policymakers to challenge conventional wisdom and start inviting the private sector into the provision of infrastructure through concessions and partnerships. Additionally, reform advocates pointed to the private sector's higher efficiency in the design and management of large and complex projects. The private sector's resources, expertise, and efficiency levels relieve the public sector from meeting these needs alone. In a nutshell, public-private collaboration promised synergistic solutions to augment the cost effectiveness of public spending with little or no loss in service and quality (Renda and Schrefler, 2006).

There is no denying the urgent needs for upgraded infrastructure to protect and enhance social well-being and economic competitiveness (table A.2). Worldwide, the demand for infrastructure reaches upwards of $2.8–3.0 trillion a year, much of it in Asia, Latin America, and Africa. While massive infrastructure investment is essential to maintain competitiveness, developing and emergent countries need to spend 5–6 percent of GDP on infrastructure, a number that rises to 7–9 percent in low-income countries, but are actually spending less than half of the $500–600 billion per year required to grow at 4 percent. In the United States, investment in infrastructure had gradually declined after the 1960s to reach 2.4 percent of GDP by 2010—compared to 5 percent in Europe and 9 percent in China, who have significantly outspent the United States partly by relying on public-private collaboration. While the Latin American and Caribbean region needs to spend $250 billion annually to erase its infrastructure deficit, government alone is generally unable to reach that level (Carranza et al., 2011).[5]

A New Generation of Infrastructure

Public infrastructure responds to basic human needs and supports economic development in several ways: increasing productivity, generating employment, and enhancing well-being. Examples abound—urban highways, subways and rapid bus systems, railroads, larger and updated sea ports and airports, sophisticated telecommunications systems, reliable energy provision, hospitals and health care facilities. The deterioration of old facilities due to wear and tear is only one of the reasons for the growing need for often large and costly infrastructure undertakings. Urgent needs also come from the convergence of long-term social transformations accelerating since the last part of the twentieth century—urbanization and demographic change, trade expansion, the information and communications revolution, and competitive pressures in the context of both global and regional dynamics. New solutions are being advanced to address these new needs and challenges, supply is far from assured due to cost and the sheer complexity and scale of these projects and technologies. Fully adequate business models have to fully emerge on a planetary scale.[6]

Transportation is a high priority worldwide. Globalization and liberalization have intensified interconnectedness (trade, travel, communication), the use of existing transportation infrastructure, the decay of old infrastructure, and regional disparities (Müller, 2004). Current needs go well beyond repair to include new and better designed, larger-capacity transportations systems—roadways, railways, bridges and tunnels, ports, logistics, urban transport, airports, and related facilities. These projects incorporate advanced technologies, while meeting demands for green energy, clean air, health and safety, environmental sustainability, human capital, equity, and liveability. Pressure for competitiveness drives national governments to give priority to new transportation and economic strategies favoring integration into the world economy through industrialization and commodities.[7]

Population growth, urbanization, and other demographic changes reshape human society and redefine social needs. World population of over 7 billion is projected to reach more than 9 billion by 2050 (US Census Bureau, 2013). The momentum of twentieth-century migration from the countryside to cities has made the world more than 50 percent urban, a number that reaches more than 87 percent and higher numbers in Latin America, Europe, North America, and a few other parts of the world. The number and size of very large cities has grown dramatically—in 1970 there were only two megacities of more than 10 million inhabitants, and by 2011 there were 23 (4 in Latin America and 13 in Asia) and was projected to reach 37 in 2015. China, the world's most populous country is a prime example. Within a few decades, it has doubled the proportion of its population living in cities and its rate of urbanization is projected to reach 70 percent by 2035. One of the top challenges worldwide is to address the especial needs (economic, energy, water, transportation, social infrastructure) of megacities and mega regions and older industrial areas.

Urbanization around older cities originally designed for administrative and commercial purposes present distinctive problems. Agglomeration brings relentless growth in the number of vehicles and the congestion of streets originally designed for other uses on a much more limited scale. Policymakers increasingly focus on the problems posed by transporting thousands or millions of people between home, work, and sites of services. For example, rapid transit systems—subway, bus, light rail—can effectively satisfy the demand of millions of urban dwellers. In many cases, however, solutions based on Bus Rapid Transit (BRT) may not be sufficient. Innovative large cities currently link metro and bus lines into integrated intermodal systems (e.g., Transmilenio and Transantiago). In addition, urban designers are called upon to develop ambitious plans to redesign and regenerate urban areas. The systems are often too complex and costly for governments to build and manage on their own.

The construction of fast urban highways with integrated toll systems requires a mix of different resources to build and manage. Large cities regularly call on the private sector to build and operate specific

Table 1.3 Latin America, country profile, 2012

	Population (million)	*Area (km²)*	*GDP $ billion*	*Urban*	*Roads* (km)*	*Paved Roads* (%)*	*Rail Freight (million ton-km)*	*Container port traffic (TEU)*
Brazil	198.7	8,459,420	2,250	84.9	1,581,181	13.5	267,700	8,864,368
Mexico	120.8	1.943,950	1,178	78.4	374,262	37.8	69,185	4,243,651
Southern Cone								
Argentina	41.1	2,736,690	475	92.6	242,481	32.2	12,111	2,245,474
Chile	17.5	743,532	269	89.3	77,603	23.8	4,032	3,588,417
Uruguay	3.4	175,020	49	92.6				895,610
Paraguay	6.7	397,300	25	62.4	32,404	15.6		8,991
Andes								
Colombia	47.7	1,109,500	369	75.6	214,433			2,498,851
Peru	30.0	1,280,000	203	77.6	129,161	13.2	900	1,887,332
Ecuador	15.5	248,360	84	68.0				1,124,415
Bolivia	10.5	1,083,300	27	67.2	82,288	11.6		

Note: GDP is in current $ billion. TEU = twenty-feet-long container unit.

* 2011 Data.

Source: World Bank Database.

components of urban road networks, in effect creating private-public authorities to manage and coordinate them.

High-speed trains and toll highways to connect cities to each other, to transportation hubs, and to recreation areas are being built in Europe and China, while Mexico, Brazil, and other countries are planning them.[8] In 2011, the US government recognized this need, though this idea has failed to gain enough congressional support. Larger and more complex airports, with dozens or hundreds of daily flights, are required to meet the long-distance transportation needs of dynamic regions.[9] Integrated networks of concessions in charge of these airports supply multiple commercial, food, and even recreational services. Fast trains often connect airport terminals to each other and to other public transportation systems. Again, solutions are increasingly hybrid, with governments rarely able to or willing to tackle alone the designing, building, and operation of these systems.

Globalization interacts with technological change and the growing scale of human settlements to accelerate rates of obsolescence and the aforementioned trends. Developed in the 1950s, the intermodal shipping container provides an illustrative example. By significantly reducing transportation costs and gradually changing shipping and logistics, containerization made a major contribution to modern trade expansion and global economic restructuring. This innovation helps explain the rise of China as a manufacturing powerhouse producing for distant markets (Levinson, 2006). Today's new containers demand larger ships, ports, and shipping.[10] In manufacturing, integrated systems for the production, trading, shipping, and distribution of goods are already present, though still expanding, in Europe, Asia, and North America.

In Latin America, trade has led to comparable dynamics. Together, the ten countries in this study increased their exports nearly fivefold between 1995 and 2011—from $206 billion to $1,012 billion (UN Comtrade).[11] Led in large part by post-1990s booms in agriculture and mining, this trade expansion poses demands for transportation and logistics facilities to connect production sites and natural resources to often distant and undeveloped port facilities (see tables A.8, A.9, and 1.3). Private operators are often called upon to upgrade, build, and manage parts of these new-generation transportation systems and logistics, often in collaboration with the public sector. In addition, economic growth and broader transformations have expanded demands for better infrastructure. In turn, concessions and PPPs have gradually become through the first part of the twenty-first century an important option for upgraded infrastructure.

Throughout the world, intensified trade and globalization have created a need for state-of-the-art transportation facilities and logistics to accommodate container terminals, shipping, transportation, and storage. These and other forms of new infrastructure require resources in short supply in most emergent and developing countries: highly specialized personnel; capabilities for management, control, interfacing, regulation, and innovation; appropriate sources of energy; telecommunications and other advanced technologies. As bottlenecks are recognized, infrastructure emerges as a top national priority, and new forms of collaboration with the private sector become clearer. Partly in response, an international or global infrastructure market of public assets has developed to the point of becoming a well-organized industry involving official agencies, construction companies, operators, financial intermediaries, and legal advice. By the end of the 2000s, the public-private provision of infrastructure has gradually spread to most parts of the developed world, as well as in transitional and emergent economies. Latin American and Caribbean countries have taken major steps in this direction—even if some cling to traditional definitions of infrastructure provision.

The impetus for public-private collaboration has come from policymakers searching for ways to eliminate infrastructure gaps. States alone have a limited ability to meet demands for elimination of infrastructure deficits, while the private sector by itself is notoriously disinterested in long-term investment and, in any case, dissatisfaction with privation have put a brake on outright divestiture. Collaborative business models reduce some risks for private sector participation in infrastructure and stretch what governments can do within the limits of often constrained national budgets.

Latin America and the New Global Context

Latin America's share of global GDP and trade decreased noticeably in the 1980s and after, in contrast to expanded trade and fast growth in East Asia and China (López-Carlos et al., 2006). That decade's fiscal turbulence and economic crisis led to a near collapse in infrastructure investment (Calderón and Servén 2004b, 2010b). In the 1990s, Latin America gradually embraced public-private collaboration in infrastructure (table 2.1). In combination with the broad liberalizing reforms of that decade, booms in minerals, soy, and hydrocarbons were major reasons for South American economic expansion after the turn of the century. Still, this growth did not erase the gaps between East Asia and Latin America, which continues to be reflected in infrastructure.

Between 1990 and 2003, more than $380 billion public-private investment went to Latin America and the Caribbean, but this seemingly impressive figure fell short of what was needed to lower transportation and transaction costs and become more competitive (IDB, 2007).[12] Less than one third of roads in the region were in good condition, while railroads, ports, airports, and related facilities remained grossly insufficient. Logistics costs of over 15 percent of product value were considerably higher than those of developed countries. Development specialists estimated annual investment needs of up to $70 billion to meet urgent infrastructure repair and improvements. As a whole, the region would need to spend at least 3 percent of its GDP on new physical infrastructure to compete with China and East Asia (Bloomgarden and Maruyama, 2008; Fay and Morrison, 2005). In Brazil, investment in infrastructure of 1.7 percent of GDP fell considerably short of China's 8.3 percent.

Still, pressures to start updating and upgrading infrastructure contributed to the shift to concessions and partnerships in subsequent years (see also CEPAL, 2010). In addition, South American countries refocused on investments in transportation infrastructure to promote regional integration and development as well as to enhance competitiveness. Though inadequate infrastructure had contributed to the substantial decrease in the region's share of world trade, external shocks at the turn of the century, and at the new commodities booms of the 2000s sharpened the need for reducing transportation costs and promoting export-led development.[13] In 2005, Peru turned to concessions and public-private partnerships for the construction and improvement of highways, and began studies to use them for the construction of new interoceanic transportation links with Brazil—while Chile and Argentina planned enhanced trans-Andean highway and railroad connections through mountain passages along their 5,200 kilometers borders.[14]

The liberalizing reforms of the 1990s created conditions favorable to private sector participation in infrastructure provision and the adoption of liberalized development strategies.[15] Public-private collaboration was flourishing where liberalization reform had become institutionalized. Mexico and Brazil, the two largest Latin American countries, gradually built programs of concessions and partnerships, as did Chile and Colombia—while a few years later Uruguay and Paraguay would take important steps toward public-private collaboration in infrastructure (table A.3).[16]

However, liberalization reforms and privatization met opposition and threats in a few countries that had moved fast toward them.[17] Ideological conflict from antimarket forces, lack of political consensus among rulers, together and deficient institutional frameworks stopped or blocked them in Venezuela, Bolivia, Argentina, and Ecuador. Argentina, a pioneer reformer, provides an interesting experience, as does Bolivia, a poor country with great needs, whose liberal reforms have been well documented. All four cases had adopted substantial liberalization measures through the turn of the century, but political dynamics turned against the reforms and for a return of statism. These reversals in the context of export booms in mineral commodities strengthen tendencies toward statism in the region (Badie, 2000). The big question is what these two sets of trends portend for future infrastructure provision and development dynamics.

China has been the main driver of commodity booms reshaping South America. The giant country emerged a trading superpower, accounting for more than 10 percent of global exports and imports. Prior to its own economic reforms initiated in 1979, China was a centrally planned economy with strict price and production controls. The country was isolated from the global economy, and foreign trade was largely limited to Soviet bloc countries. President Richard Nixon's visit to China in 1972 started a process of normalization of relations between the two countries. The post-1979 reforms included price and ownership incentives for farmers as well as special economic zones along the coast in order to boost foreign investment and trade. Trade liberalization and decentralized trade policymaking were thus key components of unprecedented growth in the ensuing decades. China gained observer status with GATT in 1986 and became a full member of WTO in 2001 after relaxing tariffs and other trade barriers.

As the country's exports rose from $266 billion in 2001 to $2.2 trillion in 2013, and imports from $243 billion to $1.9 trillion in the same period, China became the second-largest economy, largest manufacturer, and largest trading economy in the world. In the 2010s, it decided to rebalance the economy toward consumption-oriented model. Urbanization and economic growth were already fueling consumption and the rise of a middle class, in part from migration to cities. Expansion and rising domestic consumption have created a growing market for other countries' exports: meat, poultry, milk and diary products, soy and soybean meal, and the like. Soy consumption in China doubled, in part to feed pigs and other animals. So has oil. China became a net oil importer in 1993 and the largest consumer of oil-based products in 2014 (Morrison, 2013). Steel for housing, urban infrastructure, and machinery is also a main import. As discussed in this volume, China's transformation in turn led to major shifts in Brazil and South America toward specialization in commodities.[18]

State and Economy in Theoretical Perspective

Making sense of these global and internal trends and tendencies in terms of the Latin American region invites theoretical elaboration beyond established paradigms. The state figures prominently in leading approaches to twentieth-century economic development and deserves special attention. This section traces the evolution of the role of the state in development theory before further dwelling on the emerging development patterns and strategies.

Emerging from post-World War II efforts to foster nation-building and reconstruction efforts, modern theories of development had state action as a guiding premise. This assumption prevailed in the elaboration of the problematic of economic growth in postcolonial, newly emergent nation-states. In the 1930s and thereafter, Keynesianism provided the broad and compelling rationale, policy tools, and capabilities to restore economic stability in response to downturns in the economy. It was particularly suited to Western societies and played a role in the expansion of the state during and after the Great Depression (table 1.1). This broad context inspired comparable approaches to enhanced roles of the state in other world regions and in specific relation to development, a phenomenon also shaped by the rise of Marxism in various parts of the world.

Government was at the core of the development field. When economists debated "big push" versus "balanced growth" approaches to development, their focus was state policy. Other liberal, Marxian, or nationalist perspectives had statism as common ground, very often converging on how state action could best induce industrialization, modernization, and social transformation. In Latin America, the structuralism associated with the Economic Commission for Latin America and the Caribbean (ECLAC) (*cepalismo*) and dependency theory also focused on state actors and policies, highlighting their role in overcoming a fixed international division of labor with pernicious effects on developing countries. World systems theory, which emphasized the latter, came close to viewing state-making as epiphenomena to world or international dynamics, thus adumbrating the arguments of hyperglobalists.[19]

Economic historians, soon joined by comparative-historical sociology (Barrington Moore Jr., Theda Skocpol, and others), provided thick historical accounts of the roles of states in the second wave of industrialization in the second half of the nineteenth century. They drew attention to politics and state policies in Germany and Japan, contrasting them with the pattern of industrialization "from below" of early industrializers in Britain and elsewhere. Though historical sociologists also placed emphasis on social classes and class-based coalitions, statemaking and policymaking remained at the core of their concerns. Earlier, Alexander Gerschenkron (1943, 1962) had provided an influential work on the activist role of government in strategies of industrialization in Germany and Russia, which he saw as economically backward. Other political economists deepened this perspective in relation to development states ("late industrialization" after World War II) in East Asia and Latin America (Amsden, 1989). Chalmers Johnson (1982) account of late development in Japan placed industrial policy and state agencies at the center of Japan's economic success, elaborating the concept of "development state" for that kind of state. The term stuck among analysts of the Korean and other East Asian cases (Amsden, 1989; Wade, 2004; and others). This form of government interventionism was henceforth used to confront neoclassical and neoliberal approaches centered on market dynamics as well as stage theories of development (Rostow, 1960).

A conceptual bifurcation and even confusion thus set in this literature, as Latin American structural economists and social scientists had also been using the term "developmentalism" to refer to state-centered doctrines relying on protectionism (import-substitution policies) and related measures to promote industrialization, but with an emphasis on manufactured goods for domestic demand and not export promotion as in the East Asian model. Also known as *cepalismo*, Latin American structuralism had been elaborated as early as 1949, when ECLAC (best known as CEPAL) provided a highly influential critical assessment of the region's earlier liberal phase of outward growth based on commodities. Though that economic era had brought considerable development through the first part of the twentieth century, CEPAL's Raúl Prebisch and colleagues viewed it as having largely outlived its usefulness in the new post-War era and went on to sketch an inward strategy to replace the outward approach (Cardoso and Faletto, 1979; CEPAL, 2010; Love, 1980; Prebisch, 1950).

The Latin American Import Substitution Industrialization (ISI) approach had an appealing logic. Since the preceding decades of intensive export sector specialization had generated a large demand for manufactured goods from abroad, the imposition of high tariffs on imported manufactured goods together with complementary measures should be expected to provide the necessary incentives for domestic industrial production. In general, Latin American developmentalism aimed to generate a Gerschenkronian "big push" capable of overcoming diverse structural obstacles to national, industry-based development.[20]

Therein lie two key distinctions between Latin American and Asian developmentalism: (1) the inward versus outward orientation and (2) the nationalist-populist politics of the first versus the cosmopolitan dynamics of the Asian development model. These differences explain contrasting outcomes in the two regions. The East Asian developmental state concentrating on outward industrialization strategy met great success in the new era of globalization, with the Asian developmental state becoming a highly effective state-centered model as early as the 1970s. In contrast, the strong nationalist focus on industrialization for internal markets would soon hinder Latin American development.

A number of interregional comparisons have drawn out key lessons from the contrast between Latin American and Asian developmentalism. Research has explored how state-centered strategies of late industrializing in Latin America relied on protectionism and ISI throughout much of the second half of the twentieth century. Though the East Asian cases also made use of these policies, they generally did so for a shorter period.[21] Progressively shifting to export promotion, East Asian cases were able to fuel and take full advantage of the great wave of globalization opening after the 1970s. In fact, the new Asian tigers were at the center of the phenomena propelling the global expansion of production and trade in the last part of the twentieth century, preceding China in driving what came to be known as economic globalization.

Though ISI helped turn Mexico, Brazil, and possibly Argentina into "newly industrializing countries," evidence mounted in the 1980s that the East Asian approach was more successful than Latin America's. In particular, the poor economic performance from the debt crisis of the 1980s placed that region decisively behind East Asia in terms of most measures of well-being and development—economic expansion, broadening education and health, technological innovation, and infrastructure. The differences became more pronounced over time: as East Asia industrialized, much of Latin America went from the debt crisis to painful reform cycles in the 1990s and after, without experiencing fast economic recovery and expansion. In terms of shares of world trade, Latin American and the Caribbean region either remained stagnant, barely grew, or even lost ground. Ironically, economic expansion since then would be often led by the production of commodities for distant markets.

This line of comparative analysis generated ideas about the relative success of government agencies in directly organizing new industrial ventures, processes of innovation, and economic reorganization in Korea and other parts of Asia (Amsden, 1989; Amsden and Chu, 2003; Kohli, 2004; Wade, 1990, 2003; Waldner, 1999).[22] Evans' (1995) account integrates and extends results from major works on Korea and other countries. Building on Johnson's work on Japan, Amsden and others studying South Korea's export-oriented industry-based development highlight the ability of the state to use subsidies and "discipline" to cajole and pressure industrialists toward meeting and improving performance standards, while Weiss (1998, 2003) and others give more prominence to cooperation. Evans' concept of embedded autonomy identifies the institutional factors giving the South Korean state the capacity to support as well as discipline industry.[23]

Evans' institutional account of development states identifies the relationship and roles responsible for the success of the Korean and East Asian governments in promoting industrialization and development. Developmental states contrast with predatory (Congo, formerly known as Zaire) and intermediate states (Brazil and India) in reaching "embedded autonomy," a concept aiming to capture synergistic relations between the states and industrialists. Concentrating on the information technology sector, Evans identified four broad state roles in industrial transformations: direct provision, regulatory, midwifery, and husbandry. The first two are nearly self-explanatory—direct economic roles through state enterprises in the former, and rules and constrains in the second. The last two roles are less obvious: midwifery entails targeted assistance to firms in new products and sectors, while husbandry is the ability of states to guide and support businesses to maintain or enhance competitiveness in already existing products and sectors. States characterized by embedded autonomy—bureaucratic development in a Weberian sense combined with effective connections to dynamic entrepreneurs—are best able to perform these four roles and induce industry-based development.

Toward the Partnering State

For Evans, state autonomy—defined as the state's ability to achieve goals, prevent the abuse or misuse of state subsidies, and discipline industry to become globally competitive—derives above all from a strong Weberian bureaucratic form. But a highly autonomous or disciplinarian state will not elicit the needed cooperation from key economic actors. For that, the state must also be "embedded," a concept that centers on operational ties between government and the industrial business sector (Weiss, 1998). Embedded autonomy implies that effective developmental states are able to collaborate with industry, something achieved through institutional links with the private sector. The emerging "partnering" state extends the ideas of cooperation and embeddedness.

Recent patterns of development pose emergent challenges requiring elaboration in the above literature on the developmental state. A key premise here is that the new relations between state structures and the private sector are not fully illustrated under assumptions of a Weberian ideal type of bureaucracy. While a minimum level of organizational or bureaucratic development is a necessary condition,[24] a narrow or rigid bureaucratic model appears unlikely to fruitfully accommodate the new complex relationships in large infrastructure undertakings and similar projects.

For purposes of this study, embedded autonomy remains an important starting point, but some assumptions need to be relaxed, starting with the primary focus on industrialization. The roles of direct source of industrial expansion through state-owned enterprises, midwifery, and husbandry in fact declined considerably after the 1990s, partly as a result of multilateral or regional norms against protectionism from trade integration negotiations. Regulation and some forms of husbandry remain relevant to the new approaches to development based on exchange, services, and the production of goods other than manufactures.

In addition, governments are called upon to refocus and play new roles (Ayres and Braithwaite, 1992). The new forms of concessions and partnerships in infrastructure explored in this study imply collaborative and interactive, sustained, long-term public-private relationships that go beyond the state roles in the embedded autonomy construct. The regulatory functions remain pivotal for simple concessions and for the more complex sets of public-private collaboration. But emergent forms of public-private collaboration call for intense official participation in mixed capital entities and projects based on webs of public-private collaboration in which global actors may play key roles. The idea of private sector participation in infrastructure clashes with the traditional view of the latter as a public good is mostly to be provided by governments. For this reason, policymakers and other stakeholders focused on revising this traditional view lean toward flexibility on how to conceptualize the new infrastructure projects and the more complex business forms to meet these needs. Relations involving concessionaires and partnerships are often organized as networks rather than as levels in vertically aligned bureaucratic structures.

Further, in many South American countries, development is being driven by dynamic commodities sectors and by parts of the tertiary or services sector (to include new generation transportation, export logistics, and distribution centers), rather than by industry or manufacturing. But the manufacturing emphasis or bias often found in the development state literature tends to block a full appreciation of these processes and the elaboration of adequate models of the development dynamics of which they are part. The recent export-led booms based on commodities such as soybeans, minerals, and gas-oil throughout South America have been strong enough to receive theoretical attention. These leading sectors shape development paths and are implicated on major fiscal, institutional, and political dynamics, while also reshaping social stratification.[25]

The focus on institutions needs to be complemented with a better understanding of the shifting roles of civil society, social classes, and contentious politics. Other works exploring the rise or strength of the developmental state in Asia have called attention to support from industrialists and class-based coalitions. Chibber's (2006) study of the development trajectory of India argues that insufficient support from industrialists was a critical variable in the limited success of Indian developmentalism. Davis (2004) and Paige (2007) insist on how agrarian class dynamics affect social class configurations fostering the consolidation of developmental states focused on industrialization and on synergistic relations between statemakers and industrialists. Though elaborations such as these do not necessarily challenge the institutionalist approach, they make the case for broader and more flexible analytical frameworks (Thelen, 2012).

The very roles of global economic actors in emergent development models—whether based on commodities (Argentina) or manufacturing (Mexico)—imply the need to transcend or qualify assumptions of nation-based economic modernization and hard economic nationalism.

From the standpoint of developing and emergent regions, these global economic actors include international trading companies and investment banks, but also state-owned or semi-official companies from China and other countries. These actors are found not only in commodities and services, they are also actively engaged in the distinctive patterns of outward industrial expansion in Mexico and other countries linked to broad range of international partners.

Finally, a significant number of development practices and strategies are not fully captured by either the developmental state or neoliberal polarities. These ideal types may be useful to signal marked or extreme differences but they tend to draw too much attention to highly differentiated phenomena while neglecting to explore the gray area between these conceptual schemes. In that context, Chapter Three discusses challenges or limits of "post-neoliberal" accounts of regimes in the Andean region. Presumably statist Argentina also defies easy characterization. Market-oriented and state-centered practices coexist with each other in Bolivia, Ecuador, and Argentina.

The unqualified use of the above ideal types leads away from adequate analysis of these cases. Whether statist or liberalizing—existing development regimes in Latin America are more cosmopolitan, hybrid, and structurally complex than implied by those ideal types. Both the public and private sectors organize as network of diverse and complex actors whose combinations take different forms. In that broad background, manufacturing is still an option, but commodities and services can also be central. Though this volume does not address issues of class base of various approaches, these can be presumed to be more diverse and complex than any single class. To be sure, social categories in agrarian, mineral, energy, transportation, information and telecommunications, as well as manufacturing need to be considered.

This Volume

This volume focuses on public-private collaboration and infrastructure in Latin America by deepening the analysis of strategies of liberalization and market reform in several countries. Aiming at a broad framework, my discussion is informed of trends and approaches in other regions, including the European region, a pioneer and major global player.

Chapter Two discusses four early adopters—Mexico, Argentina, Chile, and Brazil—to develop a framework by which to explore other cases and programs. Chapter Three gives attention to countries in the

Andean and Southern Cone regions of South America, including main cases of reversal of liberalizing drives. Chapters Four to Six shift the focus to specifics projects and programs in Brazil and Chile.

Throughout, this book explores the links between public-private collaboration and broader processes known as market or state reform, viewed as institutional transformation and adaptation to evolving international conditions. This perspective embeds the move toward public-private collaboration in historical processes driving the region's search for an updated development model. The focus is on emerging actors, relationships, organizational forms, and policies, seeking to tease out the effects of political and institutional dynamics.

The era of globalization opening in the 1970s and 1980s has shaped these reforms and transformations. In Karl Polanyi's (1944) view, the previous grand phase of global expansion of market societies in the late nineteenth and early twentieth centuries was marked by conflicting tendencies or "double movements"—as expansion of laissez-fair or self-regulating markets triggered reactions to protect the fabric of community and social life from market forces. Few would doubt the contemporary reality of similar or comparable countermovements in defense of community control of resources (land, labor, established mechanisms of exchange). Tensions between institutional stability and openness to new processes, ideas, and actors pressures need to be examined to assess the robustness of processes of liberalization.

To endure, such transformations require realignments and learning processes on the part of politicians, political movements, policymakers, business leaders, and the public at large. The idea of partnering with the private sector may be alien to bureaucrats and the general public. Important players may often be opposed to paying road tolls, water fees, or other costs. The general public may distrust concessions. Old views and habits grounded in inherited ideological preferences about access to infrastructure services are hard to change. In addition, frustrations and failures are likely at first, and may not be easily transformed into fast and lasting learning experiences. It takes time to assimilate successes, setbacks, pressures, and shifts. That is, public acceptance of new values, norms, organizational forms, or policy paradigms is far from guaranteed.

Key actors in partnerships between public and private actors are often transnational, especially in large infrastructure projects such as new dams, energy projects, highways, and subways. Local politics often clash with global designs. In addition, the international dispersion of innovation, resources, partners, and clients by its very nature complicates the processes of learning and institutional change associated with public-private collaboration. Paradoxically, state strength—the ability to design and implement projects and develop institutional capabilities—may be in the last analysis the key condition ensuring liberalization and public-private collaboration.

This volume explores the extent to which durable shifts toward public-private collaboration are taking place in Latin America. Support and opposition usually represent the same forces advocating alternative visions of large-scale social change. Their fate is often in question. As they assess practices and outcomes, the case studies address major issues about development.

CHAPTER TWO

State and Liberalization in Latin America

In Latin America, the liberalizing reforms of the late twentieth century set the stage for experimentation with new forms of state-market relations. The decades-old state-centered economic model had brought significant forms of development and industrialization, but the crisis of the eighties signaled the need for change—as large debts, high fiscal deficits, and soaring inflation were no longer able to act as stimuli to economic growth. To reform large and often inefficient state apparatuses, policymakers launched initiatives favoring destatization and liberalization, thus widening the role of the private sector and the market in the 1990s.

In infrastructure, public-private collaboration gradually gained attention as alternative to traditional public procurement and direct government provision as well as to outright divestiture (table 2.1). Impetus for the shift came with the realization that public revenues and spending were insufficient to satisfy large and growing needs.[1] Throughout the region, infrastructure had fallen short of what was required to enhance competitiveness, grow at a faster rate, reduce poverty, and hope to catch up with East Asia's investment rates (Fay and Morrison, 2005). New thinking about fiscal constraints and the limits of state action fueled the idea of relying on private sector participation to finance, design, build, or operate large new projects.

Infrastructure needs had grown dramatically, widening the already large gaps. Expanding trade, together with other aspects of globalization, made urgent the need for efficient transportation of goods and people—highway and railroad systems, ports, as well as telecommunication and general infrastructure (Guaipatín, 2007). With population and urbanization continuing to increase in Latin America, urban

Table 2.1 Public-private investment in infrastructure in Latin America, 1990–2013, in $ millions

	Number of Projects	*Divestiture*	*Concessions*	*Greenfield*	*Management and Lease*	*Total Investment*
Brazil	693	131,864	147,780	158,517	130	438,291
Mexico	227	37,430	17,277	72,206	2	126,915
Southern Cone						
Argentina	217	23,105	41,436	28,752	615	93,908
Chile	157	10,026	9,224	23,071		42,321
Uruguay	21		811	4,129		4,940
Paraguay	5		58	16,60		17,18
Andes						
Colombia	143	10,791	7,198	19,210	36	37,235
Peru	99	14,226	5,007	13,375	205	34,718
Ecuador	28		2,073	5,230		7,303
Bolivia	26	1,542	851	3,728		6,121
Central America and Caribbean	175	9,078	4,237	204,38	6	33,759
Total	**1,809**	**247,696**	**236,354**	**357,212**	**994**	**844,161**

Note: Divestiture: Transfer of equity in the state-owned company to private entities; Concession: A private entity takes over the management of a state-owned enterprise for a given period and it also assumes significant investment risk; Greenfield: A private entity or a public-private joint venture build and operate a new facility for a given period; Management lease: A private entity manages the project while ownership and investment decisions remain with the state.

Source: World Bank, 2014a.

population was expected to add 100 million more inhabitants within a couple of decades; sprawling metropolises and larger cities cried out for massive urban renewal and such costly projects as rapid bus systems, subways, integrated transportation systems, and related innovations. The proliferation of the automobile led to the congestion of existing avenues and the eventual need for urban highways. Energy demand sharply increased as a result of economic, demographic expansion, mobility, and international vulnerability to supply shortages.

In different ways, governments in Latin America and the Caribbean began to invite the private sector into the provision of transportation, energy, telecommunications, water, sanitation services, and other infrastructure (see tables 2.2 and 2.3). This volume examines this movement toward public-private collaboration, exploring their links to institutional and political dynamics, and assessing outcomes. The analysis relies on reviews of the existing literature, field visits, interviews, and the analysis of project and country databases from the World Bank

Table 2.2 Mexico and Argentina, 1990–2013, by sector, in $ millions

	1990–1995	*1996–2000*	*2001–2005*	*2006–2010*	*2011*	*2012*	*2013*	*N*	*Total $*
Mexico									
Energy	1.0	4,335	4,535	2,283	1,207	1,326	1,937	67	15,624
Telecom	18,031	10,836	16,489	16,419	3,209	3,575	3,483	15	72,042
Transport	7,908	5,174	2,177	12,633	2,729	1,627	4,041	111	36,289
Water	560	288	524	1,290	215	0	86	34	2,963
Total	**26,500**	**20,633**	**23,725**	**32,625**	**7,360**	**6,528**	**9,547**	**227**	**126,918**
Argentina									
Energy	11,729	13,001	1,685	3,802	565	583	778	107	32,153
Telecom	11,924	9,755	3,936	6,761	2,425	2,082	2,343	7	39,226
Transport	6,119	6,511	74	1,403	235	16		84	14,358
Water	5,168	2,906	102					19	8,176
Total	**34,940**	**32,173**	**5,797**	**11,966**	**3,224**	**2,681**	**3,121**	**217**	**93,912**

Source: World Bank, 2014a.

Table 2.3 Brazil and Chile, 1990–2013, by sector, in $ millions

	1990–1995	*1996–2000*	*2001–2005*	*2006–2010*	*2011*	*2012*	*2013*	*N*	*Total*
Brazil									
Energy	614	41,244	17,715	58,123	17,742	30,438	9,472	389	175,348
Telecom		55,242	30,946	40,012	12,781	13,409	10,210	36	162,600
Transport	1,317	17,643	2,418	27,314	6,145	21,980	11,178	136	87,995
Water	157	2,408	538	1,599	128	4,573	2,947	112	12,350
Total	**2,088**	**116,537**	**51,619**	**127,046**	**36,796**	**70,400**	**33,807**	**693**	**438,293**
Chile									
Energy	2,055	6,263	784	1,663	212	1,251	6,000	60	18,228
Telecom	149	972	909	1,327	463	326	300	10	4,452
Transport	540	2,877	4,630	1,943	1137	572	678	66	12,377
Water	68	4,611	1,043	3	1,543	0		21	7,268
Total	**2,812**	**14,723**	**7,366**	**4,936**	**3,355**	**2,149**	**6,984**	**157**	**42,325**

Source: World Bank, 2014a.

and other sources. Based on a review of the four pioneering experiences, this chapter develops a framework by which to explore a total of 11 cases and programs in the region. Driven by distinctive dynamics, Chile started to realign the relative roles of the public and private sectors in the 1970s, followed by Mexico in the 1980s and Argentina in the early 1990s, while Brazil made its big move after 1994. While often seen as parts of Polanyian "double movements," market reforms and statist reaffirmations also generated distinctive turnarounds toward statism in Argentina and other parts of South America discussed (see Chapter Three).

Statism versus Liberalizing Reform

Two main lines of analysis have sought to explain the liberalizing reforms. One places emphasis on the diffusion of ideas and models from core countries, including international financial institutions like the International Monetary Fund (IMF) and the World Bank (WB). Many of these studies view national-level developments as induced by neoliberal principles and the package of advice known as the Washington consensus (Panizza, 2009). A second line of inquiry gives more attention to political, economic, and institutional dynamics at the domestic level, including their links to historical processes and responses to shifting international and global developments.

This book takes as basic premise that political and institutional processes need to be fully considered in accounts of shifts in policy paradigm and their various outcomes. The cases reviewed in this chapter acknowledge the impact of international financial agencies and the significant roles they play in the diffusion of policies, but above all they highlight how domestic institutional and political processes shape and determine reform processes. In the last analysis, and regardless of their original inspiration, endogenous dynamics are decisive in shaping and guaranteeing outcomes—I argue. Their effects are seen, for example, in the varying responses to shocks and international financial crises in 1982 and the rest of the 1980s, 1994, the turn of the century, and the post-2008 period—as several countries maintained or deepened the liberalizing drives while others downgraded or abandoned them (Correa, 2012; Lora, 2007).

The 1982 debt crisis and the "lost decade of the 1980s" were a watershed for the need for renewal in Latin America's approach or paradigm to development (Easterly and Servén, 2003; Manzetti, 2003; Oxhorn and Starr, 1999; Remmer, 1991). Throughout much of the Latin American and Caribbean region, this crisis fueled a decisive round of criticism regarding the statism prevalent after the 1930s. The economic slowdown that followed the Mexican default of 1982 lasted nearly a decade, as countries were unable to resolve accumulated bottlenecks or create conditions for faster economic development, much less improve the working of polities then characterized by authoritarianism and clientelism. Meanwhile, Latin America's old strategy based on import-substitution industrialization (ISI) now contrasted rather unfavorably with the liberalized export-oriented approaches of the emergent countries of East Asia.[2]

In infrastructure, traditional Latin American statism featured centralized and monopolized policymaking, investment, provision of services, and regulation. Evidence now demonstrated this approach's inefficiency and inability to provide solutions to new demands, unnecessary losses and high costs, loss of competitiveness, insufficient coverage, and chronic reliance on fiscal deficits. Liberalizing reforms were thus defended as vital for, both, urgently needed improvements in quality, reliability, and efficiency as well as to alleviate the strain on public finances and increase access to the poor. Policymakers in economic areas saw private collaboration as a way to increase competitiveness in the context of globalization (Correa Díaz and Rozas, 2006; Haggard et al., 1994; Leiva, 2008).

However, the South American region in particular would also become home to major opposition movements and even reversals—as liberalizing parties and coalitions lost power to these movements and their leaders in some cases. At one end, the rejection of prior process of liberalization led to the installation of decidedly statist regimes, such as the "socialism of the twenty-first century" ushered in by the victory of Hugo Chávez in Venezuela (1998). The antiliberal wave also included Néstor Kirchner in Argentina (2003), Evo Morales in Bolivia (2005), and Rafael Correa in Ecuador (2006). Lula da Silva's victory in Brazil (2002) and that of Michelle Bachelet in Chile (2006) resemble this phenomenon, but they evolved quite differently from the rest of these cases and from each other.

The decreased enthusiasm for the reform process during this period was connected to several international financial crises impacting the region—Mexico's peso or Tequila crisis of 1994, the Asian and Russian financial crises after 1997, the Brazilian turbulence of 1998, and the 2001 financial collapse in Argentina.[3] In a number of cases, the cumulative impact of these junctures contributed decisively to the success of the anti-liberalization movements of the turn of the century. The empirical association between the two is quite impressive in the cases of rejection, though the precise causal link between economic crises and contentious politics may remain in debate. In Brazil, opponents relied on the economic turbulence of the turn of the century to attack the liberalizing reform in the political debates of the 2002 elections, laying the groundwork for the election of Lula da Silva as president (Font, 2003). Blamed their 2001 crisis on the liberalizing reforms of the 1990s, many Argentines voted to put left-leaning Néstor Kirchner in office in 2003, even if a minority pointed to inadequate institutional development as the root cause of the problem.

The Andean region is particularly interesting in this regard. There, economic contractions following a period of growth fueled political opposition, weakened incumbents, and contributed to the renewed force of indigenous movements and populist politics. In 2005 or shortly after, Evo Morales became leader of Bolivia and Rafael Correa of Ecuador. Blaming "neoliberalism" for the poor economic performance, both promised a better model. Mass movements in the Andes and Southern Cone actively opposed larger roles for the private sector in water, gas, and other sectors, while left-leaning national populism drew support from international opposition to globalization.

Assessments of Latin American public-private collaboration in the 2000s reached mixed conclusions. Andrés et al. (2008) studied reforms in telecommunications, electricity, and water through 2007, comparing conditions prior, during, and post adoption phase. These authors found that the reforms generally resulted in continued expansion of services as well as gains in quality and productivity, though with some employment losses at the transition stage, as well as modest price increases. For instance, telecommunications brought positive results in most settings, though it was accompanied by some job loss and modest price increases (150). These studies acknowledged opposition to the privatization of water services, while puzzled by it considering the great needs in this area. At the same time, specialists maintained that Latin America and the Caribbean would need to spend close to $250 billion to close gaps in water infrastructure in urban areas alone. Multilateral organizations were willing to provide support of up to $2 billion per year of the total $12.45 billion needed annually for the next 20 years (Mejía, 2011) for water supply, sewerage, wastewater, drainage, new water sources, and service connections to slums. With many communities and countries reported as lacking the resources to remedy the situation, the traditional clientelistic model of connecting populations to service would need to give way to a more efficient model based on some variant of the liberalized reforms. In any case, improved governance was needed for increased investment.

If hesitation and even pessimism was heavily influenced by the Latin American economic crises and shifts to the left at the turn of the century (Arditi, 2008), placing both in a broader historical and institutional perspective can help identify the gradual economic recovery after the early 2000s and its impact on views about liberalization.

Another exogenous factor, China's rise as world economic power and consumer of commodities, was already strongly influencing developments in Latin America during this period, creating powerful incentives for the expansion of large export sectors in mineral and agricultural commodities (table A.10). Soy provides a striking illustration. The Asian giant came to represent over 60 percent of the soy trade. While in 1995 its demand was satisfied by the 14 million tons produced domestically, in 2011 it consumed over 70 million tons, though Chinese farmers still produced the same amount as in 1995.[4] In other words, China was now importing upward of 56 million tons annually. Much of that demand came from the increasingly large Brazilian harvests—with 75 percent of the latter's harvest going to China in 2013 (UN Comtrade). As discussed below, this led to diverse efforts to increase supply in Brazil—as was also the case in Argentina, Uruguay, and Paraguay. In Mexico and other industrializing parts of Latin America and the Caribbean region, the China factor also reshaped prospects for industrialization strategies.[5]

Technocracy and Reform: Mexico versus Argentina

Mexico and Argentina, two of the largest and most industrialized countries in the region, joined Chile in adopting aggressive market reforms by the first half of the 1990s. In both cases, professional economists designed changes that included a larger role for the private provision of infrastructure via outright divestiture and concessions (Basañes and Willig, 2002; Manzetti, 2000, 1999; Weyland, 2004). These destatizing measures seemed to work well at first, but they faced substantial challenges in both countries shortly after implementation. Projects involving private sector participation were delayed or failed to take hold in Argentina in the opening years of the twenty-first century. Technocratic resolve and sophistication alone thus did not guarantee success. The outcome of liberalizing reforms varied in part as a result of different institutional and political contexts, including the ability to absorb and learn from mistakes (table A.5).

Mexico: Revolution and Reform

The move to private sector participation in infrastructure in Mexico was embedded in a reform process initiated in the early 1980s. As it consolidated its hold on the Mexican polity in the 1930s, the Institutional Revolutionary Party's (PRI) dirigisme had succeeded in accelerating development and modernization through the 1970s. The oil shocks of that decade focused attention and even concern on how external forces shaped the model, but it was the hard-hitting debt crisis of 1982 that alerted Mexico's increasingly professional policymakers to the need for limits and constraints on the state's large role in economic life and near-monopoly in infrastructure (Brooks and Kurtz, 2012; Grindle, 1996; Hellman, 1988).

Also in the 1970s, the Mexican political establishment had accelerated the recruitment into the high echelons of the policymaking civil service of well-trained young economists and other professionals often holding advanced degrees from top American and national universities. This distinctive cohort received fast promotion into the high rungs of the Mexican bureaucracy—the Central Bank, the Ministry of Finance, and the office of the presidency—which allowed them direct access to political power and to specialists at international financial institutions. These reform-minded economists used the newly gained positions in the state and the ruling party to spearhead the professionalization of state and policy. After helping organize the response to the oil turbulence of the 1970s, in the following decade they elaborated a framework for policies of liberalization in response to economic crisis. Though sometimes viewed as agents of the historical leaders of the Mexican revolution, the reformers were already threatening the party's old guard by the end of that decade. Somewhat paradoxically, their rise foretold the disruption of the decades-old statist regime.[6]

The Mexican revolution of 1910 had given life to a highly centralized state bent on economic intervention. Top-down corporatism provided order and maintained peace among the factions in the political elite and the main organized social forces in the country (Cornelius, 1996). Buttressed by clientelism and the dispensation of patronage, single-party rule provided remarkable political stability for seven decades, and even developed a professional bureaucracy to foster modernization. The main challenge to centralized statism came from within, from the impatient professionals searching for a more efficient, fiscally prudent and competitive market economy. Growing progressively disillusioned with the shortcomings of homegrown dirigisme, the new policymakers were able to craft a substantial program of reforms. Economic crises after 1982 gave the new technocratic decision makers opportunities for action, but their focus on state reform put them at odds with the economic populism prevalent inside and outside the party and state. The traditional revolutionary regime may or may not have realized the incompatibility between the two policy paradigms. But the decades-old statist regime was to change in major ways.

The reform process took off during the Miguel de la Madrid six-year term or *sexenio* (1982–1988), as policymakers faced the economic crisis left by the previous government. De la Madrid held a master's degree from Harvard, while the two presidents who followed him had doctorates from Ivy League universities. Carlos Salinas (1988–1994) accelerated the liberalizing reforms, as did Ernesto Zedillo (1994–2000)—the last in the uninterrupted line of PRI presidents since 1929.

The fillip for action came from the debt crisis of August 1982 and the severe economic downturn that followed. What grew to become an international financial crisis had its roots in Mexico's inability to pay the rapidly accumulating debt owed to foreign bankers—the result of the doubling of the costs of servicing the debt largely due to fast-rising interest rates in the United States. Sharply curtailed foreign credit brought a severe recession and the need for an adjustment plan to face the complex financial and fiscal imbalances (see figure 2.1).

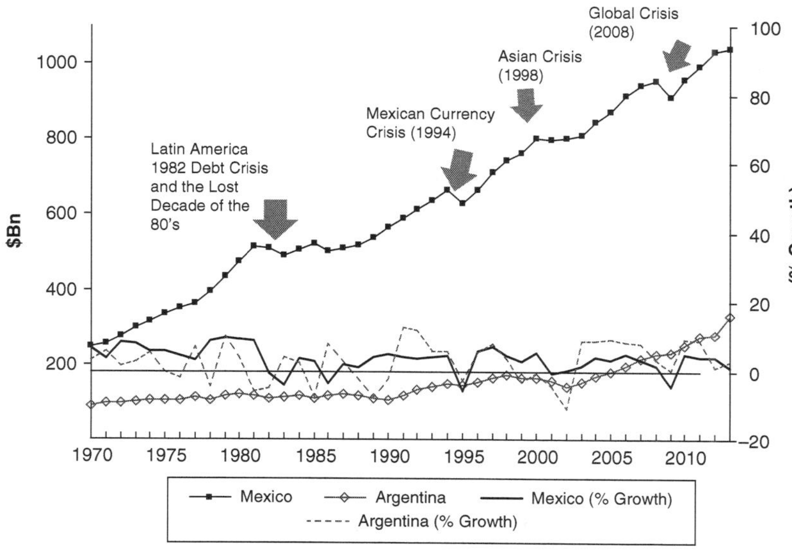

Figure 2.1 Mexico and Argentina, GDP and growth, 1970–2013.

Source: World Bank, 2014b.

Newly elected president Miguel de la Madrid sought debt alleviation through privatization. A rationale was readily at hand. In the 12 years preceding his government, the number of state enterprises had jumped from 272 in 1970 to 1,155 in 1982—while subsidies to state firms came to absorb 13 percent of GDP that last year, much of it to the financially troubled companies the government had acquired.[7] By 1985, de la Madrid's government announced a plan to merge, shut down, or transfer nearly 300 state-owned enterprises, with 57 to be converted to concessions. By the time he left office in 1988, the number of state-owned enterprises had diminished to 618 (Kehoe and Meza, 2012; MacLeod, 2004). This was indeed a major step away from the statist development paradigm.[8]

At the same time, infrastructure development had emerged as a high priority, calling for urgent attention, but the costs of upgrading roads, highways, and other transportation infrastructure would further deplete the financial resources of a government facing a severe fiscal crisis and pressures from other priorities. The federal government thus decided to explore how the private sector might become more active in infrastructure provision, opening a discussion on redefining relations between the public and private sectors. A decision was made to incorporate the private sector through concessions and partnerships in order to modernize the transportation system. By the turn of the decade, Mexico was relying on this path to rebuild the highway system.

After 1988, the Carlos Salinas government accelerated the pace of reform, focusing on 280 large firms said to represent nearly 90 percent of the value of all assets privatized or restructured up to that point (Dresser, 1991; Rodríguez, 2010). The Mexican program for highway concessions became the first in the region authorizing private operators to construct and operate roads and bridges. These measures and plans dovetailed with the objectives of the evolving negotiations for a free trade agreement with the United States, truly a sea change in the opening of the Mexican economy. To promote trade and increase competitiveness, policymakers considered it vital to improve and enlarge the highway system. Structural reforms would help increase investments, generate growth, and create up to 800,000 new jobs a year, they hoped. By then, controlling inflation had also become a priority. In this context, Salinas started the North American Free Trade Agreement (NAFTA) negotiations in 1992 and signed the agreement before ending his term (Hufbauer and Schott, 2005).

Upon taking office, Ernesto Zedillo (1994–2000) faced yet another international financial crisis having Mexico as epicenter. The sharp and sudden devaluation of the peso, from 4 to upward of 7 pesos to the dollar, detonated the new crisis. As the costs of servicing the large dollar-denominated debt skyrocketed, Mexico was forced to declare a default (technically a "moratorium") and request renegotiation and better terms. The country's international credit plummeted. Within a short period of time, the 1994 financial crisis brought GDP contraction, devaluation, unemployment, poverty, and decreased development prospects (Kuczynski, 2003; MacLeod, 2009). The crisis spread internationally. The international media dubbed the strong impact on Argentina, Brazil, and other South American countries with large debts as the "Tequila effect" (see figures 2.1, 3.1, and 3.2). Partly in response to the crisis, the Zedillo government broadened public-private collaboration and the reform process to include most infrastructure sectors—telecommunications, ports, airports, toll roads, railroads, and distribution of natural gas.

As shown in table 2.2, investments in public-private projects amounted to nearly $127 billion between 1990 and 2013, with the first phase (1990–1995) representing nearly 21 percent of the total. Subsequent five-year periods show lower but sustained levels of investment: $20.6 billion (16 percent) in 1996–2000; $23.7 billion (19 percent) in the third, and $32.6 billion (26 percent) in the 2006–2010 period—while investments for 2011, 2012, and 2013 remained high at nearly $7, $6 and 9.5 billion, respectively. This performance contrasts markedly with that of Argentina, where policymakers were not as able to assimilate setbacks, adjust to external shocks, and alleviate the economic consequences of political change. The Mexican reform process survived through diverse economic and political conditions, eventually recovering after the recession of 2008.

Zedillo would be the last president in the seven-decade uninterrupted rule by the PRI. Though political dynamics led to a slowdown of the reform process after 2000, the country had changed substantially by then. By the early years of the new century, the private sector operated much of the previously state-owned and state-operated enterprises, though the large energy and oil industry remained largely under the control of the very large, state-owned Mexican Petroleums (PEMEX) (Murillo, 2001).

The Mexican public-private program was the first in Latin America to massively rely on concessions and partnerships to expand and modernize the nation's highway system. Between 1996 and 2001, private investment in land transportation infrastructure grew from virtually nonexistent in the 1980s to triple that of the public sector.[9] With financing from local banks and individual investors, attracted by guarantees from the public sector, Mexico's first wave of concessions between 1989 and 1994 awarded approximately 52 concessions worth $13 billion and covering 5,500 km (Ruster, 1997; the World Bank database lists 51 projects worth $26.5 billion during the period 1990–1995).

However, this first wave of highway concessions resulted in a large number of outright failures, showing in part that the institutional context was still unable to guarantee sustained success. While the winning bids had promised short concessions and speeding up to complete the project, they left the operator free to impose high tolls—with users reacting by avoiding the expensive highways. Low levels of use threatened outright bankruptcy to several projects. Tolls were reduced, but to no avail. By 1997, the federal government had to step in to take direct control of 20 of the 52 concessions, transferring them to the Mexican Toll Road Bailout Fund (FARAC) at a very high cost.[10]

The political transition in 2000 toward more competitive elections did not stop the reform process during the two *sexenios* following the victory of the opposition National Action Party (PAN). Still, the presidencies of Vicente Fox (2000–2006) and Felipe Calderón (2006–2012) lacked sufficient congressional support to greatly advance their aims to deepen the reform process.[11] The Fox and Calderón governments faced substantial congressional opposition from the PRI and the emergent Party of the Democratic Revolution (PRD), which succeeded in obstructing key policy initiatives (Wise and Pastor Jr., 2005). Nevertheless, advances were made. By the early 2000s, Mexican policymakers felt they had corrected or overcome previous mistakes and were ready to renew the concessions program for highways. Between 2003 and mid-2008, a new highway concessions program invested more than $2 billion in new highways. The existing legislation allowed for some degree of innovation, and in 2002 the finance ministry designed the PPS (Projects for the Provision of Services), one of the first modern public-private partnership programs in Latin America.[12] In the PPS contracts, a private operator designs, builds, maintains, and provides a public service for normally 30 years in exchange for user fees, tolls, or government payments, while assets belong to either the government or private operator and risks are shared. Mexico used this model in roads, hospitals, and higher education.

After 2006, the Felipe Calderón presidency relied on this model to formalize a national plan for infrastructure development. Noting that Mexican infrastructure ranked 6th in Latin America and the Caribbean, and 64th internationally, the Calderón plan went on to use PPS as well as regular concessions and traditional procurement,[13] feeling that public-private collaboration would be effective in increasing highway investment.[14] The 2007–2012 national infrastructure program set goals to increase competitiveness, turn Mexico into a major logistical platform,[15] and expand exports beyond the United States and Canada, particularly to Asia and the Pacific. Notwithstanding their political differences and rivalries, the PAN and the PRI as well as part of the PRD largely agreed on this approach to reach development objectives. Meanwhile, in October 2007, Mexico awarded FARAC I, the first phase of a package of toll roads.[16]

However, the global financial crisis of 2008–2009 brought a severe economic contraction that frustrated Mexico's development and infrastructure plans. The economy slowed down to 1.4 percent GDP growth in 2008 and shrank by 4.7 percent in 2009 (see table A.11), in part due to fewer remittances, lower foreign investments, and less credit to corporations. Government revenue declined. This shock provided a truly major test of Mexico's liberalizing approach and the notion of a consensus on basic model and on the use of public-private collaboration. At first, the authorities appeared determined to meet basic infrastructure development objectives, even with the increased budgetary constraints. At the time, private investment in infrastructure accounted for less than 1 percent of GDP, much of it in energy and highway projects.

The infrastructure plan had to be adjusted but it remained in focus. The stimulus program of October 2008 called for increased public spending in that sector, modernizing the regulatory framework regarding public investment and promoting increased competitiveness.[17] The 2007–2012 national infrastructure plan was reaffirmed. The government still expected nearly 60 percent of infrastructure funding to come from the private sector, but this was unrealistic in the new financial context. Inevitably, the tightening led to project delays and complications. The FARAC highway concession program downsized. The original auction estimated at $3.5 billion was broken into several smaller packages. Phases II and III sought to maintain the initial auction dates of 2008 and 2009. FARAC II (Paquete del Pacífico) originally received two bids in September 2008, but both were for less of what the government would accept. The response was to redesign, reduce size, and minimize risk. In April 2008, a reduced Pacífico Norte package of 305 kilometers was sold to Carlos Slim's group for $238 million. Meanwhile, the secretary of Communications and Transport issued a call for bids for FARAC III. Bids for the northeast package of 46 kilometers of new roads and 180 kilometers of existing roads were rejected as too low in early 2010. Financial uncertainty led to other delays.[18]

The proximity and links to the US economy amplified the economic recession after 2008. In 2009, the federal government announced a $44.6 billion infrastructure plan and later took steps to redirect funds toward infrastructure investments. The Ministry of Communications and Transport (SCT) would increase highway spending from its budget and more actively seek to attract private interest in these projects. Meanwhile, many Mexican states accelerated their public investment plans. Enthusiasm for public-private collaboration gained momentum to include expansion at the subnational level. Several key states created their own PPS programs: Mexico (state), Mexico City (DF), Durango, Tamaulipas, Jalisco, Yucatán, and others.

But the country still needed a specific national legislation for public-private partnerships, while the institutional backbone was still lacking at all levels of government. Additional expertise was necessary to plan and model mature infrastructure projects. According to the *Economist Intelligence Unit* index (2012), Mexico's infrastructure still ranked fourth in the region and institutional conditions were not yet sufficient to attract major interest from investors. Complementary reforms would make a difference in attracting private interest in infrastructure projects. The country lacked a special unit in charge of concessions and PPP. With each ministry taking care of investments under its supervision, the institutional system for public-private partnerships gave the appearance of fragmentation with regard to planning, implementing, and supervising projects (Economist Intelligence Unit, 2010). Mexican states started to look for multilateral support to develop their PPP programs, but most investments continued to be made by the federal secretariats. The Finance and the Communication and Transport secretariats were the two most influential agencies overseeing infrastructure investments. Authorities expressed support for an agency devoted to PPS projects and public-private partnerships, but in early 2011 Mexico's lower house failed to pass a senate-approved bill formalizing the program on public-private partnerships. Having regained seats and political standing in the 2009 elections, the PRI felt it was time to flex its muscles, while internal tensions made it unlikely for the left-leaning PRD to support the PAN bill.

Still, a 2010 amendment to article 6 of the federal law of highways allowed concessions to extend or expand their contracts on public roads. Work continued on the Mazatlán-Durango stretch of a new highway in the northern part of the country connecting the Atlantic and Pacific coasts, including the imposing Baluarte Bridge, the world's tallest cable-stayed bridge. Though political and economic conditions throughout 2011 and 2012 denied national political leaders their plan to expand the public-private collaboration in infrastructure, the country was in fact taking other steps toward a new model. Various forms of public-private collaboration had come to life—including regular concessions and PSPs. All but a handful of states had developed formal legal frameworks and programs for public-private partnerships.[19] Several agencies and organizations had been formed.[20] Finally, the PPP bill passed in December 2011.

As the 2012 elections approached, five consecutive presidencies had maintained and even deepened the liberalizing reforms. The candidate of the left-leaning PRD argued for major change in policy, but winner Enrique Peña Nieto, the young candidate of the PRI, rapidly formulated a vigorous reform agenda, retaining many of the mechanisms and plans developed in the last three decades. The party that had started the reform process in the 1980s, was now back in control of Mexico's strongly presidentialist system. This was the sixth continuous liberalizing government, a pattern that contrasted with the swings of Argentina.

To bring about reforms, the new president negotiated a Pact for Mexico with the opposition PAN and PRD, complementing the reformist framework with national development and infrastructure plans. In May 2013, legislation reduced consumer costs in the telecommunications and broadcasting sector. The new government also pushed for a fiscal responsibility law to keep local government from taking too much debt, while also facilitating public access to credit.

Energy reform was a main priority. Mexico's energy sector deterioration in the previous ten years had a big impact on government's finances as oil accounts for 30 percent of government revenues. Oil production had decreased from 3.4 million barrels per day in 2004 to about 2.5 million in 2012. Foreign investors are interested in developing the large shale deposits, but oil concessions and privatization have not been popular with many Mexicans. Large private investment required a change in the constitution.

Conditions looked auspicious for Mexico's reform and development plans. The start of a new government coincided with a period of economic and political normalization, notwithstanding vocal opposition from the far left. If the 2000s had opened with economic turbulence and closed with a major crisis, both induced by external shocks, the

Mexican economy was now responding to the US's own recovery from the great recession of 2008. Trade and investment were growing. The Pact for Mexico had brought the country close to working consensus on development strategy. Hope rose about overcoming congressional gridlock on pressing policy issues such as telecommunications, education, infrastructure, labor, and oil.[21] The public-private law was being put into effect. Despite the enduring differences and political bickering, a difficult economic chapter seemed behind.

In this broad context, policymakers gave the impression to have forged a consensus on infrastructure and reliance on public-private collaboration. Legislation and a modernized regulatory framework were in place. National and local governments had gained experience in organizing programs and projects (table A.3). Key actors exuded a sense of direction on the still-emergent strategy to accelerate economic expansion.

The 2013–2018 National Infrastructure Plan reaffirmed infrastructure as a main priority. Many of the close to 500 projects across the country aim at improving competitiveness and productivity, with the stated goal for the country to rank in the top 20 percent in the World Economic Forum's Infrastructure Competitiveness Index by 2030 (in 2012, Mexico ranked 68th out of 144 countries surveyed) and similar indicators. The $315 billion plan targets roads and highways, rail lines, seaports and airports, universal access to telecommunications and boosting the energy sector. Fifteen major highways and 29 roads, as well as 16 bypasses and 7 bridges, are to complete a national road system better linking the country's regions. Four world-class ports are to increase the port system's capacity as a whole to support economic sectors, while the merchant fleet is to expand. In airports, the goals are to expand service, decrease cost, relieve congestion, and enhance regional interconnections. In addition, six Rapid Bus Systems will be built in large cities. Expected to remain at close to 5 percent of Mexico's GDP, the investment plan is considerably larger than the $200 billion in infrastructure of the Calderón years.

The plan builds on cooperation agreements with Asian countries—a mid-2013 economic accord with China promising investments of $80 billion largely in transport, communications, energy, trade, and tourism, and a $20 billion credit line from South Korea's Export-Import Bank for infrastructure related to agriculture, transportation, environment, and energy. The NAFTA had encouraged expansion in cross-border trade and infrastructure to move goods and trade with the United States grew to roughly $239 billion in 2000. By 2013, lower labor costs than China and shorter supply chains to the consumer markets of North America made Mexico more competitive.[22] By several measures, the country had entered a new chapter in the consolidation of the liberalized economic model.

Argentina: Denying Liberalism

Argentina, the third largest economy in Latin America, was a main forerunner of radical liberal reform in the region. The process started with the 1989 election of Carlos Menem, the second elected president after the democratic transition of 1983. Reacting to an economy near collapse, Menem implemented rapid and extensive privatization and other market reforms (Teichman, 2001). The speed, scope, and depth of these reforms are fully appreciated in the context of fluid political and institutional dynamics governing their adoption.

Prior to democratization in 1983, Argentina had experienced bouts of direct military rule since 1966, which inaugurated a distinctive regime self-proclaimed as the Argentine Revolution (1966–1973). The military remained close to political power in the decade that followed, and took direct reign in 1976, after a short civilian interlude. The distinguishing features of Argentina's authoritarianism were: rule by the military as an institution (rotating leadership of the military junta as opposed to personalistic rule), openness to foreign investments, focus on industrialization, postponement of redistribution in favor of development goals, and willingness to use force to maintain order. Focusing on its institutional and programmatic features, O'Donnell (1973, 1986) baptized it as "bureaucratic-authoritarianism," highlighting its simultaneous occurrence in the most industrial and developed societies in the region (Chile, Uruguay, and Brazil as well as Argentina). In the 1970s, one of the military governments implemented partial measures to better integrate Argentina to the world economy, but this limited liberalizing effort failed (Galiani and Somaini, 2010; O'Donnell, 1977).

Economic turbulence and the disastrous 1982 Malvinas war helped bring down the military regime, but democratization failed to set the country on a sustainable new course of modernization and development.[23] The "new democracy" opening in 1983 brought lingering political and economic frustration. It might be tempting to blame the leaders and movements of this period, but previous history reveals the deep-seated frustrated search for a new development model away from statism and protectionism (Korol and Sabato, 1990; Miguez, 2006; Remmer and Wibbels, 2000).

Many Argentines had welcomed dirigisme since the 1940s, when the military-populist government of Juan Domingo Perón opted for a development strategy based on protectionism and ISI. After formal adoption by the Peronist Party and allies in the labor movement and industrialists, corporatist dirigisme mustered sufficient political support to block alternative approaches. Unlike Chile, Argentina's military would largely adhere to state-centered industrialization, while the nationalist populism based on the union-based left-leaning wing of the Peronist Party was dominant in national politics. Corporatist interest incorporation, patronage, clientelism, and heavy government spending were key elements of the system (Galiani and Somaini, 2010; Smith, 1989). Economic interventionism was closely aligned with authoritarianism and centralization, with military interventions in politics becoming a recurrent phenomenon for half a century after the coup of 1930, the first of six military overthrows in the twentieth century (also in 1943, 1955, 1962, 1966, and 1976).

Perón was deposed in 1955, but his exile in Franco's Spain did not stop the pattern of statism and coups interrupted by fragile Radical constitutional governments, with the military not too far from power. In 1973–74, Perón and his third wife returned to the presidency, but disappointing results helped precipitate the 1976 military coup and the installation of the technocratic military regime governing until 1982. ISI remained national policy, though foreign investment now played a larger role (Miguez, 2006).

Democratization after 1983 opened a debate of a model now increasingly viewed as having outlived its usefulness, as was the case in neighboring countries. Criticism opened the door for ideas about a major revision, but core economic assumptions, practices, and policies were hard to change. Argentina had well-trained economists, but in contrast to Mexico it lacked the institutionalized reform-minded policymakers in the state apparatus and no political force compared to the Mexican PRI in being capable of subscribing a new approach. In contrast, Argentina was far from having a working agreement on core proposals to steer the country on a new course.

The Radical and Peronist parties opposed the post-1966 military regime but could not forge a sustained common front, while Peronist factions greatly differed in political orientation. Though leaders of some of these forces were often not too distant in doctrine, political rivalries impeded the formation of a strong reform coalition. Post-1983 Argentina was unable to organize an effective response to hyperinflation and economic turbulence, much less agree on a new economic strategy. The centrist Radicals had won the presidential elections that year, but the worsening of the economic crisis, a currency collapse in 1989, and the popular protests that followed doomed their government, with the Peronists as main beneficiaries (Belini, 2012).

The call for new elections five months ahead of schedule led to the victory of Carlos Menem (1989–1999), who brought the Peronist Party back to implement a reform process widely seen as archetypal economic liberalism or "neoliberalism." Never mind that such radical reforms had not been part of his electoral platform. After naming Harvard-trained economist Domingo Cavallo finance minister, the Menem government worked at a furious pace to implement deep and comprehensive measures to radically liberalize the economic model: end protectionism and open the economy, embrace deregulation, authorize privatization, decree a fixed exchange rate, and gain powers to rush the ambitious liberalizing legislative agenda with minimal congressional approval.[24] This was truly a comprehensive approach to reform—though it would not be able to end the large public debt owed by various levels of government.

Telecommunications and energy led the shift toward divestiture and concessions. Notorious for very poor telephone service and high prices, the national telecommunications company ENTel was divided into two segments sold as concessions (Molano, 1997). Altogether, the Argentine privatizations and concessions for 1990–2013 involved over 217 large projects worth more than $93 billion (table 2.2). The total of nearly $35 billion for the 1990–1995 period across all sectors represented 37 percent of the 22-year total, with the 1996–2000 years coming in second place with 34.2 percent. Strikingly, the projects prior to 2000 thus accounted for nearly 71 percent of the public-private investment total through 2013, reflecting a major slowdown after 2001.

Other sectors were also reorganized as concessions in the 1990s. At $21.66 billion, telecommunications was a close second to energy, followed by transportation ($12.5 billion), and water and sanitation ($7.4 billion). In energy, the government tendered concessions to operate the gas and oil industries, with a 1991 decree establishing the legal framework and an independent regulatory agency to oversee the transfer. Highly indebted and losing money, the Argentine energy company Treasury Petroleum Fields (YPF) controlled nearly two-thirds of the country's oil refining capacity. The government auctioned off 39 state oilfields and 4 large oil reserves, while government-owned shares of the two gas companies were placed on the domestic market.

State companies in the transportation sector were likewise offered as concessions. Ferrocarriles Argentinos, the largest rail company in the country with a network of nearly 35,000 kilometers, was losing $1.4 billion a year, with tracks and facilities in need of major repair.[25] The railroad network was broken up into segments and tendered through competitive bidding. Aerolineas Argentinas was put on the auction block as well. But the largest concession awarded was in water and sanitation. Signed in 1993, the Aguas Argentinas concession provided access to 2 million people and sanitation to 1 million people in Buenos Aires, with the concessionaire expected to invest heavily in improving the system.

The economy grew through 2000, turning the seemingly successful Argentine reforms into a model for the region. That year, Congress passed a law to pave the way for a new wave of concessions. The new legislation established infrastructure trust funds to guarantee future financial commitments to concessionaires as well as new regulatory agencies in sectors like transportation and water (Herrera and Tavosnanska, 2011).

But then disaster hit. The catastrophic economic collapse of 2001 submerged the country into a turbulent sea of uncertainty and despair. With the increasing foreign debt of $80 billion blocking an adequate response to the post-1998 recession and financial crisis, a forced default and major currency devaluation sent shock waves to a financial system organized under the premise of currency equivalence between the peso and the US dollar. Trust in official finances evaporated. The phenomenal crash devastated the middle class and made poverty rates soar. The Argentine "big bang" approach to reform had failed miserably (Anós-Casero and Rollo, 2010; Le Clech, 2007; Manzanelli and Martin, 2011; Saxton, 2003; Santarcángelo and Perrone, 2012).

It was now Menem's turn to see his support evaporate. Political power returned to the Radicals, but tensions between immediate popular demands and proposals for economic growth paralyzed the government. Street protest and riots became commonplace. The government's inability to end political turmoil once again drove the social democratic Radicals from power. They had not created the crisis, yet were blamed for the unresolved national catastrophe.[26] The loss of trust and a damaged reputation among international financiers explain why this time they did not come to the country's rescue. With the economic collapse seeming to have no end, desperate Argentines brought Peronists back to power in 2003, but this time with the left-leaning populism of Néstor Kirchner. Emphasis consequently shifted back toward state control of the economy (Féliz, 2012; Wylde, 2011).

Public-private collaboration became a victim of the crisis. The new Peronist government revoked the license of Aguas Argentinas in 2006, arguing that the company had failed to achieve the targets of expansion and quality under the contract. Cancellations spread, totaling 17 (8 in utilities, 3 each in roads and railroads, and 2 in electricity. An even larger number of concessions became "distressed"—23 in total, representing $16.5 billion. Needless, the period after 2001 saw a pronounced slowdown in new concessions and partnerships, with 40 projects reaching financial closure through 2010, in contrast to the 177 projects in the period 1990–2001. By the end of 2013, a total of 42 projects were distressed or cancelled (representing 27 percent of total investment between 1990 and 2013). Argentina had been a pioneer in concessions (passing its first concessions law in 1967), but now lagged far behind Chile, Brazil, and other neighbors. By 2012, it ranked a low 18th place in PPP investment climate in the region (The Economist Intelligence Unit's report). That report highlighted a very weak regulatory framework and deteriorated political support for concessions and partnerships. The innovations, institutional changes, and learning processes initiated in the early 1990s had lost their luster.

The election of Cristina Fernández de Kirchner (2007–2011) provided political and policy continuity. With the economic crisis having bottomed out, recovery contributed to her own reelection in 2012. However, continued state-centered policies strained relations with business, while many Argentines yearned for a working consensus on a coherent approach to development.[27] Cristina Fernández de Kirchner's governments continued to gravitate toward statism—as reflected in large deficits, inflation, price-setting, controls of foreign exchange, some nationalizations, and media restrictions. It remained democratic, despite the collapse of the party system and the weakened institutions (Levitsky and Murillo, 2008).

International investors worried about the renationalization of concessions; the most publicized was the 2012 takeover of Repsol's holdings of the large oil complex previously operated by the state-owned Treasury Petroleum Fields (YPF). In mid-2013, the government moved against the Belgrano Cargas railroad, which transported grains and oilseeds from 13 northern provinces to Rosario, other Paraná river ports, and Buenos Aires.[28] Latin America Logistics (ALL) was also expropriated that year. Owned by the Brazilian ALL, this concession connected western provinces to Atlantic ports, and to Uruguay and Brazil. The government revoked licences for these concessions charging them with breach of contract. The new Belgrano Cargas y Logística S.A. now controlled the holdings previously operated by ALL. China, importer of $5 billion worth of soy and other agricultural products from Argentina, provided financial support for this transaction through a $10 billion line of credit.[29] Truckers, who transported 84 percent of soy and cereals to ports and had owned 6.5 percent of Belgrano Cargas, were a main actor in this shift (Oviedo, 2013).

The Fernández de Kirchner government had additional reasons for the takeovers of these railways, especially their strained finances and complaints about service. But the nationalizations confirmed fears on the part of investors that had contracted to manage the railways since the Menem years.[30] Concessionaires and investors generally worried about a broad movement toward nationalization, the rising tide of statism, the collapse of the liberalizing impulse, and the strained relations between the public and private sectors. They lamented the absence of independent regulatory agencies and a transparent regulatory framework.

Meanwhile, industries other than the auto sector exported to Brazil had failed to expand. The industrial sector's share of GDP, which had decreased precipitously since the 1980s, did experience a recovery from 2002 to 2008 in the changed economic context (Herrera and Tavosnanska, 2011), but it decreased afterward. Economic growth after 2001 was led by exports, particularly agricultural exports such as soy, corn, and other grains (Bekerman and Dulcich, 2013; Oviedo, 2013), with agriculture representing 42 percent of exports. After decades trying to industrialize, Argentina was in fact nowhere close to an industrial take-off such as experienced by East Asia. Policymakers had shifted toward a policy of promoting agricultural and other exports combined with subsidies and tariffs to protect domestic industry (Gallo, 2012).

The country's swings in policy paradigm and in politics contrast with continuity and a sense of direction in Mexico, Chile, and even Brazil, as examined next. As of 2014, Argentines wondered whether the country had the national consensus, institutions, and momentum needed for long-term success.[31]

Democratization and Reform: Brazil and Chile

The above discussion provides a baseline to explore Brazil, the largest country and economy in the region and host to the largest program of public-private cooperation (table A.4). In turn, the three cases also invite a comparison with the Chilean approach, often treated as exemplary in the region. In Brazil after 1985 and Chile after 1990, regime change toward democracy initiated or extended the liberalizing reforms governing public-private collaboration.

The Brazilian Way

Brazil towers in levels of private investment in virtually all infrastructure sectors, with 693 projects and $438 billion in the 23 years after 1990 (table 2.3). The first great wave took place in 1997 and 1998, as part of reform initiatives of Fernando Henrique Cardoso's first term (1995–1998). Still, Private Participation in Infrastructure (PPI) increased after 2000, accounting for nearly 73 percent of the total—in contrast with only 28.5 percent in neighboring Argentina.

The Brazilian road to liberalizing reform was relatively late yet sustained despite some backlash and uncertainty shortly after the turn of the century, with the victory of a left-leaning government presided by Lula da Silva. But core elements of the liberalizing reform survived the political shift, to eventually gain momentum. The post-1985 process of redemocratization thus provides key context for the liberalizing measures that eventually led to the largest public-private sector in the region. Decentralization has been an important part of the story, as the constitution of 1988 shifted this federation of over eight million km^2 away from the centralization and statism in place since the 1930s. The new charter multiplied the centers of decision making, creating opportunities for political participation and policy innovation. While 27 state-level units and thousands of municipalities now had a great deal of authority in a considerably decentralized polity, nationally the party system expanded dramatically.

This redefined and changing polity greatly shaped the search for a new economic model. However, in the eight years after 1985, the democratizing federal government failed to stabilize the economy or generate economic growth. Clientelism and abuses of power persisted. In 1992, corruption charges after only two years in office led to the impeachment of Fernando Collor de Mello, the first president elected by direct vote. Meanwhile, the austerity measures and liberal reforms announced by Collor failed to stop hyperinflation and give the economy a clear sense of direction. Perplexed by the seemingly chronic economic quagmire, some Brazilians now wondered about the very prospects of democracy. However, the 1993 Real Plan and a broader process of state reform succeeded in defeating inflation, laying the groundwork for gradual recovery, and renewing trust in government (Font, 2003; Bresser-Pereira, 2011).

Changing macroeconomic conditions after 1994 made possible to widen and deepen the liberalizing measures. In infrastructure, Brazil's privatization program was nearly three-fifths of the region's total projects with private participation between 1994 and 2004 (World Bank, 2005, PPI Database). Telecommunications was the largest, reaching more than $55.2 billion in the period 1996–2000—of which $28.2 billion took place in 1998 alone, much of it through divestiture. Energy and transportation also received large amounts of new investment.

Though reformist policymakers since the 1980s had recognized the need to resolve infrastructure bottlenecks, insufficient public revenues had blocked decisive public intervention. The condition of the already deteriorated infrastructure worsened. The expansion of soy and other export commodities, much of it in the central-west and adjacent regions, highlighted the inadequacy of existing roads, rail, logistics, storage, and port facilities. In the 1990s, fiscal reforms and the commodities-led economic boom contributed to the government's ability to gradually regain its investment capacity. But Brazilian authorities faced a daunting task. Over the prior four decades, the country had seen a decline in government spending on infrastructure—from an average of 5.4 percent of GDP in the 1970s to 3.6 percent in the 1980s, 2.3 percent in the 1990s, and 2.1 percent in the first part of the 2000s. The deteriorated infrastructure made Brazil rank quite low in comparison with East Asia and some other emergent countries. It would take investments of upward of 4 percent of GDP for twenty years to catch up with Chile (see figure 2.2), a figure that jumped to 6–8 percent to match South Korea.[32]

Gradually, Brazilian policymakers sought to meet the challenge. After little activity between 1990 and 1995, transportation received $17.6 billion of public-private investment in 1996–2000; and though this figure contracted to $2.4 billion in the five years after 2001, it recovered to $27.3 billion in the 2006–2010 range, to then rise to $22 billion in 2012 and 11.1 billion in 2013. Energy peaked in 1996–2000, with $41.2 billion out of a total of $116.5 billion, but continued to attract investment in subsequent years (see table 2.3), receiving $58.1 billion in the 2006–2010 period and growing at an even higher rate in 2011 and 2012.

The government-owned Eletrobras had carved out a monopoly over electricity generation and transmission since its launching in the early 1960s, with distribution in the hands of state utilities. The federal government started to unbundle and privatize components of the system in 1995. But political opposition impeded fast progress in this effort. Still, nearly a fourth of the electricity generation and 64 percent of distribution were converted to concessions, while Aneel emerged as the new regulatory agency for the entire sector. Nevertheless, the

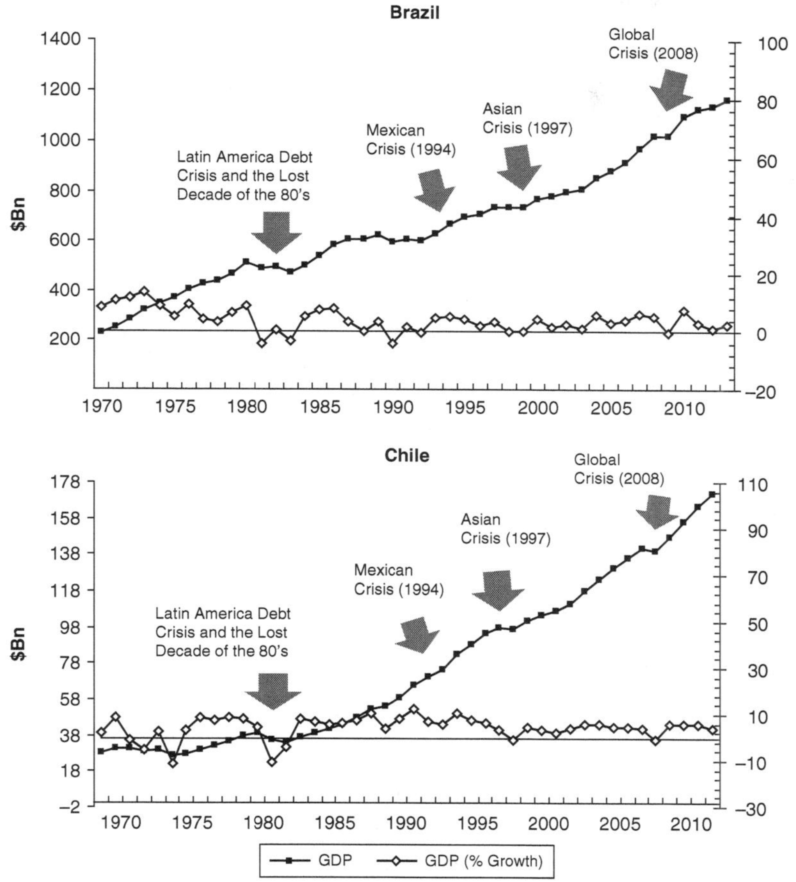

Figure 2.2 Brazil and Chile, GDP and growth, 1970–2013.

Source: World Bank, 2014b.

state-controlled Eletrobras was responsible for 58 percent of production (Andrés et al., 2008: 88)—and continued to expand in subsequent years, eventually becoming the largest power utility company in Latin America. The federal government owned 52 percent of its shares. In turn, the company had control over several subsidiaries in electricity generation, distribution, and energy research—including 50 percent of the capital stock of the trinational Itaipu, the world's largest hydroelectric plant. Its size and role made Eletrobras an important strategic actor with operations outside Brazil.

In telecommunications, the 1972 formation of state-owned Telebras as a virtual national monopoly had consolidated more than 900 different companies. In 1998, the federal government restructured the system into twelve companies—three fixed-line enterprises provided intraregional services, eight concentrated on cellular service, and Embratel itself, which handled national and international long-distance. The twelve enterprises were sold as concessions in 1998, with further measures to increase competition initiated a year later (Andrés, Diop, and Guasch, 2008: 120).

The more challenging public-private partnerships became gradually accepted and viable in the 2000s. The idea of adopting this business form in public infrastructure originally emerged in the late 1990s and was formalized as a policy concept in 2002 to address infrastructure needs at the end of F. H. Cardoso's second term (1998–2002). After 2004, the national government under the Workers' Party approved a legal framework for a new generation of concessions and partnerships. Concrete works would need to wait several years, but the new approach was taking root.

The four-year development plan through 2003 (Pluriannual Plan, PPA 2000–2003) was part of the story, as it provided a comprehensive framework shaping Brazilian thinking about infrastructure development. *Avança Brasil* built on a major planning study that identified nine national development corridors and sketched plan for upward of $20 billion annually to develop them. Competitiveness and trade expansion weighed heavily in the minds of policymakers. The plan also aimed at reducing regional disparities and better integrating the country. Expanding exports required massive improvements in transportation. For instance, export of soy alone would increase in the decade after 2000, largely due to China's demand. Awareness gradually rose about the limits of the public sector's finances, considering an increasingly ambitious national agenda and the need for innovation.

The 1998–1999 Asian financial crisis, coupled with internal political turbulence, ushered in a hiatus in public investment lasting through the early 2000s. Meantime, the boom in commodities, which had been gathering force since the mid-1990s, was thrusting the new export sector in the limelight and confirming trade promotion as a key government priority (see also PPA 1996–1999, PPA 2000–2003, and the subsequent plans of Workers' Party governments).

By the early years of the new century, policymakers grew confident that they had effectively defeated inflation, reorganized national finances, and laid the macroeconomic basis for sustained growth.

They were ready for more ambitious development goals, though federal investments were still much less than required due to high cost of infrastructure and other demands for government spending. Private sector participation grew as an attractive alternative. Public-private collaboration had contracted in the 2001–2005 but slowly began to recover in 2006.

The shift came about partly from subnational developments. In 2004, the states of São Paulo and Minas Gerais had approved public-private partnership programs, turning these two states as important leaders in this policy field. Partnerships on infrastructure provision became a national reality in 2006. Even then, the federal government wavered on the fiscal, institutional, and political commitment to invite private sector participation in infrastructure. The early Workers' Party government was not committed to the agenda defined by the outgoing authorities and lacked the internal consensus to support a program they had sharply criticized while in the opposition. Full endorsement of concessions and public-private partnerships was far from certain in 2003, though a number of important officials viewed them as desirable. Lingering statism and political rivalries slowed down the reform process and the adoption of concessions and partnerships. As a result, the nearly $51.6 billion invested in 2001–2005 was less than half the amount spent in the previous and subsequent five-year periods.

However, the discussion on using financial stimulus and guarantees to private investors had also produced a national public-private partnership program together with a legal framework (Law 11.079 of December 2004, see also CAF, 2010), as did São Paulo and Minas Gerais. Both levels of government passed laws, identified specific projects, and designed partnering programs. Other states and subnational units made similar announcements in 2005 and after. In the months that followed, a flurry of international investment gathering sought to attract external investors to business opportunities worth billions of dollars.[33] With the legislation already in place, the partnership model called for greater synergy in the planning, construction, and operational phases of the project than regular concessions. Government could offer service payments and other incentives to private operators as additional guarantees for various risks. Expectation built about the new initiative as PPA 2004–2007 repeated the call for massive investments in infrastructure.

During Lula da Silva's second term (2007–2010), the federal government moved beyond merely acknowledging the limits of government as a direct economic agent toward accepting the idea of extensive private sector participation in infrastructure. Significant progress would only be visible after 2008. But the national government was thinking big about infrastructure. In January 2007, the government launched the first of two Growth Acceleration Programs (PAC), a package of projects to eliminate obstacles to growth. PAC1 listed upward of $250 billion in roads, railways, housing, and energy while also sketching projects in finance and credit, taxation, and environmental regulations. These ideas were reaffirmed in PPA 2008–2011.

Barely 50 percent of the plan had come to fruition by early 2010, but the trend was increasingly clear. Also early that year, the federal government announced PAC2, an extended plan aiming to provide $880 billion in infrastructure and housing, health, public works, and other social areas. The plan was put together by presidential chief of staff Dilma Rousseff prior to stepping down in order to run her own presidential campaign. For the 2011–2014 period, transportation would receive a total allocation of more than R$100 billion, much of it for railroads and highways. Funds would go toward constructing 3,500 kilometer of railroad, including the Ferrovia Norte-Sul and Nova Transnordestina. Billions were also listed for a high-speed train service between Rio and São Paulo.[34] These costly packages would be financed by government, state enterprises such as Petrobras, and the private sector.

Moreover, yet other ambitious infrastructure goals evolving after 2007 allocated billions for infrastructure to host the soccer World Cup of 2014 and the Olympic games of 2016. Known as "PAC da Copa," a 2010 plan described two main types of investments. The first was new and refurbished stadiums. The second were urban mobility projects: six Bus Rapid Transit (BRT) systems and corridors, two monorails (Manaus and São Paulo), a light rail vehicle (LRV) in Brasilia, and substantial enhancements to airports. The federal government pledged R$7.6 billion of the nearly R$12 billion reais needed for the mobility projects—R$6.4 billion from the Federal Savings Bank (CEF) and R$1.2 billion from the Brazilian Development Bank (BNDES). Many warned about the dangers of overreach, but authorities shrugged off critical advice and recommitted themselves to the ambitious plan.

The public wondered about the wisdom of these expenditures and the ability to complete them on time and within the budget. By 2011, only 11.3 percent of the PAC projects had been completed, while nearly 70 percent of the transportation projects were still in the bidding process. Other investments were behind schedule, while corruption scandals subsequently caused disruptions and delays (see Chapter Four). Failure to meet environmental regulations and other criteria further slowed the process. Anxiety about the sports infrastructure would last through a few short weeks before the games. While the World Cup was expected to be R$3.5 billion over budget, the costs of financing would reach R$6.7 billion over 13 years—representing estimated total costs of R$35 billion.[35]

Chapter Four explores the role of public-private initiatives in the expansion of the railroad system to serve the expanding commodities frontier in Brazil's central region, while Chapter Five discusses subnational approaches.

The sheer size, complexity, range, and dynamics of the modern Brazilian experiences with public-private collaboration provide a near insurmountable challenge for a full assessment at this point. But this experiment is too important not to sketch an approximation.

Brazilian democratic reformers since the 1990s had sound and compelling reasons to search for infrastructure goals and new business models to accomplish them. These reasons endure, especially considering the expanding commodities frontier in the central plateau, railroad needs, and slowdowns such as after 2012. Still, issue and problem areas listed below need to be addressed for public-private collaboration to confirm its long-term viability in addressing the infrastructure question. First, institutional factors continue to limit the role of the federal government in its own sphere of policy action with planning that is not fully credible, often erring or giving the impression of being driven by political considerations. As shown in PAC as well as World Cup and Olympics projects, there have been additional problems with completion and budget projections, criteria for choosing projects, issues of corruption and accountability, and seemingly too large a role for political-electoral criteria rather than functional need or merit. Against initial hints about significant private participation, the expensive stadiums were largely paid with public funds. The country clearly needs management and planning structures and personnel with functional independence from party politics and subject to high norms of transparency and accountability. Issues of probity and accountability haunt efforts to develop projects and argue for an institutional framework less vulnerable to corruption.[36]

A parallel set of arguments pertain to the need to form effective collaborative relations with subnational authorities. Key policy areas under the jurisdiction of federal authorities all too often give the impression of being driven by political or even patrimonial interests of incumbents rather than by independent rational criteria—as in the case of rail transportation policy (Chapters Four and Five). Since both levels of government have gained skills and confidence in developing concessions and partnerships, there is an argument here for better ways of collaborating in the design and implementation of projects.

The very difficulties in attracting foreign or national private investment to these projects further indicate flaws in addressing and anticipating the concerns of prospective investors. Again, a more professional civil service is needed to explore issues of adequate financial planning, effectiveness of the bidding process, and impediments to the formation of satisfactory partnerships with the private sector. These are weighty questions posed by Brazilians themselves.

Still, a full assessment of Brazil's approach to public-private collaboration needs to fully consider its accomplishments. First, most major political currents in Brazil have come to accept and even support the liberalized model and public-private collaboration—a remarkable pattern that differs markedly from the levels of animosity at the turn of the century. Visible levels of opposition have decreased considerably. Moreover, the portfolio of projects in the pipeline has grown at a fast pace. Finally, civil service agencies at various levels of government have gained confidence and expertise, while a significant number of private and nonstate actors provide a critical mass of actors with new skills regarding risk assessment, financial modeling, financing, construction, management, and responding to environmental and community criteria and concerns.[37] More than ever, conditions exist for maintaining momentum and further advancing the social learning from mistakes and successes to craft a more innovative and effective delivery of infrastructure services.

Chile's Concerted Reforms

While several Latin American countries initiated major drives for state reform in the aftermath of the 1980s debt crisis, Chile began its reforms after the military regime seized power in September 1973. This coup overthrew the leftist coalition that had elected Socialist president Salvador Allende (1970–1973). The latter represented the peak of socialist dirigisme in Chile—a process that began to expand during the populist government of 1938 and deepened through the 1960s.[38] While Allende expanded the nationalization of large enterprises, the military regime led by General Augusto Pinochet (1973–1990) transferred public assets to the private sector and initiated a broad range of market reforms (Murillo, 2002; Paredes, 2001; Stallings, 1978, 2003).

The turn to radical economic liberalism was far from obvious or predictable. The country's armed forces had been considerably statist, as was often the case throughout the region, while no government or multilateral organization pressured the country for such a shift at the time. More likely, the reform impetus came about from the convergence of a conservative regime in urgent need of a new economic model and the existence in Chile of a group of economists recently trained at the University of Chicago under Milton Friedman (Puryear, 1994; Valdés, 1995). The adoption of these ideas by General Pinochet appears to have been more the result of Weberian "elective affinity" than of a narrowly deterministic mechanism.[39]

A further indication against overly deterministic accounts linking Chile's liberalizing project to narrow economic interests came about with democratization and the political victory of the opposition in 1990 (Budds, 2013; Ffrench-Davis, 2010; Vellinga, 1998). Instead of returning to statist or populist practices, the center-left democratizing alliance installed that year and ruling continuously until 2010 made modest changes to the core economic model. Driven by the ideas of concerted political action, democracy, and pragmatism, the Concertación political coalition, a broad coalition dominated by Christian democratic, democratic socialists, centrists and progressives, but also including communists and more radical left, retained the core of the liberalized model while seeking to make its own contribution to the country's development (Domínguez, 1997). Key elements of the liberalizing paradigm can be said to have been consolidated at that moment (Roberts, 1998).

Moreover, it was the democratizing coalition itself that opted for public-private collaboration (concessions and partnerships) to address infrastructure gaps after 1990. This was a genuine and significant policy innovation, for the military regime had neither placed infrastructure as a major priority nor adopted concessions or partnerships (Grugel, 2009). In this context of consensus, Chile's emergence as an effective pioneer and user of concessions and partnerships in South America made it an exemplary case. Even before coming to power, broad agreement had formed within the center-left democratic Concertación that neither state intervention nor the private sector alone was able to efficiently provide a range of large public goods and services such as infrastructure. Political leaders identified concessions and partnerships as major development tools in a modernized strategy (Cruz, 2002; Cruz and Barrientos, 2001).

After 1990, four consecutive Concertación administrations (Patricio Aylwin, Eduardo Frei, Ricardo Lagos, and Michelle Bachelet) relied on concessions and partnerships to build or redesign major roads and transportation facilities, as part of goals to modernize and increase competitiveness in the liberalized economy. These reformist governments also focused on the need for policies of urban development and regeneration. The shift to concessions came in the early 1990s, as the newly inaugurated democratic government of Patricio Aylwin (1990–1994) focused on the infrastructure bottlenecks caused by years of use and neglect. The concessions law of 1991 aimed at modernizing the antiquated road and transportation system while maintaining fiscal austerity. Concessions also promised to attract private capital to modernize neglected ports and airports.[40] Later, public-private partnerships as such provided further ideas about how to improve Chile's transportation infrastructure and modernize the economy, while also addressing social needs. By 1994, the country felt prepared to embark on a large program of concessions and public-private collaboration in transportation infrastructure.[41]

Leadership was another key element in the reforms of the 1990s. Germán Correa and Carlos Hurtado—ministers of transportation and telecommunications and public works in the early 1990s—were important players in the design of the new concessions. As minister of public works during the second Concertación government (Frei Ruiz-Tagle 1994–2000), Ricardo Lagos played a decisive role in developing a broad congressional and political consensus in support of concessions, the creation of a concessions agency, and the launching of the first modern projects based on concessions.[42] The broad idea was to signal to the private sector that this was to be a new programmatic direction for the country (a "proyecto país"), not just another approach to public works project (interviews with Díaz and Lagos). In 1996, changes to Law 1004–95 further opened the gate to public-private collaboration.

The Chilean concessions program became a major way to attract private capital to update long-neglected transportation infrastructure in regard to highways,[43] ports,[44] and airports.[45] By 2005, this program was responsible for 44 projects valued at $5.7 billion (about 6¼ percent of the 2004 GDP).[46] The list included 8 projects to upgrade the Route 5 highway extending the length of Chile, financed through tolls ($2 billion); additional highway projects for connecting roads to Route 5 ($1.3 billion); 10 airport projects ($240 million); 6 urban highway projects ($1.8 billion); and 9 other projects, which included prisons, public buildings, and a reservoir ($360 million) (IMF, 2005: 10).

Chile has relied heavily on the BOT concessions model (finance, build, operate, and transfer), which have gained centrality as effective ways to achieve major development goals such as increased competitiveness and economic expansion. From 1994 onward, this model was used to attract private sector investment in transportation infrastructure as a main means of repairing or rebuilding dilapidated highways, ports, and airports. Public-private collaboration has helped improve the country's transportation system, boost the export economy, and focus public sector funds on social expenditures. The new highways rely on tolls to generate a guaranteed stream of income for operators and investors. The government set up an infrastructure fund, guaranteeing minimum revenues to concessionaires.[47]

In many of Chile's concessions and partnerships, the concessionaire has complete responsibility for infrastructure services in a specified area—operation, maintenance, collection, management, delivery. The concessionaire finances investments for building, upgrading, maintaining, and expanding the system. Concessions are usually granted for 25 years (Bennett et al., 1999).

Chile has received praise for several features of its concessions and partnerships program—the Concessions Law itself, the procedures for evaluating projects, care in project design and scrutiny of bidders, contractual flexibility and provisions for possible renegotiation of contracts, clarity in definition of risks assumed by government, and fiscal transparency (Guasch, 2008). The IMF views Chile's institutional framework and fiscal transparency as lessons for other countries. The success of Chile's program is mainly attributed to a strong institutional and legal framework, respect for contracts (low levels of corruption), and political and economic stability. The Ministry of Public Works manages the concessions agency set up to develop, repair, and maintain public works that fall into the jurisdiction of the central government (Domper and Allard, 2009). The Ministry of Finance oversees bidding procedures and operations to ensure that the fiscal aspects of the concession contract are in line with economic policies. Within the Ministry of Public Works, the Concessions Agency (Coordinación General de Concesiones) established in 1991 designed and organized the bidding process, supervised the concessions program, recommended new projects, and developed norms for concessions. This agency is divided into three departments focused on projects, construction, and operations. The agency also works with agencies that enforce legal, environmental, social, and engineering standards. Since 1996, all concession projects have been subjected to environmental impact assessments contracted by the Concessions Agency, with the concessionaire being legally responsible for complying with environmental standards (Banco Interamericano de Desarrollo, 2003).

Still there is room for improvement. The IMF report lists several risks and potential pitfalls in areas such as the procedures for conflict resolution, project evaluation, design and engineering specifications, full disclosure of contracts, and fiscal dangers with the Infrastructure Fund.

Building on the success of Chile's concessions program, the Transantiago project may be viewed as a system of concessions with considerable coordination of efforts between the public and private sectors, making it a public-private partnership. Gibrán Harcha, who played a significant role in the team designing Transantiago, managed the sale of rights to commercial routes as concessions subject to a system of contracts between the concessionaires and new private economic actors yet to be created (the financial administrator and user information provider) in what Harcha called a network of interlinked contracts ("red de contratos cruzados").[48] Transantiago's implementation (see Chapter Six) deepened Chile's experience with and knowledge of concessions. Though at lower levels of investment than the 1990s, the 2000s saw continued use of concessions and partnerships as a key tool of public policy, using them in various infrastructure projects: roads, railway, water, sanitation, jails, schools, and others. In 2009, the Ministry of Public Works recommitted itself to infrastructure concessions, with a substantial increase in project investment from 2008. Despite Transantiago's complications and a three-year licitation hiatus tendered between 2004 and 2007,[49] the Chilean program has continued its commitment to the public-private model.

In December 2009, Law 20.410 further enhanced the concessions legislation. This legislation redefined the rights of government and the Ministry of Public Works to increase the technical standards governing concession bids, delineating rights of the concessionaires concerning economic compensation for unanticipated costs, fines, and termination of concessions. The law specifies that partnerships with the private sector may include substantial public resources. In the presentation of this bill, President Bachelet pondered the role of concessions in Chile's infrastructure revolution and proclaimed the need to consolidate public-private partnerships. From the perspective of Chilean officials, concessions and partnerships had enabled the government to boost economic growth and deliver infrastructure and public services.

The 2010 presidential election signaled an important change in Chilean politics. The victory of businessman Sebastián Piñera and his center-right coalition meant the end of Concertación's two-decade reign. Concertación had inaugurated the modern focus on infrastructure and urban development through concessions and partnerships, and the extent of continuity in policy under Piñera was not obvious. But reliance on concessions and partnerships policy remained stable, as the new government endorsed them. As part of the opposition, the new authorities had opposed the Transantiago system and model, but changed toward a constructive tone after taking office (see Chapter Six). Some voices from the left carped at what they called the return of privatization. However, with substantial concession legislation and policies in place, Transantiago, concessions, and partnerships continued to evolve.

In April 2010, the new regulatory framework of Law 20.410 (Public Works Concession Law) came into effect. It further improved the climate for increased construction and reconstruction projects after the early 2010 earthquake, which gave the new government additional reasons to mobilize funds for infrastructure. At that time, the country's construction industry made an important contribution to growth in the Chilean economy. But subsequent years through 2014 saw reduced action in new concessions. Chile's infrastructure gap increased somewhat, as reflected in a lower score in WEF's infrastructure ranking. Chile had invested 2.5 percent of GNI in infrastructure in the last ten years, which seemed unlikely to be sustained.

The Chilean model had gained a reputation as one with strong institution, low levels of corruption, and successful. Two caveats are in order. First, there was not much activity in the national infrastructure plan between 2010 and 2014. Second, by the time Michelle Bachelet returned to presidency in 2014, government priorities had shifted to increase taxes to finance educational access and reduce inequality. Meanwhile, the needs of big cities continued to grow. Santiago, a city of over 6 million inhabitants and 1.5 million vehicles, needed $12 billion in roads, streets, and urban highways to reduce the impact of traffic congestion. New needs had also emerged throughout the county. As of mid-decade, the expectation was that public-private collaboration would continue to play a major role in providing infrastructure.

Conclusion

The above Latin American cases show considerable, albeit uneven, expansion in public-private collaboration. Brazil and Mexico host large and diversified programs, while Chile's sustained use of concessions and partnerships has been exemplary. These three countries show leadership and momentum in adopting policy paradigms that encourage private sector participation in public infrastructure provision (Eggers and Startup, 2006). But, as argued below, the region's programs of concessions and partnerships also show diversity of process and outcome. These variations in patterns of expansion and opposition invite explanation (Domínguez, 1998; Smith et al., 1994)

In commodity-rich South America, these reforms have often taken place in the context of deepening strategies of outward or export-led development. As exemplified by Brazil, the post-1980s surge in global demand for natural resources induced a new phase of export-led economic expansion. This commodities boom placed additional pressure on the need to overcome obstacles from inadequate roads, railroads, logistics, ports, and logistics. Likewise, soy and other agricultural exports drove Argentina's economic growth and increased the need for enhanced transportation facilities. In contrast, the Mexican economic model centers on integrated manufacturing networks within North America, aiming to emerge as a hub of general economic exchange as well as tourism.

In both cases a main impetus for private engagement in infrastructure has come from the need to reduce and eventually eliminate gaps in transportation, energy, communications, water, and sanitation, now identified as development bottlenecks. However, need or demand alone hardly guarantee adoption, much less success. Where it has thrived, public-private collaboration has come about in the context of liberalizing reform processes often embedded in broader political transformations, including transitions to democracy (Estache, 2006; Latinobarómetro, 2010). The strength of the state itself shapes both liberalization and democratization, as political leadership has proven essential. Differences in these contexts account for various paths to public-private collaboration. The entire phenomenon is thus best viewed in a political process perspective that encompasses institutional change.

In addition, successful cases have sustained a reform trajectory in which divestiture, concessions, and partnerships have come in that order. The adoption of the more complex and demanding partnering programs has built on prior experience with simpler forms of public-private collaboration. In the early phase of these reform processes, governments sold assets directly to private operators, progressively shifting from divestiture toward concessions (generally some variation of the build-operate-transfer or BOT type) and public-private partnerships. Their actions were part of innovative efforts to create synergistic effects between public and private actors and as effective responses to societal needs in the context of fiscal constraints.

While successful programs of concessions and partnerships have generally built on preexisting reform processes, both have also been shaped by fiscal pressures and economic crises as well as by political dynamics. The economic turbulence of the 1980s drove governments to devise reforms that included privatization through divestiture (Eggers and Goldsmith, 2004; Stallings and Peres, 2011). But rushing to action can be perilous. Political support for divestiture support sharply declined after the second half of the 1990s. In Argentina, the first decade of the twenty-first century saw strengthened opposition to these and related liberalizing measures. Liberalization and destatization initiatives have faced opposition but with different outcomes throughout Latin America. Public-private collaboration steadied in Mexico, Brazil, and Chile, as policymakers and stakeholders learned from simple concessions, assimilated setbacks, and went on to organize more complex partnerships with the private sector.

Reform trajectories are shaped by institutional legacies, but the influence is not obvious. Legacies generally call for the replication or survival of some past patterns, but innovation means that things do not remain as they have been. Public-private collaboration requires that governing institutions develop new capabilities to design and organize effective programs and projects. Institutional adaptations need to endure in a changed context. Values, norms, and behavior need to change, as part of "deep" forms of institutional transformation (Portes, 2010). Political leadership and the mobilization of emerging economic interests are key elements, and the forging of new consensus is critical (table A.3).

In a nutshell, processes of reform require a combination of strong leadership, consensus building, and the development of policy and political backbone. Chapter Three further explores these relationships in contrasting cases of rejection and adoption in South America. Economic globalization and political transitions to democracy shaped the implementation and outcomes of liberalization policies in all of these cases. China's rise as a world economic power and source of commodity booms have added further pressure for better infrastructure. But governments alone are unable to provide infrastructure and hence launch initiatives to widen the role of the private sector.

CHAPTER THREE

Liberalization/Anti-Liberalization

While virtually all South American countries launched liberalizing and public-private initiatives by the first half of the 1990s, movements of opposition challenged them and shaped outcomes in a number of countries. Impact varied in both instances. Colombia and Peru experienced sustained liberalization and, eventually, considerable state-market collaboration. In contrast, anti-liberalization movements in Bolivia and Ecuador contributed to the rise of regimes—sometimes characterized as post-neoliberal—that significantly altered the course of reform. After discussing these two sets of Andean cases, this chapter closes with a review of Uruguay and Paraguay.

The contrast between adoption and disaffection makes South America a particularly interesting laboratory to identify conditions shaping public-private collaboration.[1] Sustained prior liberalization provides a basis for successful public-private collaboration, I argue in this volume. If so, the first task here is to identify conditions that help account for differences in reform processes. Factors such as sequencing and timing have been invoked to explain the latter's durability and need to be considered. This study explores the political and institutional dynamics of reform processes and proximate conditions shaping them. International development dynamics and policy networks have an impact on national experiences with reforms. Still, sustained cases of liberalization share a handful of endogenous conditions that mediate the impact of other variables: internal dissatisfaction with traditional statism, a shared focus on a reform policy agenda (as reflected through different presidencies), political leadership, institutional capability, and a process of social learning. The combination of institutional strength and political leaders and coalitions committed to liberalizing reforms is crucial. Policymakers are frequently motivated by the aim of increasing exports, attracting investment, increasing competitiveness in the context of pressures from globalization, improving services, ensuring macroeconomic stability, and preventing inflationary and fiscal deterioration.

South America has also attracted considerable attention because of opposition to economic liberalism. Some authors argue that the antiliberal movements clustering in a few years around the turn of the century initiated a regional trend toward "post-neoliberalism."[2] These cases of opposition and rejection share a handful of characteristics: new leftist governments, popular movement participation, the search for alternatives to the liberalizing doctrines associated with the Washington Consensus and neoliberal economics (Margheritis and Pereira, 2007; Rodrik, 2006; Rovira Kaltwasser, 2011; Silva, 2009a). These shifts demonstrate the negative impact of liberalizing reforms and the breakdown of the political consensus supporting them. That is, liberalizing reforms are taken to have lost credibility and effectiveness—with backlash against policies presumed to have resulted from exclusionary and elitist agreements among experts and transnational capital opening the way for alternatives. Though the concept of "post-neoliberal state" lacks precise definition, it contrasts with those of developmental state or neoliberal state in several main ways—ending economic liberalism as dominant policy paradigm, reasserting the role of the state, a political turn to the left, link to popular movements (particularly ethnic communities), social-democratic welfare measures, and opposition to US hegemony.

The post-neoliberal literature concentrates on the election of several presidencies after 1998 inaugurating government sharing these characteristics. That year Venezuelans elected Hugo Chávez. In Ecuador, the overthrow of Jamil Mahuad in 2000, and the truncated presidency of Lucio Gutiérrez between 2002 and 2005 opened the door for the election of Rafael Correa in December 2006. The Argentine debt default and street protests of December 2001 were followed by the election of Néstor Kirchner in 2003 and Cristina Fernández de Kirchner in 2007. In Bolivia, social movement protests in 2003 followed by the resignation of Gonzalo Sánchez de Lozada led to the election of Evo Morales in 2005. In addition, the election of Tabaré Vázquez to the Uruguayan presidency in 2004 brought a leftist coalition to power, though one only partly sharing the above traits.

These are the main cases taken to demonstrate the negative impact of economic reforms and the breakdown of the consensus on liberal economic policy. To explain these shifts, Silva (1999) and others highlight the role of popular contention opposed to market or neoliberal reforms presumed to have had for poor economic performance. Anti-neoliberal mobilization objected to the foreign imprint, economic costs, social impact, or unpopularity of neoliberal reforms. Particularly in the Andes, the new movements demanded redistribution, expanded government, revision of property rights to benefit indigenous communities, and direct popular participation (Lucero, 2009). These popular movements often aimed at replacing neoliberalism with a mixed economy and a larger welfare state rather than with necessarily advancing a purer socialist model. In any case, political and ideological reactions to neoliberalism are at the core of the shifts to the left, according to post-neoliberal authors. These authors see the slow or negative economic growth after 1997 as evidence of the failure of the liberal reforms of the 1990s and thus a main reason for their rejection.

There are several grounds for doubting a hard version of the anti-liberalization or post-neoliberal approach. First, such a position would be pressed to explain why liberalizing reforms endured in countries also experiencing major economic contractions and highly mobilized social movements favoring alternative development approaches. As discussed throughout this volume, Mexico and Brazil, by far the two largest countries in the region, experienced reform survival under these conditions. Liberalization turned out to be quite deep and durable in both cases as well as in Chile. And it also survived and even thrived in Colombia, Peru, Uruguay, Paraguay, and other countries with major opposition movements. Policy stability in these and other cases following the economic turbulence from the global economic crises of 2008 and subsequent years further challenges the idea of a region-wide post-neoliberal trend.

Factors other than popular contention played roles in the above political shifts. Flores-Mecías (2010) views returns to statism as more likely in countries where leftist turns from diverse causes coincide with weak party systems—Bolivia, Ecuador, and Venezuela, contrasting them to Brazil, Chile, and Uruguay. Other authors highlight the links of these leftward or populist swings to the political economy of resource nationalism and commodity booms in agriculture, mining, and oil (Blanco and Grier, 2013; Fishlow, 2006; Kaufman, 2011; Murillo et al., 2011; Manzano and Monaldi, 2008; Ocampo, 2007). Liberalizing reforms have floundered as a result of various other conditions and interactions (Flores-Mecías, 2010; Manzano and Monaldi, 2008).[3]

Explanations of regime change as direct and inexorable outcomes of the failure of liberalizing reforms take the poor economic performance and downturns found throughout Latin America during and after the late 1990s as confirmation of the misconceived character of market reforms. As noted, a great many Latin American economies experienced economic downturns (as well as antimarket sentiment and rising opposition) during this period without making major changes to economic strategy. In several cases, fiscal measures adopted in the earlier wave of liberalization effectively contributed to this relative economic buoyancy in the context of severe international financial crises. The reform process initiated in the 1990s prepared Brazil for resuming economic expansion. This and other South American economies returned to growth after 2002–2003, with export booms and expanded trade driving the upturn.

The post-liberal approach highlights the role of popular movements in the demise of liberalism, with Ecuador and Bolivia, home to massive popular mobilizations, as key examples. But this view might be tempered by a careful examination of several other factors known to have shaped collective action during this period. A new wave of popular social movements sprang throughout much of Latin America in the 1980s and the 1990s in the context of political liberalization and democratization—a phenomenon that reduced the costs of mobilization, widened public space for participation, and created political opportunities for political mobilization and the expansion of civil society. Institutionally strong polities experiencing democratization were ultimately able to respond constructively to these and other expressions of citizen participation without major discontinuities in the political process or development model.

The changing political context in these new democracies, including decentralization, facilitated and shaped civil society activism and contention to amplify their impact on policymaking and politics. The birth and rapid expansion of the Brazilian Workers' Party or the Mexican PDR are good examples of political organization rooted in trade unions, social movements, and expanded civil societies in changing polities. New urban and rural social movements emerged in both countries. Popular mobilization and contentious politics, including opposition to liberalization, are in fact quite common and normal in democratic orders. But the broader political process and the strength of political institutions can greatly channel the impact of these and other expressions of political participation and thus define their broader significance.

Yet another problem in the above interpretations is the tendency to ignore the role of exogenous factors in the configuration of conditions leading to poor economic performance or slowdown of liberalization reforms just prior to the above political shifts. That the peak in antiliberal shifts took place toward the turn of the century and in countries that differed in scope or intensity of the reforms is telling in this regard. After 1997, external shocks, amplified by the institutional weaknesses in some of these democratizing societies, worsened economic, social, and political conditions. The Asian financial crisis jolted the entire region after that year, with impact dependent on financial and fiscal vulnerability. In addition, El Niño and other natural phenomena had a highly significant impact, particularly in the Andean region at approximately the same time. The exceptional climate turbulence of 1997–1998—rainfall, floods, mudslides, as also droughts, unusually high temperatures, forest fires, and other abnormalities in climate and weather patterns—contributed to the economic woes visiting these countries (table 3.1).[4]

The international economic crisis and the climate events of the turn of the century led to poor economic performance and substantial economic contraction. In Ecuador, the economy downsized 4.7 percent in 1999, while growing by only 1.1 percent in 2000, while Bolivia had five consecutive years of slow growth starting in 1999. After a meager 0.6 percent growth in 1998, Colombia's GDP decreased by 4.2 percent in 1999, to then grow at slow rates in 2001 and 2002. Likewise, the Peruvian economy contracted by 0.7 percent in 1998. It grew only by 0.9 in 1999, to then return to slow growth through 2001. Argentina, the most heavily affected by shocks, had four consecutive years of negative growth in 1999–2002, culminating in a disastrous 10.9 percent reduction in 2002. Uruguay was equally devastated, while Paraguay and Venezuela were severely affected (see tables A.11, A.12, and A.13). As discussed in Chapter Two, Chile, Brazil, and Mexico did not escape the impact of international crises.

Table 3.1 Impact of El Niño, 1997–2001, Andean region, in $ million

	Bolivia	*Ecuador*	*Peru*	*Colombia*
Economy	261.5	1,517.5	1,626.6	148.6
Infrastructure	248.1	828.4	954.4	315.4
Social	5.3	207.4	485.2	44.4
Cross-sector	12.3	331.2	433.7	55.1
Total	**527.2 (3.95% of GDP)**	**1,881.8 (12.19% of GDP)**	**3,500.0 (5.91% of GDP)**	**563.5 (.53% of GDP)**

Source: Value of post-disaster damage and losses, needed by international organizations, as compiled by GFDRR (Global Facility for Disaster Reduction and Recovery), country tables, www.gfdrr.org.

These external shocks greatly strained the already difficult processes of liberalization and democratization throughout the region, substantially increasing the probability of government or even regime change in vulnerable cases. Countries with pronounced fiscal and monetary imbalances (debt, fiscal deficits, inflation, and current account deficits), particularly those in the middle of politically difficult liberalizing reforms, were especially at risk. Those polities with reasonably strong political institutions were able to survive the considerable strain from these external or exogenous shocks.[5]

Bolivia and Ecuador illustrate the relationship between state weakness, exogenous shocks, contention, and the likelihood of significant regime change in the context of democratization. Relatively small and poor, both countries had been prone to political and institutional instability before deciding to implement liberalizing reforms. As discussed below, that background shaped democratization and related political transformations attempted in the 1980s, as new political forces, including indigenous social movements and leaders, rose to prominent roles (North, 2004). Bolivia and Ecuador went on to revise or reject market reform policies of the 1990s, including public-private collaboration in infrastructure. In both countries, these policies and the broader movement toward liberalization faced a nationalist and populist backlash. Increasingly focused on the exploitation and distribution of natural resources, these new populist political movements undermined and reshaped the inchoate institutional framework governing questions about ownership rights, particularly of large, often foreign, private producers. Their demands contributed to a shift toward statism on the extraction and sale of oil, gas, water, mining, and other commodities.[6]

But, again, socioeconomic conflict and new social movements also emerged elsewhere in Latin America but did not have the same impact. Neighboring Peru and Colombia stand out. Perhaps even more than Mexico, Brazil, Chile, or even Ecuador and Bolivia, they experienced major new forms of activism, conflict, and political turmoil without the outcomes of the latter two.

The contentious political mobilization of indigenous peoples in the context of the still institutionally weak democratizing polities contributed to political volatility in Ecuador and Bolivia. Often embedded in specific ethnic groups and territories, these national movements would find themselves taking direct part in bids for power, including a series of government coups. Leaders and movements representing the indigenous communities had incentives and opportunities to thereby escalate their claims. In the context of economic strains, fledgling democratic regimes with weak political parties and state institutions turned out to be quite vulnerable. Instability returned.[7] Sometimes quite suddenly, weakened governments in these cases were directly exposed to great pressure and demands about deep and long-held grievances regarding poverty, discrimination and social exclusion, unemployment, land distribution, and elite dominance.

The distinctive dynamics of Ecuador and Bolivia did not quite match those in the rest of the Andean region (Peru, Colombia, and Chile), where considerable opposition and popular political mobilization did not stop liberalization and public-private collaboration. There, institutional and political actors, together with various socioeconomic groups were able to retain and further develop economic models based on liberal principles.

Moreover, it would take considerable qualifications to characterize these governments and reform processes as either neoliberal or post-neoliberal. In fact, Ecuador and Bolivia, as well as Argentina and even Venezuela, have retained significant market or liberal principles and public-private collaboration in combination with emergent statism. Likewise, many governments and leaders elsewhere in the region do not fit their framing as neoliberal. Public-private collaboration and aspects of the state reforms of the recent past endured throughout the Andes and Southern Cone regions—for example, dollarization (Ecuador), fiscal austerity (Bolivia), trade orientation, economic openness, and

Table 3.2 Public-private investment in infrastructure in Andes and Southern Cone, 1990–2013, in $ millions

	Number	*Concessions*	*Divestiture*	*Greenfield*	*Management and Lease*	*Total Investment*
Southern Cone						
Argentina	217	41,436	23,105	28,752	615	93,908
Chile	157	9,224	10,026	23,071	0	42,321
Uruguay	21	811	0	4,129	0	4,940
Paraguay	5	58	0	1,660	0	1,718
Andes						
Colombia	143	7,198	10,791	19,210	36	37,235
Peru	99	5,007	14,226	15,280	205	34,718
Bolivia	26	851	1,542	3,728	0	6,121
Ecuador	28	2,073	0	5,230	0	7,303
Total	**714**	**67,060**	**69,324**	**107,956**	**856**	**245,196**

Source: World Bank, 2014a.

regulatory frameworks. Often aiming at increasing competitiveness, policies often target four basic infrastructure sectors: transportation (of goods and people), telecommunication, energy, as well as water and sanitation (see table 3.2). Increasingly, policymakers have come to seek private collaboration to finance, design, construct, or operate infrastructure. As part of the process, they have separated policymaking, regulation, and service provision, seeking to increase competition in all of these areas (Andrés et al., 2008: 80).

Faltering Liberalism in the Andes

The trajectory and fate of reform in Bolivia and Ecuador deserve closer attention. In both, governments relying on newly installed, somewhat improvised technocratic teams and international advice pushed through broad liberalizing programs in the 1980s and 1990s. In infrastructure, later reforms sought to expand the supply of services and improved quality and productivity. Public opinion turned against the reforms as a new century opened. Andrés, Diop, and Guasch (2008) dubbed this turnaround "the privatization paradox," puzzled by rejection despite early relative successes and the urgent need for infrastructure. But, as shown in table 3.3, the phenomenon of decreased public enthusiasm for liberal reforms was common throughout the region shortly before or after the turn of the century. While democratizing polities elsewhere in South America were generally able to absorb opposition and decreased support for market reforms through the end of the 1990s and beyond, left turns contributed to the shifts in Bolivia and Ecuador as well as in Venezuela (1998) and Argentina (post-2001), stopping the momentum toward public-private collaboration.

Evo Morales and the Movement toward Socialism (MAS) emerged as central actors in the Bolivian shift. As labor leader in the 1990s and after, Morales coordinated protest movements making demands on behalf of Bolivia's disadvantaged indigenous communities: land reform, redistribution of income and wealth from natural resources, in addition to more political power. An Aymara Indian himself and leader of the indigenous movement of coca leaf farmers, Morales was elected president of Bolivia in 2005. In Ecuador, the striking rise of an indigenous movement was also a key component in the broad coalition that catapulted Rafael Correa, an economist with a PhD from the University of Illinois, into the presidency in 2006. As a result, the country moved in a new direction.

Table 3.3 Public support for "privatization," 1998–2013, as percent of polls

	1998	*2000*	*2001*	*2002*	*2003*	*2005*	*2007*	*2009*	*2010*	*2011*	*2013*
Brazil	50	32	39	38	33	41	45	50	51	45	44
Mexico	50	37	30	28	31	38	40	37	41	38	35
Southern Cone											
Argentina	39	26	17	14	12	25	19	18	30	32	20
Chile	51	32	43	22	29	37	33	26	34	20	18
Uruguay	29	26	23	16	17	36	ND	ND	ND	ND	
Paraguay	45	37	33	19	24	22	22	29	37	40	19
Southern Cone Average	41	30	29	18	20	30	25	24	34	31	
Andes											
Colombia	39	30	14	23	24	40	35	34	30	37	27
Peru	44	38	22	31	22	31	32	28	31	39	31
Ecuador	52	40	31	40	21	33	45	26	53	50	57
Bolivia	49	35	24	23	19	26	43	ND	45	42	
Venezuela	51	54	48	38	32	44	47	ND	43	45	
Andes Average	47	39	28	31	24	35	40	29	40	43	
Central American Average	45	34	ND	ND	ND	ND	31	38	38	36	

Note: ND = No Data.

Source: Latinobarómetro (2010: 107) and other years. Percent of sample agreeing with "privatization of state enterprises has been beneficial."

The political movements led by Morales and Correa found geopolitical support from the prior or parallel turns to the left in oil-rich Venezuela, where Hugo Chávez proclaimed the advantages of a new kind of "twenty-first-century socialism" over "neoliberalism" (de la Torre, 2000). They were also inspired by Argentina, where the precipitous economic collapse in 2001 led to the repudiation of the liberalizing reform of the 1990s and the reassertion of statism. Brazil's election of left-leaning Lula da Silva as president in late 2002 further broadened regional support for these movements.

Bolivia: State, Market, and Community

Bolivia hosted a pioneering technocratic process of fast and comprehensive liberalization in the 1980s, one deemed well-conceived and effective by international specialists like Jeffrey Sachs. The first issue is thus to explore why and how the reform movement may have ultimately backfired (Arce et al., 2009; Gamarra, 2003; Silva, 2009a). As in much of the region, Bolivia's economy was having difficulties servicing its external debt and controlling inflation in the years preceding the liberalizing reforms (table A.12). With hyperinflation and currency depreciation hindering the country's ability to pay its debt, Bolivia became the first in South America to implement the "shock therapy" approach to economic reform. The bold reform program was set against the background of institutional and political instability—14 presidents in the 11 years after 1978, following a military dictatorship in the preceding 7 years. Bolivia's patterns of regional and ethnic differentiation between the western highlands and eastern lowlands fueled these political shifts. Upon coming into office, the recently elected government of Víctor Paz Estenssoro (1985–1989) took the first steps in the new economic model based on trade liberalization, privatization, restructuring of the public sector, loosening government control of financial institution, and deregulation of the economy.

As planning minister in the Estenssoro government, businessman Gonzalo Sánchez de Lozada had supervised the new liberalizing drive. He deepened these reforms during his two presidential terms (1993–1997, 2002–2003). Bent upon turning the country into a modern market economy, Sánchez de Lozada was viewed as the main architect and embodiment of the economic reforms. In this process, Congress approved the legislation to privatize parts of six major state-owned companies: YPFB (oil and gas), ENDE (electricity), ENTEL (telecommunications), LAB (airlines), ENFE (railroads), and EMV (tin). The liberalizing government put a new regulatory system in place to oversee the changing relations between the private sector, consumers, and government in major economic sectors.

As a core program of privatization through divestiture advanced, Bolivian policymakers sought new ways to invite the private sector into infrastructure. In 1998, the authorities passed a law of concessions and public works (Law 1874) to expand private sector participation in public-private collaboration. The concessions program between 1990 and 2005 focused on energy ($3.6 billion), telecommunications ($1.0 billion), water-related ($682 million), and transportation ($186 million).

But fortune turned against reformers. Economic blows after 1998 ushered in a few years of slow growth. External shocks from the Asian financial crisis and losses from weather disturbances slowed down the economy (table 3.1; Vos et al., 1999). Many large public-private projects had come into existence in the 1990s, but already by 2000, several were cancelled and others began to fall into the distressed category. Public-private collaboration wilted after that period.

Moreover, the eruption of internal conflict around the turn of the century directly challenged the liberalizing reforms. In 2000, the

Cochabamba indigenous communities mobilized to protest the privatization of the municipal water supply (Klein, 2003; Roberts, 2009). Protest spread nationwide. Water issues inspired mass movements in La Paz and other cities. In the interior, opposition to policies for the eradication of coca planting led to sustained protests organized by Evo Morales. The "gas war" of 2003 protested the distribution of income from the rapidly expanding gas sector then in private hands.[8] In 2003, indigenous farmers, miners, and urban public workers demanding higher salaries brought Bolivia to a standstill, as they joined forces to stage strikes and block roads. Violent confrontation and repression stoked contentious politics, turning historical resentments of Indian communities into powerful broad movements demanding the reorganization of national politics.

Gonzalo Sánchez de Lozada's resignation and exile in October 2003 did not calm the situation. Emboldened social movements escalated their demands to include the full nationalization of gas deposits and power to the indigenous majority. The more systematic exploitation of gas reserves and the construction of a gas pipeline to Brazil led a new exports boom based on this commodity. With gas emerging as pivotal issue, a referendum in mid-2004 drove the Bolivian Congress to enact a hydrocarbons law in 2005 to increase government royalties from natural gas exploitation. A coalition of these old and new political forces elected socialist Evo Morales in 2005, and by May 1, 2006, the new government signed a decree announcing the nationalization of gas reserves. Morales was reelected in December 2009 and Bolivia realigned itself internationally with the more radical left in Latin America. Needless, the liberalizing process came to a halt—though the fiscal prudence in place since the 1980s survived.

Morales argued that the preexisting "neoliberal model" was broken and that a new economic strategy would center on the preservation of indigenous communities. In 2006, the government moved to renegotiate contracts with private companies in the hydrocarbon sector and sharpened the goals to have enterprises produce 82 percent of the oil. The government drafted a new constitution granting specific rights to indigenous peoples, a process completed in 2009.

Declaring Bolivia a plurinational country, the Constitution of 2009 enhanced the power of the state. While calling for a mixed economy based on state, private, and communal owners, it set limits to land ownership, recognized local and departmental autonomies, and declared natural resources to be the exclusive dominion of the Bolivian people to be administered by the state. The new charter had grown out of the issues raised during the gas conflicts since 2003. Morales, who had been elected to implement demands from the social movements, remained faithful to his pledge once in office.

Protest and increasing opposition to privatization delayed and then stopped the concessions program. Instead of working on public-private collaboration in infrastructure, the authorities gave priority to measures to strengthen small producers, cooperatives, and communitarian enterprises. While much of the economy remained in private hands, it initiated the nationalization of recently privatized enterprises in oil, telecommunications, mining, electricity, and airports.[9] Still, the Morales government retained fiscally conservative practices.

Bolivia had started to grow quite fast soon after the very early 2000s, fueled after 2002 by the global markets boom in hydrocarbons, soy, and other exports. As a result, total exports expanded from $1.3 billion in 2002 to nearly $12 billion in 2012. That year, oil and gas accounted for $5.8 billion, or 49.8 percent of commodities exports—with tin representing 10 percent, silver 12 percent, and soybeans 7 percent.

As a result, Bolivia's GDP grew by an average of 4.8 percent between 2004 and 2008—contrasting with the previous level of less than 2 percent between 1999 and 2003 (table A.12). After a slower rate of 3.4 percent in 2009 (an echo of the global crisis), growth rates recovered to the 4.8 percent average between 2010 and 2012 and 6.8 percent in 2013 (see figure 3.1). International demand for gas and other commodities was now aided by larger soy harvests in making exports an impressive growth engine.

Government revenues also increased, further driven by the Bolivian state's raised share of revenues from natural resource extraction in the form of higher taxes on firms and control of nationalized firms in the expanding mining and hydrocarbons sectors (Sinnott et al., 2010). Government budget thus increased approximately fivefold in absolute terms from 2003 to 2012—and from 25 percent to 38 percent as share of GDP (IMF, 2014). The expansion of the state brought a recovery of direct state investment, which grew from nearly 15 percent in 2005 to nearly 20 percent in 2012.

While tilting toward its own brand of socialism, the new Bolivian regime has been able to coexist with international investors, entrepreneurs, and the middle class. The market remains an important part of the economy, though antiliberal sentiment has not abated.[10] In 2012, the government converted several foreign-owned mining companies into joint ventures, while the state-owned Corporación Minera de Bolivia gained prominence. The foreign and national private sectors

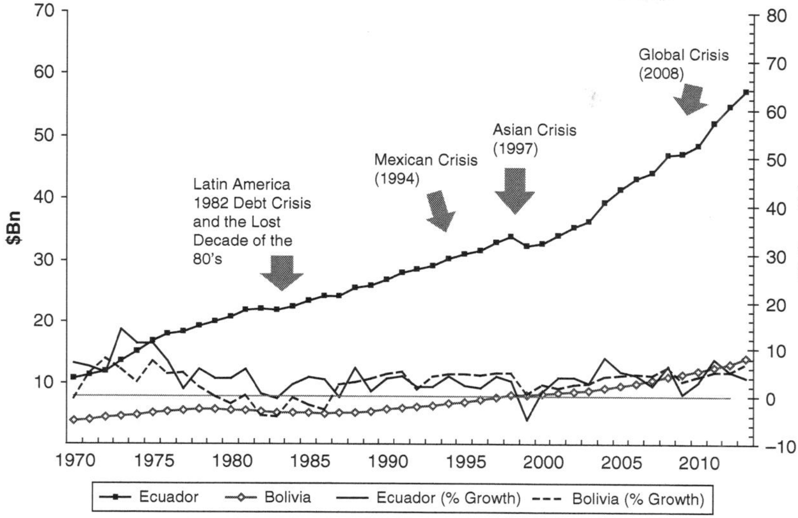

Figure 3.1 Ecuador and Bolivia, GDP and growth, 1970–2013.
Source: World Bank, 2014b.

feared for their investments and cancelled large projects. At the same time, the country attracted $860 million in net foreign investment in 2011, while Chinese companies in particular were drawn by the prospects of long-term profits from the extraction of natural resources.[11]

Soy had gradually expanded after the early 2000s, becoming the country's most important crop and turning Bolivia into the 7th largest world producer. Much of the Bolivian soy is produced in the eastern lowlands in the state of Santa Cruz, home to the opposition. In 2012, production exceeded 2 million tons, with 65 percent of the harvest exported to Andean countries and the rest consumed domestically. There are approximately 14,000 soybean producers in Bolivia—77 percent of which own less than 50 hectares, while 2 percent own farms of more than 1,000 hectares. A quarter of the soy is produced by Brazilian farmers. Soy has brought new attention to better access and logistics to the shipping ports in the Parana-Paraguay waterway for transhipment in the deep port of Rosario, Argentina (USDA, 2012). Though projected to grow further, several impediments stand in the way of soy expansion. Bolivia would need better roads, logistics, port and transportation linking it to shipping ports. Other obstacles include hostile financial climate and a stiff regulatory framework regarding reforestation, export restrictions, land tenure insecurity, and pending issues on use of biotechnology.

The Bolivian government under Morales has relied on direct government procurement to address its infrastructure gaps, an approach made easier by the increased government revenue from the hydrocarbons boom. The country lacks mature agencies and regulations for a program of public-private collaboration (The Economist Intelligence Unit did not even include Bolivia in its 2012 Infrascope report). Weak governance structures and poor infrastructure hinder economic and social development, according to many specialists. However, in 2013, transportation accounted for 30 percent of public investment (more than 3 percent of GDP), while significant amounts of state investment have also gone to energy, housing, and education.

The Morales government has received criticisms from all sides of political spectrum. Some reflect opposition from the market-oriented, dynamic, and economically liberal eastern part of the country (half of the population and economy), which presses for autonomy.[12] In contrast, leftist intellectuals and activists dwell on what some see as survival of neoliberal policies and others decry intolerance toward diversity (Kennemore and Weeks, 2011; Mejido Costoya, 2011). The national government also found resistance from Amazon communities demanding direct control over natural resources. In 2011, the government suspended the construction of the $451 million highway linking the departments (states) of Beni and Cochabamba, under pressure from affected indigenous communities.[13] By now a political veteran who has survived many political battles, in mid-2014, Morales was confident of his reelection in October of that year.

Ecuador: Search for National Focus

Responding to the interests and demands of three very different geographic zones has been a main historical challenge for Ecuadorian policymakers.[14] With its center in the commercial city of Guayaquil, the eastern lowlands along the Pacific coast are market driven and outward oriented. That port city is much more economically liberal than the capital of Quito and the indigenous civilizations stringed along the Andean highlands. In turn, both regions differ markedly from the large western lowlands merging into the Amazon basin. The political and economic challenge has been for the country's diverse components to coalesce into a common vision and purpose. For decades, populist leaders rising to fit this bill have driven the nation into fiscal deficits, inflation, large debts, and recurrent economic dislocations.

Ecuador started to implement a structural adjustment plan in the early 1990s and seemed to be making some progress in that regard. But economic and political instability derailed this process. Both had deep-seated roots. Unstable military rule from 1960 to 1978 had failed to erase institutional weaknesses inherited from decades of populism. Though the return to democracy in 1978 promised to bring a new, more modern order, it too ultimately proved frustrating, as new shocks interacted with domestic dynamics to undermine efforts at political and institutional modernization as well as the very process of economic development.

While Ecuador benefitted by higher oil prices in the 1970s, the end of the decade brought a reversal toward higher inflation, an expanding national debt, and slow growth or stagnation. The debt crisis of 1982 and lower oil prices precipitated the end of the developmentalist approach more or less in place since 1950 (Carvajal, 2011). GDP growth rates fell to 0.6 percent in 1982 and −0.3 in 1983, while the debt reached 73.3 percent of GNI (see table A.12). Forced into an unpopular adjustment program, the government decreed austerity measures and took steps toward privatization and state reform. In this context, policymakers invited the private sector to operate a substantial number of state-owned enterprises, hoping to attract new investments and increase competitiveness. It also took steps to decentralize. Through 2005, authorities persisted in the liberalizing reform effort, seeking to end the seemingly endemic climate of economic and political instability.

However, modest but volatile economic growth between 1983 and 1997 was again punctuated by recurrent bouts of low or negative GDP growth rates of −0.3 percent in 1987, 1 percent in 1989, 2.1 percent in 1992, and 2.0 percent in 1993. Macroeconomic adjustment programs after 1992 also faced headwinds hampering economic growth, while shocks in the late 1990s added to economic and fiscal deterioration—with GDP contracting by 4.7 percent in 1999 and growing by only 1.1 the following year (see figure 3.1). The Asian financial crisis had a big part in the decline, costing the country up to $8 billion.[15] Natural disasters once again caused major damage (table 3.1), as droughts crippled some hydroelectric power plants and floods hit other areas, while the eruption of two volcanoes disrupted major population centers. Furthermore, prices of main exports (petroleum, bananas, shrimp, coffee, and cacao) had fallen.[16]

Institutional weakness continued to constrain the development process, with the country ranking very high in corruption. Generalized bribery meant lack of trust on government officials, while distrust of public officials made it difficult for the privatization program of the late 1990s to attract major private sector interest and participation. Laws regulating private investment remained woefully inadequate. Against this context, the coup d'etat in 1998 brought increased uncertainty. In an attempt to stop further currency instability and stem a banking crisis, the presidency of former Quito mayor, Jamil Mahuad adopted the dollar as national currency in early 2000. A few days later, a military coup under pressure from indigenous movements and other forces overthrew the government. But the Ecuadorian economy gradually recovered after 2000 and dollarization remained in place. Price stabilization created conditions for economic growth rates in subsequent years, with higher prices for other exports, remittances, higher government revenues, and public spending contributed to the recovery.[17] Elected president in late 2006, and aided by the economic bonanza of the 2000s, Rafael Correa pushed for a new economic model.

Political and institutional vulnerabilities provided a large part of the explanation for this shift in economic model amid the economic boom. The militarism of 1972–1979 and the four decades of populism starting in the 1920s had left a legacy of poorly developed institutions, while the post-1978 process of democratization ushered in an era still dominated by political parties organized around factions representative of specific regions or social classes.[18] The polity was characterized by high levels of corruption, ineffectual governance, frequent changes of constitution, and coups d'etat involving popular movements and mid-level military officers. But Ecuador's democratization after 1978 also created opportunities and conditions for indigenous and popular mobilization, including the emergence of powerful movement organizations in the Sierra or highlands. Founded in 1986, the Confederation of Indigenous Nationalities of Ecuador (CONAIE) grew to coordinate major initiatives advancing a wide range of economic, cultural, and political rights (from land and autonomy to political power). By 1996, the indigenous movement was ready to contend for direct political power (Zamosc, 2007),[19] as its organizations also demanded control of their natural environments and a share of proceeds from natural resources. Indigenous communities competed with other interests in the distribution of income from oil, which nearly doubled the GDP between 1999 and 2008. Correa's presidency drew strength from these social movements and the commodities bonanza.

Rafael Correa inaugurated a policy of selective reversal of liberalization—an approach maintained after his reelection in 2009, under a new constitution, and then again in 2013. In late 2008, his government shrewdly defaulted on a $3.2 billion of sovereign debt, arguing that it had been agreed to by despotic and corrupt governments and was thus illegitimate, but only to buy back the sharply discounted debt instruments several months later. Attacking existing policies as part of the Washington Consensus, Correa announced plans to adopt "a socialist revolution."

Correa's government annulled some existing concessions and moved to nationalize natural resources, while retaining the dollar regime. Having grown in importance through the mid-2000s, concessions and public-private collaboration remained significant. Of the total $7.3 billion invested between 1990 and 2013, more than $4 billion went to the telecommunications sector and $2.16 billion to transportation, while water received $510 million and energy $461 million. Still, in 2011 The Economist Intelligence Unit ranked Ecuador's laws and regulations last in Latin America in terms of facilitating public-private partnerships. The same report diagnosed as very poor the regulatory system and the investment climate. A subsequent announcement of a project to build a metro for the capital city of Quito faced difficulties in attracting private investment but proceeded as a traditional public procurement undertaking financed by the national government and the city.

Meanwhile, the economy had nearly doubled between 1999 and 2008 and responded well to the global economic crises of 2008–2012—after falling 0.6 percent in 2009, GDP growth rose 2.9 percent in 2010, 7.8 percent in 2011, 5.1 percent in 2012, and 4.0 percent in 2013. Driven by tax revenues from oil, public spending for roads, education, healthcare, and infrastructure emerged as a main engine of growth after 2007.[20] Government spending rose to 15 percent of GDP—which, added to the 13 percent from the private sector, brought the national investment rate to 28 percent of GDP. In 2014, the collapse in the price of oil and other commodities brought uncertainty about fiscal equilibrium, high levels of government expenditures, and economic growth.

Summary Assessment

Assessments of the Morales and Correa governments in Bolivia and Ecuador acknowledge their success in inaugurating dynamics and promises for expanded equity, representation, and rights to disadvantaged groups, and for formalizing them in new constitutions. Both leaders gained considerable popular support as the expansion of natural resources led economic growth.

While Ecuador's approach has been to raise taxes on foreign companies carrying out oil and gas exploration and extraction, the Bolivian state has aimed at a larger direct role in extractive industries without gaining complete control. Both seek a larger role for state role while retaining market-driven dynamics and private economic actors. That is, neither has aimed at a deep socialist transformation. Some critics point that these approaches fail as alternatives to the extraction of natural resources, while fiscal dependence on foreign investment to maintain public spending raises questions regarding long-term sustainability. Others believe that promised environmental initiatives clash with the reality of continued extraction of natural resources. Both cases show poor implementation of reforms and conflictive politics (Kennemore and Weeks, 2011).

Various assessments highlight the populism and personalistic rule of these two leaders (de la Torre, 2013). Still, the Morales and Correa governments differ somewhat in terms of their support as well as opposition. In Ecuador, the movement against the previous liberal order came about not so much from within elite factions as from indigenous and environmental groups making various demands, who framed their attacks in terms of opposition to neoliberalism. But Correa's "citizen revolution" also drew much of his support from urban middle classes, the same sector of the population that brought down the Gutiérrez government in 2005, promising alleviation from the economic and social costs of structural adjustment. Mining and water legislation and related policies would eventually alienate members of the coalition.

Morales rose to national politics as leader of the coca growers union and later, of the MAS political coalition. To enhance its bid for national power, the coalition put together by Morales incorporated diverse leaders of indigenous movement, other popular organizations, women, and nonindigenous figures. After gaining the presidency, the more radical factions of the ruling coalition push for broad reforms, while indigenous leaders tend to focus on narrower regional demands rather than broad agendas of social change. Regionalism is a source of polarization and friction between the central government and the four provinces in the eastern lowlands known as the Crescent or "Media Luna" region: Santa Cruz, Beni, Pando, and Tarija. This cleavage has hampered the full implementation of agricultural and other reforms, while groups from this region accounting for nearly half of the country's GDP feel inadequately represented. As in Ecuador, political tolerance in Bolivia ranks low and is often seen as endangering the democratizing premises of "twenty-first-century socialism." Finally, these two governments have also come short of fully addressing the infrastructure needs of their respective societies, while the reform process remains constrained.

Judging these leaders and governments by how close they come to end liberalization sets the bar too high, while the persistence of liberalizing policies are more interesting as a pragmatic acknowledgment of the importance of market mechanisms. A more fruitful task may be to assess the changing roles of the state and the extent to which they represent durable good governance.

In both cases, policies and performance respond in large part to exogenous factors: international financial crises, ebb and flow of commodity booms, climate events, and various aspects of globalization. Interactions between local institutions and global factors need to be further studied to clarify these roles and relationships. Research is needed to update the understanding of the impact of commodity market cycles as well as of climate events.

Isolating domestic actors, choices and dynamics in this broader context remain another challenge. The debate about the politics of transformation in the Andes points to the need to explore the relationship between these governments and processes of democratization. Conflicts are vital and inevitable aspects of economic and social life. Confrontations with groups such as those representing the eastern lowlands in Bolivia, indigenous social movements, or with urban middle classes raise questions about the extent to which political institutions and processes in new democracies are able to channel them constructively into effective policies (Yashar, 2005). The balance between the participation of previously unincorporated sectors and the development of a collaborative framework to effectively address fundamental development challenges is part of that research agenda.

Colombia and Peru: Conflict and Consensus

In contrast to Bolivia and Ecuador, the larger Colombia and Peru stand out as examples of remarkable continuity in their liberalization, as well as in the development of public-private collaboration (despite a background of internal conflict and violence). Distinctive political and policymaking processes marked the path of liberalization driving these two countries, separating them from the above Andean cases. Large in terms of population and economic size, economic expansion led in large part by exports has been a central concern to policymakers.

Colombia: Reaffirmed Liberalism

In 1990, newly elected president César Gaviria (1990–1994) inaugurated a restructuring plan to open the economy (trade expansion, tariff reduction, free trade agreements), liberalize economic relations, and privatize state-owned enterprises in Colombia, formally opening a process of liberalizing reform.[21] Nearly 40 percent of public spending would be decentralized, aiming at a more nimble state better able to promote competitiveness. The strategy shifted the economic development model away from its relatively modest version of the import substitution industrialization (ISI) approach since the 1940s.[22] In the early twentieth century, the coffee-centered export economy did not prevent industrial development and import substitution policies, but the role of the state in favor of industrialization did not reach the levels of Argentina, Brazil, or Mexico (Kalmanovitz, 2010: 197).

Unlike many of its neighbors, Colombia did not suffer a major economic contraction in the 1980s.[23] The above change in economic policy responded to dissatisfaction with economic conditions related to slow growth, increased debt, fiscal imbalances, and vulnerabilities since the early part of the decade (appendix A and table A.12). Having presided over decades of sustained export-led growth based on coffee, policymakers were predisposed to openness. The market reforms of the 1990s reflected a rejection of protectionism and economic statism, though state strength was also a main concern. With public security and social issues tending to strain the public sector, the reforms aimed at strengthening the state and democracy (Easterly et al., 2003a; IDB, 2010). A revision of the constitution in 1991 included provisions for an independent judiciary, proscribing presidential reelection, and expanding political rights.

The governments that followed Gaviria provided continuity to development policy. Presidents Ernesto Samper (1994–1998), Andrés Pastrana (1998–2002), Álvaro Uribe (2002–2006 and 2006–2010), and Juan Manuel Santos (2010–2014) all maintained the focus on liberalizing reforms to deepen the free market economy, expand trade and financial liberalization (selectively in agriculture), privatize state-owned firms, and strengthen relations with the United States. Though these presidencies differed in various ways—social policy, strategies to pacify the country, and the precise limits of national deficits—economic liberalization remained on course.[24]

The reform process initiated in the 1990s created conditions for private investment in infrastructure through public-private collaboration (see table 3.2). By 1995, the country had invested $4.38 billion in such projects, adding an additional $9 billion during 1996–2000. Telecommunications, energy, and transportation led the way. Between 1993 and 1998, the government sold assets and concessions in power, natural gas, transportation, and manufacturing. The constitutional reform had introduced new rules for property rights regarding public services and public infrastructure, as well as the creation of a regulatory framework for the oversight of concessions. Still lacking specific legislation about concessions, the government relied on the general procurement law governing contracts for the provision of public services (Basañes and Willig, 2002).

External shocks and other problems during the second half of the decade significantly slowed down this process.[25] After expanding through 1995, the economy grew by only 0.6 percent in 1998 and by −4.2 percent in 1999, as the country fell into a short recession (table A.12). A modest recovery and expansion took place after 2000, making it possible to keep the fiscal deficit below 2.5 percent of GDP (IDB, 2012: 2) even while fully engaged in a protracted internal conflict with guerrillas and drug-trafficking groups. In the context of stability, faster economic expansion gradually resumed, with GDP growth peaking at 6.7 percent in 2006 and 6.9 percent in 2007, to then expand at only 3.5 percent in 2008 and 1.7 percent in 2009 (largely in response to the global economic slowdown), after which it averaged 8.9 percent between 2010 and 2012 (see figure 3.2).

Exports expanded from $13 billion in the early 2000s to more than $58.8 billion in 2012, with oil alone bringing $39.2 billion.[26] Expanded export receipts responded to incentives to private producers, enhanced security, and reforms of Ecopetrol and the regulatory framework. The construction of pipelines and transportation infrastructure also mattered (Steiner and Vallejo, 2010; UN Comtrade).

Investments in public-private projects recovered to nearly $12.9 billion for 2006–2010 compared to the $2.45 billion in the 2001–2005 period. By 2010, Colombia ranked fifth in Latin America in terms of the total public-private investments in infrastructure. Telecommunications, transport, and energy became leading sectors in public-private investment.[27]

Moreover, public-private collaboration also gained institutional space. The 2003 National Institute of Concessions (INCO, or ANI after 2012)[28] procured, administered, and regulated national infrastructure projects. To free up government resources for other priorities, this agency attracted private investment for infrastructure development—though the lack of cohesion in the legislation governing concessions and partnerships had posed a main challenge to expanded private

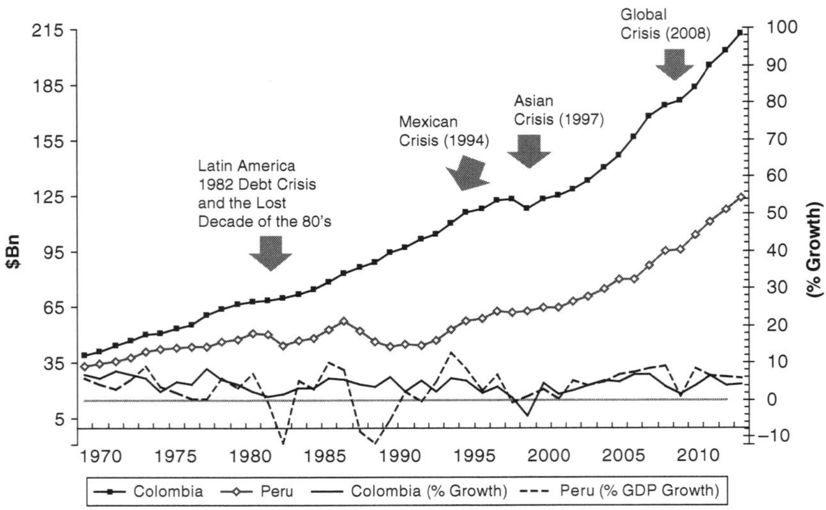

Figure 3.2 Colombia and Peru, GDP and growth, 1970–2013.
Source: World Bank, 2014b.

participation in infrastructure.[29] Complexities in the legal framework, including different regulatory and contracting authorities at different levels of government, hampered the effective coordination of the system of concessions.

The national development plans of 2002–2006, 2006–2010, and 2010–2014 called for expanding the role of private investments in infrastructure, with planners giving priority to infrastructure and physical capital to increase competitiveness and trade. The development plans aimed for investment of $106.2 billion, with at least $10 billion for transportation infrastructure. Financing was to come from public and private participation, with the former to provide up to 55 percent of needed funds. The plan identified pressing needs to address the inadequate ports and weak export capacity, announcing a review of preexisting concession contracts to ports. The upgrading of ports went hand in hand with the goals of better transportation and communication infrastructure.

Meanwhile, Colombian cities and regions had also engaged the private sector in the design and implementation of innovative infrastructure projects. Transmilenio, Bogota's rapid bus system, stood out in this regard and came to be viewed as the country's most successful public-private partnership after its opening in 2000—its 9 lines covering 54 miles serve the 7 million inhabitants of the capital and providing more than 1.6 million trips daily. As of 2011, the project had been partly financed with bonds sold in local and international markets, with local pension funds buying half of them. Subsequent expansion was contemplated.

Though some aspects of these public-private projects have been widely debated, the overall outlook appeared quite positive in 2010 and after. That year, Colombia ranked as the top country in the region in terms of the quality of the regulatory framework governing concessions and partnerships, according to the World Economic Forum (WEF). The Santos administration (2010–2014) introduced reforms aimed at improved state efficiency and expanded infrastructure. From the standpoint of institutions, a review process led to the transformation of INCO into ANI (National Infrastructure Agency) and the ministry of transport into the ministry of infrastructure and transport. In addition, it created new agencies to supervise ports and transportation as well as infrastructure. A new procurement agency attached to the national planning department was set to monitor and manage public purchases. The review of preexisting concessions led to the removal of a government concessionaire in charge of the highways. The international airport in Bogotá was reassigned to a new private contractor.

In 2012, the government passed a law for public-private partnerships (Law 1508), with the goal of attracting private investors to the infrastructure sector. The plan was to invest $56.2 billion in highways, ports, and railways over ten years. A new network of highways, including 760 kilometers with 100 tunnels and more than 700 bridges, would better connect various parts of Colombia.

The ANI had confirmed the government's decision to invest 1.5 percent of the national GDP in infrastructure in 2012 and 2013, with the goal of raising it to 3 percent in 2014, the level required to maintain a sustainable economic growth and to close the infrastructure gap.[30] ANI announced considerable investor interest in a list of 30 cutting-edge highway concession projects—especially Highways for Prosperity, a 8,000 kilometer of highways with investments of 44 billion pesos.[31]

By mid-2013, Colombians thus seemed confident of continuity. Policymakers had gained experience and accumulated lessons from the country's programs and projects. Growth was restored. Sustained institutional and policy stability appeared likely. Yet, the very success in opening the economy and emphasizing exports of primary products posed risks. Foreign investment in oil and mining strengthened the Colombian peso, which in turn threatened price-sensitive exports such as flowers. The search for policies to devalue the national currency had to be balanced against the possibility of economic downturns from adverse global conditions. Policymakers continued to bet on infrastructure and other ways to enhance competitiveness.

Three international events organized by Colombia in 2012 and 2013 indicated the country's commitment to overall liberalization: the hemisphere Summit of the Americas (Cartagena, April 2012), the 2013 public-private partnership summit of Cartagena (co-organized with the Inter-American Development Bank [IDB]), and the Pacific Alliance Summit of 2013 (Cali). These gatherings focused on physical and regional integration and economic cooperation to foster development. The PPP Americas 2013 was organized by the IDB and the national planning department of Colombia to share knowledge and skills regarding public-private partnerships. Finally, the gathering of the Pacific Alliance featuring heads of state and diplomats discussed free trade and economic integration within the Pacific region. Throughout, government officials extolled free trade agreement and the process of liberalization.

Colombia had come a long way in reaffirming a path of liberalization, rebalancing the roles of state and market. Agencies and a mature regulatory framework were in place. Policymakers exuded clarity of purpose about development goals. They had gained experience in planning large new generations of infrastructure projects. Decision makers from different political orientations seemed to share a working consensus on major economic issues. In this context, the 2014 presidential elections were unlikely to reverse course.

Peruvian Choices

Peru's distinctive trajectory to market reform has been punctuated by even more political suspense and uncertainty than that of Colombia, with which it shares a pattern of internal conflict. The last part of the twentieth century forced the choice among three rather different prototypical models: nationalistic statism, Maoist socialism, and liberalization (Sheahan, 1999; Stephan, 1978; Weyland, 2002; Wise, 2003).[32] Initiated in the difficult decade of the 1990s, Peru's support for liberalization was on a path of convergence with neighboring countries such as Chile and Colombia.

This process of liberalization had as backdrop the failure of two episodes of statism that preceded it: seven years of military-authoritarian dirigisme after 1968 and the two populist presidencies of the 1980s. The military government presided by army general Juan Velasco Alvarado (1968–1975) had as centerpiece an interventionist development model built around ISI, expropriation of foreign companies, and nationalization of economic sectors designated as strategic, enlargement of the state apparatus, elaborate central planning, agrarian reform, price controls, and general economic regulation. Velasco came to power through a coup that he and his followers justified in terms of the shortcomings of the first Fernando Belaúnde Terry presidency (1963–1968). But Velasco's left-leaning nationalism also failed to spark sustained growth and development. The public debt expanded and the currency lost value, while critical economic sectors such as agriculture and fisheries performed poorly. Overthrown by a coup, another military government lasting five years sought to reverse course but lacked the legitimacy and ability to be effective.

The reformist populism of the constitutional governments of the 1980s greatly frustrated expectations, failing miserably in setting Peru on a path to sustained development and bringing disgrace to two major parties. The presidencies of Fernando Belaúnde Terry (1980–1985) and Alan García (1985–1990) were unable to respond effectively to the shocks of the debt crisis and failed to eliminate internal bottlenecks to development. In 1982 and 1983, the economy contracted by 0.6 percent and 11.8 percent—to then continued to contract by 8.7, 11.7, 5.1, 2.2, and 0.4 percent in the five years between 1988 and 1992 (table A.12). As had been the case in the 1960s, political rivalries between García's APRA (American Popular Revolutionary Alliance) and Belaúnde's AP (Popular Action) parties blocked coherent reforms from either government. Vulnerable, the economy succumbed to economic turbulence, with inflation and the foreign debt mounting to new heights. Economic hardship was now joined by the violent Maoist insurgency of the Shining Path movement in the list of woes visiting the country.

In particular, the García presidency of the 1980s brought the country quite close to economic disaster, political turmoil, and spiraling social unrest. Hyperinflation peaked in 1990, as GDP contracted by 5.1 percent and hard currency reserves all but disappeared (table A.12). Increasing poverty fueled the explosive growth of the rebel movements and the spiral of bloody conflict. To make things worse, a furious cascade of corruption charges were directed at García himself. Poor overall performance cast a dark shadow on Peru's two main parties, on the democracy they represented, and on government institutions themselves. Conditions were ripe for something different.

An unexpected shift came with the 1990 election of Alberto Fujimori, an agricultural engineer, mathematician, and university administrator of Japanese descent—that is, a political outsider to traditional Peruvian politics, in great contrast to his predecessors. While declaring open war on the guerrilla movement, Fujimori also took major steps toward economic liberalization: privatize state-owned enterprises, end price controls and protectionism, open the economy to foreign investment, decrease regulation and bureaucracy. Many of these ideas had been appropriated from the program of the candidate he had defeated, writer Mario Vargas Llosa, another outsider to mainstream politics. Whatever its failings, Fujimori's ten-year rule achieved two elusive goals—macroeconomic stability and defeat of the powerful leftist insurgency.[33]

Though the Fujimori presidency would end in disgrace, by then Peru has a new and different economic model. Key features included liberalized trade and reintegration into the global economic system, openness to foreign investment, privatization, replenishing hard currency reserves, smaller bureaucracy and government budget, reformed administration, and expanding infrastructure (roads, schools, communications). The free market economic policies remained hotly debated, but the economy had grown by more than 3.7 percent annually between 1992 and 2001. Mining, tourism, fisheries, and agro exports helped drive the economy. Poverty, which had increased dramatically during the 1980s, decreased.

Still, Fujimori was driven to resignation, exile, and eventual imprisonment on charges of corruption and human rights abuses during his presidency. Liberalization brought economic expansion during the 1990s (table 3.2), but it also did not help that the economy declined by 0.7 percent in 1998 and stagnated at a meager growth rate of 0.9 percent in 1999 and 0.2 percent in 2001—with the slow growth resulting in no small part from the shocks of the Asian financial crisis and the weather adversities related to El Niño (table 3.1). Together with accusations of corruption and abuse in battling insurgents, the stalled economy helped bring yet another outsider to the Peruvian presidency in the 2000 elections.[34]

Alejandro Toledo (2001–2006), the first indigenous president in South America and also another outsider to mainstream Peruvian politics, maintained the liberalization drive and the overall economic model. Born into a large and humble Quechua-speaking family, Toledo experienced poverty and hardship in his early years. After attending a Peruvian university, he went on to earn a master's and PhD degrees in Economics at Stanford University. His government further privatized state-owned companies and deepened the liberalizing reforms—even as opposition over layoffs, higher energy prices, and the lingering charges of corruption from previous government blocked some of these initiatives.

This government's renewed emphasis on democracy made the opportunity structure more conducive to popular mobilization and social movement leverage (Arce, 2008). As collective action and popular participation expanded, it included protest by civil servants and others making demands on public spending, but the Toledo administration retained its focus on fiscal balance and tax reform. The economy continued to grow, accelerating to an average of slightly less than 6 percent, while inflation and the fiscal deficit remained low and unemployment and poverty decreased. Toledo did not enjoy great popular support during his presidency, but the economy expanded, democratization deepened, social initiatives were launched, the state apparatus improved somewhat, and the new economic approach remained on course. Still, the president left office with very low approval ratings.

Suspense built up with the election of Alan García in 2006, as many Peruvians feared a return to the ineffectual policies and utter failure of his first government in the second half of the 1980s. But, surprisingly, Alan García's second presidency (2006–2011) maintained the basic liberalized economic strategy of the previous two governments, veering away from the populist statism of his first term. Policy continuity lends support to the notion of a nascent core consensus around the goals of expansion of exports, the opening of the economy, competitiveness, and overall liberalization. Altogether, the Peruvian economy had grown by 4 percent in the decade after 1997, more than doubling the performance of the previous ten years, and now continued to expand. Growth of 8.9 percent in 2007 and 9.8 percent the following year were the highest in Latin America. Despite the global financial crisis and contraction of 2009, the nation's economy actually grew by nearly 1 percent that year, returning to a fast rate of annual percent growth—8.5 in 2010, 6.5 in 2011, 6.0 in 2012, and approximately 5.8 in 2013 (see figure 3.2). Meanwhile, the fiscal deficit and inflation remained low.[35]

In 2011, uncertainty returned with the election of Ollanta Humala, a nationalist politician with strong leftist leanings, as Peruvians anxiously debated the future of the liberalizing model pursued since the 1990s. A former army officer, Humala was yet another relative outsider to mainstream politics. He won a tight race over Keiko Fujimori in heated and polarizing elections in which Humala shed his prior revolutionary persona in favor of a milder one: a politician closer to Brazil's Lula da Silva than to Venezuela's Hugo Chávez. His appointment of moderates to key economic posts allayed anxieties about his policies—though many Peruvians still remained leery of his true intentions and even larger numbers held their breaths about his presidency. But the Humala government maintained the open and liberalized economic model sympathetic to business as previously set by the Fujimori, Toledo, and García governments. It identified infrastructure as a priority, deciding to spend heavily on roads and rails, airports and seaports (McKeigue, 2013).[36]

The sustained economic model created a context in which concessions and public-private formulas asserted themselves as major ways to build large-scale infrastructure projects (table 3.2). First, it had to overcome setbacks, for example, loss of investor interest in several state-owned electric companies led to the cancelation of projected conversions to concession in the early 2000s, while earlier public protest in favor of protecting national industries stopped the $167 million sale of a state-owned power company. These and other instances of public and investor resistance reflected distrust of the idea of privatization or even public-private collaboration through the early 2000s (table 3.3). Still, infrastructure, telephone, and telecommunications provision improved and the bulk of the program continued. Perhaps more importantly, mining and energy extraction (gas, copper, zinc) began to expand after the first wave of privatization and concessions (table 3.4).

As closer relations with the private sector grew and concessions became more normal, policymakers took steps to formalize a more adequate legal, regulatory, and institutional framework for public-private collaboration. The public-works concession law of 1996 allowed public works to be contracted out to the private sector. But private sector interest in the infrastructure program began to expand rapidly after the rules of 2005 guaranteed government compensation to concessionaires if revenues failed to reach a defined target, while enabling these operators to issue bonds to finance parts of the contract, thereby making it possible for them to augment the financing of projects.[37] In 2008, legislation to provide more flexibility regarding financing and risk allocation further strengthened the legal framework governing concessions and partnerships.[38] Also that year, the government created ProInversion, an official agency for attracting private participation in large infrastructure projects—advising on risks and responsibilities between the state, private investors, and multilateral banks, and providing expertise for the design of public-private models.

Table 3.4 Andes, 1990–2013, by sector, in $ millions

	1990–1995	*1996–2000*	*2001–2005*	*2006–2010*	*2011*	*2012*	*2013*	*#*	*Total*
Colombia									
Energy	1,813	5,821	270	1,180	684		1,400	37	11,168
Telecom	1,552	1,299	1,459	6,953	2,096	1,532	1,994	9	16,885
Transport	1,015	1,530	450	4,461			789	46	8,245
Water	3	360	272	305				51	940
Total	**4,383**	**9,010**	**2,451**	**12,899**	**2,780**	**1,532**	**4,183**	**143**	**37,238**
Peru									
Energy	1,208	2,596	2,151	2,221	657	2,019	2,292	53	13,144
Telecom	2,569	4,455	1,638	3,285	774	583	1,081	9	14,385
Transport	7	86	523	3,290	860	983	916	32	6,665
Water			152	120	150	105		5	527
Total	**3,784**	**7,137**	**4,464**	**8,916**	**2,441**	**3,690**	**4,289**	**99**	**34,721**
Ecuador									
Energy		30	302	129				6	461
Telecom	52	693	338	2,004	327	299	460	5	4,173
Transport	13	687	695	766				13	2,161
Water			510					4	510
Total	**65**	**1,410**	**1,845**	**2,899**	**327**	**299**	**460**	**28**	**7,305**
Bolivia									
Energy	252	2,650	720	138				14	3,760
Telecom	38	652	379	284			141	5	1,494
Transport		186						5	186
Water		682						2	682
Total	**290**	**4,170**	**1,099**	**422**				**26**	**6,121**

Source: World Bank, 2014a.

Peru's current regulatory framework for concessions[39] contains guidelines and incentives for the partnering of the state and the private sector in the provision of infrastructure and public services. Continuity in policy and macroeconomic stability, together with institutional development and the assimilation of early setbacks opened the way to new concessions and partnerships. It also helped that inflation remained low, while the national debt fell to less than 25 percent of GDP, a far cry from the much higher levels before 2003.

Throughout the dozen years after 2001, vigorous debate had not stopped major investments in public-private collaboration. The $4.46 billion total investments in 2001–2005 were the highest for the Andes region. Encouraged by the improving institutional framework, investments have grown, reaching a total of $34.7 billion through 2013.

Transportation picked up momentum after 2005, increasing from $523 million in the first half of the 2000s to $3.3 billion in the second. Several water projects and water transfer systems were finally approved as concessions.[40] Peru came to rank sixth among Latin American countries in terms of total public-private investments in infrastructure.

In this trajectory, the ambitious Integration of Regional South American Infrastructure (IIRSA) initiative provided a major test of the country's capabilities. This IDB-sponsored program includes two bold trans-Andean toll roads in its first phase—a 960 kilometer northern road passage as well as a 700 kilometer southern route between Peru and Brazil. Prioritized by the government as being of national strategic significance, these roads will link transportation networks connected to Pacific and Atlantic ports, giving Peru access to direct trade with and through Brazil and northern Bolivia. Concessionaires signed on to build, maintain, and operate the various sections of the toll road project. After the completion of the northern branch in 2006, it was time to start the $630 million southern passage. The concessionaire Buena Pro was awarded five stretches of the larger highway network stretching over 2,586 kilometers and worth $1,091 million—the 25-year BOT concession makes this firm responsible for improving, maintaining, and operating this stretch of highway. By early 2010, 13 highway concessions had been either tendered or were under advanced study, including the remaining IIRSA branches. The total planned investment in national transport projects reached $4.9 billion[41] (though only one project was implemented, according to the WB database).

By 2007, Peru had effectively emerged as one of the most attractive countries in Latin America for private investment in transport and infrastructure (Mia et al., 2007). The improved investment climate was responsible for an upward trend in private investment, while the binding bilateral agreements made it difficult for future governments to change the current framework favoring public-private cooperation.

By 2012, the mining boom—gold, copper, silver, and other minerals—had been responsible for a decade of fast annual economic growth of more than 6 percent. That year, the government proudly announced new plans for $50 billion mining projects.[42] Updated plans to improve the country's infrastructure gap underscored the country's pressing needs for private participation.

Although the Peruvian program of public-private participation had expanded and gained institutional support and political commitment, it still faces challenges. The country still lacks a full partnership law and appropriate institutional framework. ProInversion has drawn criticisms for lacking the proper technical and fiscal capacity to coordinate investment efforts. Its mission has been delayed by ministries without experience with partnerships, with projects behind schedule.

A number of projects have been approved without adequate environmental and social impact study. For instance, mass protest movements against large global mining projects have emphasized their damage to local communities and environments. In 2011, these protests put a stop to a large silver mining project by a Canadian company. The following year, opposition from activists stopped the $4.8 billion gold-copper Conga mine, a top project in the country's $57b mining portfolio. Humala had opposed as a candidate, but decided to support it after becoming president. Still, the project was postponed, following violent marches leaving five fatalities. The widespread community opposition in Cajamarca (78 percent rejection rate) framed its arguments in terms of the dangers to water supply from the plans to drain four small lakes. Sponsors and authorities tried to respond to demands from communities before attempting to restart the project.[43] A well-designed environmental impact study would have addressed these issues before approving the project (The Economist, 2013a).

Still, awareness of infrastructure needs and commitment to specific plans for addressing them augur well for public-private collaboration in Peru. AFIN (Association for the Development of National Infrastructure) pressed for investing $88 billion to close the infrastructure gap by 2021—$33 billion in energy, mostly in electricity; $21 billion in transportation; and $19 billion in telecommunications—urging the use of public-private partnerships. In 2013, the Peruvian minister of Economy and Finance identified 28 infrastructure projects to be financed through public-private partnerships. The list included roads, airports, and natural gas pipelines to enhance competitiveness. The specific list of projects included a second gas duct linking the coast to production fields in the Peruvian jungle, 500 kilometers of roads, a logistics zone connecting the port of Callao and Lima's international airport, and irrigation of 100,000 hectares of arable land. Private concessionaires would be able to use infrastructure investments as tax write-offs.[44] Other organizations continue to lobby for a broader range of projects.[45]

But stakeholders seem to have assimilated these setbacks. In early 2014, Proinversion announced a $12 billion portfolio of projects for 2014–2015, with the construction of a second line for Lima's subway to absorb nearly half of this investment. At that point, Fitch commented positively on the county's experience with public-private collaboration.

As in other Latin American countries, the Peruvian expansion of infrastructure and development plans aim at increased production and competitiveness in the market-oriented model. That is, they are focused on trade as an engine of growth. An eventual tapering of the mining boom will test the economic model and the strategy based on the export of commodities.

Southern Contrasts

While Argentina and Chile, the two largest Southern Cone countries, contrast in their experiences with public-private collaboration (see Chapter Two), smaller Uruguay and Paraguay have taken steps toward its expanded use while maintaining policies of economic liberalization.

Uruguay: Social Democracy and Reform

Uruguay's small size as well as historical similarities and closeness to Argentina, have not prevented it from pursuing a distinctive path to reform. Throughout much of the twentieth century, Uruguay enjoyed high levels of modernization and development comparable to those of its large neighbor to the south. Besides large shares of European immigrants in their populations, Southern Cone countries also had similar historical development paths led by large export sectors—beef and grains in Argentina and Uruguay, and minerals, wine, and fruit in Chile.[46] Despite their higher levels of economic, institutional, and social development, these countries experienced repressive military regimes in the 1960s, 1970s, and parts of the 1980s (O'Donnell, 1973, 1977, 1993). This episode interrupted decades of democracy in the case of Uruguay.

Redemocratizing transitions in the 1980s were accompanied or followed shortly after by liberalizing state reforms, but Uruguay advanced at a more gradual pace (Blake, 1998). There, redemocratization after 1984–1985 proceeded with remarkable continuity, surviving a major political realignment in 2005. In the first phase, political leaders from the traditional Colorado and National parties took turns in the four presidential terms opening the new era of democracy—Julio María Sanguinetti (1985–1990), Luis Alberto Lacalle (1990–1995), Julio María Sanguinetti (1995–2000), and Jorge Batlle (2000–2005). Starting in 2004, two candidates of the leftist Broad Front were elected in succession: Tabaré Vázquez (2005–2010) and José Mujica (2010–2015). The 2004 elections also gave the new Broad Front coalition a majority in both houses of Parliament.

Surprisingly, the first Broad Front president stuck to the gradual and consensual approach to a liberalizing economic model. As commodity prices soared and the economy recoiled from recession, the Vázquez government claimed credit for tripling foreign investment, reducing the public debt from 79 percent of GDP to 60 percent, and keeping inflation low, while also cutting poverty and unemployment (The Economist, 2009a). After winning in 2009, Broad Front's José Mujica, a leftist militant who spent almost 15 years in prison during the years of military rule, maintained the liberalizing approach. That the two leftist presidents respected the democratic institutional context and maintained the evolving market reforms is evidence of the consolidation of both processes, as all major parties since the restoration of democracy were now also on record as agreeing on the new development model. Uruguay was thereby affirming a gradual but sustained approach to state reform that gave priority to public consultation—a contrast with Argentina's reformist big bang under a technocratic model. The differences in the reform trajectories of these otherwise comparable cases show the decisive role of domestic political contexts (Blake, 1998).

The public works and concessions legislation of 1984 (Law 15,367) and 1991 provided the legal framework to attract private partners to infrastructure project. Through the 1990s, Uruguay invested nearly $487 million in diverse sectors, including mobile telephony, airport, highway, and gas. Five road concessions were launched shortly after 1995. For several years after 1997, four external shocks brought economic turbulence: the Asian crisis at the end of the twentieth century, the devaluation of the Brazilian real, Argentina's financial collapse in 2001, and low commodity prices (see figure 3.3). The severe Uruguayan recession of 2002 brought about a 10 percent contraction in the economy, very high unemployment, a poverty rate of over 30 percent, and years of only modest infrastructure investments (Meyer, 2010). Despite public discontent, by 2000–2001 the country had been able to launch concessions for natural gas, airport expansion, and a seaport terminal. Shortly after, over $160 million were invested in the country's international airport, $20 million in a seaport terminal, and $20 million in telecommunications, while plans were made for concessions to develop the transport corridor of Río de la Plata.

However, reflecting the mood in Argentina and Brazil, many Uruguayans now soured on privatization and economic liberalization,

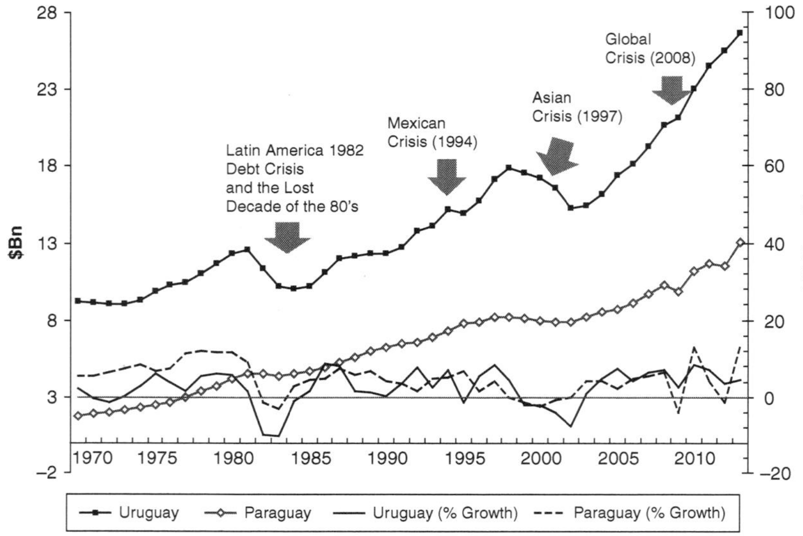

Figure 3.3 Uruguay and Paraguay, GDP and growth, 1970–2013.
Source: World Bank, 2014b.

blaming the "neoliberal" policies for their economic woes. Mobilization against the privatization of water and petroleum drew large numbers. In 2004, voters approved a constitutional reform that declared water resources to be public goods not open to the private sector and authorized the government to terminate concessions that threatened this principle. The large Uraguayan water utility and treatment project was cancelled. These actions built on the 1991 referendum declaring water a human rights issue and another referendum in 1996 restricting privatization in the oil sector.

In this context, the liberalization process entered a period of suspense with the 2004 victory of the Broad Front coalition, as it had included the strong movement opposing the privatization of water and petroleum. Shortly after, the government turned 1,300 kilometers in its highway concessions system into a state-controlled mixed-capital company.[47] Though technically open to private investment, most infrastructure sectors (water, power, railways) continued to be run as state-owned companies. Public opinion appeared unsympathetic to programs to privatize infrastructure. Uruguay's gradual liberalization thus faced a major test with the election of the Broad Front presidents. Firmly supportive of its European-style social democracy, public opinion seemed to want as little change as possible in its traditional procurement practices. In this context, public-private collaboration could only hope to expand very gradually.

However, doubts about the compatibility between the leftist government and Uruguay's distinctive social democracy and political civility disappeared as these governments retained the dual commitment to democracy and economic liberalization. Though the private sector did remain somewhat reluctant to invest in infrastructure, international financiers gradually returned to the perception of Uruguay as having a favorable investment climate. Through 2008, Uruguay developed 13 public-private projects worth $1.5 billion. These were distributed in the energy (gas), telecommunications, transportation, and water sectors.

Upon assuming office in March 2010, President José Mujica argued that Uruguay urgently needed $2 billion of new infrastructure investment and that concessions and partnerships would be adopted for that purpose since the state lacked enough funding. In November, his government sent a bill authorizing the creation of public-private partnerships. The public workers trade union and two other unions mobilized against the bill, maintaining that public-private collaboration was detrimental to labor. The government insisted on the reasons for public-private collaboration: the urgency of new infrastructure investments, the state's fiscal limitations and need to reduce the public deficit, and the priority focus on security and social policy. New investments from abroad were required to turn the country into a major regional center for logistics, maintained the government.

After extended debate, the Uruguayan lower house approved the Law for Public-Private Participation in May 2011. The bill approved public-private partnerships in a wide range of areas: roads, rail, airports, navigation projects, water treatment, sanitation, jails, health, education, sports, and urban development. Political support from the Broad Front and the Colorado, National, and Independent parties ensured passage. The senate gave its nearly unanimous consent in early July 2011, adding a clause indicating that the government could not unilaterally annul any contract. The law authorized investments up to 7 percent of GNP, with the annual cost to the government to not exceed 0.5 percent of GNP.

Uruguay's program of public-private collaboration is embedded in a gradual, but sustained, reform process in which a strong executive leadership has been decisive. In the context of democratic stability, the country now had a mature framework for collaboration between the public and private sectors. Uruguay ranked a modest 85 in competitiveness and 55 in infrastructure in the 2013–2014 report (World Economic Forum) and sixth in investment climate in the South American region (The Economist Intelligence Unit). That year the country invested $2.4 billion in infrastructure.

In the early 2000s, soy rapidly displaced other crops and land uses in western Uruguay as the country took off as a significant exporter of soybeans in 2003, becoming the world's seventh largest exporter by the following year. Soy became Uruguay's top export by 2008—much of it to China and Europe. Soy acreage had grown to 863,000 hectares and total production to 1,293,000 tonnes in 2009–2010, up from 309,000 hectares and 632,000 tonnes of soybeans in the 2005–2006 harvest (see also UN/ FAO-STAT database).

Paraguay: Soy and Globalization

Paraguay is traditionally viewed as, in contrast to neighboring Uruguay and Argentina, a country of low socioeconomic development, high levels of poverty and inequality, low levels of modernization, ineffective governance, landlocked geography, and isolation. Politically, its trajectory since the nineteenth century and for much of the twentieth century was marked by high levels of authoritarianism, conflict, and instability. At least 16 of the 31 presidents met forced removal between 1903 and 1954—and that year, General Alfredo Stroessner's coup launched a harshly authoritarian regime that lasted until 1989. A difficult search for democracy opened since then, including the adoption of a new constitution in 1992. The country had relatively free elections since 2000, though punctuated by the removal of an elected president in 2012.

One of the long-held stereotypes that needs a clearer revision is that of the country's economy as chronically stagnant and backward. In fact, Paraguay's economy has often outperformed its neighbors in recent history. First, construction of the trinational Itaipú dam meant faster growth in the 1970s, as the sale of its share of electric power to Brazil made Paraguay the world's second largest exporter of electricity. As a result, the country weathered the challenges of the 1982 international recession and the low commodity prices for cotton and soybeans, two crops whose price and yield volatility had battered the economy in the past. Second, sustained commodity-led export booms after 1984 fueled recovery and expansion, driven by the gradual expansion and modernization of its soybeans and other agricultural sectors. Partly for these reasons, the slowdown of 1998 was less pronounced than those of Uruguay and Argentina.

Soy emerged as a main engine of national transformation thrusting the country into the dynamics of the global economy. By 2012–2013, Paraguay's soy harvests of 8–9 million tons were considerably smaller than the 80–85 million tons of Brazil or 50 million tons of Argentina, but they had increased by 10 percent annually in the prior decade and promised further expansion. That year, the large soy harvest represented upward of $2 billion. Demand from China and Europe had turned the country into the world's fourth largest exporter of soy. In addition to soy, more than 600 farms export organic crop such as sesame, sugar, and the sweetener stevia, while beef remained an important export.

Having expanded at a substantial rate between 1970 and 2009, the economy grew 13.1 percent in 2010 and 4.3 percent in 2011, to contract somewhat in 2012 and then expand at 13.6 percent in 2013 (see figure 3.3). Forecasts remained generally optimistic, despite the recent shock from the global slowdown and a drought. This very expansion placed the spotlight on infrastructure bottlenecks constraining it. In the 1990s, Paraguay had invested $1.1 billion in concessions for the new cell phone systems (1992, 1997, and 1998). Clearly, a major need now was for better transportation and logistics to improve competitiveness in the production of commodities for distant markets.

Geography dictates a narrow set of options in this regard. Two major South American rivers define its territory and choices rather decisively—the Paraguay dividing it into two parts and the Parana separating it from Brazil and northeastern Argentina. Together with their tributaries, they are major sources of food, water, energy, and transportation. They provide this landlocked country with its access to the Atlantic through the Río de la Plata Basin, a route traveled by 80 percent or so of the country's trade. Rising in Brazil's Mato Grosso, the Paraguay river flows in a southwest-southward direction for 400 kilometers through the middle of the country, neatly dividing it into two main parts: the eastern half, home to more than 95 percent of the country's 6.5 million inhabitants, and the much poorer and unsettled Gran Chaco region to the west. The river's next 275 kilometers draw part of the border with Argentina's northeast, to then merge with the equally majestic Paraná, as both now flow in a southwestern direction before turning to the Platine basin. Upstream and to the east of Paraguay, the Paraná River separates it from Argentina and Brazil, but Itaipú and other hydroelectric dams and falls interrupt navigation. The merged forces of the great Paraguay-Parana waterway flow toward the Atlantic Ocean under the latter's name. This river system is thus the main shipping and transportation corridor for Paraguay and adjacent areas. Through it, the country's river ports are connected to the gateway of world trade at the Plata basin.

However, effective access is constrained by Argentina's jurisdiction over much of the Paraná River, by congested ports, and by navigability problems in parts of the entire waterway requiring periodic dredging due to sedimentation. River barges and deep-water vessels crisscrossing the main Paraguayan waterways depend on Argentina for effective trade, as shipments to global markets must rely on the latter's ports for transhipment or passage. Paraguay thus needs joint ventures and partnerships with Argentine counterparts to develop and maintain the Rio de la Plata basin as an international corridor. As major interested parties, traders ADM, Cargill, Bunge, Louis Dreyfus, and other global commodity companies work with governments in the region in maintaining and enhancing this vital transportation channel. The first three handle 70 percent of Paraguayan soy exports. ADM alone processes about 30 percent of Paraguay's output of grain and oilseeds, operating more than 25 grain stations near the waterways, a trucking company, a river fleet of 10 or so tugboats and 171 barges, as well as the port it owns and the other three that is leases. Further expansion of the Paraguayan economy thus depends on solution to complex transportation and logistic bottlenecks.

To address its infrastructure gaps, the Paraguayan government has sought to create investment opportunities attractive to private sector participation. The 2000 law on concessions and public services (Law 1618) provides a legal framework for concessions. Line ministries are responsible for undertaking preliminary studies, qualifying proposals, and executing the contracting process through a mandatory public bidding process. This arrangement survived the period of political tension after 2008, when leftist Fernando Lugo won the presidential elections after 61 years of rule by the conservative Colorado Party. Though some feared a sharp reversal of development strategy, the new president surprised critics by supporting private investments in infrastructure. In 2010, policymakers drafted a new legal framework and guidelines for authorizing concessions. Inspired in the Chilean case, and with the support of multilateral development banks, the ministry of public works drafted a concessions plan to improve the country's roads, better integrate its regions, and provide access to the Atlantic as well as to Brazil, deemed its main strategic and economic partner. International advisers helped develop projects and tenders were prepared under the 2000 law, though additional legislation would be needed for a legal framework for public-private collaboration appealing to key stakeholders.

Soon after, the government announced several projects: Silvio Pettirossi International Airport, improvements in the Paraguay-Paraná waterway, and upgrades to five highway stretches connecting major production areas to this key transportation corridor. The IDB, CAF, other regional and multilateral financial institutions, and local banks addressed financial aspects of the new projects, with an eye on competitiveness and long-term economic growth. Local banks were reported as planning to invest up to $1.7 billion in major infrastructure projects (Desantis, 2010). Policymakers also began to refine public-private projects to improve urban infrastructure, including public transportation. A $125 million grant from the IDB targeted a larger and more effective bus service in the capital city of Asunción (IDB, 2010), with a broader urban plan to construct pedestrian walkways and bicycle paths, restore historic buildings, develop government office space, and upgrade public places. However, actual movement in public-private collaboration was slow (The Economist, 2013). The list of failed or delayed projects included those to expand the international airport, build highways and better waterways. Some political forces distrusted the idea of public access by the private sector.[48] In addition, political instability following the removal of Fernando Lugo in 2012 created uncertainty.

In 2013, the outgoing interim president and the recently elected one worked with Congress to pass a PPP law with a main focus on roads and highways. The lower house voted the law in June 2013.[49] New president Horacio Cartes used his inaugural speech to support the law of public-private partnerships and announce a 10-year infrastructure investment plan of nearly $10 billion. More than half of the funds would be used for improvements to the Paraguay-Parana waterways, rail, airports and other transportation projects—while energy would attract a fourth and water services 10 percent of the investments. The government continued to work with the IDB, CAF, and investors to develop the long-term logistics plan.[50] By early 2014, this effort had created a list of projects worth $12 billion, to include a handful of major roads, highways, and bridges.

At face value, these plans fit the country's urgent needs for infrastructure. Still, Paraguay's low level of institutional development (e.g., ranking 150th place among 176 countries in corruption and tax evasion, according to Transparency International) places in question its very ability to develop long-term associations requiring great trust.[51] But public-private collaboration was poised for expansion, even if Paraguay lacked the institutional backbone and stability of Chile or Uruguay. It was taking major steps to engage the private sector in the provision of infrastructure, a choice that by now had been confirmed by different presidents. Several of the main plans for transportation infrastructure hinged on global demand for its soy and other commodities. But what ultimately mattered most were political leadership, institutional competence, and the policy momentum to work with national and international actors toward widening the paths to develop this historically isolated part of the South American heartland.

Conclusion

As discussed above, public-private collaboration has followed diverse paths in Latin America. In the Andean region, Chile, Colombia, and Peru have robust programs showing long-term commitment and a list of projects completed or in progress. Uruguay and Paraguay have taken significant steps toward adoption of public-private collaboration, though still in the early stages. The picture is quite different in Argentina, Bolivia, Ecuador, and Venezuela, which reversed early liberalization strategies in favor of statism without necessarily abandoning some types of concession in the provision of infrastructure (tables A.6 and A.7).

Meanwhile, Brazil and Mexico, the two largest countries in the region, already host large, elaborate, and by now quite mature programs. On balance, the idea of public-private collaboration appears nearly consolidated, with momentum toward an adequate regulatory framework and poised for expansion—though debate, slow growth, or opposition endure in a few cases.[52]

In Brazil, Argentina, Uruguay, and Paraguay, soy and other agricultural export booms made clear the need for major improvements in transportation infrastructure—roads, railroads, logistics, bridges, and ports. Likewise, the mining and hydrocarbon booms in Peru, Colombia, Ecuador, Bolivia, and Chile have demanded port terminals, pipelines, transportation, overall modernization, and the like. Governments responding to pressures for increased competitiveness and development have also targeted communications, energy, and water for investment. Some sectors have done better than others. Telecommunications attracted widespread attention and support between 1991 and 2004, while water and energy are prone to opposition.

Need alone has not guaranteed adoption or success. In Latin America, public-private collaboration emerged in the context of sustained liberalizing reform processes often embedded in successful political transitions toward democracy (Milner and Mukherjee, 2009). State strength is a key variable in the success of both democratizing and liberalizing reforms. Effective institutional capabilities or governance make them more likely. Inadequate institutional strength often leads to disaster. Different combinations and sequences have led to varying outcomes. In unconsolidated democracies, ambitious liberalization and public-private reforms have generally wavered or failed. They have also faltered when both sets of reforms have been implemented simultaneously or when bold liberalizing reforms are attempted in the context of incomplete political transitions or bold liberalization drives were attempted by governments in the initial or early-middle stages of democratic transitions. In contrast, liberalization has tended to survive in two other situations: organizationally effective authoritarian regimes, like pre-1990 Chile or pre-2000 Mexico, and in democracies in advanced stages of consolidation—as in post-1990s Chile, Uruguay, and Brazil, which maintained the course on liberalizing policy and withstood the strains of economic shocks.

The vagaries of the global economy help explain reform outcomes. International crises and other unexpected shocks, such as those at the turn of the century, help explain shifts away from liberalization processes and public-private collaboration. They weakened the political position of reformers and worsened the fate of various social groups. Opposition movements thus peaked precisely when reforming incumbents were particularly vulnerable. "Reform fatigue" set in during or shortly after 1997–1998. Whipsawed by the above movements, vulnerable polities succumbed to unstable dynamics. Unpredictable outcomes and unusual political change occurred when major slowdowns from external shock interacted with political processes to fuel political contention. Antiliberal political reversals in Argentina, Bolivia, and Ecuador can be understood partly in those terms—as can that of Venezuela, where corruption, waste, and an ineffective bureaucracy also undermined the legitimacy of its party system and democratic polity at a critical moment for its process of liberalization.

However, fiscal and economic crises and other external shocks have often contributed to the adoption of concessions and partnerships. Governments responding to the economic turbulence of the 1980s devised reforms that included privatization through divestiture. These forms of privatization reached limits in terms of political support in the 1990s. Political backlash in the first decade of the twenty-first century strengthened opposition to these and related liberalizing measures in Venezuela, Bolivia, Ecuador, and even Argentina.

But public-private collaboration became a robust trend in Mexico, Brazil, and Chile, where experience learned from simple concessions, including the assimilation of setbacks, led to more complex relations with the private sector through public-private partnerships. This is not automatic; processes of change and reform require considerable political leadership and commitment. They work through a combination of strong leadership, consensus building, and the development of political-institutional backbone. Sustainability also builds on public support. Democratic consultation is one. Domestic civil society has not been fully incorporated into these new forms. This would be an effective way to further consolidate the learning process, create durable policy network, and build competencies.

In any case, learning to design and implement simpler concessions appears to be a necessary building block before more complex partnerships are attempted. Effectiveness and capability enhancement in public-private partnerships seem to require prior expertise in launching a successful concessions program. This is the sequence found in Mexico as well as in Chile and Brazil. This learning process may take considerable time. Global or international policy networks and the transborder diffusion of models shape the initiation and sustainability of concessions and partnership models. In Latin America and the Caribbean, international development banks and institutions have often performed this function. Though some countries have acquired knowledge and expertise relevant to other cases, multilateral organizations, business summits, and professional gatherings frequently bring together private and public actors to network, share opportunities, and learn about practices that have worked well in other settings.

In closing, it is appropriate to explore the extent to which and why the external shocks related to the financial crisis of 2008 have not brought about a new round of crisis or an acceleration of statism in Latin America. Through 2013, slowed growth had increased joblessness and generated unusual demands on governments, but a good number have responded by further subscribing to collaborative projects with the private sector. The successful cycles of reform of the 1980s and 1990s help explain this response to crisis, but not alone. In addition, sustained demand for the region's commodities has also been of major significance. After 2002 or so, commodity booms in many South American countries decisively contributed to economic recovery and economic growth during the following decade. This phenomenon coincides with China's growing interest in South American commodities, as reflected in large purchases of soy and minerals.

Would an eventual shift away from export booms, such as from changed conditions in China, subvert the reforms associated with public-private collaboration? Drawing from discussions in this volume, it can be surmised that policymakers in the region are now more likely to stay the course in the presence of such adverse conditions. They have generally come to agree that better infrastructure is essential and that governments alone are unable to underwrite very large infrastructure projects required for competitiveness, sustained development, and modernization. To that extent, public-private collaboration in infrastructure provision may prevail or even expand in the context of an eventual economic slowdown. But the wager here hinges on political and institutional dynamics.

Chapter Four further explores how agricultural and mineral booms expose needs and shape plans for better infrastructure. Soy expansion in Brazil pressed for transportation infrastructure to keep up with global demand. It also explores how institutional and political variables shape the role of the private sector in the provision of such infrastructure.

CHAPTER FOUR

Commodities and Rail in Globalizing Brazil

Brazil's boom in commodities during the last part of the twentieth century put its central plateau on a path of transformation and prominence in national development. This potential hinges on railroads and roads to move grains to ports on the Atlantic and thence to the outside world. After discussing agrarian expansion in the untamed savannahs of central Brazil, this chapter focuses on two railroad projects: a private initiative to connect the key state of Mato Grosso to the port of Santos and a federal alternative to reach ports in the north. Together with a rail bypass around the São Paulo metropolitan area, these projects help address key questions about public-private collaboration in infrastructure.

The inauguration of the new capital of Brasilia in 1960 drew attention to the vast but traditionally isolated and undeveloped central plateau or *Cerrado*, bringing demographic and economic expansion to the state of Goiás. Three decades later, commercial farming was turning this state as well as Mato Grosso and Mato Grosso do Sul—the three main units in the central-west region—into the heartland of the boom in soybeans and a main engine of economic growth (figure 4.1 and table 4.1). Soy led the march of the new agricultural frontier. Responsible for a mere 1.1 percent of national soy production in 1970, the midwest's share expanded rapidly—11.8 percent in 1980, 28 percent in 1985, 46 percent in 1991, and more than 50 percent by the mid-2000s. In the state of Mato Grosso alone, soy harvests of less than 100,000 tons before 1980 grew to 1.6 million tons in 1985 and 2.74 million tons in 1991, to then jump to more than 15 million tons in 2006 and 26 million tons in 2014 (table 4.1). Transportation infrastructure to connect this isolated region to global markets emerged as an increasingly pressing issue—building

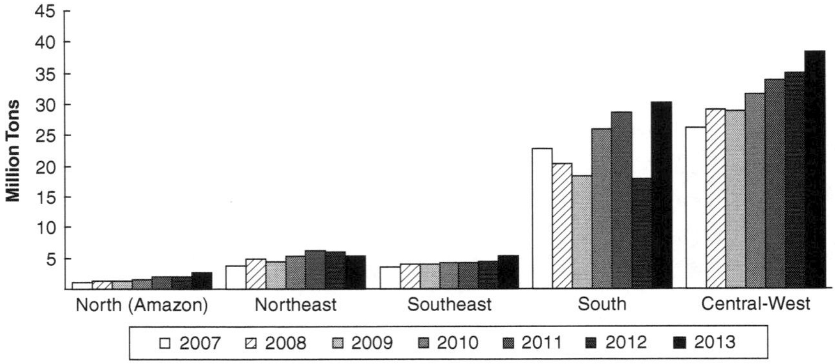

Figure 4.1 Soybean production in Brazil's five regions, 2007–2013.
Source: IBGE-Municipal Agricultural Production (PAM), 2007–2012.

new railroads, repairing or upgrading dilapidated roads, and using rivers and waterways to provide access to shipping ports near the coast.

The New Agrarian Frontier

Occupying more than a fifth of the country's 8.5 million square kilometers, the *Cerrado* is the country's second largest ecosystem after the Amazon. Much of it lies in the three states in the midwest, particularly Mato Grosso.[1] This tropical savanna differs markedly from the humid Amazon rainforest to its north and west. It also contrasts with the semi-arid *sertão*—the landmass of nearly 650,000 square kilometers, largely unsuitable for sustained commercial agriculture due to frequent droughts, separating the central plateau from the densely settled northeastern coastline. The more humid *Cerrado* sustains a great deal of biodiversity, though its traditional isolation and climate of short rainy summers and longer dry winters had also led to a reputation as unsuitable for large-scale commercial agriculture. But that view changed in the 1970s with the development of new soy seeds and soil treatments adapted to the savanna.

Together with government incentives, the new seeds and techniques developed by the Embrapa research institute made possible large-scale production of soy in this part of the country.[2] They were necessary but not sufficient conditions for fast expansion, as harvests of less than a million tons in 1968 grew to more than 31 million tons 30 years later. Though modest levels of financing contributed to gradual growth

Table 4.1 Soy Production in the *Cerrado*, main states, in million tons, 1970–2014

	1970	*1980*	*1985*	*1991*	*1996*	*2006*	*2007*	*2011*	*2012*	*2013*	*2014*
Mato Grosso	.01	.09	1.61	2.74	5.03	15.60	15.27	20.80	21.84	23.42	26.36
Goiás	.01	.37	1.16	1.66	1.96	6.02	5.94	7.70	8.37	8.90	8.83
Mato Grosso do Sul	–	1.04	1.81	2.02	2.00	4.15	4.85	5.08	4.59	5.78	6.28
Bahia	–	–	.06	.44	.70	2.00	2.30	3.51	3.21	2.76	3.98
Maranhão	–	–	.01	.01	.14	.93	1.13	1.57	1.64	1.59	1.88
Tocantins			.03	.01	.01	.74	.73	1.20	1.29	1.50	1.82
Piauí	–	–	–	–	.02	.54	.48	1.14	1.24	.92	1.49
Sub-total	.02	1.50	4.68	6.88	9.86	29.98	30.70	41.00	42.18	44.87	50.64
Total Brazil	**1.88**	**12.75**	**16.73**	**14.94**	**23.15**	**46.20**	**58.38**	**74.81**	**65.70**	**81.70**	**86.60**
Share of total production (%)	1.1	11.8	28.0	46.1	42.6	64.89	52.6	54.8	64.2	54.9	58.5

Source: IBGE: PAM (Produção Agrícola Municipal), several years; 2006 Agricultural Census; 1996 Agricultural Census; Indicadores Agropecuários 1996–2003; Indicadores IBGE: Estatística da Produção Agrícola (novembro de 2012, janeiro de 2013, maio de 2013), June 2014.

through the 1970s (Frechette, 1997), faster expansion in the 1980s and 1990s came about with the financing, fertilizers, and pesticides often provided by trading companies (Bickel, 2003). Macroeconomic stability in 1994 and currency devaluation in 1999 widened the window of opportunity, but soy's rapid expansion in the *Cerrado* since then responded above all to the dramatic rise in global demand led by China, which very rapidly emerged as the main importer of Brazilian soy.

The central plateau replaced the southern region as Brazil's capital of soy toward the turn of the century (see figure 4.2 and table 4.1). This region's 50.6 million tons of soy in 2014 represented 58.5 percent of Brazil's soy and more than half of the country's grains and oilseeds. As central Brazil consolidated its standing as a global soy producer, Brazil's soy crops reached 46 million tons in 2006, 74.8 million tons in 2011, and nearly 87 million in 2014, to become a close second only to the United States as top soy producers. With the increased soy harvests in the *Cerrado*, the central-west states rose to 48 percent of the nation's total. Mato Grosso alone represented more than 30 percent of Brazil's total between 2011 and 2014, that is, nearly half of the *Cerrado* as a whole.

Total land use in soy in the three midwestern states increased from less than half a million hectares in 1977 to 10.5 million in 2009 and almost 14 million in 2014. The region also produced corn, cotton, meat products, and other agricultural goods.[3] The fast-moving agricultural

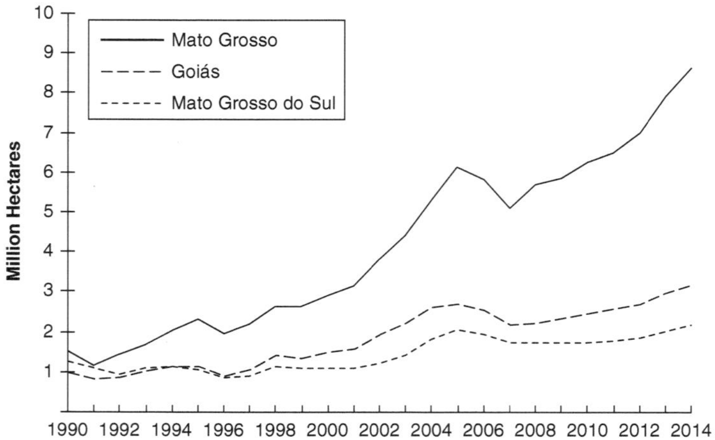

Figure 4.2 Growth of the soy frontier in Central-West, 1990–2014.

Source: IBGE, "Levantamento Sistemático da Produção Agrícola" (LSPA), several years.

frontier and unrelenting occupation of idle land reached the northeast and then the Amazon rainforest.[4] Mechanization and capital intensive practices have been key elements in this tendency. Though smaller producers were part of the process, large farmers occupy most of the land. Very large farms of more than 1,000 hectares claim nearly 80 percent of Mato Grosso's soy. Global trading companies—Cargill, ADM, Bunge, Louis Dreyfus, Maggi, and others—own or finance a good number of the warehouses and terminals dotting the changed landscape, including grains-loaded trucks crisscrossing roads and highways at harvest time.

In this dynamic context, economic actors press for adequate transportation and logistics.[5] Since distance and geography had traditionally kept the central plateau in relative isolation, upgraded and new roads and railroads to Atlantic ports are now essential to consolidate the central states as engines of export-led development. This is a particularly urgent matter for growers and traders, whose transportation costs of 30 percent or so of prices are four to five times those of the United States. They also complain about the routine delays for their grains to reach ports and buyers.[6] Large parts of the expanding agricultural frontier in northern Mato Grosso and beyond can still face difficulties in accessing road or railroad services in the rainy season, when unpaved roads may be nearly unusable.[7] The World Economic Forum's 2012–2013 report placed Brazil 107th out of 144 countries in quality of overall infrastructure, a drop from 104th place in 2010.[8] There is agreement about the infrastructure needs of export agriculture: expand and improve railroad, roads, highways, intermodal capabilities, and port capacity. While government agencies estimate investments of $400 to $500 billion to end the transportation gap, plans for 2013–2016 call for $104 billion (BNDES; MF/Seae, 2013; Coutinho, 2013).

Soy is not the only commodity demanding better transportation infrastructure. Iron ore and concentrates top the list of Brazilian exports, accounting for 13 percent of its value, that is, more than soy's 10 percent. The average of 117 million tons of ore exported in the early 1990s grew nearly threefold to reach 329 million tons on average between 2011 and 2013, or, more dramatically, from $2.4 billion to $35 billion in terms of value (UN Comtrade). A few companies control iron production, most of which were originally owned by the state before the reforms of the 1990s. Technically privatized in 1997, the Companhia Vale do Rio Doce (Vale) is the world's top producer of iron ore and derivatives, which command 65 percent of its revenues. This mining conglomerate has an important stake in national rail policy and plans, since transportation and logistics are big aspects of iron's product chain.[9] Vale operates the Carajás Railroad (EFC) carrying iron ore from its huge mines with the same name in Pará to the port of Itaqui in Maranhão. It is also the owner or main shareholder of three other railroads servicing its mining operations: the Centro-Atlântica (FCA); the Vitória-Minas (EFVM); and MRS Logística. Through these companies, the mining giant operates in 16 Brazilian states and owns or controls the ports of Itaqui (Ponta da Madeira terminal), Tubarão, Sepetiba, and large terminals in Santos and other ports. Vale, CSN (Companhia Siderúrgica Nacional), USIMINAS, and other mining companies have a strategic stake in controlling railway and shipping facilities (table 4.2).

Representing 5 percent of national exports, sugar and ethanol are other significant stakeholders in national railroad and logistics plans. This sector concentrates much of its activities in the state of São Paulo and thus relies heavily on access to the port of Santos provided by the rail concession operating the São Paulo export corridor, Latin American Logistics (ALL). In late 2013, Cosan, co-owner of the world's top ethanol and sugar producer, made a multibillion offer to merge ALL with its own logistics operation. This takeover was approved on February 11, 2015. This industry wants to ensure that rising transportation demand from grains and minerals does not diminish its own logistics and export capabilities.[10] China is yet another global stakeholder interested in transportation and logistics issues affecting Brazilian commodities. Authorities and companies from the Asian giant aim at cost-reducing transportation initiatives and greater control over vital food and mineral imports. China rapidly became Brazil's largest trading partner shortly after the turn of the century. Trade between the two countries jumped from $3.2 billion in 2002 to $83.3 billion in 2013. That year, China represented nearly a fifth ($46 billion) of Brazil's total exports, including nearly half of its iron exports and three-fifths of its soy exports (Jenkins, 2012; UN Comtrade). In a mid-2014 visit, Chinese president Xi Jinping pledged over $8.6 billion in investment and credit, including a multibillion credit line to Vale, Brazil's largest exporter, to obtain large vessels, as well as a $3.2 billion order of Brazilian jet planes. Xi also repeated Chinese interest in hydroelectric plants and railway connections to Atlantic and Pacific ports.[11]

Powerful global actors are playing growing roles in the country's development and modernization driven by the export of commodities. Under this condition, Brazilian railroads and transportation infrastructure has become a global concern.[12] In this context, a big question is the ability of Brazil's political dynamics and institutional development to effectively reconcile diverse views and interests from different sectors

Table 4.2 Post-reforms railroad concessions, as of 2013–2014

Concessionaire	*Older Name (1990s)*	*Owners/Products*	*Km/Main Ports*
ALLMN (América Latina Logística: North Net)	Ferronorte	ALL/soy, cellulose, corn, containers	754/Santos
ALLMP (Paulista Net)	Ferroban (Bandeirantes)	ALL/sugar, ethanol, other fuels	1,989/Santos
ALLMO (West Net)	Novoeste (Ferrovia Novoeste)	ALL/iron, cellulose, ethanol, other	1,945/Santos, Corumbá, Bolivia
ALLMS (South Net)	ALL (América Latina Logística do Brasil)	ALL/soy, sugar, corn, fuels, cargo	7,265/Paranaguá, Rio Grande
EFC (Carajás Railroad)	Estrada de Ferro Carajás	VALE/iron, fuels, copper	892/Itaqui (MA)
FNS (North-South Railroad)	Ferrovia Norte-Sul	VALE/soy, iron, corn, fuels	720/Itaqui (MA)
FCA (Centro-Atlântica Railroad)	FCA (Ferrovia Centro-Atlântica)	VALE/iron, soy, grains, sugar, ethanol, bauxite, cargo	7,427/Tubarão, Bahia, Sergipe, Rio, Santos
MRS Logística	MRS Logística (EF Rio-SP-MG; EF Santos-Jundiai)	VALE, CSN, USIMINAS & mining co./ iron, coal, sugar	1,674/Rio, Sepetiba-Itaguaí, Angra, Santos
EFVM (Vitória e Minas Railroad)	EFVM (Vitória e Minas RR)	VALE & mining co/ iron, other minerals, coal, wood, cellulose, oils, passengers	905/Tubarão
TLSA (Transnordestina Logística)	CFN (Companhia Ferrroviaria do Nordeste)	CSN, Valec/iron & minerals, oils, grains, cotton, limestone, cargo	4,207/Pecém (CE), Suape (PE), NE
FTC (Tereza-Cristina Railroad)	FTC (Ferrovia Tereza Cristina)	/coal, containers, cargo	164/Imbituba, Santa Catarina

Source: ANTT, 2014. "Evolução do transporte ferroviario."

and regions of the country as well as national debate over alternative views of the economic role of the state. Key players have accepted that public-private cooperation is a vital component of the country's strategy for infrastructure development. An important challenge now is to strengthen the agencies and institutions responsible for managing programs and projects.

Reforms and Railroads

By revealing gaping transportation bottlenecks, the expansion of grains in the midwest put the spotlight on Brazil's low levels of public investment, which had fallen from 1.1 percent of GDP in 1998 to 0.5 percent in 2005 (Blanco and Santiago, 2006; Resende, 2009). Private participation gained appeal in the context of fiscal constraints and other government priorities. But private investors are notoriously averse to costly infrastructure projects. While it takes many years to recover investments in transportation and logistics, uncertainty comes from a long list of risks, among them, currency fluctuations and economic crises, natural calamities, construction problems, changes in political conditions, and delays in obtaining permits and licenses. An adequate legal framework and practices allowing partners in public-private undertakings to assess and share risks should in principle contribute to private sector interest. But such arrangements also require substantial levels of trust as well as significant long-term commitments and capabilities from the government.

Private sector participation in infrastructure is hardly new in Brazil. Throughout the nineteenth century until the 1930s, international and domestic financiers and entrepreneurs launched initiatives to provide energy and build railroads, ports, and public transportation. In fact, transporting commodities was a key factor in the early development of the country's railroad system. In the 1860s, private financiers built the railroad connecting the port of Santos to the nascent coffee frontier in the western plateau of that state, ushering in a great wave of railroad construction to link agricultural expansion in diverse parts of the western hinterland to the outside world. By the early twentieth century, this dynamic state had the largest and most modern railway network and port facilities in Brazil. But this era ended in the 1930s, as the economic crisis at the start of the decade and the political revolution it helped precipitate swung the pendulum toward centralized and interventionist state rule.

Railroads entered a long process of contraction and decay in the 1930s, punctuated by national consolidation in 1957, when the 18 or so lines under federal jurisdiction were merged into the Federal Railroad Network (RFFSA). In 1971, the state of São Paulo integrated its five main railroads into the FEPASA railroad system.[13] Brazil would now have two main rail networks until the 1990s, but none could restore the stagnating systems to their former days of glory. Meanwhile, state governments, particularly in the southeast, built roads and highways.

The federal government claimed a near monopoly in railroad and other infrastructure provision through the 1980s, when the oil shocks of the 1970s and the fiscal crisis that followed signaled the need for change. Combined with the mounting backlog in infrastructure, fiscal dynamics led to renewed acceptance of private participation in the 1990s. With its railroad network significantly smaller than in the 1920s (Murphy, 2012), Brazilian authorities decided on a new model friendlier to the private sector. The reforms of the 1990s completed the transfer of railroads to the federal government, which then proceeded to tender them as concessions. In São Paulo, this move was part of a repayment agreement to alleviate mounting debt, chronic deficits, and collapsing service. The central government consolidated the national rail network into one and proceeded to break it up to correspond to the relevant macroregions. Completed by 1999, the main reforms launching the concessions also inaugurated a national regulatory and management system. By the late 1990s, 11 lines or stretches became privately operated regular concessions, carrying freight rather than passengers. Eventually, ALL emerged as the largest concessionaire, with a network of 11,738 kilometers, while Vale and other mining companies gained control over several of the other railroads (tables 4.2 and 4.3).

In the 2000s, as midwestern Brazil leveraged its economic expansion to press for better transportation, national policymakers were thus inclined to the idea of relying on concessions and partnerships to expand the nation's rail network. Mining giant Vale was in a good strategic position to deliver access to shipping outlets for those parts of the *Cerrado* relatively close to ports and railroads it owned (the Carajás in the north as well as the Vitória-Minas and Mid-Atlantic railroads), while it was also a major shareholder of concessionaire MRS Logística. Controlled by CSN, the northeastern rail network developed plans for a newer version of Transnordestina (TLSA) linked to North-South Railway (FNS) as well as to ports in the states of Ceará and Pernambuco. In São Paulo itself, ALL took longer to become holder of the state's main rail concession and of Ferronorte Railroad (Ferronorte).[14]

Table 4.3 Federal institutional framework for transportation

Type	*Name*	*Sector*	*Functions*
Ministry or cabinet secretariat	MT—Transportation Ministry	Railroads, roads, waterways, airports,	Formulate and implement sector policies
	SEP—Ports Secretariat	Ports and terminals	
	SAC—Civil Aviation Secretariat	Airports	
	MF/SEAE—Monitoring Secretariat	All sectors	Monitors regulatory agencies to improve regulation and competition
Regulatory organizations	ANTT	Railways and roads	Regulatory agencies in transportation sector
	ANTAQ	Ports and waterways	
	ANAC	Airports	
	TCU—General Accounting Office	Congressional authority to oversee regulatory agencies (legal, accountability, efficiency)	Oversight of concession contracts and agencies
State enterprises	DNIT	Roads, railroads, and waterways	Implement initiatives with public funding
	Valec	Railways	
	Infraero	Airports	
	EPL	Multiple sectors	Planning: multimodality and fast trains

Source: Brazil, Ministry of Finance/SEAE, 2013, p. 3.

The shift to concessions and partnerships in transportation infrastructure also led to the creation of regulatory agencies and public companies to aid the government's role in setting and implementing rules, formulating policy, and coordinating other aspects of the new transportation system (table 4.3). In 2001, National Ground Transport Agency (ANTT) emerged as the national regulatory agency for land transportation. The National Department of Transport Infrastructure (DNIT) was created as a state enterprise to manage the federal program of highways and intermodal traffic. Valec, which had been in existence since the 1970s, now gained prominence as the state enterprise for planning, construction, and operation of railways. Though these entities, the Ministry of Transportation wields enormous authority over strategic planning and management. Two cabinet-level secretariats in charge of ports (SEC) and civil aviation (SAC) extend federal authority over regulatory agencies for waterways (ANTAQ) and civil aviation (ANAC, created in 2006)—while public enterprise Brazilian Airport Infrastructure Company (Infraero created in 1972) has authority over commercial airports, and Brazilian Logistics and Planning Company (EPL) handles long-term planning for multimodal transportation. Some of these agencies manage concessions. Federal Auditing Court (TCU) exercises auditing oversight over these and other public agencies.[15]

Initial public reaction was generally favorable in terms of customer satisfaction. Traditional opponents did continue to criticize public-private collaboration through the 2000s, attacking it as liquidation of the public patrimony, but various observers documented positive outcomes, including productivity increase and the expansion of railroad service. Under the new system for railroads, concessionaires invested nearly R$2 billion in urgent repairs and basic improvements from 1996 to 2004 (Silva and Marujo, 2012).[16] But federal authorities after 2003 took considerable time to ponder the role of direct public procurement, the advantages of different forms of public-private collaboration, and the relative benefits of rail and highways. They hesitated, but did not block the idea of concessions and public-private partnerships, which gradually gained salience as part of strategies to modernize and expand Brazil's transportation system.

By default, roads were the main mode of transportation for moving soy from the midwest to shipping ports. Nationally, rail was second to roads in freight, with approximately 28.5 thousand kilometers of tracks transporting around 460 million tons annually (Silva and Marujo, 2012). But the new railroad concessions met significant success in terms of productivity, capacity, and related criteria, as rail's share of freight transport grew to 25 percent in 2005.[17] The new companies often reduced operational deficits and expanded service,[18] even if additional investments were needed for new rail equipment, upgrades to loading facilities, and other improvements. All in all, public-private collaboration was emerging as an option to direct procurement, having shown that it could help address bottlenecks.

Together, the pressing need for better transportation and the performance of concessions made it reasonable to expect a new era of major railroad expansion under the concessions model. But the federal authorities controlling railroads and ports moved too boldly in planning and too cautiously on implementation. The Lula presidency (2003–2010, reelected in 2006) maintained the concessions program and supported the 2004 law providing for federal public-private partnerships, implicitly revising the traditional emphasis of government as provider of infrastructure. Lula's first four-year plan (PPA 2004–2007) projected public-private partnerships to mobilize R$11.3 billion for railroads (Brazil/Ministério do Planejamento, 2003). But actual progress was very slow.

The three rail projects discussed below—North-South Railroad (FNS), Ferronorte, and São Paulo's Rail Bypass (Ferroanel)—were in the original list of government priorities for implementation as public-private partnerships.[19] However, momentum in the new public-private initiative slowed down in 2005 as the federal government focused on electoral issues, other policy priorities, and on a major political corruption scandal. Notwithstanding the promises of massive support for all the public-private partnership projects announced in the 2003–2005 period, only FNS received sustained federal attention, during this period. None of these made great advances through 2008.

The Growth Acceleration Program (PAC) of 2007–2010 renewed expectations of a major wave of investment in transport infrastructure, as did the legislation enacted in 2006 (Law 11297) and 2008 (Law 11772). The latter strengthened Valec as a state enterprise in charge of executing the proposed plans, while consolidating the role of the transportation ministry as a preeminent actor in railroad policy.[20] The commodities boom of the 2000s had fueled economic growth and strengthened state finances, emboldening planners. In 2010, the government announced major additions to the already grand plans for the FNS railroad. At approximately the same time, federal officials announced yet other major infrastructure projects for the 2014 World Cup and the 2016 Olympics. Skeptics continued to wonder about the country's ability to successfully implement all these ambitious undertakings simultaneously, seemingly unrealistic timelines, and issues of long-term sustainability. But the rail megaproject was taken to be a powerful magnet attracting regional political support. As Lula's chief of staff and heir to the presidency, Dilma Rousseff was a key player in the expanded scope of the rail network. Her revised PAC for 2011–2014 further amplified plans for railroads and other transportation infrastructure. Known as PAC2, it became the official plan for the Rousseff presidency (2011–2014), calling for investments of R$959 billion during this period, with transport logistics to receive more than R$104 billion (Tavener, 2012; Wheatley, 2010).

But progress continued to be very slow, and key parts of the transportation plan would still be in the study, design, or pre-bidding phases in 2014.[21] There were diverse reasons for the delay. Within the first year of Rousseff's presidency, the key federal agencies in the railroad sector—Valec, the Ministry of Transportation, and DNIT—were involved in a corruption scandal. Investigations by federal prosecutors, the federal police, and the TCU uncovered fraudulent overpricing of up to 25 percent and other irregularities in the construction of several FNS stretches.[22] Under pressure, the president of Valec and top authorities in the Ministry of Transportation resigned.[23] That the accused individuals were from a political party in the ruling national coalition turned this situation into a political crisis. But the FNS-Valec affair raised questions about the readiness of state institutions. Brazilians wondered why the country lacked a more determined focus on the development of a professional civil service, on ensuring transparency and value for money. At issue was how institutional and political dynamics shape public-private collaboration and the country's ability to address pressing infrastructure needs.

Additional reforms for a better institutional framework to boost public-private collaboration were clearly needed. But it was also significant that infrastructure expansion had continued to take place.[24] To what extent and how is further assessed here through a more detailed inspection of the main railroad projects.

Ferronorte

Ferronorte started in 1989 as a private sector project to connect Mato Grosso to the state of São Paulo's railroad network. In 1901, acclaimed writer-engineer Euclides da Cunha first envisioned the idea of extending the Santos rail corridor in a northwestern direction, and three quarters of a century later Mato Grosso congressman Vicente Vuolo convinced Congress to include it in the 1976 national transportation plan. But Ferronorte as such came about as a brainchild of entrepreneur Olacyr de Moraes, who won rights to the line in 1989 and built much of the first stretch through Mato Grosso do Sul along its border with Goiás. Moraes lost his concession after falling into bankruptcy, but the first step had finally been taken.[25]

The bridge connecting Ferronorte to São Paulo was completed in 1998 while the first terminal in Mato Grosso opened a year later in Alto Taquari—near the borders with Mato Grosso do Sul and Goiás, approximately 410 kilometers from the state of São Paulo. Opening in 2003, the second terminal in Alto Araguaia could handle 700 truckloads of grains daily, more than twice the capacity of the first station 71 kilometers away.

Financing became more difficult in the context of financial turbulence from 1997 through 2003 and the change of government in Brazil. In addition, Ferronorte and São Paulo's old rail network were still going through changes in ownership after the privatizing reforms of the late 1990s. First taken over by Ferroban, then by Brasil Ferrovias, and finally by ALL in 2006, after which Ferronorte's official name changed to ALL-Northern Network (ALLMN). Mato Grosso's soy boom and the inclusion of the project in the original list of federal public-private partnerships of 2004 raised expectations about federal support, but delays continued as the Union focused on the North-South Railway and its branches. Though only 36 miles away, Ferronorte's third grain terminal in Itiquira only opened in 2012. The R$40 million facility could move 100,000 tons of grains per day. That year, Ferronorte was hauling more than half of Mato Grosso's expanding soy harvests, with trucks transporting much of the rest.[26] Sill, soy's explosive expansion soon overwhelmed the capacity of the three facilities, leading to heavy congestion and long waiting lines for trucks loaded with soy.

Finally, the opening of the much larger grains terminal and complex in Rondonópolis in 2013 alleviated the problem. The fourth Ferronorte terminal in Mato Grosso is amodern facility of 365 hectares capable of handling greater amounts of grains and other goods. It can simultaneously unload six trucks on two trains—more than a thousand trucks daily. Located 47 miles from the Itiquira station, the R$750 million complex is close to BR-163, the main, though still incomplete, south-north national highway crossing the state. Though mainly designed for grains and agro-industrial goods shipped to Santos, the complex can handle containers and manufactures and has capabilities for processing and storing wood products, refrigerated containers, oil derivatives, fertilizers, and the like. Its 18 or so plants will employ a few thousand workers, including a soy crushing and processing facility operated by Nobel, a Chinese biofuel firm. Rondonópolis would now have three crushing plants—the other two by the Bunge and ADM trading companies—and four grain terminals (the last two as well as Cargill and Maggi). This rising city of 205,000 residents, the second largest in the state, is thus consolidating its role as a main agro-industrial center in the strategically located southern *Cerrado*.[27]

At this point, Ferronorte/ALLMN had a length of 474 miles from the state of São Paulo border (see figure 4.3). Its trains moved mainly soy and grains, fertilizers, and fuel. Local stakeholders demanded further expansion to reach the Mato Grosso capital of Cuiabá only 134 miles away. Some insisted on the original plan to next reach the northern port

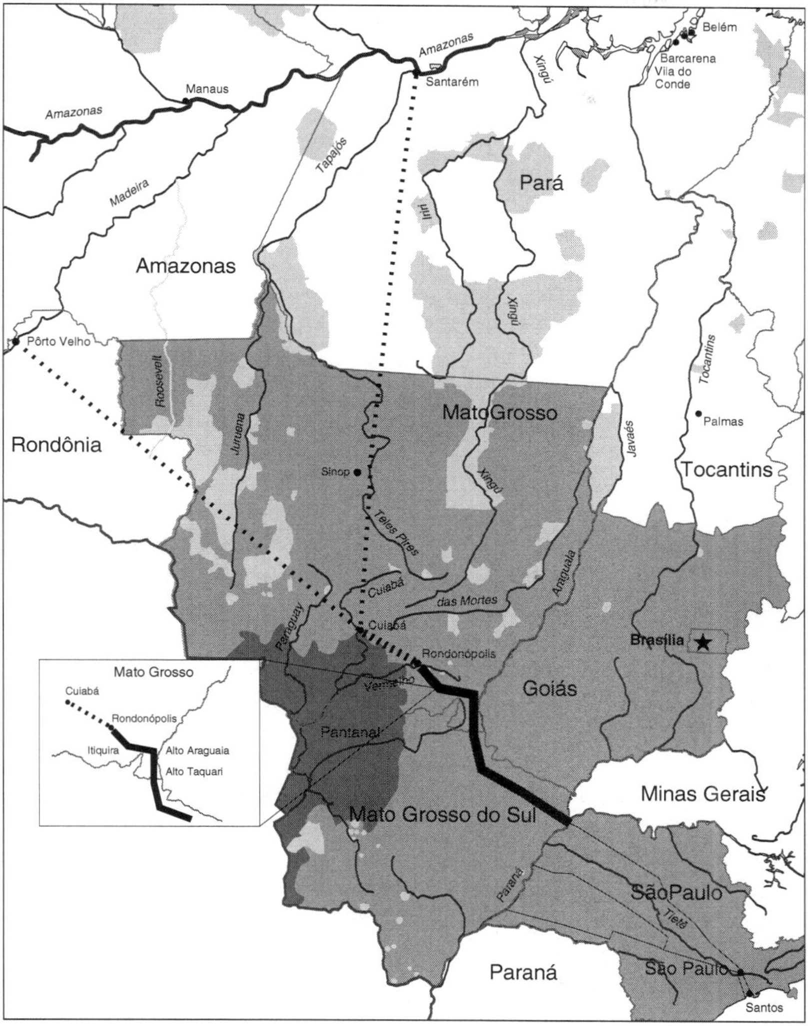

Figure 4.3 Ferronorte Railroad.

Source: Ministério do Transporte.

of Santarém, on the confluence of Tapajós and Amazon rivers, halfway between Manaos and Belém. Stakeholders reasserted arguments for infrastructure to meet the needs of this dynamic region and reminded politicians of past promises. Federal authorities responded with benign promises, but further expansion of Ferronorte beyond Rondonópolis was in fact doubtful in mid-2014. Heavy spending on the sports infrastructure for the 2014 World Cup and the 2016 Olympics, as well as on other railroad projects and priorities had depleted federal resources, while the Brazilian economy had just entered a phase of slow growth and inflation.

Comparing Ferronorte/ALLMN with the operating northern segment of FNS from Açailândia to Palmas in terms of their cargo volume further illuminates this performance (table 4.5). These two lines were of similar lengths and both served agricultural zones dominated by soy, corn, and other grains.[28] While Ferronorte started to be built somewhat earlier, it lacked the support bestowed on the FNS project. Ferronorte's cargo growth and higher levels between 2006 and 2014 confirms the view of the private sector in creating viable options for such large projects. If the slower growth and smaller cargo of the FNS segment underscores ALLMN's performance, it also raises questions about state-led initiative. The contrast is striking considering the government's caution in underwriting the private initiative. Ferronorte moved faster in reaching Mato Grosso, with its four terminals being able to process most of that state's soy harvest. Ferronorte's performance shows that public-private collaboration led by the private sector can give effective answers to Brazil's needs for new and better railroads.

Ferronorte's successful expansion into Mato Grosso highlighted the role that private collaboration can play in this type of project (see figure 4.3). This railroad had been a pioneer in the regeneration of the Brazilian railway system while providing port access to central Brazil's growing harvests (see table 4.4). Private actors had gained experience and confidence in the use of concessions to build an important railway, overcoming uncertainties about short and long-term risks and payoffs.

However, Ferronorte's future looked uncertain in the 2014 election year. Its extension to Cuibá and beyond was not as high a federal priority that year as various other rail branches linked to FNS.[29] In addition, it was not clear how freight demand would be affected by other government-sponsored railway plans to connect Mato Grosso to outlets in the north, northeast, and east (see figure 4.4). Global investors with stakes on the expanding soy and commodities frontier were

Table 4.4 Two new railroads for Brazil's central plateau

	Ferronorte (ALLMN)	*North-South Railroad (FNS)*
Length and status (mid-2014)	(977 km to Cuiabá)	(4,156 km when complete)
	726 km to Rondonópolis and 3 other terminals functioning	First section: 719 km from Açailândia to Palmas, Vale concession since 2007
	Extension to Cuibá pending	Second section: 855 km from Palmas to Anápolis, finished/pending concession
	Extension to Porto Velho and Santarém pending	Third section: 680 km from Anápolis to Estrela d'Oeste (São Paulo), some construction
Main purposes	Soy, grains & ethanol to Santos; supplies & manufactures to interior	Soy, grains and minerals to northern ports; national integration; strategic and international plans
Construction	Ferronorte/ALL	Vale (Carajás) and government (Valec)
Operator	ALLMN since 2008	Vale (2008 concession to Palmas), other stretches pending
Main ports	Santos	Sao Luis/Itaqui (Maranhão), Barcarena (Pará), Northeastern ports
States served	Mato Grosso, Mato Grosso do Sul, Goiás, São Paulo	Pará, Maranhão, Tocantins, Goiás, Mato Grosso
Links	ALL networks, MRS	MRS, FCA, EFC, TLSA, new east-west lines
Extensions or branches planned	Santarém (PA) and Porto Velho, via Cuiabá (MT)	North extension of FNS E. F. 151 to Barcarena (PA) (450 km, delayed, under study)
		West-East Integration Railroad E. F. 334 (1,490 km) (delayed or under study)
		Central-West and Transcontinental E. F. 354 (partly delayed, under construction, under study)
		Panorama (SP) to Porto Murtinho (MS)
		E. F. 267 (under study)
		Panorama (SP) to Rio Grande do Sul (under study)
Comments	Private sector initiative since 1989	Public initiative since 1987, partnership with Vale

helping develop competitive waterway solutions to the transportation needs of northern and western Mato Grosso.[30] Moreover, a sugar and ethanol producer had just made a seemingly successful bid at merging Ferronorte/ALL to its own logistics operation. Finally, important

Table 4.5 Ferronorte and FNS, cargo in thousand tons (TU) and million ton/km (TKU), 2006–2014

	2006	*2007*	*2008*	*2009*	*2010*	*2011*	*2012*	*2013*	*2014**
ALLMN (TU)	5,551	6,928	8,232	10,072	10,498	11,611	13,952	14,416	4,385
TKU	7,446	9,394	11,297	13,887	14,618	16,073	19,451	20,594	6,689
FNS (TU)	0	0	1,424	1,639	2,012	2,541	2,934	3,114	1,092
TKU	0	0	1,026	1,155	1,524	1,874	2,322	2,377	879

TKU = tons x distance; * = through April, 2014.

Sources: ANTT "Evolução do transporte ferroviário," June 2, 2014, p. 5; ANTT "Acompanhamento das concessões ferroviárias," 2013.

improvements to the Santos export corridor, such as a metropolitan rail bypass and port upgrades, had yet to be implemented. Singly or jointly, these developments would affect the role of Ferronorte in relation to the expanded soy and commodity production in Brazil's heartland.

The North-South Railway (FNS)

In contrast, the federal government showed growing enthusiasm for the railroad to connect the *Cerrado* to a northern port. As proposed in 1987 by then-president José Sarney, the FNS was to extend for 932 miles south of the northern port of Itaqui (Maranhão) to Anápolis, near the nation's capital in the state of Goiás (figure 4.4). The main stated purpose was to open an export corridor for the *Cerrado*, particularly northern Goiás, northeast Mato Grosso, Tocantins, and adjacent states. Trains would transport minerals and agricultural products to Itaqui, while carrying fertilizers, fuel, and general cargo from that port to the interior.

FNS was prominently included in the original list of public-private partnerships in 2004, but attracted only modest interest from private investors. This did not prevent fast expansion in the scheme. Soon after, the Lula government embraced an even bolder plan with two major upgrades—a longer transcontinental railway crossing the *Cerrado* in an east-west direction and an extension of FNS toward southern Brazil (first to São Paulo and later to Rio Grande do Sul). The government would design and build the network, tendering completed segments as concessions. The expanding plan proved popular with various stakeholders in the regions to be served. While local politicians and groups pleaded for inclusion in the expanding rail network, congressional leaders lobbied for enhancements. Within a short time, the official plan covered nine states and all five regions in the country.

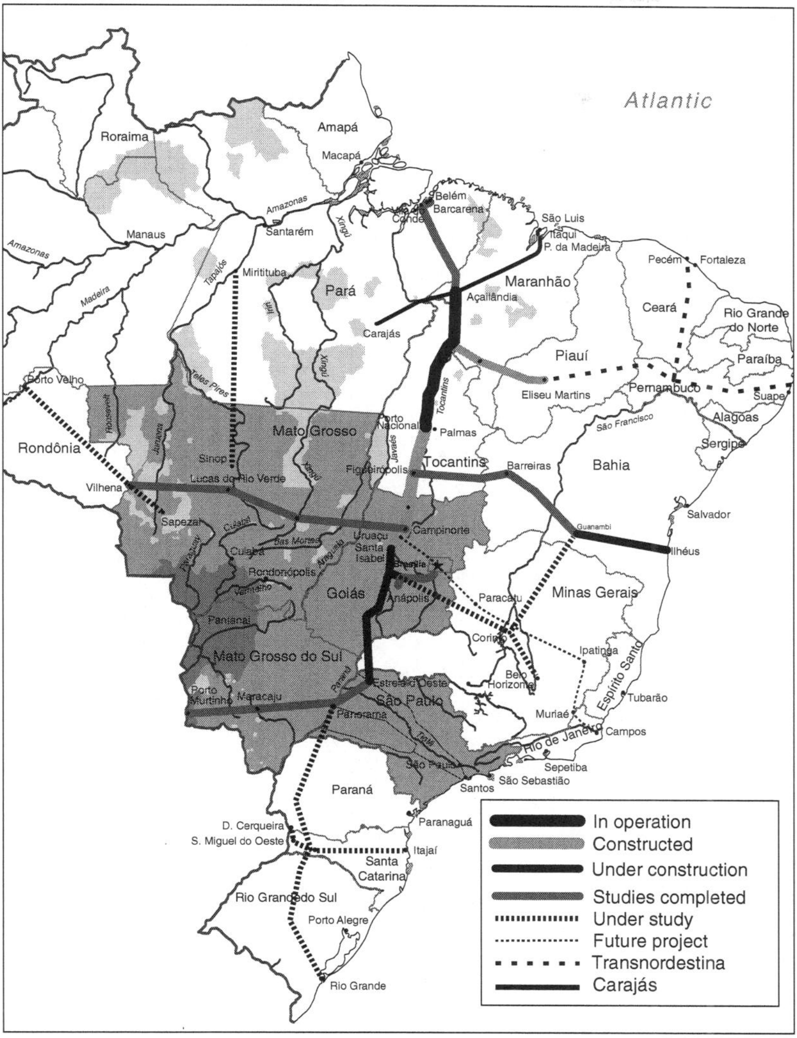

Figure 4.4 North-South Railway (FNS).

Source: Adapted from Agencia Nacional de Transportes Terrestres ANTT.

Agricultural producers are not the only or possibly the main actors influencing the effort to design and construct a new national rail network. Grain trading companies and Chinese enterprises focused on commodities emerged as important players in transportation policy, as discussed below. Above all, a handful of large mining companies are key parties in rail policy. Vale is particularly prominent in this regard. Since 1985, this company owned and operated the Carajás railroad (EFC) carrying iron ore from the huge mine of the same name into its Ponta da Madeira terminal next to the public port Itaqui.[31] Its influence reflects close ties to government. Though technically privatized in 1997, the government continued to exercise a great deal of control through an investment entity holding more than half of the Vale shares owned by the Banco do Brasil's pension fund and the Brazilian Development Bank (BNDES). Moreover, the federal government owns "golden shares," allowing it to veto any major decision by the company. Vale emerged from the reforms of the 1990s as owner or main shareowner of three other railroads servicing its enormous mining operations: FCA (Centro-Atlântica); EFVM (the Vitória-Minas); and MRS Logística. Vale's control of the northernmost segment of FNS and improved connections to the Transnordestina and Centro-Atlântica railroads further enhance an already preeminent role in the rail network, providing access to mid-Atlantic and northern ports.

Other economic groups have major stakes in the expanded FNS-centered megaproject. Meanwhile, the federal government continues to seek investors for the new rail network, working on the premise that it has major international and global implications for commodities, particularly more efficient and less costly access to the middle and north Atlantic.

The original 2004 government plan assumed that FNS' northern segment presented the greatest cargo potential and should be the first to be implemented. Preliminary figures indicating low rates of return[32] was a main reason for listing FNS as a public-private partnership that year. That choice of business model seemed justified when Chinese officials and companies hinted at heavy investment in transportation infrastructure for commodities destined for Chinese ports,[33] but these talks did not progress as hoped. The project was taken off the list of public-private partnerships in 2005, after the CAF regional development bank advised that a concession model was better suited. Valec proceeded to auction off the concession to FNS' northernmost segment between Açailandia and Palmas (capital of Tocantins). Vale won the concession. This was expected, considering that the mining giant was the only bidder, had strong ties to the government, and this segment extended the railroad it already owned and operated to transport minerals to its terminals in Itaqui (see table 4.4).

The public sector did not hide its intention to play the key role in designing, constructing, and regulating the railway system (see Law 11297 of 2006 and the initial PAC of 2007). The government focused on designing and building the network by itself, to then sell completed segments as concessions. Valec, the construction company under the Ministry of Transportation and owner of the concession of the new system, was to construct segments before tendering them as sub-concessions to private operators. While revenue from these sales would be used for building new segments, BNDES was to provide financing to concessionaires.

But the rest of the original FNS plan made slow headway. Deadlines for reaching Palmas by December 2007 changed several times, as President Lula criticized the idling and dawdling and urged a speedier process. Despite the delays and other problems, plans for FNS continued to expand, eventually becoming monumental. A year after the 2007 decision to extend FNS by a thousand kilometers to reach the state of São Paulo, with the redesigned FNS now to be approximately 3,000 kilometers in length, new decrees and legislation (Law 11772 of 2008) granted authorization for northern and southern extensions of FNS to Belém-Barcarena and to São Paulo's Panorama. Furthermore, the new version of the plan enlarged and complemented the evolving FNS-centered system with three east-west branches:

- The West-East railway (E. F. 334, or Ferrovia Oeste-Leste, also known as West-East Integration Railroad)—a 1,527-kilometer line linking FNS from Figueirópolis (Tocantins) to the Atlantic port of Ilhéus (Bahia).
- The Central-West railroad (E. F. 354, or FICO)—a 1,641-kilometer stretch from Campinanorte (Goiás) to Lucas do Rio Verde (Mato Grosso) and from there to Vilhena (Rondônia). This line was conceived as a segment of a new transcontinental railroad from northern Rio de Janeiro to Peru.
- "Pantanal" Railroad (E. F. 267)—750 kilometers from Panorama (SP) to Porto Murtinho (Mato Grosso do Sul, border with Paraguay).

Altogether, the extended railroad plan called for 4,650 kilometers of new railroad and improvements to the existing system at an estimated cost of upward of R$16 billion.[34] The 2008 legislation also turned Valec into a state enterprise with wider powers and gave the Ministry of Transportation enhanced authority over the design of projects. The 2006–2008 measures announcing these projects were consolidated in the official national transportation program.[35] This master plan confirmed Valec's role in constructing the entire network to then transfer rights of operation to concessions, though it was still vague about the government's financial commitments and what models of public-private collaboration would be ultimately used.

The continued slow progress of the ambitious and complex design did not prevent yet other ambitious additions. In 2010, an election year at the end of Lula's second and last term, the expanded list in PAC2 provided for additional extensions at both ends: from São Paulo to Brazil's southernmost state of Rio Grande do Sul and a link to the Transnordestina railroad in the north. At this point the basic FNS alone would have 4,156 kilometers. At the same time, the government confirmed a series of additional transportation projects for the World Cup and the Olympics.

After Dilma Rousseff's election, the Logistics Investment Plan (PIL) of August 2012 further expanded the list, calling for partnerships with the private sector to expand the national railroad network and enhance connectivity between roads, waterways, and ports. PIL listed plans to invest R$99.6 billion in construction or improvements of 11,000 kilometers of rail and formulated a new concessions approach separating railway construction from the provision of train and logistics services, with Valec having responsibility for construction and sub-concessions. A June 2014 decree formalized a regulatory framework for the new approach.

The dizzying succession of increasingly ambitious railroad plans did little to speed up implementation. As of mid-2014, FNS was functioning only in the northern stretch of 447 miles between Açailândia and Palmas (TO) managed by Vale. Though Valec had recently announced the completion of 531 miles between Palmas and Anápolis (Goiás), there had been limited investor interest in the concession. The 424-mile FNS stretch to Estrela d'Oeste, the first contact point with the São Paulo rail system, was now to be completed by 2015, according to officials (see table 4.4).

In mid-2014, federal authorities welcomed proposals for six rail segments received from 19 invited groups. Most of these reconfirmed projects already in the PIL list, but some were redefined so as to appear new. The 284-mile extension of FNS north of Açailandia ending in

Barcarena/Vila do Conde in Pará now responded to rapidly evolving recent plans for use of northern waterways as logistic corridors. That was also the case with two other rail proposals linking large soy counties in central Mato Grosso to river ports in the Amazon river system, especially on the Madeira and Tapajós tributaries. The 615-mile segment from Sinop to the Tapajós river port of Miritituba (Pará) responded to initiatives from Bunge and other trading companies to enable grains shipment on the Tapajós river, relying on new transhipment terminals and navigation system for transporting grains to a new export complex in Vila do Conde. The 590-mile line from the municipality of Sapezal to Porto Velho (Roraima) would be part of a comparable system in the Madeira river. These two stretches overlap with the two final components in Ferronorte's original plan, which they effectively preempt.

Two other projects enhanced the connection of FNS to the ports in the mid-Atlantic, especially those served by the Centro-Atlântica railroad. The 482-mile segment between Anápolis (part of FNS) and the Corinto station in Minas Gerais was also part of the Transcontinental railroad megaproject of 2,774 miles between the states of Rio de Janeiro and Acre. A second 525-mile link would interconnect the FCA (from Belo Horizonte) and the West-East Integration Railroad (at Guanabi, southern Bahia). These plans further strengthen FCA's role in both lines through the strategic nodes in Corinto and Guanabi.[36]

The mushrooming railroad plan addresses interests of diverse consequential economic groups and other constituencies, but it has been less useful as a blueprint for implementation. The rather long list of subprojects lacked clear sense of priorities. Key components experienced substantial delays, often due to inadequate feasibility studies (engineering, economic, and environmental). Past failure to obtain licenses give grounds for skepticism about meeting deadlines and timely progress, while doubts persist about capital and technical capacity for so many big and complex undertakings. Irregularities and corruption issues raise more fundamental questions about the broad institutional framework.[37] Meanwhile, the role of government expands as it accumulates functions in designing and managing the railroad network.

Assessments of PIL's railroad plan especially apply to risks and challenges in FNS and its extensions, the plan's core component. Armando Castelar, a former BNDES specialist, takes issue with the new "open source" approach splitting railway concessions from transportation operators: while infrastructure managers receiving a standard fee for maintaining rail facilities do not have incentives to attract new customers, train operators providing the actual transportation services lack incentives not to abuse tracks and facilities, something likely to result in increased accident rates. The preexisting vertical model offering "economies of scope" is thus more desirable. Further, with little evidence of political consensus around the current plan, future governments may not agree to pay subsidies to at least some concessionaires or remain committed to specific projects, business models, or even the overall plan itself (Castelar, 2013).

Other analysts underline the extent to which pronounced state intervention as seen in FNS and its offshoots have not been greatly successful in managing Brazil's railroad system (Accioli and Monteiro, 2012: 14–15). The "Valec risk" is a focal question in this regard: whether the state-owned enterprise with past problems of probity can rapidly regain and maintain the high levels of trust required of an effective broker for the sale of railway freight capacity.

Planners have often failed to anticipate the difficulty of preparing engineering and environmental impact studies acceptable to regulatory and auditing agencies, as was the case with the northernmost stretch of FNS to the Barcarena area and major segments of the West-East Integration Railroad (Castelar, 2013). In addition, plans have not fully taken into account various impediments to reliable port access and capacity and other sources of delays. Improving institutional capacity for preparing better feasibility studies and speeding up environmental and other licenses is no doubt a priority. Enhanced institutional capacity is also essential for generating financially sound projections and business models that take demand risk into fully account, a problem with several key railway segments.

Financial planning faces other challenges. The heavy reliance on loans from BNDES may be too optimistic a long-term assumption, while the sustained use of such subsidized rates inhibits the role of private capital, thus blocking the goal of attracting long-term private finance. Related questions have been raised about the likely market success in infrastructure bonds, insurance policies, and other instruments, as well as the very ability of BNDES to securitize them.

Economic slowdown and adverse international capital markets present doubts about adequate levels of funding for the above projects. Regardless of the likely performance of the FNS-centered rail network, but particularly if delays continue, a pivotal issue is how to improve the ability of existing export corridors to provide port access to the growing production from Brazil's hinterland. This question returns the spotlight to the Santos export corridor.

São Paulo's Rail Bypass

Though São Paulo's railroad corridor may still be considered among the best in Brazil, it needs upgrades to meet the growing demand from the state itself and from the midwestern part of the county. Nothing is more pressing than building a rail bypass around metropolitan São Paulo, a project presented with a sense of urgency in 2003 and in the original list of public-private partnerships,[38] while the port of Santos itself is waiting for substantial improvements (DuisPort, 2012).

For more than a century, the state capital has been Brazil's leading hub of commerce, industrial production, consumption, and communications.[39] Over the years, this success attracted migrants and capital from many other countries and parts of Brazil. Greater São Paulo is home to more than 20 million residents in 39 municipalities. Its location turned this dynamic metro region into a huge source of congestion and transportation problems. Partly surrounded by mountains, and at the center of the main available pathways for the flow of goods and people to and from the port of Santos and in a north-south direction, highways and railroads must both currently pass through or near the core of the metropolis. Bottlenecks from congested transportation systems reached critical levels in the first decade of the twenty-first century. With the ever larger fleet of vehicles straining the congested urban highway system in the sprawling city, this rail beltway will reduce overall congestion and improve access to Santos.[40]

Ferroanel is a national priority, considering the strategic location of metropolitan São Paulo and Santos in the national flows of goods and people. But the state government has been unable to convince the Union and MRS, holder of the rail concession, about constructing the two segments of the bypass (figure 4.5).[41] Until it is built, trains loaded with millions of tons of grains, minerals, sugar, ethanol, and other export commodities from the interior will continue to follow the only existing route to Santos through the middle of the city, where they compete with an equally large and expanding number of passenger trains. Completing north and south stretches of the bypass will shift freight trains around the city, reserving the existing tracks for passenger trains. The bypass is thus an urgent matter for both freight and passenger traffic.

Ferroanel was considered urgent enough to be included in the original list of federal public-private partnerships, but has remained under study through 2014.[42] Stakeholders include all railroad companies operating in metropolitan São Paulo—not only ALL and CPTM

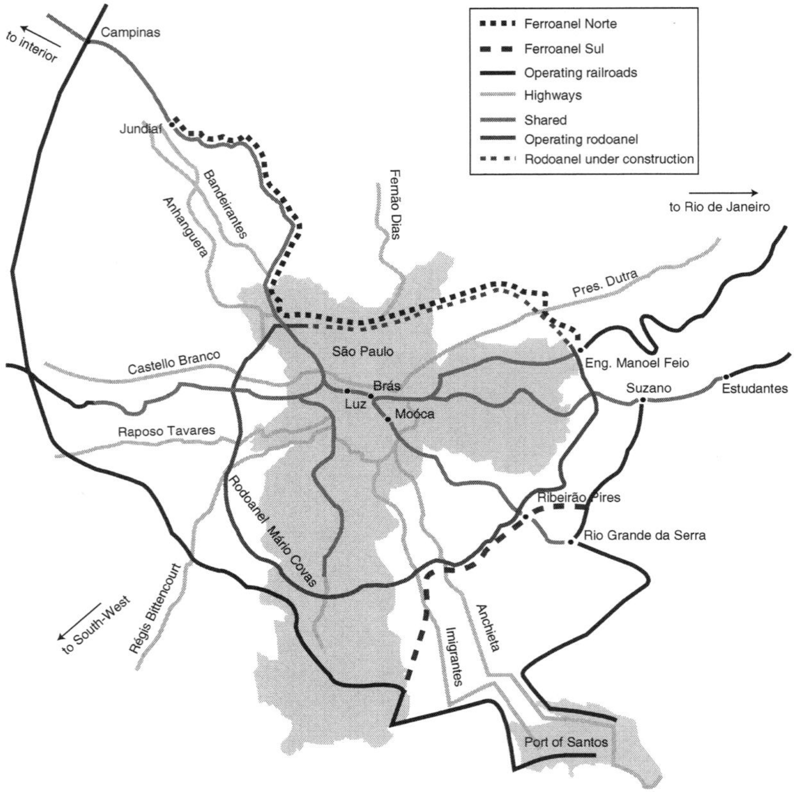

Figure 4.5 Metropolitan São Paulo Rail Bypass (Ferroanel).

Source: Governo do Estado de São Paulo, Unidade de Parcerias Público-Privadas.

(metropolitan passenger service owned by the state of São Paulo), but also the large and powerful MRS Logística. Other interested parties include port and logistics operators, as well as local governments in the metro region.

MRS Logística has been in operation since 1996, when a consortium of large mining companies bought the concessions to the pre-reform southeastern lines and thus came to own much of the rail access to Santos, including the planned bypass. In 2005, Vale became MRS's main shareholder after buying out MRB, while mining companies CSN, USIMINAS remained major partners. MRS operates in the states of Minas Gerais, Rio de Janeiro, and São Paulo—hence the name MRS. Its 400 locomotives and 13,000 cars move 10 million tons of cargo on its 1,643 kilometers of track. Iron ore, other minerals, and steel products account for 60 percent of the cargo, with agricultural products and containers accounting for much of the rest. The São Paulo-Rio trunk line controls main lines of access not only to the ports of Santos, but also those of Rio de Janeiro (including Sepetiba-Itaguaí and a private ore terminal in Angra dos Reis).

One early source of disagreement was MRS Logística's preference for the northern stretch of the bypass, while the state of São Paulo gave priority to the southern segment. The northern stretch would augment the system's transportation capacity by several million tons and benefit in particular economic actors using other ports in Rio de Janeiro.[43] With an extension of 29 miles, the southern bypass will move ALL cargo in particular, including grains and other agricultural goods from the midwest.

The São Paulo rail bypass has been discussed since the project's conception in 2003, when Geraldo Alckmin proposed it in his first term as governor. After the 2006 elections, the federal government announced a commitment to build Ferroanel. BNDES recruited engineers at the University of São Paulo to conduct feasibility studies. But the federal authorities continued to ponder on what business model to use (public-private partnership, concession, or something else). Despite its urgency, the incomplete assessments and other delays at the federal level put the project in suspense.[44]

In summary, Ferroanel is essential to alleviate the flow of people and goods, improve metropolitan living, and promote competitiveness and development. Its construction hinges in part on reconciling the interests of three powerful sectors: grains from the midwest, minerals from Minas Gerais and north, and sugar and ethanol from São Paulo itself. A second challenge comes from varying political and institutional interests at the federal and state level. In the long run, progress and effective operation requires a better-articulated institutional framework between the federal, state, and metropolitan agencies and authorities.

Conclusion

The agricultural boom in Brazil's plateau redefined its role, created new economic dynamics, and altered local identities. Coinciding with a gradual decline in the industrial sector,[45] soy-led expansion sharpened the country's global role as an exporter of commodities. As domestic and global interests pressed for access to previously remote parts of the *Cerrado*, political actors became drawn to the process of providing transportation infrastructure, hoping to harness new demands and contention into durable alignments. The central government's response has been marked by increasingly ambitious plans and public expressions of enthusiasm for private participation, even portraying infrastructure expansion as a leading sector in national economic development (Coutinho, 2013).[46]

Comparing Ferronorte and FNS brings out lingering issues about state and private control, as well as between the federal concentration of functions and decentralization. A private initiative from its beginning, Ferronorte became the first to provide an outlet for the exporters of southern Mato Grosso and the adjacent midwest. By 2014 it had the momentum to handle a major part of the anticipated growth in grain harvests. But the federal government had not effectively responded to needs of the São Paulo export corridor: construction of a rail bypass around metropolitan São Paulo and further extension toward Mato Grosso's capital, and improvements to the Santos port complex.

In contrast, the national government displayed enthusiastic leadership in designing and building the North-South Railroad and the ambitious enhancements linked to it—east-west rail branches, upgrading a large number of northern ports, and improved connection to the Transnordestina and FCA railroads. Evolving from the original focus on providing transportation for midwestern commodities, the mission of the emergent FNS-centered railroad network grew to encompass several other aims: regional development of the northeast, national territorial integration, strategic access to Andean countries and Pacific ports, and even South American integration. To the extent that meeting the needs of soy, other grains, and minerals from central Brazil was the main original purpose, this expanding undertaking may have represented a case of goal displacement. The grand rail plan appealed to diverse constituencies and may have sketched worthy long-term goals, but it came short as a strategy for implementation. Multiple goals led to the allocation of scare resources among many projects rather than to a narrow focus on clearly identified bottlenecks. This dispersal of effort helps explain the false starts, incomplete work, delays, cost overruns, and other problems that plagued most components of this network. The far-flung network formed by FNS and connected undertakings were mostly at early stages in the mid-2010s, not close yet to become a mature network.[47]

Meanwhile, frustration had mounted with the unresolved transportation problems in light of the faster increase of soy harvests after the early 2000s. Growers' truck drivers protested the poor conditions of roads and terminals and the long waits for unloading soy, minerals, and other products.[48] Resistance from indigenous communities and environmentalists blocked projects penetrating the Amazon rainforest.[49] In addition, many voices had been concerned over the large public expenditures on stadiums and other infrastructure for the 2014 World Cup and the 2016 Olympics, without thorough consultation with citizen groups.[50] The Ministry of Transportation put in charge of investments of $92 billion in new railroad and logistics between 2013 and 2016 was still battling charges of political patronage and corruption. With modest progress reported in mid-2014 and few finished projects ready for inauguration in the upcoming October elections, federal authorities could do little for now but make new promises about investment plans.

These problems and issues point to a still inadequate institutional framework governing railroad and infrastructure policy. The TCU and the media showed the extent to which office holders used their authority as opportunity to replenish political party coffers and personal gain rather than to better governance and decision making on behalf of the public. This behavior is partly the result of using high-level appointments as reward or incentive for political support and coalition building.[51] Corruption scandals are only the most visible consequences of this practice. More corrosive is its impact in undermining efforts to develop a professional civil service. Politicization of public infrastructure provision is also suspect in decisions to excessively favor some localities and projects over others. Generally, there are grounds for concern about insufficient cooperation with state and local governments. As discussed below, São Paulo and other Brazilian states have developed expertise in designing concessions and public-private partnerships in highways and other infrastructure. In this context, it is puzzling that the federal government has been unable to work with state administrations to complete the clearly urgent Ferroanel and the upgrades to Santos. Another challenge is to attract higher levels of international investment and know-how (Coutinho, 2013).

Still, political leadership and continuity in basic policy have played a big role in the adoption and spread of public-private collaboration in Brazil. Ferronorte is an example of how public-private collaboration led by the private sector, sustained over two decades, has resulted in effective answers to urgent needs for better infrastructure. Something similar may be foreseen for at least parts of the government-built FNS-centered railroad system (through central Goiás and then São Paulo) and the east-west branches depending on sustained global demand for commodities. Political differences and rivalries have not stood in the way of the new approach, even if commitment and consensus have come somewhat short of ensuring effective outcomes. Though Brazil's political and policy consensus on public-private collaboration in railroad expansion seems broad, the problems and challenges discussed above show the need for a more robust institutional framework.

Brazil's network of railroads and highways is gradually expanding, and creditable objectives have been advanced. In this context, further progress in the planning and regulatory frameworks governing transportation infrastructure are due for assessment and improvement. Auditing agencies have carved out an important institutional presence that needs to be further promoted. Capabilities for project evaluation and risk assessment appear insufficient for a successful implementation of partnerships. Time also seems ripe for improvement of relations with state-level authorities, independent civil society organizations, and specialists on defining national priorities and the institutional mechanisms for infrastructure development.

Finally, commodity exports to global and national markets have been a main engine of economic development in Brazil and other parts of South America. Driven by global demand, soy and minerals have created conditions for railroad and logistics expansion. Commodities booms usually end in substantial market corrections or even world price collapse as in earlier decades. When that happens, policymakers should hope that superior infrastructure of rails, roads, and ports may contribute over time to broader forms of sustainable development adaptable to changed international economic conditions.

CHAPTER FIVE

Subnational Brazil

Though most Brazilian states are exploring the use of public-private collaboration in infrastructure, large states have been able to launch the most significant subnational initiatives, with those in the southeast taking the lead (table 5.1). That these relatively large and prosperous states have developed programs and projects and the smaller or less developed ones have not suggests that a critical mass of resources and institutional development shapes outcomes in a major way. But state-level programs are vital components of Brazil's overall experience with public-private initiatives.

The populous southeastern states of São Paulo and Minas Gerais pioneered the adoption of public-private partnerships at the subnational level. These cases stand out as interesting phenomena of their own and as exemplars for other states. This chapter pays special attention to these two cases, with particular emphasis on trends and proximate conditions shaping outcome. The discussion highlights the interplay between local state-level dynamics, institutional context, and relations with the federal government. Representing a third of the national economy, the spotlight is on São Paulo.

A great deal of political leadership has been necessary to spread public-private collaboration in Brazil. From the 1930s through the military regime ending in 1985, the country experienced political centralization and a distinctive approach to statism. This economic model gave clear signs of exhaustion in the 1980s, but the democratizing era formally beginning in 1985 had to wait until the 1990s to take steps toward a coherent alternative model. Deeply embedded in the political system, old practices refused to die. Moreover, the new constitution of 1988 itself banned close partnerships between government and the private sector.

Table 5.1 Public-private investment in Brazilian states, 1990–2013, in $ millions

State	*1990 to 1995*	*1996 to 2000*	*2001 to 2005*	*2006 to 2010*	*2011 to 2013*	*$TOT 1990–2013*
Southeast						
São Paulo	394	38,482	10,264	33,291	34,909	117,341
Rio de Janeiro	1,002	8,058	3,220	6,808	9,556	28,644
Minas Gerais		1,998	1,360	2,285	422	6,065
Espírito Santo	387	755	186	913	906	3,147
South						
Paraná	118	4,162	774	74	253	5,381
Santa Catarina	168	1,953	1,704	1,559	968	6,352
Rio Grande do Sul		7,585	1,727	1,549	3,064	13,925
North						
Pará		388	164	1,502	15,741	17,795
Amazonas		653	1	7,006	1,476	9,136
Tocantins		840	433	106	83	1,463
Central-West						
Goiás		1,880	160	1,618	1,266	4,924
Mato Grosso		1464	308	2,018	2447	6,237
Mato Grosso do Sul		995	212	664	691	2,562
Northeast						
Bahia	2	2,516	1,330	4,098	5,954	13,901
Ceará		1,132	915	3,991	2,560	8,598
Pernambuco		1,004	417	1,012	3,153	5,585
Maranhão		289	507	2,676	3,133	6,605
Rio Grande do Norte	2	693	227	1,015	5,494	7,430
Rondônia	12	65	226	74	127	505
Multistates		32,500	21,843	33,037	32,460	119,840
Other		9,122	5,267	21,477	16,327	52,193
Total Brazil	**2,085**	**116,535**	**51,245**	**126,773**	**140,990**	**437,629**

Source: World Bank, 2014a.

Still, the new charter restored a substantial part of the regional vitality that Brazilian regions, states, and even counties had before the centralizing drives of the twentieth century. The national reforms of the 1990s set a new tone and provided an overall framework for the development of subnational reform initiatives (Kingstone, 1999). In addition, in 2003 several prominent members of the outgoing administration of F. H. Cardoso took their reform ideas with them upon moving to influential government positions in several states. These and other reformers developed subnational reforms that in some cases came to include public-private collaboration.

São Paulo

The state of São Paulo has long been Brazil's main economic leader, to such an extent that it might be seen as a region in itself. Coffee-led agricultural expansion after the 1860s followed by industrial development made it reach that status early in the twentieth century. As the country's prime exporter, São Paulo urgently needed major investments in transportation and other forms of infrastructure—from passenger and freight transportation, to ports, urban redesign, and more. While the state remained Brazil's largest economy through the twentieth century, its share of national exports has recently declined, from 35.6 percent in 1998 to 33.3 percent in 2002 and 23.3 percent in 2011.[1]

Exports to global and national markets have been the main engine of modern economic development since the second half of the nineteenth century, transforming a previously undeveloped region into the country's economic heartland (Font, 2010). Railroad infrastructure was a key factor. In fact, the story of modern São Paulo can be said to have begun in the 1860s, when a concessionaire built the São Paulo railway, linking the port of Santos to the capital city and further west to Jundiaí. In rapid succession, Paulista entrepreneurs and their allies built additional railways into the fertile and gracefully undulating temperate plateau to the west, converting it into a highly dynamic expanding frontier led by coffee.

Because of the expanding rail network, coffee and other commodities could henceforth flow toward the capital, to then be funneled down the steep 800-meter escarpment of the Serra do Mar and then reach the port of Santos. Immigrants, ideas, and foreign capital arrived in the other direction. Upon landing in Santos from long voyages originating in Europe, the Middle East, and Japan, they could now rely on rail rather than mule to climb to the state capital, to then spread throughout the growing hinterland to the west.

Becoming a Global Metropolis

Modernization made the Paulista nineteenth century fade away faster than elsewhere in Brazil. In rapid succession, the state capital transformed itself from an administrative capital to a commercial entrepôt, to then emerge as an industrial powerhouse, financial center, and global metropolis. The city of São Paulo synthesized much of the state's political, economic, and social energy. The larger metropolitan region eventually became the most important hub in the increasing flows of west-east and north-south commerce in the country. Fast growth from internal migration and other sources eventually made it the largest megalopolis in the country.

By the last part of the twentieth century, the São Paulo metropolitan region had consolidated its standing as a large global metropolis. Expansion and success came at a price. As the twenty-first century approached, transportation bottlenecks threatened to asphyxiate this global city. Heavy investments were needed to alleviate congestion and effectively allow for the flow of goods shipping through Santos. Though the latter had expanded into a large transshipment complex, it needed major investment for improved access, more capacity, and upgraded port facilities. Together with complementary investments in transportation and other infrastructure, these improvements were now needed to increase or even maintain the competitiveness of the state's large and changing industrial sector, one shaped but also threatened by global trends, institutional shortcomings, and currency appreciation. Major improvements were also needed to transport and ship the soy and other export goods from the expanding frontier in central Brazil. With freight, urban dwellers, and suburbanites competing for access to the routes and even trackage laid out decades earlier, a large part of the challenge boiled down to opening new pathways for transporting goods and people through and around the megalopolis of São Paulo.

Liberalization

São Paulo had the momentum for continued innovation in infrastructure. Brazil's new era of political and economic reform since the 1970s had strong roots here. Key movements and top leaders of the Brazilian transition to democracy and subsequent economic reforms originated in this state, where they remained prominent in its political landscape. This was exemplified by the political success of the Brazilian Social Democratic Party (PSDB) and the Workers' Party (PT), both sharing the state as their birthplace.

The redemocratizing era in this state had an auspicious beginning with the election of André Franco Montoro as governor (1983–1987). The first democratic government set high standards and goals for a state that had been rocked by populist or authoritarian rule since the 1930s, but hopes were dashed after 1987 by eight years of local politics dominated by patronage and practices associated with the worst side of populism, including charges of corruption. These conditions interacted with the national fiscal crisis of the late 1980s, with hyperinflation, and with the frustrating collapse of the Collor de Mello presidency to generate a crescendo of political and even moral gloom (Baer, 2008; Bresser-Pereira, 1996). The state's political institutions and general morale deteriorated.

The two consecutive terms of Mário Covas (1995–1999, 1999–2001) aimed at a new course for the state of São Paulo to rebuild political institutions and general morale in the context of liberalization. Its reforms paralleled those at the national level after 1993. A close ally of national president F. H. Cardoso, and both members of the reformist PSDB, Covas' leadership marks a turning point. Subsequent governors from the same party built on this legacy.

Taking over a bloated, nearly bankrupt, and outdated state apparatus, Covas focused on administrative reforms, liberalization, and the creation of a favorable environment for public-private collaboration in infrastructure. A vocal critic of populist politics, statism, and the political abuse of patronage, the governor reduced the size of the state and relied on privatization and other means to restructure the bloated governing machine and root out corruption. The state laid off thousands of civil servants, while a 1996 law authorized the expanded use of public-private cooperation. More than 80 percent of the state's total public-private investments in infrastructure in 1990–2010 were made in the first five years of the Covas government including the divestiture of telecommunications (Ferreira and Hamilton, 2005).

São Paulo's fiscal problems in the mid-1990s were emblematic of those of the country at large—incumbents relying on state banks to finance uncontrolled and politically motivated spending during electoral cycles, working on the assumption that the federal government would reschedule and eventually assume debts. The worsening of these practices in the 1980s left mounting deficits and public debt. Covas organized the state destatization program (PED), while his vice governor and future governor Geraldo Alckmin implemented it. It was the first such federally mandated adjustment program to reach its goals (Engler, 2001).

This was no minor accomplishment. Responding to financing needs and the centralization of resources at the federal level, subnational governments had borrowed heavily from national development funds and foreign sources. São Paulo's total debt in 1996 reached R$82.3 billion (Mora, 2002). By 2000, São Paulo's destatization program had yielded R$32.9 billion since its start in 1995, much of this as part of a debt repayment agreement. The state government transferred Fepasa,

Ceagesp, part of Cesp, and Banespa to the federal government for that purpose. After a brief transfer to the federal government, Banespa state bank was sold to a private operator, with proceeds from the sale and from the early private participation program used to reduce the state debt and implement a fiscal adjustment. In 2000, the federal Law of Fiscal Responsibility compelled states to curtail such debts and limit expenditures to revenues.

In 2004, São Paulo used shares of state-owned companies to capitalize the PPP fund—especially from Sabesp (Companhia de Saneamento Básico de São Paulo) and Banco Nossa Caixa. The reform drive continued after Covas' death in office in 2001, when vice governor Geraldo Alckmin became governor. After winning the governorship race in 2002, Alckmin moved to reduce the state payroll, simplify procurement, and launch the state's public-private partnership program, while maintaining state investments in health and education. São Paulo's priority on fiscal responsibility renewed the focus on public-private collaboration. It had already made use of the 1996 law of concessions to attract new public-private investments to run and develop its main highways. After the slowdown of public-private infrastructure investment of the early 2000s, the state government's public-private partnership program of 2004 induced fresh thinking on how to address pressing infrastructure needs. Several top officials from the outgoing national government furthered the adoption of this program during Geraldo Alckmin's first term as governor in 2001 to 2006, and who returned to the governorship in 2011 and was reelected in 2014.[2]

The state's public-private partnership program inaugurated in 2004 consisted of three main components: the PPP unit itself to study and approve projects, a management council, and the Partnership Company of São Paulo (CPP, Companhia Paulista de Parcerias). The public-private partnership unit was officially launched that year as part of the planning and finances secretariat. Early momentum came from plans for concessions on state highways and natural gas distribution.[3] Administered by the CPP, the trust fund was to be capitalized by a sale of concessions, shares of the state energy company CESP, and of other public assets. The port of São Sebastião itself would be converted to a concession.[4]

The public partnership law of 2004 in conjunction with the concessions law of 1996 provided the legal framework. The state of São Paulo recognizes two main forms: (a) sponsored concession (*concessão patrocinada*), a contract in which the private partner is paid by a combination of collected fees complemented by the government; and (b) administrative concession (*concessão administrativa*), where the state government is the main direct or indirect user of the public service and pays the private partner for specific services.[5] Other measures sought to eliminate problems in the tax system, refine the control of public expenditures, enforce mechanisms to guarantee the flow of contracts, risk allocation templates, and refine priorities (Melo, 2003). The government of José Serra, the PSDB national leader who succeeded Alckmin as governor in 2007, maintained the preexisting public-private initiative, though with some changes.

In São Paulo, state-level public-private investments in infrastructure totalled $19 billion between 1996 and 2013, or 55 percent of all state-level investments during the same period. This movement was uneven. The substantial amount allocated in the first five years was similar to that of 2006–2010, but the rhythm of these two moments was interrupted by the much lower levels of investments of the intervening years (see table 5.2).

Table 5.2 State of São Paulo public-private investments, by source and sector, 1990–2013, in $ millions

	1990–1995	*1996–2000*	*2001–2005*	*2006–2010*	*2011–2013*	*Total*
State						
Transport		4,454	534	7,515	2,324	14,827
Energy		1,201	547	1,052	990	3,790
Water and Sewerage			361	156	517	
Subtotal		**5,655**	**1,081**	**8,928**	**3,470**	**19,134**
Federal						
Transport		1,765			13,178	14,943
Energy	210	8.787	1,504	5,702	3,985	20,188
Subtotal	**210**	**10,552**	**1,504**	**5,702**	**17,163**	**35,131**
Local						
Transport			12		11	23
Water and Sewerage	45	28	50	163	612	898
Subtotal	**45**	**28**	**62**	**163**	**623**	**921**
Other						
Transport	28	976	51	662	1,048	2,765
Energy		293	21			314
Telecom		20,393	7,120	17,973	12,700	58,186
Water and Sewerage	112	472	427			1,011
Subtotal	**140**	**22,134**	**7,619**	**18,635**	**13,748**	**62,276**
Total	**395**	**38,369**	**10,266**	**33,428**	**35,004**	**117,462**

Source: World Bank, 2014a.

The internal debate during Lula's first term as president further contributed to tentative movement in creating incentives for private participation in the provision of infrastructure.[6] Public private investment in São Paulo totaled $38 billion during 1996–2000, after which it dropped to near $10 billion during 2001–2005, to then recover to $33 billion the next five years. It then climbed to $35 billion in the three years between 2011 and 2013 (table 5.2).[7]

In a long-term perspective, São Paulo's program of public-private participation in energy, transportation, and provision of infrastructure was far from new. Nineteenth-century concessions built much of the railway and energy in the state's development through the mid-twentieth century. The railroad system largely built by private companies through the 1920s opened the planalto to intense commercial settlement.[8] Though representing a major break with the immediate past, the 1998 devolution of the large state railroad (Fepasa) as concessions (via a brief phase of consolidation of rail by the government) thus represented a return to the original business model (Oncala, 2004).

Much the same story can be said in regard to the energy sector. The state's first gas company had been formed as a concession awarded to the British São Paulo Gas Company in 1872. Decades later, this company was nationalized as Comgas and subsequently incorporated under CESP. In electricity, the concessionaire São Paulo Tramway, Light and Power Company formed in 1899 helped open the impressive modernization of the state capital. "Light," as it was popularly known, changed hands in 1970 when the military regime used the end of the 70-year concession to merge it into the fledgling Eletrobrás, to then become Eletropaulo in 1981 when the state of São Paulo acquired it.

Likewise, the PED destatization program initiated the modern phase of public-private collaboration in energy in the 1990s (Tankha, 2009). State authorities auctioned off Comgas as a concession in 1999 (Sant Ana et al., 2011). The program converted other power companies to concessions. The list included CPFL, Eletropaulo, Elektro, Empresa Bandeirantes de Energia, and parts of CESP. These measures were gradually accepted or even well received by many users, thankful that the new investments modernized and expanded services in the greater São Paulo region. Also part of São Paulo's PED of the late 1990s, the devolution of Eletropaulo to the private sector came about as a complex process in which the giant company was first split up into four enterprises. In 1998, the state privatized AES Eletropaulo, the company servicing 16 million people in the expanded metropolitan area, transferring full stock ownership to Lightgás.[9]

Highway Concessions

The state of São Paulo itself built much of the original state highways throughout the twentieth century, with an important start in the 1920s. The shift to concessions came in 1996–2000, with a sharp acceleration in 1999. In this first wave, the Bandeirantes, Anhanguera, Anchieta, Imigrantes, and other highways were sold as concessions to 12 private companies for a total of R$3.9 billion.[10] From 1998 to June 2011, R$12.9 billion had been invested in the conversion (Artesp).

The second major wave in public-private investments in highways took place after the relative lull during the 2000–2005 period. Much of it happened in 2009, with the west portion of Rodoanel Mário Covas and five other highways—Dom Pedro I and Ayrton Senna/Carvalho Pinto on the northeastern and northern part of the state, Raposo Tavares on the south/southwest direction, and Marechal Rondon on the west/northwest. This wave of state-level concessions drew to the highway network $6.7 billion of the nearly $8.9 billion spent on infrastructure during the 2006–2010 period (see table 5.3). Transportation thus accounted for nearly 78 percent of the $19 billion total investment between the 1990s and 2013.

Announced in 2011, São Paulo's third wave of highway concession includes public-private partnerships and regular concessions. Before resigning as governor to run for president in 2006, governor Alckmin had prioritized five highway concessions in the northeastern part of the state: Dom Pedro I, Ayrton Senna/Carvalho Pinto, Tamoios, and a highway through the north shore. But as of 2010, these projects had made slow progress. Together with the upgrading and expansion of ports and logistics, the new Alckmin administration sought to give high priority to the project of turning the northern littoral region into an important export platform capable of promoting economic development in Campinas, São José dos Campos, and nearby centers of industrial innovation. Projects for the northern coast and the area of São Sebastião were planned as public-private partnerships worth billions, including the duplication of the 78-kilometers of Tamoios highway.

The state government approved ten public-private partnerships for implementation and eight for study, as well as three concessions for implementation and nine for further consideration.[11] In August 2011, it announced the tender of the northern segment of Rodoanel, the R$5.3 billion highway bypass for alleviating traffic in São Paulo's Metropolitan Region (RMSP). Public-private participation thus appeared

Table 5.3 Total state investment by sector, other top states, 1990–2013, in $ millions

	1990–1995	*1996–2000*	*2001–2005*	*2006–2010*	*2011–2013*	*Total*
Minas Gerais						
Transport				366		366
Energy		1,115	982.2	1,256	228	3.581
Telecom		1,537				1,537
Water and Sewerage		2.8	1.5	383	195	583
Total		**2,655**	**984**	**2,009**	**423**	**6,071**
Rio de Janeiro						
Transport	1,002	1,613	358	3,868	5,503	12,344
Energy		5,824	2,853	2,659	2,405	13,741
Telecom						
Water and Sewerage		655	9.4	281	1,648	2,593
Total	**1,002**	**8,092**	**3,220**	**6,808**	**9,556**	**28,678**
Pará						
Transport						
Energy		389	162	1,502	15,679	17,732
Telecom						
Water and Sewerage			1.7		62	63.7
Total		**389**	**164**	**1,502**	**15,741**	**17,796**
Rio Grande do Sul						
Transport		102				102
Energy		3,065	1,036	1,549	2,905	8,555
Telecom		4,419	691			5,110
Water and Sewerage					160	160
Total		**7,586**	**1,727**	**1,549**	**3,069**	**13,927**
Bahia						
Transport		37	56	1,578	1,796	3,467
Energy	2.3	2,347	1,275	2,388	4,159	10,172
Telecom						
Water and Sewerage				131		
Total	**2.3**	**2,384**	**1,330**	**4,097**	**5,955**	**13,770**

Source: World Bank, 2014a.

to have firmed up as a main way of providing transportation infrastructure during the first months of the new Alckmin administration.

The state of São Paulo relied on concessions and partnerships in other forms of transportation. The completion of Metro Line 4 (Yellow Line) stood out in the state's list of projects under contract in 2011. The Yellow Line represents a major addition to the capital's 70-kilometer subway system. In need of urgent expansion, the total number of passengers reached 11.5 million in 2010, making São Paulo's subway one of the most crowded in the world. Modeled as a public-private partnership, its 12.8 kilometers and 11 stations along the west side of the capital started to be built in 2004 and were close to completion in late 2010. Major stations finally opened in early 2011 (e.g., on the Faria Lima and Paulista avenues), with others scheduled within a few months. Delays pushed completion to a later date, partly to add some extensions. When finished, Line 4 would connect the Luz train station in the downtown area to stations several kilometers to the southeast. The concession was granted to ViaQuatro, a concessionaire owned by CCR, the private infrastructure company that also operated 15 percent of the highways converted to concessions in Brazil, including the western stretch of Rodoanel.

The Yellow Line overcame several challenges during construction, including delays from political opposition, and an accident taking the lives of several workers. In the launching phase, the World Bank (WB) and Japan's JBIC provided $200 million each, with private investors responsible for $340 million and the São Paulo state for the rest. Its estimated cost in 2011 was nearly three times as high as in the original plan. In 2006, an election year, the Line 4 extension suffered short strikes from subway workers protesting "privatization," with support from the Workers' Party candidate for governor, who also objected to the level of public investment in this project. Opponents filed a suit against the project, but the courts dismissed it. Meanwhile, state policy makers took progress as evidence of success and made plans for the further expansion of the metro system.

The completion of Rodoanel, the 178-kilometer highway bypass around metropolitan São Paulo, also ranked high in the list of state projects in 2011. This urgent project was essential to alleviate the traffic of trucks passing, in particular through the Marginal Tietê and Marginal Pinheiros, the two main metropolitan motorways adjacent to the rivers serving as historical boundaries to the city on the north and west. The bypass was only half-built early that year, when two of its four segments or stretches had been completed. The 32 kilometers of the West stretch absorbs and channels the large flows of traffic to and from five major highways radiating from the city toward the west and south. The concession contract was signed in 2008 and that same year it began service to nearly 80 million vehicles annually. In March 2011, concessionaire SPMar signed a contract to operate the 61.4 kilometer of the already built Rodoanel South.

The new state government gave priority to the remaining two segments—the east and north stretches. SPMar also won the contract to construct and operate the east stretch (40.6 kilometers) within

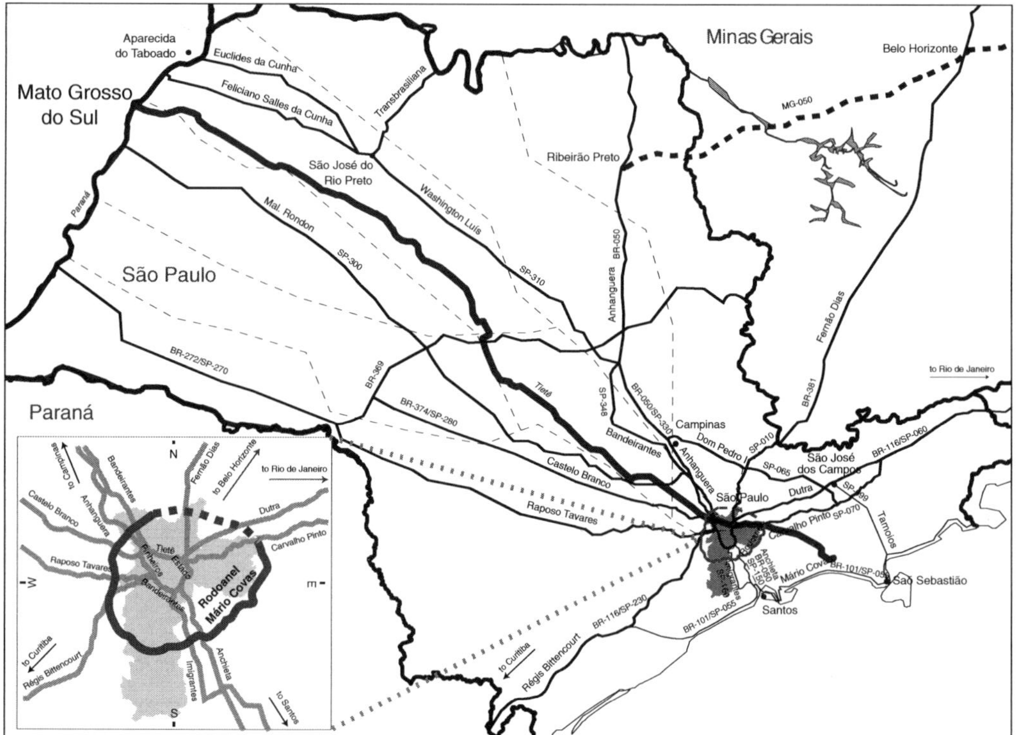

Figure 5.1 São Paulo's Rodoanel and main highways.

Source: Google Maps.

36 months. With an estimated annual traffic flow of 98 million vehicles, the R$5.5 billion invested in the south and east stretches will serve trucks moving around the city, the industrial counties to the east of the metropolitan region, and general vehicular flows to Santos and the shore. Connecting the highways to Rio de Janeiro and the Guarulhos airport (the Dutra and Ayrton Senna systems), the eastern segment will link them to the two highways leading to the port of Santos—Imigrantes and Via Anchieta.

Rodoanel North, the last segment, suffered the most delays, though it is urgently needed to alleviate the dense traffic flow connecting the busy Dutra and Fernão Dias highways to other routes to the interior of the state as well as to the south and south-west of Brazil. This 44-kilometer stretch includes a passage through the Serra da Cantareira mountain range to the Fernão Dias highway. Despite delays stemming from environmental concerns, the Alckmin government committed itself to initiate works by the end of 2011 and to complete it by 2014, but work started in early 2013 and was scheduled for completion in 2016. The Interamerican Development Bank announced financing of $400 million for the R$6.1 billion northern stretch (IDB, 2011). As approved by the Senate in May 2012, Rodoanel North would include a loan agreement between the state of São Paulo and IDB, federal funding, and support from the state government. At an investment of R$6.8 billion, this was the country's largest road construction project at the time (Bland, 2012). Over 20 bids were received and a decision was made in the third quarter of 2012.

These two projects confirm that the state of São Paulo's program of public-private investments had made strides in restructuring the transportation sector. Between 1998 and 2010, highways had attracted R$12 billion in investments, with most projects taking the form of regular concessions. In addition, the state's rail system had returned to private operators. Notwithstanding delays and adjustments, both were doing well in terms of improvements in the quality and quantity of infrastructure. Likewise, metro Line 4, a public-private partnership, had successfully expanded the coverage of the city's underground train network.

Presented in August 2011, São Paulo's Pluriannual Plan (PPA) 2012–2015 continued to emphasize transport infrastructure investments, including urban mobility. The plan allocated R$30 billion for transportation projects, 31 percent of all PPA funds,[12] in addition to the R$15 billion to come from public-private initiatives. Two secretariats—Metropolitan Transport and Logistics and Transport—are to share resources to add 30 kilometers to the metro, upgrade the metropolitan

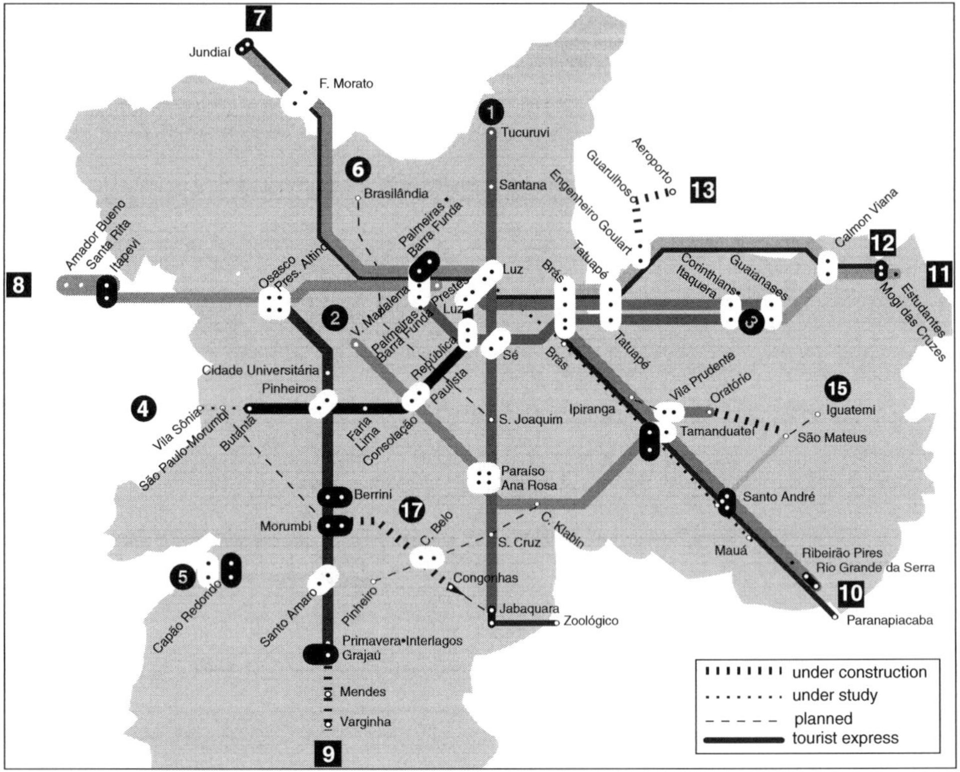

Figure 5.2 São Paulo's metro, 2014.

Source: Governo do Estado de São Paulo, 2014.

train system run by CPTM, complete the eastern segment of Rodoanel, and duplicate the Tamoios highway. It also stated the readiness of the state of São Paulo to build itself the rail bypass known as Ferroanel (see Chapter Four).

Discussion on São Paulo

São Paulo's program of public-private collaboration in infrastructure of the 1990s returned to more decisive growth after 2005, after the slowdown of the previous five years.[13] Private investment in the energy, transportation, and telecommunications sectors increased considerably in the ensuing years. By 2014, the state's Rodonanel "Mario Covas" had made considerable progress and aimed at completion of the entire bypass by 2016.

The 2006–2010 period also marked the start of modest but credible public-private investments in the state's water and sewerage sector. The $524 million for that period focused on large metropolitan areas. Water and sanitation projects for these areas were also well represented in the 2011–2013 list of public-private partnerships and concessions in the state of São Paulo, while total investment in this sector between 1990 and 2013 reached $2.4 billion. The state's performance on water treatment becomes more clear after taking the municipal level into account. São Paulo represents more than a third of the county-level public-private investments in Brazil, which had grown from $45 million in 1990–1995 to $775 million in the 2006–2013 years. In São Paulo, municipal water and sewerage projects represent much of the public-private investment at this level. The municipality of Rio Claro illustrates a pioneering example in water and sanitation services as a public-private partnership. This county of nearly 200,000 inhabitants offered the PPP as a 30-year concession requiring a private investment of $30.9 million, though the final cost was more than twice.[14] A consortium formed by Odebrecht and Lumina won the concession. In 2011, a new local government questioned the commitments made by the city and criticized the PPP project, even with talk of judicial action to change the profitability guarantee made by the local government. Still, there was support for the idea of using public-private investment for local economic development.

In summary, the state of São Paulo government approved various public-private projects in infrastructure after 2005, with the growth of the subway and urban highways (Rodoanel) as leading undertakings. To that effect, it developed state agencies such as Dersa and appointed qualified personnel in the transportation and logistics secretariat. By 2014, this program appeared to be on the path to successful consolidation. In addition, the state of São Paulo had worked with the federal government in the construction of a R$890 million stadium to host opening ceremonies and some games of the 2014 World Cup. Federal support was expected for the development of the Tietê-Paraná waterway.

But state authorities have focused much of their attention on the four stretches of the Rodoanel Mário Covas. The federal government finally agreed to use PAC2 funds to share the costs of building the northern stretch of the bypass. Redefined to share its terrain layout with a future Ferroanel, Rodoanel North will cost R$5.9 billion, including construction as well as asserting public domain over 3,000 compensated and relocated households, environmental mitigation, and the like. The 44-kilometer segment' three or four lanes in each direction will connect Rodoanel West and other highways from the west to the national and other highways to Rio, the northern littoral, the Guarulhos airport, and Rodoanel East (to be completed in 2015 at a total cost of R$3.2 billion). The cost will be covered with funds from the state and federal governments as well as the Interamerican Development Bank. Responding to delays due to environmental concerns over the Serra da Cantareira, the project was shifted to clear most of the sensitive areas. It started construction in early 2013 and is expected to be completed by 2016.[15] When finished, the entire Rodoanel Mário Covas will consist of a 180-kilometer ring around the metropolitan region.

Stable political consensus, leadership, expertise, and strategy for developing governance institutions made a difference, allowing the reform process to gain new traction in the state. The foundations for continuity were laid by governor Mário Covas and his successors Geraldo Alckmin, José Serra (2006), and once again Geraldo Alckmin (2010, reelected in 2014), all of whom were elected with strong public support. In addition, reform coalitions have remained strong in the state legislature. These conditions augur well for the continuity of the program and for the very large commitments already made to the public-private program. Though the state of São Paulo is thus poised for sustained momentum and leadership in this policy domain, entanglements with the federal government have yet to reach an optimal form.

Toward Assessment

Important highway and subway contracts have been signed and implemented in São Paulo as concessions and partnerships, but a detailed exploration of these early infrastructure projects paints a less rosy picture (Benvenuto et al., 1997). In particular, transportation projects in the state's large metropolitan have not advanced nearly as much. By 2012, the list of active projects still under study went beyond the 2011 list to include such undertakings as a suburban train to the airport, upgrading the airport itself, enhancing the metropolitan rail network, improving regional bus transportation, and bus-metro integration. A full assessment needs to include the entire range of initiatives.

Through 2014, Ferroanel remained one of the least successful undertakings. Under federal jurisdiction, the critically important Ferroanel metropolitan rail bypass had failed to make much progress, seemingly victim to the rather broad list of federal objectives. While São Paulo state had decided to approve funds to build it itself if needed, the federal government had jurisdictional control of the railroad system. Rail connection to the Guarulhos international airport was also a source of frustration. In 2008, the CPTM had developed the technical plans for the construction and operation of a high-speed train to connect downtown São Paulo (Luz terminal) and the airport through a 20-minute rail trip. Together with a feeder line, this project will require R$567 million from public funds. Announced as a 35-year concession, the Brazilian holding company CCR (winner of Line 4 bid) had expressed early interest in the airport link as a public-private partnership. Initially, CPTM announced construction contracts to be signed in 2007 and expected a 2009 completion. The bidding was suspended and the business model was being revised in mid-2011. By early 2013, CPTM announced that the express train had been cancelled and would be replaced by an airport extension of a future Line 13. Also in 2011, the delays in completing the highway bypass around the city stood out. Notwithstanding the progress reported above, it was only in 2010 that the state announced the public hearing for Rodoanel's east and north segments, its two remaining major stretches.

In summary, if the critically needed north and east segments had not been constructed, neither had the express service to the airport and Guarulhos, a major corridor in Campinas and yet other projects, while the Ferroanel rail bypass remained a concept. Meanwhile, the metropolitan region reported worsened traffic, congestion, and citizen satisfaction with the congested system of public transportation resulting from the above bottlenecks. Urbanization, demographic growth, industrialization, increased agricultural production, and changed patterns of settlement had worsened the logistical bottlenecks. Getting commodities and other exports from Brazil's vast interior to ports had reemerged as a major challenge. The delays included slow progress in the northern export corridor to the port of São Sebastião, a key item in the original list of public-private partnerships. The expansion of port infrastructure had been viewed as vital to continued growth by the state of São Paulo but remained an incomplete agenda. Considering the importance of increased export capacity for economic development, vital needs were going unmet.

Modernizing ports, multimodal transportation, and logistics were listed as priorities in multiyear plans (PPAs) for 2004–2007[16] and 2008–2011. These documents called for the improvement of existing roads and railroads, the elimination of bottlenecks in the network of roads to access Santos, and the upgrading and integration of the ports of São Sebastião and Santos. Public-private collaboration was identified as essential to repair and restructure the roads, railroads, waterways, and ports in the network.[17] Santos had steadily expanded to meet growing demand and was the most important shipping and entry point for goods in Brazil.[18] If it was due for a major upgrade, the state needed additional facilities.

As originally conceived, the northern export corridor called for enhancements to the port facilities of São Sebastião located some 200 kilometers from the capital. Integrating the expansion of freight capacity with improvements in the network of highways providing access to other ports was also needed (see figure 5.1). Owned and managed by the state, the port of São Sebastião's traffic load was 878,000 tonnes in 2012; the state plan was to enlarge capacity to eventually reach 1.5 million containers per year.[19] In addition, several highways needed to be upgraded and interconnected—Dom Pedro I (SP-65), Ayrton Senna (also known as Trabalhadores)-Carvalho Pinto (SP-70), and Tamoios (SP-99).

The idea is for the enhanced system to connect the Campinas region to the highways running toward Rio de Janeiro, with the Tamoios providing the key link to the northern shore and São Sebastião. Extending west, the latter would also give access to new port facilities to the emergent industries in the São José dos Campos and other areas to the northeast of the state. The goal will be to rely on partnerships with the private sector to provide the transportation enhancements and general infrastructure to serve the new export-oriented facilities and communities as far west as Campinas and north-northeast through the Vale do Paraíba. The plan would also encourage economic development in other counties in the northeastern part of the state.

In summary, the expanded network would substantially reduce transportation costs, alleviate the congestion in Santos, and open up an alternative shipping route for soybeans from the central-west, the products and services from the large metropolitan area of Campinas, and the large industrial areas in the Paraíba Valley.[20] The northern export corridor would be linked with MRS Logística rail network as well as with the airports of Viracopos and São José dos Campos.[21]

But prior to 2011, port modernization had been very slow, with state policymakers opting for gradual and relatively modest improvements in the transportation corridor to Santos, including avenues on the port perimeter, small enhancements to rail access, and the construction of facilities for the regulation of freight traffic.[22]

Unresolved debates about environmental impact and social benefits to surrounding communities contributed to the standstill of the program for the expansion and improvement of the port of São Sebastião.[23] Questions about sustainable infrastructure and the impact on local populations posed unexpected challenges, magnified by political debates on the merits of public-private collaboration.[24] Part of the northern export corridor would require widening a highway and building alternative routes through the Serra do Mar forest reserve,[25] a project with environmental consequences and likely to involve the resettlement of populations. Critics pointed to shortcomings in the institutional apparatus to administer public-private partnership projects.

With a relatively strong institutional and regulatory framework already in place, as well as considerable momentum,[26] the expectation was that São Paulo would move swiftly to implement the above priorities. However, the northern export corridor failed to make fast progress. While the state government focused on the expansion of the subway system and other priorities, upgrades to the Tamoios highway providing access to São Sebastião and the northern littoral and related parts of the northern export corridor project experienced progress after 2006. After being reelected governor in 2011, Alckmin rekindled the focus on the development of the northern shore but nothing had happened by 2014.

Other Brazilian States

Public-private collaboration in infrastructure spread throughout Brazil after 2005, and by 2010 most other states had taken steps to organize public-private partnerships. Regional dynamics, institutions, ideologies, and interests shaped reform initiatives across the nation. The Brazilian federation is comprised of 26 states and a federal district often differing in marked ways. These states vary in the depth of their involvement and their performance in public-private collaboration.

The southeast and south regions represent 72 percent of the country's GDP and enjoy the highest standards of living.[27] Together, they represent nearly 68 percent of the nation's total public-private investment in infrastructure from 1990 to 2013.[28] The southeast claims 23.6 percent of the national territory and the smaller south 6.6 percent. Their shares of public-private investment in infrastructure from 1990 to 2013 amounted to 58 percent and 9.9 percent of the total for all regions, respectively.

Together with São Paulo, the states of Minas Gerais and Rio de Janeiro showcase the southeast's active involvement in public-private initiatives. As of early 2011, Rio was second to São Paulo in overall activity, having launched a program in 2007. This state invested $40 billion in public-private projects, with an additional $281 million from local sources. The small state of Espírito Santo also developed a public-private partnership program.

The state of Minas Gerais was a pioneer in the adoption of public-private finance for developing infrastructure in 2003.[29] It is the second most populous state in all of Brazil and is home to many industries and infrastructure projects. Strategically located next to prosperous São Paulo and Rio, Minas has the largest road network in Brazil and operates 21 airports, while its roughly 5,300 kilometers of railways are 18 percent of the national network.

The state's western region is home to an important and diverse economy—mining, sugarcane, alcohol, and textile sectors. Transportation infrastructure is a pressing matter. Originally built as a single-lane road, a busy artery suffering from extreme traffic and high accident rates, the duplication of Highway MG-050 was chosen as Minas' first public-private partnership project. Operational costs had risen and infrastructure remained precarious in spite of investments of between 1993 and 2003. The highway currently spans 370 kilometers through 50 counties, from the state capital of Belo Horizonte to the border with São Paulo. The 25-year partnership project for the upgrading of MG-050 was delivered to a winning consortium in May 2007. The concessionaire would invest $370 million in exchange for tolls and a fixed payment from the state government. The task included repaving and expanding, signaling, drainage and crash barriers, bridges, pedestrian walkways, u-turn facilities, hard shoulders, access roads, and long-term highway repair. The expectation was that traffic flow would increase significantly. But actual improvements have come rather slowly and much work remains to be completed. In 2012, for example, only 10 percent of drainage works and 40 percent of road paving goals had been completed.[30]

The Development Bank of Minas Gerais administers the contract and disburses the state contributions to the project. While the federal government had been able to negotiate road concessions with lower tolls, the authorities defended Minas' model as a way of guaranteeing the necessary private investments[31] with modest public participation. In general, Minas' PPP fund relies on financing from the state, which is linked to its budget. With support and advice from IDB specialists, private bank UNIBANCO was contracted to design the proposal for an independent PPP fund from the sale of stocks of CEMIG (Companhia Energética do Minas Gerais), support from the World Bank, royalties, and funds from the state economic development company CODEMIG.

Minas built on the MG-050 project to develop other public-private undertakings. It encourages local governments to initiate programs and legislation based on concessions and public-private partnerships. The 2006–2010 period saw substantial investments in energy as well as water and sewerage. Other public-private partnerships in the state include five penitentiaries, public health facilities, and the Mineirão soccer stadium for the 2014 World Cup. A federal project, the Confins/Tancredo Neves International Airport began to operate as a concession in late 2013, with the aim of upgrading it to handle 16.5 million passengers annually instead of the current 10.2 million.[32]

In Brazil's south region, the state of Rio Grande do Sul made early progress, voting a law and launching a program for public-private partnerships. While Paraná and Santa Catarina also passed enabling legislation in 2004F, the latter created a public company to promote public-private collaboration in infrastructure, though neither has developed broad portfolios beyond concessions.

The north and midwest regions have experienced expansion, but not nearly as dramatic as parts of the southeast. In the north, the states of Amazonas and Pará—large territories and low population density—are home to the construction of large hydroelectric dams and transmission lines. In terms of number of projects, these represent modest shares of total public-private investment in the 1990–2010 period. While the north region claims 10.6 percent of investments, the midwest represents 5.1 percent (table 5.1). The state of Amazonas passed legislation in 2008 and eventually started a federally funded monorail in Manaus. Tocantins instituted a program in 2009 and developed plans for the administration of a prison and other projects.

Likewise, the midwest states of Goiás (2004) and Mato Grosso do Sul passed legislation and made plans to attract private investment, but the federal government has provided the most investments, often focusing on telecommunications and hydroelectric plants.

The nine states in the northeast form a distinctive block holding 28 percent of the population and 18.3 percent of the national territory but only 16 percent of the total public-private investment in infrastructure in this period. Traditionally seen as underdeveloped economies with very high rates of poverty, states in this macro region have been expanding since the 1990s. Three northeastern states represent the most progress. Bahia passed legislation in 2004, made plans for public-private partnerships, and emerged as a leader within this region. In 2008, a loan from IDB allowed this state to include a partnership program in the context of plans for fiscal reforms and modernization of the state apparatus. The state PPP program has two main projects under its administration: the highway BA 093 and the underwater sanitation project. The highway project was designed in cooperation with BNDES and the International Finance Corporation (IFC). Massive federal support helped build a large sports complex as part of the international sports projects of 2014 and 2016. Pernambuco adopted appropriate laws in 2005.

After passing legislation in 2009, Ceará authorities collaborated with the Bank of the Northeast (BND) and IDB, which led to the organization of seminars drawing on specialists from Minas, São Paulo, and government agencies. Smaller or less prosperous states have also taken some steps for developing public-private infrastructure. In Piauí, the state government announced a $1 billion PPP project for the production of oil in the northern city of Parnaíba, aiming to export production to Japan. This project proposal includes the construction of a direct pipeline between Parnaíba and port facilities as a public-private partnership between Petrobras (50 percent, viewed as the private entity), the federal government (40 percent), and the state government (10 percent).[33]

Conclusion

Public-private collaboration in infrastructure has gradually spread throughout Brazil. Haltingly and unevenly, programs have emerged in most states and a number of cities. The 2000–2005 dip that followed the enthusiastic takeoff of the prior decade proved temporary. By 2004 or shortly after, São Paulo, Minas Gerais, and other influential states passed laws and identified public-private partnerships. The rebuilding of subnational governance institutions after decades of authoritarian and populist national excesses shaped this process. Political pragmatism, institutional development, and the strength of liberalization have made a difference in the timing and rate of adoption of concessions and partnerships. Sustained political leadership has proven critical in maintaining momentum. In terms of sectors, energy, transportation, telecommunications, water, and sanitation have received the most attention.

At the same time, delays and lack of adequate financial guarantees have been frequent sources of concern for the private sector. Environmental impact has emerged as an important criterion in project assessment, with more assertive agencies to grant licenses and permissions. Lack of agreement among decision makers, private operators, and civil actors have led to delays in construction. In addition, large projects needing federal financing have remained unfunded.

In São Paulo, political leadership, institutional development, and a mature liberalization framework have contributed to successful public-private partnerships. In other cases, lack of these conditions have acted to inhibit the success of these measures. Further comparison of subnational experiences is a fertile field in which to further explore these differences. Ferroanel illustrates how diverging interests between state and federal agencies can complicate initiatives deemed critical by specialists. Lack of consensus between the federal and state governments has often blocked growth in other areas, with the perception that agencies often favor political criteria in investment policies. Discrepancies between national and provincial governments in regard to priorities can become roadblocks to subnational public-private projects. Adequate mechanisms are not yet in place to ensure coherence between federal and state policies.

Institutional and political dynamics at the subnational level can also hinder public-private initiatives. Plenty of ideas come to the surface at that level, but local governments frequently lack the institutional capacity and other conditions for long-term success. Considering their proximity to local needs, multilateral organizations and policy organizations are called to support initiatives at this level. Limited expertise impedes programs at small or poorly funded levels. While a few state governments have been able to build effective infrastructure programs and projects, frameworks for implementing partnerships still seem an elusive goal in many others. Private stakeholders point to the deficiency in public administration and the inefficient process of environmental licensing as prohibiting a greater participation of the private sector in infrastructure.[34] Public-private collaboration needs an institutional and societal learning process, which is taking time to solidify.

CHAPTER SIX

Transantiago: Urban Development in Chile

Chile's capital city of Santiago is home to over 6 million of the country's 17 million inhabitants—roughly half of all urbanized Chileans.[1] As late as the 1990s, Santiago's urban infrastructure sorely lagged behind the dense concentration of people, buildings, and vehicles. Thereafter, this picture began to change rapidly with the implementation of a massive public works program created by the democratic reformers in power since 1990. By early 2005, residents of Santiago[2] were experiencing a sense of wonder and suspense as the completion of an interconnected urban expressway network opened a period of transformation in urban life.

Costanera Norte, a dazzling expressway along and under the Mapocho River, was inaugurated on April 12, 2005. It ran through the heart of Santiago on its main east-west axis connecting the downtown area with several outlying areas and with each other. The middle- and upper-class residents from the eastern neighborhoods could now access the western side of the expanding metropolis in a matter of minutes. They could easily reach the international airport, major highways running on the north-south axis, and the popular coastal area around Valparaíso and Viña del Mar (Hinojosa and Gómez-Lobo, 2000).

The majority of Santiago's residents rarely owning cars had relatively less to gain from the new toll roads at the time, but they expectantly awaited for Transantiago, the new public rapid bus transportation system more directly affecting their lives. Transantiago promised to relieve congestion, air pollution, public safety, and noise[3]—terms used by the general public to describe the city's transportation system (Cruz, 2002).

Chile's economic growth provides the background for the great effort at urban regeneration. The model of development had been built on macroeconomic and institutional stability, economic liberalization, and the opening to international markets. It gradually changed the economy and society as a whole and substantially reduced poverty (Solimano, 2012).[4] As a result, Santiago contrasted favorably with other large cities in the region in terms of well-being, less gross poverty, and public insecurity, notwithstanding the claims of many urban dwellers. On the other hand, in terms of air pollution, traffic congestion, and other urban problems, Santiago ranked as high as Mexico City, São Paulo, Bogotá, and other Latin American cities.

In this context, Santiago's public transportation system operating during the last decade of the twentieth century was woefully inadequate for the new realities and aspirations of the country. Having experienced a great deal of economic and political modernization, Chileans wanted more.[5] At the same time that the number of private vehicles was rapidly increasing, seemingly out of proportion with the traditional design of the city,[6] the new mass transit system promised to substantially improve access and connectivity throughout the city, while reducing the high levels of noise and air pollution (see figure 6.1).

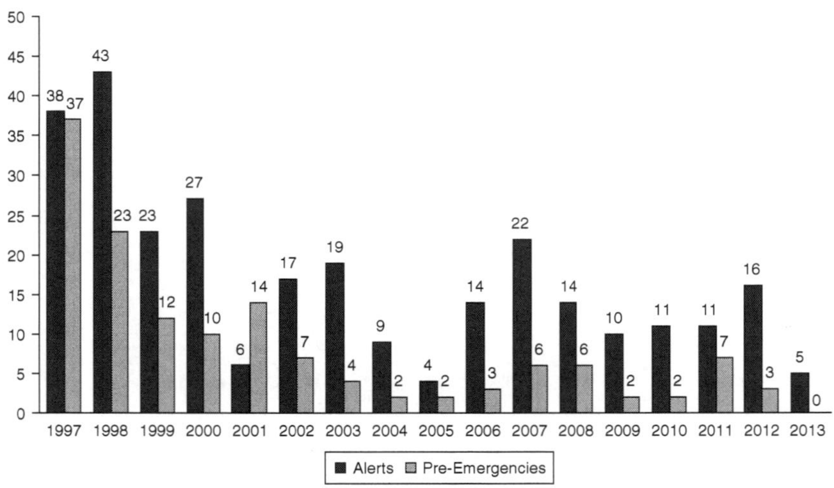

Figure 6.1 Air contamination events, 1997–2013.

Source: Ministerio del Medio Ambiente, Gobierno de Chile, 2013.

Turning the sprawling capital city into a more liveable and appealing world-class urban center was the self-avowed goal of democratic reformers who gained control of the government in the 1989 presidential elections. The modernization of Santiago went hand in hand with plans to turn Chile's capital into a major and competitive global metropolis.[7] The great wave of change took place under the four successive Concertación administrations between 1990 and 2010. They fostered innovative concessions and public-private partnerships to build and redesign major transportation facilities and projects.

In 2005, Santiago's transformation included the construction of more than 210 kilometers of tolled urban highways, doubling the size of the subway system, the expansion and major improvements of the international airport, and the redesign of streets and public spaces among other related changes. In addition, the Greater Santiago area was benefitting from improvements in health, housing, waste disposal programs, and other improvements.[8]

Transantiago was to build and maintain new infrastructure—segregated bus lanes, road connections, two large bus-metro stations, and 27 bus transfer stations. It would also modernize the bus fleet and sharply reduce the number of bus companies to ten or less.

Scattered voices expressed misgivings about the massive changes, but Chileans as a whole welcomed the effort to modernize the capital. In 2005, during his last year in office, President Ricardo Lagos, a center-left politician, basked in the progress of projects he saw as part of his legacy. He stepped down with huge popular support, even if Transantiago and several key projects had yet to be completed. It would be up to his successor, President Michelle Bachelet, to finish and inaugurate Transantiago in 2007.[9] Overconfidence and inexperience exacted a high cost. After a massive debacle upon launching, Transantiago became a nightmare for mass transit users as well as policymakers.

Public Transport in Historical Perspective

Santiago's public transportation had been organized in terms of three very different models since its start in the 1920s. The Chilean state directly provided transportation and regulated transit fares, routes, and operating licenses in Santiago until 1979. Inadequate supply of buses was chronic during this first phase; many complained that buses were overcrowded and that service was very poor.

The pendulum between state and market swung widely in 1979 when the military regime radically liberalized fares, routes, and bus frequency. Supply increased under a system of highly competitive fares. According to Germán Correa,[10] extreme liberalization in this second phase led to a veritable chaos. Driven by fragmented and narrow decisions, the number of small-scale operators increased out of control and by 1990, there were 13,698 buses circulating in the city. Traffic congestion, old and unsafe buses, expensive costs to the public, and pollution became major issues.

The third phase began with the use of private concessions during 1990–1991, leading to the design and implementation of the Plan for Santiago's Urban Transportation (PTUS) in the early 2000s. As part of the Concertación's task force to create a government program for the return to democracy, the mass transit problems rapidly emerged as a key priority.[11]

In 1990, the system began to modernize under a concession model that determined the contracts and bidding of the bus routes. Despite stiff opposition from the *micreros*,[12] President Patricio Aylwin enacted several laws to regulate the emissions and life span of the buses. Within four years, the enforcement of increasingly higher standards (EPA-91 and EURO-I in 1993, and EPA-94 and EURO-II in 1996) resulted in the removal of 4,600 older buses from service. This initiative gave impetus to the modernization of the system, showing policymakers that concessions of routes provided a powerful new tool for the administration of public transportation (Paredes and Sánchez, 2004). Still, problems with excessive supply and duplicated routes, congestion, and pollution persisted. Nearly 70 percent of the buses belonged to very small companies that owned an average of 2.1 buses.[13] Policymakers were concerned with the high degree of informality in the sector.

In theory, the lack of economies of scale led to the high level of informality. Since operators in a given line shared administrative costs, there were no incentives to improve the system through a more concentrated ownership pattern. The decentralized system resulted in an unnecessarily high number of buses. Since individual bus owners did not coordinate how many buses operated at a given time, a large number of buses thus competed for users. Fare evasion was high, while individual bus drivers often charged passengers a fraction of the real ticket price, either to pocket the money or to attract more passengers to their line or route.

Between 1991 and 1998, the government relied on 15 auctions to induct operators into a few modern companies. It demanded that individual bus owners have legal representation and an agent to manage and fulfill the new contracts. This was intended to bring organization and accountability to the sector.

Still, the goals of the Concertación for reforming the public transportation system originating in the Patricio Aylwin administration (1990–1994) were not fulfilled during his presidential tenure. The first licitations were not able to solve the core problem of restructuring the routes. With very limited information about the public's needs and patterns, the government conducted the Origin-Destination poll in 1991, which gave the first quantified vision of the system. The next step was to organize a comprehensive plan, the PTUS. However, transportation failed to become a main concern during the Eduardo Frei administration (1994–2000) and the plan was not implemented.[14]

Transportation returned as a top priority during the Ricardo Lagos administration (2000–2006). Shortly after its inauguration, the Lagos administration reinitiated government studies to find ways to use concessions in the transportation sector. In 2001, a second Origin-Destination (EOD) poll was conducted to provide the basis for an urban transport plan. The second poll, tracking people and vehicles traffic, served as basis for a new task force to design the PTUS. Following the appointment of Javier Etcheverry as minister of Public Works, the PTUS was implemented in early 2002 to address transportation bottlenecks and serve as the foundation for Transantiago.[15]

The task force established the pressing need to balance service, transport, and public resources among urban zones. Services and access tended to concentrate in the central region of Santiago to the detriment of new residential areas growing in expanding urban peripheries. This caused an increasing shift in mobility and movement from the periphery to the central zones, creating an uneven flow of people and vehicular traffic. Seventy percent of the population traveled by means of public transportation, with 46 percent of those earning less than $500 a month strained by the weight of transportation expenses on family budgets. This underscored the importance of creating a more efficient and accessible mass transit system.

The policy of low entry costs and unrestricted competition applied in the 1990s allocated resources inefficiently—competition among the buses, metro, and taxis generated a disorganized, nonintegrated system that forced users to assume a major monetary expense and use multiple forms of transportation. Additionally, the overlap of different routes led to excessive supply and inefficient use of road infrastructure, causing unnecessary congestion.

To counteract these problems, the PTUS implemented measures that affected bus routes, bus drivers, user information, supervision and control, and financial requirements; the plan called for 11 programs, including Transantiago. The focus was to decongest the streets of Santiago—outlining interurban and rural-city transport, limiting bus stops, improving road network structures, regulating automobile traffic and vehicle standards, promoting nonmotorized forms of transportation and authorizing public spaces for pedestrians, telecommunication, and implementing new environmental regulations. In this way, the PTUS framed Transantiago in a larger governmental plan to improve Santiago's public transportation—the goal was to make the city's public transit more efficient and accessible.

Transantiago

Created under an evolving framework for urban transportation based on public-private collaboration, Transantiago became one of the top priorities of the Concertación government after 2003.[16] It entailed a complex network of institutional, business, and public actors running and supervising its components. It represented a major reform by the Concertación to improve overall living conditions, mainly traffic congestion, quality of public transportation, and high air pollution (see figure 6.1). Much of the early impetus took place under the presidency of Patricio Aylwin, as new policymakers focused their attention on public transportation.[17]

Transantiago included several discrete elements: a system of main bus lines connecting to the metro and the local feeder lines; new buses replacing the fleet of more than 8,000 antiquated buses; easily accessible modern bus stations; new management and information center for the fleet; integration with the subway system; and a smart card fare system. At the outset, this modernization of the public transport system was to cover 24 of the 54 municipalities in the greater Santiago.

The new payment method based on a smart card system promised faster bus-subway integration, improved access, and increased safety. It was seen as a major innovation compared to the old system where passengers paid cash directly to the driver for each trip, which attracted unnecessary robbery and was generally perceived as disorganized.[18]

Initially owned and operated by ten large private concessionaires, the system would eventually be supervised by a new metropolitan transportation authority.[19] The idea was to sharply reduce the number of different bus operators, eliminate the duplication of low-level service, and improve strategic planning. Transantiago anticipated that as a result, the city would experience a rise in the number of users of public transportation.

The system was to be developed in stages after a formal opening in 2005 and was expected to be completed by 2010, although a number of delays slowed down full completion.

Indeed, Transantiago experienced delays in the construction of stations as well as in the implementations of the smart card technology. The scheduled inauguration for May 27, 2005, was postponed twice. As the fog of pollution hung over the city in the winter of 2005, residents were told to wait for the grand inauguration until October 2006. To some, this was an omen of failure. The construction of exclusive lanes for the bus networks, the installation of both filters for particulate matters and Euro II technology, as well as the removal of the old buses, resulted in more delays. This pattern of postponements affected not only the operation of the new buses but also increased air pollution. Finally, Transantiago was inaugurated on February 10, 2007.

Inauguration: Debacle and Debate

The much heralded launching of Transantiago turned out to be a huge collective disappointment. It opened with an insufficient number of buses, long waiting lines at subway stations, unfinished bus stations, no GPS, few segregated bus lanes, long delays in getting to work and getting home, scathing criticism by users, and general public perplexity. The system would not work properly for a considerable time, turning Transantiago into a fiasco. The debacle turned into a growing national debate and eventually a major political problem.

Following the initial period of great confusion, President Bachelet, who had taken office in 2006, named René Cortázar as minister of Transportation and gave him complete authority over Transantiago.[20] The new minister presided over a series of improvements including a larger bus fleet, accelerated construction of stations and related facilities, and the redesign of bus routes. However, progress was not fast enough for critics and the opposition; by mid-2008, a year before the presidential elections of 2009, Transantiago had become a political nightmare for the authorities.

The issue of financing a large deficit took center stage in late 2007 and through 2008. The original expectation was that Transantiago would be financially self-sustaining, but a monthly subsidy of $30 million to $50 million was needed to keep the system on track. The government tried different solutions, but Congress, which was then controlled by the political opposition, blocked these proposals. In 2008, the government announced a $570 million loan from the Inter-American Development Bank and BancoEstado but the courts declared this measure unconstitutional. As the matter continued to be debated in Congress, the Concertación government was forced to finance the deficit via the national emergency fund. This was a bitter pill to swallow as it reinforced the perception that Transantiago was a national calamity. This solution could not be invoked permanently. The national debate became acrimonious—by September 2008, the opposition felt strong enough to call for the demise of the entire system.

The woes of Transantiago figured prominently in the celebration of Chile's Independence Day on September 18, 2008. It appeared in the homily by the influential Archbishop of Santiago as well as in similar statements by Evangelical Bishop Emiliano Soto a few days earlier in his church's own Te Deum. Cardenal Francisco Javier Errázuriz in his discussion of the challenges facing the Chilean nation highlighted the debate about the mass transit system and called for a return to political civility, open dialogue, and national agreement. Chile's media reported the reactions of key members of all parties attending both celebrations. President Michele Bachelet and members of her cabinet reminded Chileans of the need to maintain a consensus and act responsibly, acknowledging that Transantiago and public transport had become a national issue and challenge (Correa, 2010).

National discussion dominated the headlines, affirming that the fate of Transantiago had become a top national issue, highlighting the political differences between Concertación and the conservative opposition. The immediate concern was the pending congressional decision to provide a permanent subsidy to the fledgling public transport system. The lower house had in fact approved a bill supporting the subsidy; however, it was a Senate subcommittee that first challenged the interim loan from the Inter-American Development Bank, revealing a strong anti-Transantiago sentiment in the Senate. Sensing the political vulnerability of the Concertación government, opposition senators forcefully argued against the system. Some of the most recalcitrant senators came from a new faction, known as Regionalist and Independent Party, which called for a return to the bus routes used before Transantiago, the end of the present concessions, and the creation of a new institutional authority to coordinate a new multioperator system.

Faced with the likelihood of defeat, government officials moved to prevent or delay the vote in the Senate, acknowledging that more political work was needed to obtain broad support. Meanwhile, they agreed to use the government's discretionary fund to cover Transantiago's deficit, but this too was an uncertain decision.

Minister Cortázar's government found itself in a very difficult position as concessionaires such as Buses Gran Santiago were not fully complying with their obligations. Drivers mobilized in demand for better working conditions and users expressed anger at the slow pace of improvement. Swayed by a great deal of criticism and attacks, the tide of general public opinion seemed to turn against Transantiago—the system's very survival seemed uncertain.

Political interests were blocking key measures to fund the system. The question was whether the Chilean political class as a whole would be willing and able to put politics on hold and regain trust and faith in Transantiago. A final compromise was not reached until the summer of 2009; after a prolonged and often heated debate between Concertación and Alliance for Change/Coalición por el Cambio, the IDB loan was approved.

Assessing Transantiago, 2006–2008

A fair evaluation of Transantiago turned out to be a bigger challenge than anticipated at the beginning of this study. In the context of general frustration with the system, the debate through 2007–2009 became highly politicized. As the ruling Concertación alliance faced an unprecedented level of vulnerability since 1990, the opposition turned relentlessly critical, attacking every pro-Transantiago initiative in Congress. In this context, evaluation has become a highly contentious matter.

Five main dimensions are considered in this tentative exercise, including environmental impact, success of technological implementation, overall user satisfaction and public opinion, financial performance, and political consequences and impact on institutional and legal frameworks.

Environmental Impact

In 2006, National Environmental Commission (CONAMA) contracted a team of independent air quality consultants[21] to conduct an evaluation of air decontamination and pollution prevention and to provide an independent measure of environmental conditions in Santiago. The study reported that the air contaminants in the capital had decreased since 2000. However, PM10[22] levels were 75 percent above the Chilean norm of 150 ug/m^3, which in turn is three times more than the European norm of 50 ug/m^3.[23] The audit also detected significant budget cuts in the departments responsible for carrying out environmental policies, with the budget for personnel decreasing by 42 percent and the research funds decreasing by 50 percent. Nonetheless, the audit confirmed that two unexpected external factors had contributed to the scarce improvement in air pollution—the setback in the implementation of Transantiago and the introduction of natural gas for industrial use.[24]

After Transantiago's delayed implementation, studies conducted in mid-late 2008 showed that environmental improvements had in fact been observed in the metropolitan area. Such reductions were compatible with the environmental goals set by Transantiago. In August 2008, a study released by a private environmental research center showed improved quality of air in the Greater Santiago area, in which ultrafine particle PM0.1 contamination had decreased by 30 percent from July 2006 to July 2007.[25] According to Minister Cortázar, Transantiago was meeting its objectives, as public transportation emissions—particularly at street level—decreased significantly with the implementation of the new system.[26] Alejandro Smythe, the director of the Regional Environmental Commission (COREMA), agreed that Transantiago was helping address Santiago's environmental problems. Smythe cites his own studies that if the old yellow buses were still in use, there would be many more environmental alerts if Transantiago were not in place.[27]

In 2011, CONAMA's report on critical environmental episodes pointed to a decrease in the number of alert from 22 in 2007 to 11 in 2011—in accordance with the general trend that began in the early 2000s. According to this data, the winter months of 2008 saw better air quality, which coincided with favorable meteorological conditions. By 2012, environmental readings from Santiago's monitoring stations registered an improvement in air quality index with a reading of 59.3 MO10 compared to 73 in 2007.[28] However, when compared to European norms and World Health Organization guidelines, air quality level was still a regional issue.[29]

A 2009 study reported a 65 percent decrease in pre-emergencies and a 30 percent decrease in environmental alerts. Following the announcement of this study and resultant data, the *intendente* of the metropolitan region credited the continued improvements in environmental episodes to a process initiated in 1997 and solidified under President Bachelet. The minister of the environment, Ana Lya Uriarte, attributed the new improvements to the implementation of government policies coming to fruition, directly citing the regulation of the transport industry, further restrictions of catalytic automobiles, and Transantiago itself.[30]

As of 2014, Transantiago has indeed played an important role in the improvement of the city's air quality by the reduction and modernization of the bus fleet. On the other hand, this decrease has been offset by an increase in the total number of vehicles, particularly an increase of diesel vehicles that are not buses (Gramsch et al., 2013).

Technological and Operational Goals[31]

The technology component of the Transantiago system is a key element to the overall success of the project. The smart card fare and collection system was introduced in certain locations as early as January 1, 2007, and has since been considered the best working feature of the Transantiago technology. The smart card system is completely automated, and as of February 2008, there were close to 2,000 card charge points and 1,307 Bip! service stations in operation.[32] According to a December 2007 poll conducted by the Central University in Santiago, public satisfaction held strong with 5.53 out of 7 in public scoring—the highest rating recorded in the survey. However, in March 2011 when the Bip! card charges broke down and passengers were unable to use their cards, the minister of Transportation threatened to fine and not review the contract with Transantiago Financial Administrator (AFT) upon its expiration date.[33]

In fact, at the end of 2012 and after a year of negotiations, the contract to manage the Bip! card and its card charging network was transferred to Santiago Metro which had already been responsible for 70 percent of card charges. Instead of contracting with AFT, which in turn outsourced special services to third parties, the state would now deal directly with each specialist entity allowing for a faster response from service providers. Patricio Pérez, coordinator of Transantiago, explained that the new structure would allow for more supervision of the contractual agreements and the ability to impose proportional fines as well as incentives. Most importantly, it was announced that the new infrastructure translated into $8 million in annual savings.[34]

As of January 2014, there were 1,675 card charge points, to be increased by 800 (48 percent) in February of the same year as announced by Metro. At the same time, users were very pleased to learn that they would be able to charge their Bip! cards over the Internet. This service, implemented by the Webpay system, requires that the cards be validated at a *tótem* in a Metro station or at an *Infobip!*[35]

In contrast to the success of the smart card system, ambitious plans to install advanced GPS and up-to-date technologies had not been implemented in the majority of the buses. More than 6,400 buses will have to be updated, as the current technology is outdated and cannot be reused. The newest forms of the software will include advanced GPS, Euro IV technologies, and renovated consoles with precise buttons for easy interaction. The GPS will allow drivers to know exact distances and times that separate every bus travelling the same route.

Beyond bus and metro activity, supervision and information were in short supply. A deficient information system for users and operators was in place, with a lack of operating security cameras, passenger counters, variable information panels, and emergency panic buttons. Additionally, only ten fleet management centers were functioning, all without the proper fleet management software.[36]

On its second anniversary, Transantiago underwent new modifications under Minister Cortázar's 2009 plan. In an attempt to bypass political agendas and definitively normalize the transport system, the plan called for adding 216 new carts to the most-used Metro lines, adding 1,000 new buses, and eliminating close to 30 percent of the old ones, expanding and charging the smart card sites by 20 percent, and more. A high priority for 2009 was the enactment of a new law to create the much-anticipated metropolitan transport authority, both in Santiago and in surrounding areas. Ultimately the plan was not implemented in part due to party politics and policy road blocks.

In addition to these alterations, further advancements were initiated in December 2009 to complete Transantiago's operational and technological objectives. Of the 1,700 old yellow buses still running in the capital, only 300 would be in circulation by early 2010, and would be replaced by 1,130 modern vehicles with Euro III technology.[37] Filtering systems were to act as purifiers, eliminating more than 70 percent of smog and fine particulate matter.

Late February 2010 saw further regulations to the operational system of Transantiago, as eight new routes and modifications to seven other routes were initiated to increase coverage in the most inhabited areas of the capital. This new plan will benefit 500,000 people in the 20 most inhabited municipalities.

After a permanent subsidy guaranteed the future of Transantiago through 2014, a new series of technological and operational improvements were issued to public transportation to drastically reduce waiting time during nonpeak hours (nights and weekends), which has previously experienced significant delays. The plans will increase the frequency of buses for over 146 routes, create four new nocturnal routes, and improve the nighttime coverage of over 32 other services in the metropolitan area. These changes are expected to reduce wait time by at least 20 percent depending on the route.

While progress and advancements having been made since its initial launch in February 2007, original design and operational goals for Transantiago are still far from complete. The technology system now in place is not complete in terms of the initial design and implementation; it is incapable of responding to the needs of Transantiago. The pending and future plans seek to rectify and update the current system in line with the original technological goals.

User Satisfaction[38]

In an early June 2007 poll issued by the CEP,[39] 61 percent of the people surveyed disagreed that Transantiago has positively affected the quality of their lives—though 67.4 percent asserted that Transantiago was a good idea that just needed to be perfected. When asked about the main problems with Transantiago, 43.9 percent of those surveyed cited poor execution and 28.5 percent cited poor design. According to a follow-up November-December poll, when asked about improvements in travel time, quality of buses, and form of payment (i.e., the smart card system) with the new Transantiago system, the majority of the respondents reported that travel time was worse (47.1 percent), quality of buses was worsening (41.2 percent), but that the smart card system was an improvement (43.6 percent). Finally, when asked if Transantiago had been functioning well, average, or poorly, 76.6 percent of people surveyed ranked it as functioning poorly in November and December, showing little improvement from the 78.6 percent who answered the same question in June. After initial structural modifications and improvements, polls continued to echo similar public disapproval and frustration. According to late 2008 Adimark polls,[40] general disapproval ratings for the transport plan were up 10 points from June, as

79.6 percent of those surveyed disapproved of Transantiago in October 2008. A complementary national survey issued by the Center for the Study of Contemporary Reality (CERC) in September 2008[41] confirmed that Transantiago continued to be a national issue, as 46 percent of participants reported that the problems with the transport system could not be resolved. User dissatisfaction was further evidenced by the 42 percent of respondents who said that Transantiago was the biggest problem affecting the country—a figure larger than that of unemployment (32 percent) and inflation (29 percent). About 28 percent of participants blamed President Bachelet (compared to 32 percent who blamed ex-president Ricardo Lagos), while only 10 percent of those polled approved of Bachelet's management of Transantiago (see figure 6.2).

The polls of November 2009, following financial resolutions and increased transport alterations, indicated marked improvement in user satisfaction. Approval ratings for Michelle Bachelet's management of Transantiago maintained their highest numbers through fall 2009—over 33 percent approval in October and 30 percent in November.[42] Moreover, a similar study conducted in summer 2009 further revealed image improvements, reporting that only 7.3 percent of those surveyed felt that Transantiago was Chile's biggest problem,[43] a decrease from the 42 percent in 2008. Though these figures still showed the complexities and problems with the Transantiago system, user satisfaction and public approval ratings had never been higher, and maintained their level through 2009.

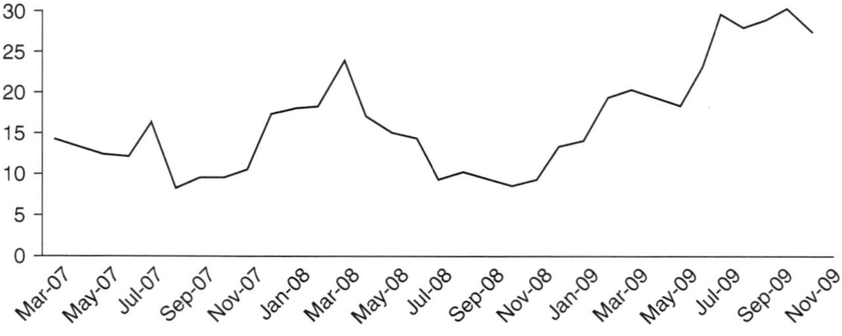

Figure 6.2 Approval rating for Michelle Bachelet's handling of Transantiago, 2007–2009.

Source: Adimark GfK, "Encuesta Evaluación de Gestión del Gobierno: Informe mensual Noviembre 2009," November 2009.

Financial Performance

Since Transantiago was expected to be financially self-sufficient, failure to achieve this goal proved costly to policymakers. The substantial monthly subsidy required since the official launch in February 2007 frustrated the original plan and fueled the political debate about the very viability of the system.

Covering the deficit emerged as a top political issue in late 2007 (see figure 6.3). Authorities explored internal and external alternative sources once it was clear that fare increases would be too unpalatable to the public and that fare collection would not suffice to cover the deficit. In December 2007, the Senate failed to approve a subsidy bill for Transantiago and public transportation after the bill passed the lower house by one vote. In May 2008, the IDB and BancoEstado approved loans, but challengers from the opposition succeeded in a legal suit to declare this measure unconstitutional in September. Finally, President Bachelet authorized the use of a national emergency fund set aside for disaster relief and other emergencies. A large deficit continued to accrue through 2008.

Fare rates played an important role in Transantiago's financial situation. Fixed at $380 pesos in February 2007, actual costs were later estimated to be $400–$422 pesos. Policymakers decided to hold fares down to promote ridership and prevent popular protests. In fact, immediately following the unsuccessful February 10, 2007, implementation, fares

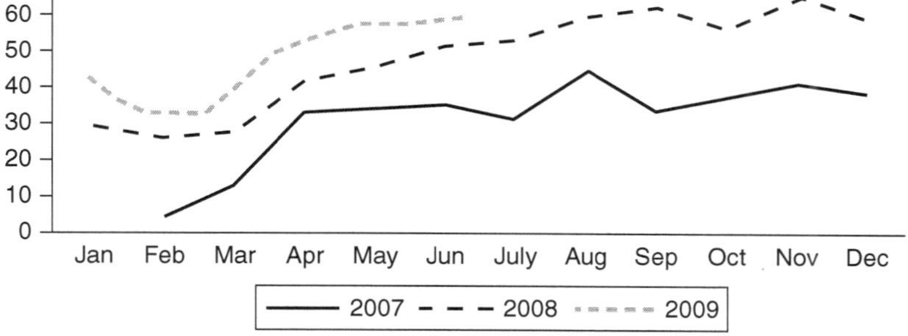

Figure 6.3 Transantiago's deficit in $ millions.

Note: In August 2009, permanent subsidy for Transantiago was approved.

Source: *El Mercurio*, April 23 and August 2, 2009.

were waived, and many riders used the system free for nearly ten days at a cost of one million dollars a day, according to the financial administrator (AFT). Fare evasion became a problem, as it significantly contributed to lower than expected revenues while higher gasoline prices aggravated Transantiago's deficit in 2008 (see figure 6.3).[44] Government projections indicated a $1.076 million fiscal deficit to have accrued by 2010. The Concertación's 2009 plan hence called for fare increases (estimated at $40 pesos above the previously fixed $380 peso fare) as well as stricter anti-evasion programs. As a political alternative, the Alianza opposition (now known as the Coalición por el Cambio)[45] called for a new transport plan under an altogether new administration.

As 2008 wore on, the government and a growing number of experts seemed to reach a consensus that Transantiago would need a substantial subsidy in the foreseeable future. But opponents argued that Transantiago was a total fiasco, continuing to point their fingers at the Lagos and Bachelet governments.

Financing Transantiago and resolving the veritable crisis surrounding it had become a major challenge for the government. After five months of negotiations between House and Senatorial committees, Minister Cortázar submitted a proposal in March 2009 that similarly failed to reach a consensus. The proposed plan, which called for incremental spending to absorb the debt within several years, did not progress. This funding impasse continued, underscoring the party rivalries and political posturing before the December 2009 presidential election.

By May 2009, however, the Coalición por el Cambio opposition submitted its own proposal, posing a new agenda to finance the multimillion dollar deficit of Transantiago. The proposal outlined a new autonomous organism to improve service, adjust price based on real costs, and explore legislation for permanent subsidies and sovereign bonds to finance the accumulating debts. After presenting the proposal at the congressional headquarters, members of the Coalición por el Cambio rode on a Transantiago bus, paying with smart cards. Among the senators, politicians, and leaders involved, presidential candidate Sebastián Piñera led the group on a short trip applauded by bystanders and reported by the media. While the opposition's motion was not approved, the proposal and symbolic bus ride implied the possibility of an impending compromise to the logistical and political impasse plaguing Transantiago. These implications highlighted a new willingness on both sides to cooperate, but did not overshadow each party's own agendas and priorities for the upcoming presidential election and the following administration.

By mid-July 2009, a financial resolution was finally reached. The senate approved a previously submitted proposal by the Concertación government to establish a permanent subsidy of the transport system within Santiago and the surrounding regions. The proposal was initially introduced months before and underwent subsequent modifications based on continuous negotiations led by senatorial committees and complemented by government technicians and the opposition. The bill was first passed by the Chamber of Deputies with 43 votes in favor, 37 against, and 3 abstentions, and with the subsequent modifications to the proposal, the bill was passed in the Senate with 68 votes in favor, 12 against, and 1 abstention. The approved bill outlines financing of $3.460 billion between 2009 and 2014, subsidies guaranteeing the operation and funding of the Transantiago system for the next five years.[46] The initiative called for further construction of exclusive corridors and preferential scheduling for transit buses to alleviate city and regional congestion. However, both parties did not reach an agreement on two points: the creation of the Metropolitan Transport Authority and the payment of the BID and BancoEstado debts. Regardless, the political agreement was seen as a significant step in the development of transportation politics.

Despite the agreement, the Concertación and Coalición por el Cambio presented far from a united front. In announcing the new agreement reached by both parties, presidential candidate Sebastián Piñera (from the Coalición por el Cambio) called his own press conference, declaring, "Not always do the ones responsible for the problem make the announcement; sometimes, the one responsible for the solution is the one that makes the announcement."[47]

Political Consequences

It is difficult to underestimate the significance of Transantiago as a political issue affecting the very standing of Concertación. President Bachelet's high levels of approval upon taking office dropped in the ensuing months, partly as a result of what opponents saw as the Transantiago debacle. In August 2008, Bachelet's approval ratings were down to 42 percent, with the same polls showing a relation to the low approval rates for Transantiago (see figure 6.2). However, while rates of disapproval reached 46 percent in August, they dropped to 38 percent in September.[48]

Alianza por Chile and its allies in the opposition argued for the outright dismantling of the Transantiago system, maintaining that the original design as well as implementation was fatally flawed. Transantiago had become a rallying point against the administration. Meanwhile, debate raged within the ruling Concertación itself. Former president Lagos maintained that the original design of Transantiago was sound and was gaining international recognition, pointing to the implementation phase as the source of its major problems. President Bachelet and her cabinet sought to share responsibility with the Lagos administration for Transantiago.

Ricardo Lagos' popularity sank in late 2008 and he decided not to run for president in the 2009 election. Meanwhile, former president Frei proposed the creation of an independent public corporation similar to the one used in the metro system. Others demanded that the government pressure concessionaires to fully comply with contractual agreements or be eliminated from the system.

The financing issues raised by Transantiago had created political consequences and impeded progress. With each party blocking the other's proposals, Transantiago served various political agendas. Alianza insisted on the failure of Transantiago, advancing itself as the only alternative to fix the problems and penalize those responsible. Concertación worked hard to resolve problems, improve Transantiago, save face, and bolster ratings. The interface of finance and policy magnified political consequences and Transantiago's setbacks.

Overall Performance

The charged political debate surrounding Transantiago makes it very difficult to reach a balanced assessment. The very inadequacy of the public education campaign contributed to the criticism of such a momentous change of routes, bus frequencies, stops, and overall system operation (Figueroa and Orellana, 2007). The exclusive bus lanes, stops and advanced stations, new technology, and the elimination of old buses either had experienced costly delays or remained incomplete. These problems plagued the system since October 2005, the original launch date of the system delayed until February 2007.

Despite these problems, however, improvements were made through 2007–2009 and continue to take place. For instance, in September 2008, Transportation Minister Cortázar announced a round of substantive changes that included increased competition and flexibility in feeder lines connecting passengers to Metro stations and main bus lines. Enacted in response to recommendations from a panel of independent experts in January 2007, the measures included the threat to cancel one of the main concessions (Buses Gran Santiago) because of failure to run the number of buses to which they had agreed. In December 2009, the Supreme Court confirmed that several Transantiago bus operators, Express Santiago 1, STP, and Gran Santiago would have to pay fines totaling $700 million pesos. The fines were issued after an initial verdict from the Santiago Court of Appeals for problems with bus frequency, plan operation, and technology failures. The Supreme Court decided that it was the responsibility of the operators, not the Transantiago system and the national emergency funds, to cover the cost. As such, the operators were ultimately ordered to pay fines totaling $1.4 million.

After his inauguration, President Piñera named Felipe Morandé as his new minister of transportation. The first major initiative of the new team was to launch a new plan to reduce the high number of Transantiago's fare evaders. As of February 2010, the level of evasion had risen to 17.8 percent, which corresponds to a loss of $3.6 billion pesos. In the anti-evasion plan, evasion infractions would be fined between $73,300 to $184,300 pesos. Additionally, those who failed to pay the fines would be subject to community service or denied access to certain governmentally granted social benefits. The plan called for an increase in the number of supervisory agents, increasing from 30 to 60.

At the same time, Transantiago experienced two consecutive fare increases. The second increase was justified as a way to reduce the system's deficit because Transantiago was "financially unsustainable." Explaining the recent fare increases and anti-evasion fines and stringency, Minister of Transport Felipe Morandé said that "the reality of finances is worse than what was estimated from the outset of Transantiago." Transantiago's deficit was $365 billion pesos as of May 2010, attributed largely to high evasion and to the previous government's unwillingness to increase fares during its last year in office. According to evaluations from the Piñera administration, Transantiago cost the government $800 million (an amount said to have equalled the cost of building eight hospitals). Still, Minister Morandé stated that the plan was to gradually diminish the deficit by 2012, the year set as the goal date to improve the transport system. But deficits continued.

The progress and evaluation of Transantiago continues to be both intertwined with political agendas and the resultant political consequences. In fact, new realities and dynamics in public transportation are in place. Specialists agree on the viability of an improved Transantiago and return to the old system appears highly unlikely.

Conclusion

This study of urban transformation in Chile's capital city provides a preliminary description and assessment of the planning and implementation phases of Transantiago and of the system of concessions and partnerships on which it is based. This system appears consolidated in Chile, where the concept of concessions and partnerships have come to be accepted.

Fifteen years after its inauguration in early 1993, Chile's concessions and partnership programs served as a model for other countries to study. It was featured as the region's paradigm at a CEPAL meeting in November 2008. Minister of public works Sergio Bitar pointed out that the concessions program had provided $11.4 billion in public infrastructure through that year. The US Treasury Department gave Chile's program an enthusiastic endorsement. Still, the Chilean government aimed to improve the law of concessions in regards to resolving conflicts between the public and private sectors.[49]

Other tentative conclusions can be arrived at. Continuity in high-level leadership had been a noteworthy aspect of the concessions and partnerships program. The policymakers of Concertación provided bold political leadership creating the legal and regulatory conditions required for the design and implementation for urban reform and related projects. By the same token, the shortcomings of Transantiago were also related to leadership factors. The political vacuum surrounding the last year of Lagos presidency and the first of Michele Bachelet's was an important component. In the context of a succession, implementation had moved to a lower level in the bureaucracy and was placed in the hands of young and promising staff unprepared for the serious challenges posed by Transantiago's launching. High-level members of the cabinet ultimately addressed the problems and took responsibility of Transantiago.

A presidential order of April 16, 2013, created the Metropolitan Public Transportation Board (DTPM) to provide a better institutional framework to Transantiago. The DTPM replaced the Committee of Urban Transportation Ministers of Santiago. The board's major tasks are to articulate, coordinate, and follow up the transportation actions, programs, and measures taken and developed by the various public and private actors responsible for the city's transportation plan.

The list of remaining challenges is long. The nature of the contracts with concessionaires and partners is a critical matter—flawed contracts with Transantiago providers are blamed for additional risk exposure. Well-designed regulatory regimes are needed to help steer projects out of major problems such as those of Transantiago. Regulatory frameworks with a solid legal base are financially capable, and have operational autonomy, succeed in avoiding certain risks and in bringing rates of return in line with the cost of capital. Improvement in government capabilities is essential, as are further investments in financial experts and personnel.

Chilean politicians soon learned that failures can have very high, unexpected costs. Michelle Bachelet had to endure low ratings. So did former president Ricardo Lagos, for whom Transantiago may have cost the possibility of running again in 2009 as his candidacy was unable to gather sufficient support.

Still, concessions and partnerships firmed up as a key tool of public policy. New infrastructure projects relied on them: roads, water, sanitation, jails, and schools, among others. Indeed, 2009 reports from the Ministry of Public Works project a renewed commitment to infrastructure concessions and a 136 percent increase in project investment from 2008. Despite Transantiago's complications and a three-year period between 2004 and 2007 without tendered projects,[50] the Chilean program remained committed to public-private collaboration.

In December 2009, President Bachelet signed a bill revising the Concessions Law, allowing the government and particularly the minister of public works to increase technical standards for concessions and refine the rights of the concessionaires in cases of economic compensation for unanticipated costs, the reduction of fines for certain highway concession infractions, as well as the termination of a concession for the public good by offering compensation to match investments. This bill used the lessons learned from Transantiago, identifying mistakes and implementing measures to prevent recurring mistakes. During the presentation of this bill, President Bachelet had cited that over the last 20 years Chile had lived through an infrastructure revolution in which the concession model made a major contribution.

Chilean policymakers have had to reevaluate basic assumptions leading to Transantiago. Original plans failed to work and major adjustments needed to be made, especially in terms of finances. A World Bank report argues that infrastructure concessions in Latin America are in fact highly risky as investment projects. While up to 40–50 percent may never be sufficiently profitable, those that become profitable do so only after ten years. The rate of renegotiation in infrastructure concessions within three years of signing contract reaches 42 percent.

The more complex the form of public-private collaboration, the more likely it is that they should be framed as part of learning processes involving the development of realistic assumptions, new institutional capabilities, and trained new staff with technical expertise—all of which need to be codified into government institutions. Chile must digest all these experiences, both its successes and failures, in order to arrive at a fully successful new approach to as complex an infrastructure project as Transantiago.

CHAPTER SEVEN

Conclusion: Changing States

Latin American states responded to cycles of crisis and globalization since the 1980s by refining their roles in economic and social development. These reform processes aimed at economic growth, stabilization, and competitiveness, but also equity and environmental sustainability. Infrastructure ranked high in this regard. Mexico, Brazil, Chile, Colombia, and Peru built on liberalizing reforms initiated in the 1980s to launch public-private collaboration initiatives to expand infrastructure provision. In a few other cases, such programs met difficulties, backlash, and seemingly Polanyian opposition. This volume has explored ten key cases to identify proximate political and institutional conditions affecting outcomes. Figure B.1 presents a working framework organizing the part of the analysis focused on institutions, while discussions have explored evolving relationship between them and political economic dynamics.

The above review of programs and projects permits several statements about magnitude, characteristics, and trends in the adoption of public-private collaboration in infrastructure. On balance, these experiments have gained considerable momentum and appear set for further expansion. A main force in this trend is the need for a new generation of infrastructure from global interconnectedness together with a new realism regarding the limits of state action (Cipoletta et al., 2010; ECLAC, 2010a).[1]

International financial crises after 1997 brought down but hardly stopped the rate of adoption of concessions and partnerships. The global economic crisis of 2007–2008 was not able to stop the trend toward concessions and partnerships partly linked to the commodities booms of the 2000s. Their number across countries discussed in this volume increased from an yearly average of 58.6 projects and $25 billion reaching financial closure between 2000 and 2007 to 78.5 projects worth $28 billion between 2008 and 2013.[2] External shocks related to financial crisis did not necessarily stop collaborative projects with the private sector or return to the prior levels of state-centrism in Argentina, Bolivia, and Ecuador.

Latin American economies responded generally well to the global recession of 2008 due in large part to previous cycles of reform in response to crises in the 1980s and 1990s as well as to subsequent commodity booms driven by Asian markets.

Beyond demonstrating its significance, this study situates the phenomenon of public-private collaboration in a dynamic analytical context. Learning to overcome failures and shortcomings to design simple concessions was a requirement for more complex partnerships and programs in Mexico, Chile, Brazil, and some Andean cases. Prior experience in launching successful concessions program creates capabilities essential to the implementation of effective public-private partnerships. While Latin American policymakers have come to agree about the urgent need for better infrastructure, many of them have also concluded that the state alone cannot underwrite such large investments required by development and modernization. Problems in cases where domestic civil society is not fully incorporated into these initiatives show that consultation is necessary to further consolidate the learning process, create durable policy consensus, and build sustained competencies; the idea has thus also spread that sustainability builds on public support. In this context, public-private collaboration in infrastructure provision appears likely to expand.

International policy networks and the transborder sharing of models shape the initiation and sustainability of concessions and partnership models, at least in the short run. Global policies support domestic experiences in several ways, including the diffusion of paradigms, practices, and resources encouraging private sector participation in public infrastructure. Concessions and public-private partnerships are spreading in part because of sustained contacts with such sources as the Inter-American Development Bank, the Andean Development Corporation, the World Bank, or other international agencies. Business and professional groups are important. Their international meetings and forums explore and compare individual regional experiences, share lessons and best practices, promote networks, and generate better understandings of the paths and paradigms developing in the region. All Latin American cases in this volume acquired or are obtaining knowledge and expertise from other experiences. Cooperation agreements between North and

Latin American countries or within the latter have not served quite the role of those used by the European Union as part of its economic cooperation and integration efforts. Still, business and regional summits regularly bring together private and public actors in the Americas. This integration from below lacks the conditionalities and broad impact of the European patterns, though agencies at all levels of government develop links to multilateral and regional development organizations.

In the above framework, the government develops skills as regulator or partner of private operators. This shift needs to be better understood. The combination of bureaucratic development with effective connections to dynamic entrepreneurs, broadly what Evans called "embedded autonomy" works in public-private collaboration for infrastructure in a manner somewhat similar to the information technology explored by Evans. But the new forms of collaboration require distinctive institutional frameworks and mechanisms. Coordination goes beyond, with traditional techniques provided by market or hierarchical governance. It calls for sustained long-term networks that are flexible and responsive to long-term adaptation to the uncertain environment. Trust between partners is a crucial factor reducing transaction cost. Functions to coordinate these means new competencies: training appropriate personnel and placing them in strategic positions in the public bureaucracy. Transparency and accountability are essential to prevent selective relationships with the private sector from lapsing into traditional rent-seeking behavior and outright corruption. That is, sustained private participation raises distinctive issues.

In addition, planning and strategic thinking are needed to identify and assess changing national priorities and demands from sectors, regions, and cities. Large, dynamic, and central metropolitan areas such as São Paulo and Santiago have exceptional needs in transportation and logistics projects. Policymakers need to open channels to public opinion and address issues of public perception and societal concerns as public support is essential. Public discontent increased throughout Latin America even after relatively successful implementation of projects entailing private operators due to perceptions of corruption, community and environmental impact, higher costs, or animosity toward foreign investment and the wealthy.

While new agencies, often linked to finance ministries and able to work with line ministries and planners, are needed to manage concessions and partnerships, these can be difficult to achieve as some developing countries are still struggling to create functional basic bureaucracies and a civil service. Below a certain level of administrative development, inadequate institutions can be an insurmountable handicap.

New practices thus imply new structures and functions. The partnering role calls for organizational development to design an effective framework delegating responsibilities to private actors. Above all, political actors need to build a national consensus that endures across governments.

Capabilities reflect the underlying strength of the state as an institution. But relatively weak national bureaucracies and insufficient expertise can result in unbalanced negotiations and conflict between the public and the private sectors. The public sector is often at a disadvantage as project managers in the private sector are more experienced and better prepared than government representatives. Lack of managerial skills and experience in the public sector reduces the ability of public officials to monitor and control projects in the operational stage.

The Latin American cases discussed in this volume confirm that savings achieved through concessions or partnerships can readily disappear when all factors are taken into account. The cost of Transantiago greatly increased after taking into account the adjustments and renegotiation to make the system function. Cost overruns are also common in Brazil. The acquisition of managerial competence by public officials remains a significant challenge in Latin America, where there is great need to train cadres in ministries and specialized units. The review of cases tends to confirm that specialized units within the public service are needed to create conditions for success. Chile does not have one, but the transportation and public works ministries have been in charge. In Brazil, where one was announced, effective control of specific projects is exercised by the ministries in specific infrastructure sectors.

Governments in these emergent or developing societies wanted to solve infrastructure problems rapidly, but they lacked professional project managers. The results were often hasty tendering and contracting processes, cancellation of projects, politically influenced decisions, corruption, and excessively high costs to government. In turn, these outcomes fueled a very negative public reaction or backlash of public opinion about partnerships (Brenck et al., 2005).

A main challenge of public-private partnerships is proper risk allocation. Uncertainty or scare knowledge are risk factors that need to be distributed between public and private parties. The rule is to distribute risks to the actor most capable of managing them at the lowest costs—conditioned in reality by the government goal to transfer financial risks to the private sector. Improper risk evaluation and allocation do result in higher costs.

Political Dynamics

The cases discussed in this book tend to confirm the centrality of political dynamics in the reform processes leading to public-private collaboration. In Chile, the reformist Concertación alliance governing the country between 1990 and 2010 provided essential leadership, political commitment, and sustained support, effectively framing policy innovations in this area as key part of a national policy. In this context, policymakers were able to design and implement ambitious infrastructure and development plans and mechanisms for collaboration between the public and private sectors. Transantiago is illustrative. If political leadership was critical in the Transantiago plan, political and institutional lapses at a later point contributed to a disastrous inauguration and subsequent public dissatisfaction. The relaxed political leadership during the last year of the Ricardo Lagos administration and the first year of Michelle Bachelet's first administration created a costly vacuum at a moment requiring sustained leadership in such a large undertaking, that is, well-conceived and institutionalized support from those in high-level position in government and the public bureaucracy. In Chile, lapses in political leadership might have been partly compensated by a strong institutional presence.

In contrast, Brazil's problem was in part for policymakers who proceeded with too much caution or even timidity as they officially embraced public-private partnerships and a wider use of concessions. Lukewarm national leadership through 2006 led to delays and confusion about the program. The concessions program took off on a larger scale in 2007–2008, during Lula da Silva's second term with the announcement of the PAC program. Infrastructure investment became a main element of cabinet member and prospective presidential candidate Dilma Rousseff's bid to succeed Lula as president. A large number of plans were made prior to 2010, but their intimate association with the political ambitious of incumbents led to problems. Long-term projects often experience several election cycles before they are completed and national consensus may be essential for their continuity. Private contractors and the general public pay these extra costs. Still, there are grounds to surmise that Brazil may remain on course. The Lula presidency's eventual embrace of private sector provision of infrastructure pointed toward the appropriation of yet a reform mechanism initially conceived and launched in the context of the state reforms of the 1990s. Some analysts remain skeptical of PAC's megaprojects, launched as they are in a political year and directly associated with the political platform of an official candidate, but they do reflect a growing consensus about national priorities.

In other Latin American cases, plans for concessions and partnerships with the private sector has brought acrimonious and enduring tensions with opposition parties. In the absence of a working consensus among consequential political actors, long-term stability may be compromised. Political or policy disagreements often lead to low levels of public support. In the 2000s, distrust of Mexican policies viewed as favoring business owed in large measure to political tensions between the three major parties. Even though major parties agreed on policy, political conditions did not allow decisive leadership. These failures were due in part to instabilities inherent in its dynamics of democratization.

Political impetus by a single leader or party often backfires, as new governments are tempted to renege on the initial contract. Breach of contract by the public sector can result in lawsuits and possible compensation for private actors, further increasing public costs. As noted, both major political alliances in Chile agree on basic policy in this area.

Leadership goes beyond nominal support for policy. Above all, it means the deployment of political capital to launch and protect a state reform initiative even in the presence of debate. Political leadership is the willingness to mobilize and allocate necessary resources and implement programs and projects. High levels of leadership and long-term commitment are needed for serious private investors to participate. Developing and transitional societies in particular are often lacking in this regard.

Effective advocacy networks and public support can be decisive. Failure of civil society to participate in the design and implementation of projects can result in major setbacks. Governments have major responsibility to actively involve civil society actors in the design and implementation of projects at the beginning. For example, omitting environmental activists, interest groups, or local communities in an early phase can result in major setbacks. Twentieth-century statism is a lingering legacy throughout the world, not just in transitional societies. Public-private participation is shaped by the larger context, including the level and features of democratization, the prevalence of a technocratic ethos, political coherence, and the like. Governments are often expected to provide infrastructure and the private sector is often distrusted. These beliefs are more marked in Brazil than in Chile. Political movements in favor of larger state roles relative to private sector set back the reform process in Venezuela, Bolivia, Ecuador, and other countries, as discussed in Chapter Three.

Learning to Partner

Economic, political, and social environments are likely to change during the lifespan of long-term partnerships, thus creating multiple sources of uncertainty affecting outcomes. Authorities and partners need strategic flexibility to address unexpected obstacles and unintended consequences. Realistically, programs of public-private collaboration evolve over many years. The willingness to accept and learn from unexpected challenges calls for a learning approach taking considerable time to mature.

The political and institutional dynamics in the creation and consolidation of public-private partnership is normally embedded in a state reform process in which values, norms, and organized behavior need to change for the reforms to advance and take hold. The state itself is the locus of transformation.

In this broader context, the very concepts of private infrastructure investment and business-government collaboration may be at issue. Most modern societies have a permanent debate about the scope of the private sector in both respects, including what roles the state should play in public service. In changing or developing societies, these questions are often part of polarizing debates about values and political doctrine or ideology. Highly developed democratic societies may indicate paths to resolve such debates and provide practices and policies to be emulated. Some Latin American countries already provide examples of help to others. But the simple adoption of "best practices" from countries facing different political, economic, or cultural scenarios is fraught with major risks from the different political and institutional realities. To a considerable extent, each needs to develop its own way of translating them into lasting local solutions. Above all, successful programs are unlikely to take root without a long endogenous process of social learning regarding complex issues such as the acceptance of a large number of economic freedoms giving private actors control of the spheres of production, exchange, finance, and innovation. Venezuela, Bolivia, Nicaragua, Ecuador, and Argentina provide examples of societies with strong populist and statist movements with animosity toward the very idea of expanding the role of the private sector. In these cases, the kind of learning conducive to partnering values will be slow at best. Lasting state reform is unlikely in the absence of political support, but even then concessions and partnerships can survive. Deeper forms of institutional learning can take place at the proper time.

In general, Latin America societies are experimenting with partnerships between the public and private sectors, but this process needs to be nourished. A next big step is to expand norms, organizations, and practices favoring transparency and openness, civil service development, clear property rights, and more effective rule of law to regulate interactions between economic and political actors.

More effective government agencies and organizations is particularly pressing. Important capabilities—expertise, risk evaluation, cost assessment, and financial modelling, new corps in the civil services with high-level skills and organizational abilities—are often in short supply. Frustrated expectations and failure are likely in the absence of institutional development. As discussed, unintended consequences, setbacks, surges in opposition, and changed parameters impede sustained expansion of projects and programs.

Consider the learning and strategic effort to effectively deal with issues of cost assessment. Maintaining a partnership between private and public actors is more costly in a PPP project than in a traditional short-term contract or a simple regular concession. More so in the latter, the public party needs to take additional measures to monitor performance, regulate the policy field, flag deviations from objectives, and take remedial action. This calls for clearly specified outcome or performance indicators. But contracts are unlikely to anticipate changed conditions in two or three decades. It is more difficult to monitor the performance of private actors in fast-changing fields such as IT and other technology-related sectors. In sectors where public objectives could generally enter into conflict with cost-saving measures by private parties (health care, education), monitoring also becomes problematic and contractual renegotiations are needed. For these and other reasons such as underestimated inflation, full project costs often exceed expectations (Reeves and Ryan, 2007).

As conditions change, there must be a mechanism by which the partnering arrangements can be adjusted or updated. Often, this means refinancing. While the goal is to reduce renegotiations that benefit private operators, clauses regulating renegotiation may reduce the possibility of demands ("extortion") for more financing by the private party.[3] At one extreme, the absence of refinancing or renegotiating options might cause serious damage to public-private projects. Disagreements frequently escalate into legal conflict between the public and the private parties, while court litigation is generally slow and costly. Part of the answer is to prescribe clear channels and mechanisms for how the partners will discuss and negotiate contract modifications and how independent mediators can help develop rapid compromises between the parties.

Though institutional legacies shape reform trajectories, these often reflect institutional patterns in need of change. New capabilities and institutional adaptations need to endure in a changed context. In turn, these "deep" forms of institutional transformation take place through unusual forces like political leadership and action and coalitions with powerful economic interests (Portes, 2010). Aspects of globalization may contribute policy networks and advice to embed domestic experiences.

Globalization

On balance, international responses to the global financial crisis and recession of 2007–2008 reinforced a broad policy consensus to maintain preexisting patterns of trade and open investment, resisting calls for economic autarky and protectionism. Latin American leaders and delegations to world summits, such as G-20 gatherings or Asia-Pacific economic cooperation, endorsed building international ties and resisted new export restrictions or trade barriers.[4] These international forums underscored the need for infrastructure development, foreign investment and trade, support for capital market expansion, and the role of the private sector in national development, and public-private collaboration.

Initial worries about the crisis' impact on Latin America had been ameliorated by the commodities boom that survived from 2009 to early 2013, as Asian economic and demographic expansion continued to drive the high demand for minerals, soy, and other natural resources. In addition, anticrisis stimulus plans called for massive investments in infrastructure throughout many parts of the world, such as China's stimulus package increased spending in roads and rail infrastructure, while the United States announced spending as a response to the global downswing.[5] Though not fully considered, Latin America's dependence on commodities and Chinese economic relations presented important risks as of late 2014. The international prices for iron ore, copper, and other minerals were experiencing severe downswings, while soy and other crops faced different conditions. Was this part of a traditional "boom and bust" pattern of commodity-led economic growth cycle? What would be its economic impact? Which countries would do well? The close dependence on Chinese markets is likely to act as a transmission belt for factors shaping economic demand, such as change in development strategy, demographic ageing and other problems. As a whole, the Latin American cases discussed in this volume confirm the worldwide shift toward partnership through 2013—adding to the literature on public-private collaboration, the various forms it takes, the conditions under which they blossom, and the challenges they create. Capabilities and dynamics vary substantially across national and subnational programs, responding in part to the processes of public sector reform and innovation in which they are embedded. Success in partnering programs entails complex changes at the institutional, political, and cultural levels. These processes are historically situated in the great transformations associated with the era of reform and globalization in the 1970s and 1980s. In general, these changes take time to consolidate themselves.

Open systems of governance rely on organizational cohesion, social societal receptivity to new ideas and actors, and trust in government institutions. As open-ended processes of innovation in systems of governance, capabilities represent but also reinforce broader processes of institutional change. They aim at increasing adaptability to evolving environments and conditions. Learning processes drive institutional change. These innovations advance as a result of learning on the part of politicians, public officials, business leaders, and the public at large. Partnering with business is often a revolutionary idea that may be alien to bureaucrats and the public. Players may have internalized biases against such ideas as paying tolls to concessionaires to use roads and bridges—particularly when public authorities are implicated in the scheme. These views may be grounded in inherited ideological preferences regarding the roles of government and business in the provision of infrastructure.

The new learning is also increasingly global—as the innovations, resources, partners, and clients are widely dispersed throughout the world. Large infrastructure projects are often embedded in global or transnational networks about which considerable amounts of knowledge need to be learned. A relational or networking approach may thus helps connect and better understand the multiplicity of the new actors and relationships in this changing policy domain. The challenge here is to map out the core universe of consequential actors, relationships, and organizational forms embedded in preexisting institutions as well as in emergent developments. Besides trade expansion, aspects of globalization such as transnational production, finances, innovation, other responses to crisis, and the like lead to new, more complex, and more dynamic policy domains.

Advocates of the state need not fear its withering away as a result of the expanding role of civil and private society actors and economic globalization. Enhanced and sophisticated institutional capabilities are necessary to plan, launch, and manage large-scale concessions and partnerships. Instead of contracting, these imply considerably state development, though in new ways.

APPENDIX A

Tables and Graphs

Competitiveness and Public-Private Collaboration

Table A.1 Public-private investments (1990–2013), developing/emergent countries, in $ billions

	Number	*Divestiture*[a]	*Concessions*[b]	*Greenfield Projects*[c]	*Mgt/ Lease*[d]	*Total*
Latin America	1,841	251.7	236.9	355.4	0.38	845.1
Europe and Central Asia	849	123.8	29.7	190.1	6.1	349.7
East Asia and Pacific	1,779	76	51.5	254.9	0.22	382.7
Middle East and North Africa	151	20.1	10.3	67.2	0.2	97.9
South Asia	1,027	20.8	64.2	288.6	0.2	373.9
Sub-Saharan Africa	499	25.4	10.3	113.8	0.1	149.7

Note: a. A private entity buys an equity stake in a state-owned enterprise through an asset sale, public offering, or mass privatization program.

b. A private entity takes over the management of a state-owned enterprise for a given period during which it also assumes significant investment risk.

c. A private entity or a public-private joint venture builds and operates a new facility for the period specified in the project contract. The facility returns to the public sector at the end of the concession period.

d. A private entity takes over the management of a state-owned enterprise for a fixed period while ownership and investment decisions remain with the state.

Source: World Bank, 2014a.

Table A.2 Competitiveness ranking, 2005–2014. Based on WEF Global Competitiveness Index

	2005 *(122)*	*2006* *(122)*	*2007* *(131)*	*2008* *(134)*	*2009* *(133)*	*2010* *(139)*	*2011* *(142)*	*2012* *(144)*	*2013* *(148)*	*2014* *(144)*
Chile	27	27	26	28	30	30	31	33	34	33
Mexico	59	58	52	60	60	66	58	53	55	61
Brazil	57	66	72	64	56	58	53	48	56	57
Peru	77	74	86	83	78	73	67	61	61	65
Colombia	58	65	69	74	69	68	68	69	69	66
Ecuador	87	90	103	104	105	105	101	86	71	71
Uruguay	70	73	75	75	65	64	63	74	85	80
Bolivia		99	105	118	120	108	103	104	98	105
Argentina	54	69	85	88	85	87	85	94	104	104
Paraguay		107	121	124	124	120	122	116	119	120
Venezuela	84	88	98	105	113	122	124	126	134	131
Panama	65	57	59	58	59	53	49	40	40	48
Costa Rica	56	53	63	59	55	56	61	57	54	51
Guatemala	95	75	87	84	80	78	84	83	86	78
El Salvador	60	61	67	79	77	82	91	101	97	84
Nicaragua	96	95	111	120	115	112	115	108	99	99
Dominican Republic	91	83	96	98	95	101	110	105	105	101
Honduras	97	93	83	82	89	91	86	90	111	100

Note: Weighted average of 12 components: Institutions, infrastructure, macroeconomic stability, health and primary education, higher education and training, goods market efficiency, financial market sophistication, technological readiness, market size, business sophistication, and innovation.

* Number of countries included in that ranking.

Source: World Economic Forum (2005–2013), *The Global Competitiveness Report*.

Table A.3 PPP Readiness Index 2012

	Rank	*Score*	*Main Challenges*
Brazil	2	71.3	Laws/regulation, political consensus, financial facilities
Mexico	4	63.8	Investment climate, regulatory framework
Southern Cone			
Chile	1	76.4	Regulatory checks, subnational adjustment
Uruguay	6	49.5	Operational maturity, financial facilities, subnational adjustments
Paraguay	14	28.9	Operational maturity, institutional framework, subnational adjustments, other
Argentina	18	17.5	Political will, financial facilities, subnational adjustment factor, other
Andes			
Peru	3	69.6	Subnational adjustments, planning capacity.
Colombia	5	59.5	Laws/regulations, operational maturity
Ecuador	17	19.9	Institutional framework, laws/regulations, investment climate, others
Bolivia	NA	NA	NA
Venezuela	19	5.1	Institutions, operational maturity, investment climate, other
Central America			
Costa Rica	8	38.8	Regulatory framework, subnational adjustment, investment climate
El Salvador	9	38.2	Laws/regulations, investment climate, political consensus, other
Honduras	12	33.7	Laws/regulations, financial facilities, other
Panama	11	34.0	Institutional framework, operational maturity, subnational adjustment
Guatemala	7	43.2	Financial facilities, subnational adjustment, operational maturity.
Nicaragua	16	20.4	Financial facilities, investment climate, other.
Caribbean			
Dominican Republic	15	25.7	Laws/regulation, institutional framework, operational maturity, others.
Jamaica	13	30.0	Operational maturity, financial facilities, other
Trinidad and Tobago	10	34.3	Operational maturity, investment climate, other

Note: Report ranks nineteen countries. Weights of ranking criteria: legal and regulatory framework (25 percent); institutional framework (20 percent); operational maturity (15 percent); investment climate (15 percent); financial facilities (15 percent); subnational adjustment factor (10 percent).

Source: Economist Intelligence Unit, Infrascope 2012.

Table A.4 Brazil and Chile, public-private collaboration in infrastructure by subsector, 1990–2013

	Brazil		*Chile*	
Sector	*Num*	*$ million*	*Num*	*$ million*
Energy				
Electricity	373	166,493	53	16,403
Natural gas	17	8,854	8	2,672
Subtotal	**390**	**175,347**	**61**	**19,075**
Telecom	36	162,600	10	4,451
Transport				
Airports	14	15,411	15	617
Railroads	18	28,258	4	128
Roads	64	33,225	35	9,761
Seaports	53	11,100	12	1,869
Subtotal	**149**	**87,994**	**66**	**12,375**
Water				
Sewerage	14	696	3	68
Utility	98	11,654	18	7,202
Subtotal	**112**	**11,350**	**21**	**7,270**
Total	**694**	**438,291**	**158**	**43,171**

Note: Num = number of projects.

Source: World bank, 2014a.

Table A.5 Argentina and Mexico, public-private investment in infrastructure by subsector, 1990–2013

	Argentina		*Mexico*	
Subsector	*Num*	*$ million*	*Num*	*$ million*
Energy				
Electricity	93	21,856	39	12,456
Natural gas	15	11,144	28	3,166
Subtotal	**108**	**33,001**	**67**	**15,622**
Telecom	7	39,226	15	72,042
Transport				
Airports	5	2,381	6	3,324
Railroads	18	5,574	8	6,168
Roads	45	5,507	70	24,658
Seaports	16	894	27	2,139
Subtotal	**84**	**14,356**	**111**	**36,289**
Water and Sewerage		–	29	2,712
Utility	19	8,176	5	250
Subtotal	**19**	**8,176**	**34**	**2,962**
Total	**218**	**94,758**	**227**	**126,915**

Note: Num = number of projects.

Source: World Bank, 2014a.

Table A.6 Andes countries, private collaboration in infrastructure by subsector, 1990–2013

	Colombia		*Peru*		*Ecuador*		*Bolivia*	
Sector	*Num*	*$ million*	*Num*	*$*	*Num*	*$*	*Num*	*$*
Energy								
Electricity	26	10,108	51	12,154	6	461	11	548
Natural Gas	11	1,059	2	990			3	3,211
Subtotal	**37**	**11,167**	**53**	**13,144**	**6**	**461**	**14**	**3,759**
Telecom	9	16,884	9	14,384	5	4,171	5	1,494
Transport								
Airports	8	1,374	4	687	3	665	2	117
Railroads	25	500	4	352			3	69
Roads	2	4,033	19	4,424	6	730		
Seaports	11	2,337	5	1,201	4	765		
Subtotal	**46**	**8,244**	**32**	**6,664**	**13**	**2,160**	**5**	**185**
Water								
Sewerage	3	168	3	334				
Utility	48	772	1	72	4	510	2	682
Transfer			1	120				
Subtotal	**51**	**940**	**5**	**526**	**4**	**510**	**2**	**682**
Total	**143**	**37,235**	**99**	**34,718**	**28**	**7,303**	**26**	**6,121**

Note: Num = number of projects.

Source: World Bank, 2014a.

Table A.7 Uruguay and Paraguay, public-private collaboration in infrastructure by sector, 1990–2013

	Uruguay		*Paraguay*	
Sector	*Num*	*$ million*	*Num*	*$ million*
Energy				
Electricity	8	3,164		
Natural Gas	3	416		
Telecom	2	615	4	1,660
Transport				
Airports	2	195		
Roads	2	85	1	58
Seaports	2	87		
Subtotal	**6**	**367**		
Water				
Utility	2	378		
Total	**21**	**4,940**	**5**	**1,718**

Notes: Num = number of projects.

Source: World Bank, 2014a.

Table A.8 Trade patterns, Brazil, Mexico, Chile, as percent of total trade, 2012

	Brazil		*Mexico*		*Chile*	
Main trading partners	*Import*	*Export*	*Import*	*Export*	*Import*	*Export*
European Union	21.4	20.2	11.0	5.9	13.4	15.3
United States	14.6	11.1	50.1	77.8	22.2	12.3
China	15.3	17.0	15.4	1.5	18.2	23.3
Argentina	7.4	7.4	–	–	6.6	–
Brazil	–	–	–	1.5	6.5	5.5
Japan	–	3.3	4.8	–	–	10.7
Main group (shares)						
Agricultural products	5.9	35.6	7.3	6.2	8.0	24.2
Fuels and mining products	20.9	27.0	11.6	17.8	24.4	60.4
Manufactures	73.1	33.8	78.2	72.7	67.5	13.3
Share in world total	1.25	1.38	2.04	2.01	0.43	0.43

Source: World Trade Organization Statistics Database, current as of March 2014.

Table A.9 Trade patterns, Argentina, Colombia, Peru, as percent of total trade, 2012

	Argentina		*Colombia*		*Peru*	
Main trading partners	*Import*	*Export*	*Import*	*Export*	*Import*	*Export*
European Union	17.9	14.7	12.6	15.1	11.9	17.1
United States	12.4	5.1	24.3	36.9	19.0	14.2
China	14.5	6.2	16.5	5.5	18.5	17.1
Brazil	26.1	20.4	4.8	–	6.1	–
Mexico	3.3	–	11.0	–	–	–
Main group (shares)						
Agricultural products	3.6	53.3	10.5	11.0	11.3	16.8
Fuels and mining products	15.8	10.2	8.8	66.7	15.3	50.2
Manufactures	79.6	31.2	79.6	17.3	73.2	11.5
Share in world total	0.44	0.34	0.32	0.33	0.23	0.25

Source: World Trade Organization Statistics Database, current as of March 2014.

Table A.10 Main commodity exports, 2012

Country	*Exports (% GDP)*	*Top five commodities (% of exports)*	*Main commodities*
Argentina	19.7	45.1	Soybeans and derivatives (22.4%), vehicles and trucks (9.7%), corn (6%), wheat (3.8%), petroleum (3.2%)
Brazil	12.5	35.3	Iron ore (12.8%), crude petroleum (8.4%), soybeans and derivatives (7.1), sugar (4.1%), poultry (2.9%)
Chile	34.2	65.4	Copper and derivatives (53%), fish (4%), minerals (3.3%), wood pulp (2.9%), wines (2.2%)
Colombia	18.2	74.9	Petroleum and derivatives (51.9%), coal (12.1%), gold (5.6%), coffee (3.2%), flowers (2.1%)
Ecuador	31.1	81.9	Petroleum and derivatives (56.9%), sea food (11.5%), bananas (8.7%), flowers (3.2%), gold (1.6%)
Mexico	32.8	35.3	Crude petroleum (12.7%), vehicles (7.8%), vehicle parts (5.1%), computers (5%), broadcasting devices (4.7%)
Peru	25.6	59	Copper and derivatives (22.6%), gold (21.1), derivatives from petroleum (7.1%), lead ore (4.3%), animal meal (3.9%)
Venezuela	26.1	98.5	Petroleum and derivatives (93.6%), coal tar (3.3%) natural gas (1%), iron ores (0.6%)
Bolivia	47.2	82.1	Petroleum and gas (54.8%), platinum (9.4%), soybeans and derivatives (9%), zinc (6.9%), tin ore (2%)
Uruguay	26.2	45.6	Beef (16.1%), soy (16%), rice (5.2%), wheat (4.5%), milk and derivatives (3.8%)
Paraguay	46.6	77.1	Electricity (30.7%), soy (23.6%), beef (10.4), corn (7.5%), wheat (4.9%)

Source: Export (% GDP) data from World Bank. Commodities data from Economic Commission for Latin America and the Caribbean, Databases and Statistical Publications, 2014.

Economic Growth, Inflation, and Debt, 1980–2013

Table A.11 GDP growth (G), inflation (I), external debt (D, as % GNI)

	Brazil			*Mexico*			*Chile*			*Argentina*		
	G	*I*	*D*	*G*	*I*	*D*	*G*	*I*	*D*	*G*	*I*	*D*
1980	9.1	–	31.7	9.2	26.4	30.6	8.1	35.1*	46.0	4.2	100.8	35.8
1981	***−4.4***	101.7	32.4	8.8	27.9	32.7	4.7	19.6*	50.8	***−5.7***	104.5	46.6
1982	***0.6***	100.5	35.3	***−0.6***	58.9	53.4	***−10.3***	9.9*	78.1	***−5.0***	164.8	55.3
1983	***−3.4***	135.0	51.7	***−4.2***	101.7	66.7	***−3.8***	27.2*	100.3	3.9	343.8	47.0
1984	5.3	192.1	52.9	***3.6***	65.5	57.4	8.0	19.8*	115.5	***2.2***	626.7	65.4
1985	7.9	226.0	49.4	***2.6***	57.7	55.3	7.1	30.7*	142.1	***−7.6***	672.2	61.1
1986	8.0	147.1	42.8	***−3.8***	86.2	82.9	5.6	19.4*	134.4	7.9	90.1	49.7
1987	***3.6***	228.3	42.6	***1.9***	131.8	82.2	6.6	19.8*	112.5	2.9	131.3	55.4
1988	***−0.1***	629.1	37.2	***1.2***	114.2	56.5	7.3	14.6*	86.7	***−2.6***	343.0	49.0
1989	***3.3***	1430.7	25.6	4.2	20.0	43.8	10.6	17.0*	68.5	***−7.5***	3079	93.3
1990	***−4.3***	2947.7	26.8	5.1	26.7	41.2	3.7	26*	64.7	***−2.4***	2314	46.3
1991	***1.5***	432.8	30.5	4.2	22.7	37.3	8.0	21.7*	52.2	12.7	171.1	35.7
1992	***−0.5***	951.6	33.8	3.6	15.5	31.8	12.3	15.4*	45.1	11.9	24.9	30.6
1993	4.7	1928.0	33.8	***2.0***	9.8	33.3	7.0	12.7*	43.5	5.9	10.6	27.7
1994	5.3	2075.9	28.5	4.5	7.0	33.9	5.7	11.4*	42.2	5.8	4.2	29.6
1995	4.4	66.0	21.2	***−5.7***	35.0	60.5	10.6	8.2*	32.1	***−2.8***	3.4	39.0
1996	***2.1***	15.8	22.0	5.8	34.4	49.0	7.4	7.3*	37.5	5.5	0.2	41.8

1997	***3.4***	6.9	23.3	6.9	20.6	38.0	6.6	6.1★	33.7	8.1	0.5	44.2
1998	***0.0***	3.2	29.3	4.7	15.9	39.0	3.2	5.1★	43.5	3.9	0.9	47.9
1999	***0.3***	4.9	43.1	2.6	16.6	35.7	***−0.8***	3.3★	49.4	***−3.4***	−1.2	54.3
2000	***4.3***	7.0	38.7	5.2	9.5	26.6	4.5	3.8★	51.7	***−0.8***	−0.9	53.1
2001	***1.3***	6.8	43.0	***−0.6***	6.4	27.3	3.3	3.5★	58.6	***−4.4***	−1.1	57.4
2002	***2.7***	8.5	47.7	***0.13***	5.0	25.0	2.2	2.4★	64.2	***−10.9***	25.9	154.0
2003	***1.1***	14.7	44.1	***1.4***	4.5	23.9	4.0	2.8★	61.7	8.8	13.4	132.5
2004	5.7	6.6	34.3	4.2	4.7	22.6	6.0	1.0★	50.0	9.0	4.4	114.4
2005	3.2	6.9	22.0	3.0	4.0	21.1	5.6	3.0★	40.4	9.2	9.6	72.0
2006	4.0	4.2	18.3	5.0	3.6	18.6	4.6	3.3★	36.9	8.5	10.9	56.7
2007	6.1	3.6	17.8	***3.2***	4.0	19.6	4.6	4.4★	36.5	**8.0★**	8.8	47.1
2008	5.2	5.7	16.3	***1.4***	5.1	19.2	3.7	8.7★	38.3	**3.1★**	8.6	38.4
2009	***−0.3***	4.9	17.7	***−4.7***	5.3	23.0	***−1.0***	1.4★	43.3	***0.9★***	6.3	42.8
2010	7.5	5.0	16.7	5.1	4.1	23.8	5.8	1.4	40.4	**9.1★**	10.8	32.7
2011	2.7	6.6	16.6	4.0	3.4	25.2	5.8	3.3	41.0	**8.6★**	9.5	28.3
2012	0.9	5.4	19.9	4.0	4.1	30.6	5.4	3.0		0.9	10.0	26.3
2013	2.5	6.2		1.1	3.8		4.1	1.8		3.0		

Source: World Bank, 2014b.

Table A.12 GDP growth (G), inflation (I), external debt (D, as % GNI)

	Peru			*Ecuador*			*Bolivia*			*Colombia*		
	G	*I*	*D*	*G*	*I*	*D*	*G*	*I*	*D*	*G*	*I*	*D*
1980	3.1	59.1	48.4	3.7	13.0	53.2	***−1.4***	47.2	61.3	4.1	26.5	21.5
1981	7.2	75.4	36.5	5.6	16.4	58.1	***0.3***	32.1	52.6	***2.3***	27.5	24.8
1982	***−0.6***	64.4	45.7	***0.6***	16.3	62.9	***−3.9***	123.5	65.6	***0.9***	24.6	27.8
1983	***−11.8***	111.2	64.0	***−0.3***	48.4	73.3	***−4.0***	275.6	79.4	***1.6***	19.7	31.2
1984	5.2	110.2	66.5	***2.6***	31.2	79.8	***−0.2***	1281	76.9	3.4	16.2	33.4
1985	***2.8***	163.4	73.9	3.9	28.0	81.6	***−1.7***	11749	99.0	3.1	24.0	43.6
1986	10.0	77.9	87.8	3.5	23.0	101.2	***−2.6***	276.3	155.4	5.8	18.9	46.4
1987	8.0	85.8	77.2	***−0.3***	29.5	130.8	***2.5***	14.6	146.0	5.4	23.3	49.7
1988	***−8.7***	667.0	167.1	5.9	58.2	135.4	2.9	16.0	115.3	4.1	28.1	45.7
1989	***−11.7***	3398	106.0	***1.0***	75.6	136.5	3.8	15.2	94.7	3.4	25.9	45.5
1990	***−5.1***	7481	79.2	***3.7***	48.5	133.1	4.6	17.1	94.5	6.0	29.1	45.6
1991	***2.2***	409.5	64.4	4.2	48.8	122.4	5.3	21.4	81.5	***2.3***	30.4	44.1
1992	***−0.4***	73.5	58.5	***2.1***	54.3	111.0	***1.6***	12.1	79.4	5.0	27.0	37.0
1993	4.8	48.6	71.3	***2.0***	45.0	99.4	4.3	8.5	79.6	2.4	22.4	35.0
1994	12.8	23.7	61.9	4.3	27.4	85.1	4.7	7.9	85.7	5.8	22.8	27.5
1995	8.6	11.1	60.4	***2.2***	22.9	72.2	4.7	10.2	82.5	5.2	20.9	27.7
1996	***2.5***	11.5	53.8	***1.7***	24.4	59.3	4.4	12.4	72.9	***2.1***	20.8	30.2

1997	6.9	8.6	51.8	4.3	30.6	56.2	5.0	4.7	68.7	3.4	18.5	30.5
1998	***−0.7***	7.2	55.0	3.3	36.1	57.6	5.0	7.7	68.2	***0.6***	18.7	34.1
1999	***0.9***	3.5	58.2	***−4.7***	52.2	87.6	***0.4***	2.2	69.9	***−4.2***	10.9	39.7
2000	3.0	3.8	55.5	***1.1***	96.1	78.8	***2.5***	4.6	72.0	4.4	9.2	33.9
2001	***0.2***	2.0	52.5	4.0	37.7	60.8	***1.7***	1.6	60.4	***1.7***	8.0	36.9
2002	5.0	0.2	51.3	4.1	12.5	59.4	***2.5***	0.9	66.2	***2.5***	6.4	34.1
2003	4.0	2.3	51.0	2.7	7.9	53.8	2.7	3.3	75.3	3.9	7.1	39.6
2004	5.0	3.7	48.1	8.2	2.7	50.4	4.2	4.4	74.9	5.3	5.9	33.0
2005	6.3	1.6	39.3	5.3	2.4	43.8	4.4	5.4	75.9	4.7	5.0	26.4
2006	7.5	2.0	34.5	4.4	3.0	38.6	4.8	4.3	52.9	6.7	4.3	24.0
2007	8.5	1.8	32.6	***2.2***	2.3	36.4	4.6	8.7	42.9	6.9	5.5	21.7
2008	9.1	5.8	29.4	6.4	8.4	26.2	6.1	14.0	36.8	3.5	7.0	19.7
2009	***0.9***	2.9	31.5	***0.6***	5.2	21.6	3.4	3.3	36.1	***1.7***	4.2	23.4
2010	8.5	1.5	29.6	2.9	3.6	22.4	4.1	2.5	32.2	4.0	2.3	23.2
2011	6.5	3.4	27.5	7.8	4.5	21.5	5.2	9.8	28.4	6.6	3.4	24.0
2012	6.0	3.7	29.3	5.1	5.1	20.3	5.2	4.6	27.	4.0	3.2	22.4
2013	5.8	2.8		4.0	2.7		6.8	5.7		4.3	2.0	

Source: World Bank, 2014b.

Table A.13 GDP growth (G), inflation (I), external debt (D, as % GNI)

	Uruguay			*Paraguay*			*Venezuela*		
	G	*I*	*D*	*G*	*I*	*D*	*G*	*I*	*D*
1980	5.8	63.5	17.3	11.7	22.4	22.8	***−4.4***	21.3	43.6
1981	***1.6***	34.0	20.1	9.2	13.0	21.3	***−0.4***	16.2	42.3
1982	***−9.8***	19.0	29.7	***−1.4***	5.1	25.4	***−2.1***	9.6	42.8
1983	***−10.3***	49.2	68.8	***−3.0***	13.4	26.5	***−3.8***	6.2	50.1
1984	***−1.1***	55.3	73.4	***2.8***	20.3	35.6	***1.4***	12.2	68.5
1985	***1.5***	72.2	89.8	4.5	25.2	60.8	***0.2***	11.3	63.5
1986	8.8	76.4	70.2	***5.0***	31.7	61.9	6.5	11.5	59.9
1987	8.0	63.6	61.1	7.6	21.8	71.8	3.6	28.1	79.1
1988	***1.5***	62.2	48.7	5.9	22.6	61.7	5.8	29.4	61.3
1989	***1.1***	80.4	55.4	6.9	26.4	55.2	***−8.6***	84.4	81.4
1990	***0.3***	112.5	49.6	4.1	37.3	40.4	6.5	40.6	71.7
1991	3.5	102.0	38.5	3.5	24.2	34.6	9.7	34.2	66.7
1992	7.9	68.5	36.4	1.7	15.2	26.4	6.1	31.4	66.7
1993	2.7	54.1	33.0	4.9	18.2	23.8	***0.3***	38.1	66.6
1994	7.3	44.7	29.7	5.3	20.6	30.5	***−2.3***	60.8	67.6
1995	***−1.4***	42.2	28.1	6.8	13.4	32.0	4.0	59.9	49.0
1996	5.6	28.3	29.2	***1.6***	9.8	27.9	***−0.2***	99.8	52.2
1997	8.5	19.8	28.2	***4.2***	6.9	27.3	6.4	50.0	47.9
1998	4.5	10.8	30.1	***0.1***	11.6	34.1	***0.3***	35.7	49.7
1999	***−1.9***	5.7	33.3	***−1.4***	6.8	44.6	***−6.0***	23.5	45.1
2000	***−1.9***	4.8	37.3	***−2.3***	9.0	44.2	3.7	16.2	36.6
2001	***−3.8***	4.4	44.7	***−0.8***	7.3	42.2	3.4	12.5	32.7
2002	***−7.7***	14.0	74.7	***0.0***	10.5	53.1	***−8.9***	22.4	41.2
2003	***0.8***	19.4	95.3	4.3	14.2	59.7	***−7.8***	31.0	46.9
2004	5.0	9.2	90.0	4.1	4.3	53.7	18.3	21.7	36.1
2005	7.5	4.7	66.3	2.1	6.8	44.1	10.3	15.9	31.6
2006	4.1	6.4	53.4	4.8	9.6	36.9	9.9	13.6	24.1
2007	6.5	8.1	52.5	5.4	8.1	28.0	8.8	18.7	20.9
2008	7.2	7.9	39.1	6.4	10.2	24.1	5.3	30.3	17.0
2009	***2.4***	7.1	44.9	***−4.0***	2.6	28.0	***−3.2***	27.1	18.8
2010	8.4	6.7	36.8	13.1	4.7	27.3	***−1.5***	28.2	16.8
2011	7.3	8.1	31.6	4.3	8.3	23.8	4.2	26.1	22.7
2012	3.7	8.1		−1.2	3.7	27.1	5.6	21.1	19.4
2013	4.4	8.6		13.6	2.7		1.3	40.6	

Source: World Bank, 2014b.

APPENDIX B

Framework

By public-private collaboration this volume means any of several possible arrangements in which public and private actors agree to pool resources and share risks to deliver some service or facility. In most cases, these forms of private sector participation in infrastructure require a new institutional framework. State agencies, national and foreign investors and entrepreneurs, civil society organizations, and all other actors need a conceptual and legal map that goes well beyond the delimitation of the public and private spheres used in traditional procurement (Levy, 2006; Maman and Rosenhek, 2011; O Riain, 2004; Pang, 2000; Schamis, 2002; Weiss, 1998, 2003; Wong, 2004). In terms of concrete institutional forms, the changed framework includes new and effective mechanisms for planning, designing projects, structuring processes of bidding, supervision, and monitoring of projects and facilities. It also means bridging traditional cultural and ideological lines separating the public and the private.

Though partnerships and concessions vary greatly in terms of size and complexity (Renda and Schrefler, 2006a), they share characteristics and challenges for which a broad framework is needed. The idea is to develop and create conditions ensuring outcomes. Partnerships entail hybrid organizational forms in which key sectoral ministries develop capacities, while the finance and planning ministries develop organized capabilities to manage concessions or partnerships. These separate agencies need to be coordinated. This can be a formidable challenge in developing countries still struggling to create functional bureaucracies and an adequate civil service. Figure B.1 presents a working framework to organize the analysis. Below a certain size and level of complexity, inadequate organizational development may pose insurmountable

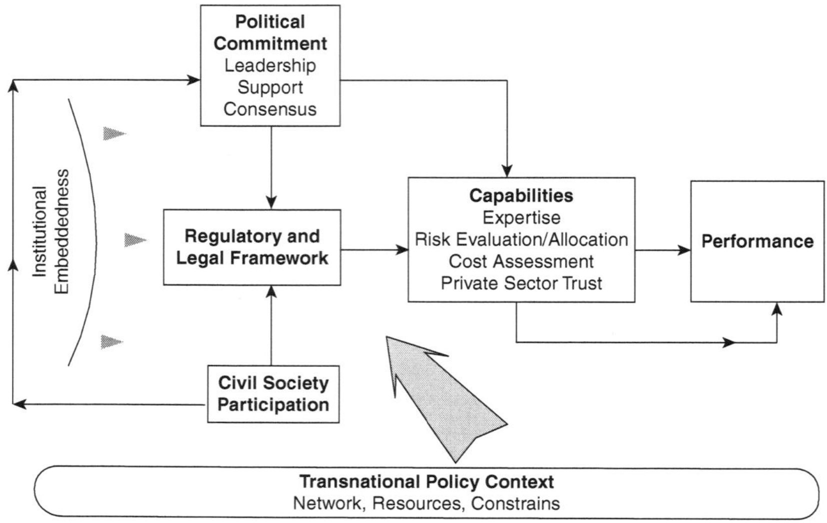

Figure B.1 Basic analytical framework.
Source: Forrer et al., 2010.

handicaps. Still, it may be wise to keep in mind that some types of concession and partnership may call for distinctive approaches.

The European Commission distinguishes two main types of PPP: *institutional* and *contractual* (Commission of the European Communities, 2004). The institutional forms are newly established organizations jointly held by public and private operators while contractual partnerships are agreements in which private operators provide some kind of service in exchange for compensation by users or by the public authority itself.

Partnerships may thus cover a wide range of organizational forms and business models in the spectrum from public to private. For example, in Brazil they take on a narrower meaning that does not include regular concessions, joint ventures, outsourcing and other forms of financing partnerships. From the standpoint of policymakers, their purpose is generally to transfer as much risk and responsibility as possible to the private sector, though risks can be shared between the two sectors. But models differ in the degree to which the public or private sector designs, finances, operates, owns, participates in the revenues, and controls service fees and tolls. When revenues are insufficient to maintain financial returns, the public sector often offers financial complements. Partnerships frequently seek private efficiency with long-term public perspectives.

The most basic form of public-private collaboration is the *simple service contract*: an agreement between two parties in which the private actor procures, operates, and maintains an asset for a short period of time, while the public party is responsible for management and investment. This model is often found in toll collection services. Another form is the *operation and management contracts*, which are agreements where the private party is responsible for both operation and management. The duration is also relatively short, but longer than in simple service contracts. The public party bears the financial and the investment risks. These types of agreements are often seen as privatization. In *leasing contracts*, private sector operators lease an existing asset from the state, and the private actor usually renovates, modernizes, or expands this asset.

Build-operate-transfer (BOT) is a more sophisticated concession model in which the private actor has responsibility for design, construction, and operation, while the public party may bear some or even most of the financial risks. By paying for operating costs, the private party faces incentives for better planning and management. When the operating contract ends, the private party transfers the asset to the public actor. BOT has been widely used in infrastructure projects, including waste and water treatment.[1]

The Design-build-finance-operate (DBFO) is a complex concession that often takes the form of a public-private partnership While this model provides the operational features and effectiveness of previous models, it also ensures opportunity for new sources of capital. The private actor or consortium of actors designs, builds, owns, develops, operates, and manages an asset for a long period (25–30 years). The public sector actually owns the asset and actively regulates the project to ensure quality standards of service and consumer protection from monopolistic prices. This model of public-private partnership is often found in large-scale infrastructure projects such as railroad, roads, water and waste treatment, prison complexes, and the like.

Depending on the project and the focus of the program, standard ways of measuring outcomes and performance include financial success, expansion of the project, public support, impact on development, impact on the poor, and environmental impact. Performance criteria are strongly dependent on the main purposes and goals of the particular project.

The PPP field of action or policy domain is populated by diverse national, regional, and multilateral organizations, including development banks, business networks, and firms that claim major parts. These and other organizations are often part of policy networks, linking transnational and national actors.

Together, these networks and actors generate resources, knowledge, and relationships that enhance the ability of policymakers and elected officials to develop regulatory frameworks and generate projects. This entails contracts, advocate and plan for specific projects and agendas, create commissioning units to attract foreign investment, and the like. Participation in these networks allows stakeholders to learn about triumphs and pitfalls of public-private collaboration around the world. Knowledge thus gained leads to more efficient procurement practices and implementation.

Development banks and other international financial institutions and business fora are critical. The World Bank stands out at the multilateral level, as do the International Monetary Fund (IMF) and the World Economic Forum (WEF). Regional development banks are involved in this international policy field. In the Western Hemisphere, the Inter-American Development Bank has produced numerous documents concerning the specific purpose of helping public officials bent on launching PPP programs and projects.[2] So has the Corporación Andina de Fomento (CAF).

Business organizations take a supportive or proactive stance in the adoption of programs and projects. Consulting agencies with specialized legal and finance teams are hired to review and advise in legal contracting, bidding consortium, and procurement. For example, PricewaterhouseCoopers has become a major consultant in the Brazilian state of Minas Gerais. The company sees itself as the foremost private authority on partnerships. Legal contracts are the foundation for successful PPP projects, and for-profit consulting agencies, including finance and law firms, have a large role in this aspect of PPPs.

Some of the most important exchanges of PPP-related information and ideas involve country-based officials and agencies with experience or interest in them. Groups focus on urban development and the environment.

Governments often send groups to other countries to give presentations on their own partnership experience. In the development of PPPs, possibly the most important exchange of information and ideas involve these agencies with experience designing and implementing PPP programs. The United Kingdom, Ireland, and several other countries maintain PPP-specific websites that provide access to useful reports, information on PPP processes, and listings of investment opportunities.[3] The list of cooperation agencies includes the Canadian Agency for International Development, the German Agency for Technical Cooperation (GTZ), the German Ministry of Economic Cooperation and Development (BMZ), the German Investment and Development Company (CDEG), the Reconstruction Loan Corporation (KfW), the International Finance Corporation (IFC), and the Private Finance Initiative (PFI) of Britain. Indeed, partnerships have a larger role in the context of efforts to reconstruct the international order toward cooperation. In the United States, the World Bank and the IDB has preempted much of this space, but forums and organizations have emerged.

Private firms and trade associations also play important support roles in the PPP process. Consulting agencies (legal and finance teams) are hired to review and advise in legal contracting, organizing bidding consortia, and procurement. Further work is needed to probe the role of transnational policy networks in specific projects and programs and to advance the understanding of the dynamics leading to effective identification of problems, solutions, and best practices.

Analytical Framework

This appendix reviews general conditions affecting outcome in a large number of cases.

Institutions and regulatory framework

The regulatory and institutional context directly governing the design and creation of partnerships is a pivotal factor affecting performance and outcome. The British legislation is widely seen as providing a exemplary framework. The main piece of legislation in this case is the Private Finance Initiative of 1992, which eliminated major legal and institutional barriers to private participation in public projects and public service provision. This initiative sketched criteria for regulatory frameworks: clearly defined public sector goals and objectives, effective and transparent bidding processes, competent authorities, formal rights of the concessionaire, and opportunities for renegotiation (Leahy, 2005).

Poor legislation thus increases costs to the public. If the regulatory framework is not appropriate, private contractors will add a risk factor in their bids. Exit strategies should specify what to do in cases of bankruptcy of the project company.

In all advanced adopting countries, governments have created special partnership units within the state administration. These units become "knowledge organizations" in which PPP expertise and competence are developed and centralized. They have an important role in encouraging public and private sector innovation for the improvement of efficiency and quality of public service. The numbers of projects and the ability to attract private investors have significantly increased in countries where partnership units have been established (Renda and Schrefler, 2006b). These experiences have led to the recommendation of an institutionalized national public-private partnership coordinator.

Enabling legislation

Public-private partnerships are special types of concessions. A preexisting law of concessions represents a preestablished legal context in which to elaborate the necessary new laws and decrees.

Political commitment

Both institutional and programmatic development depend on a cluster of political conditions conceptualized here as political commitment. Political support is one aspect of political commitment.

The likelihood of sustained *political consensus* among critical political actors is also a substantial risk in the design of partnership programs and projects. Long-term projects often experience parliamentary election cycles before they are completed. Newly elected governments may renege on the initial contract. The breach of contract by the public party often results in lawsuits and possible compensation for private actors, further increasing public costs. Private contractors and the general public pay these extra costs. Since public-private partnerships often draw debate and opposition, consensus among the main political parties is often decisive. Political conditions, especially *political leadership*, are of particular importance in transitional and developing societies. Several cases point to the significance of political leadership, which may be the single most important factor.

In Britain, for example, bold political leadership by four consecutive prime ministers—Margaret Thatcher, John Major, Tony Blair, and Gordon Brown and David Cameron—was decisive in the adoption as well as continuation and development of public-private partnerships. Leadership is more than nominal support or reflection of consensus; it means the deployment of political will and political capital to launch, organize, and protect a state reform initiative likely to generate considerable opposition. Political leadership determines societal willingness to mobilize and allocate resources to programs and projects, and is thus crucial to the success of public-private partnerships.[4] This is a dynamic process requiring permanent revision and development, for example, in 2011, the British conservative government introduced a full assessment of the 20-year experiences in PFI and implemented significant reforms in the program.

Capabilities

Capability is different from political leadership or commitment. Rather, it has to do with the effectiveness of agencies and personnel. It is intertwined with the preexisting institutional frameworks and preexisting reform dynamics in which concessions and partnerships are embedded. More broadly, it is a reflection of the strength of the state as an institution.

Different levels of *expertise* can result in unbalanced negotiations and conflict between the two parties. The public sector is often at a disadvantage in that project managers in the private sector are often more experienced and better prepared than government representatives. Lack of managerial skills and experience also reduces the ability of public officials to monitor and control the project in the operational stage. The acquisition of managerial competence by public officials remains a significant challenge in Latin America, where there is great need to train cadres.

Acquiring managerial competence in partnership programs is a particularly significant challenge for public sector officials. These different backgrounds can result in unbalanced negotiations, tension, and conflict. British PFI-PPP projects tend to perform better and achieve greater value for money than traditional procurement in the design and construction stages, but a number of projects showed much less efficiency in the operational phase. Cost and poor contract management on the public side has been deemed responsible for this unbalanced outcome (Nao, 2010; Renda and Schrefler, 2006b). The lack of managerial skills and experience can reduce the ability of public officials to monitor and control the project in the operational stage. The

Table B.1 Risk allocation in typical concession and partnerships contracts

Risk	*Allocated to*
Design	Government/concessionaire
Financial	Concessionaire
Traffic/use revenue	Government/concessionaire
Construction and engineering	Concessionaire
Inflation	Government
Exchange rate	Government/concessionaire
Institutional	Government
Force majeure	Concessionaire

UK review of the PFI program concluded that a deficit in the public sector skill was a crucial issue, resulting in the 2012 launching of the Major Projects Leadership Academy at Oxford's Saïd Business School in order to build the skills of senior project leaders across government to deliver complex PFI projects. Other European experiences confirm that special units within the public administration are needed to foster competency and train the specialists necessary for the project's success.

The core challenge of a public-private alliance is *risk evaluation and allocation* between parties. The partnership design aims to redistribute particular risks to the actor most capable of managing them at the lowest costs, constrained in turn by the government's desideratum that financial risks be transferred to the private sector. However, improper risk evaluation and allocation can result in higher costs than in a traditional public project.

Risks can be divided into five basic types:

- Construction risk—related to the design and construction phase
- Financial risk—related to unpredictable interest, prices, and exchange rates
- Performance risk—related to poor service provision or quality standards
- Demand risk—linked to the actual consumption of the service
- Residual risk—related to the future market price of the asset; relevant if the property will be transferred into the public party at the end of the contract.[5]

Developing countries, particularly in Latin America, face difficulties in reducing the financial risks involved in long-term, large-scale infrastructure projects such as railroads. Insufficient guarantees on returns by the public sector has delayed the constructions of strategic railroad projects in Brazil as private investors hesitate. The Brazilian federal concessions law contains clauses in which the public administration has the unilateral power to revise service fees if necessary to maintain the economic and financial viability of the project. Such clauses have deterred private sector long-term investments.

Cost savings (*value for money*) can be better achieved through partnerships than through traditional public procurement (Leahy, 2005). Public-private partnerships may not always be the best solution. Special transaction costs often emerge in establishing and maintaining a partnership between private and public parties. Transaction and other indirect expenses can add substantially to the total cost. These costs result from organizing the bidding process, participating in it, negotiating the contract between the public sector and the winning bidder, monitoring the private sector partner's compliance with the contract, and renegotiating the contract during its life cycle (Dudkin and Válilá, 2005). They include legal and broker fees and enforcing contracts. Due to their long-term character and risk-taking features, tendering, bidding, negotiating, and monitoring processes can make them more expensive than traditional short-term contracting. Care needs to be taken to avoid the erosion of savings achieved through a public-private partnership project.

Establishing and maintaining a partnership between private and public parties will have unexpected transaction costs. Transaction and renegotiation costs can greatly inflate their final costs and undermine their claim to provide greater value for money than traditional public procurement. Partnerships can be more expensive than traditional short-term contracts.

The size of the project is also important in determining cost. For instance, British projects with a capital value below £25 million have significantly higher transaction costs than larger projects. Procurement time can also affect the cost of partnership projects. Costs appear to be significantly higher in projects that take longer than 50 months to procure. Interestingly, the number of bidders does not significantly affect the costs of projects (Dudkin and Válilá, 2005).

Broader Social Impacts and Local Benefits

Large projects, regardless of the specific form taken by public-private collaboration, are increasingly required to meet standards in regard to social environmental and social impact, sustainability, safety, sanitation, and related local concerns. For instance, in projects related to the 2012 London Olympics, a high priority was to involve small and medium enterprises and the local labor force, making efforts to develop better relationships with local residents and a supportive culture within the workforce. The projects also aimed to minimize negative impacts on the environment. For example, more than 98 percent of materials from demolition were reused on the Olympic Park. Poor planning and execution can lead to costly delays and sanctions.

APPENDIX C

Brazil: Planning for New Infrastructure

Brazilian policymakers gradually altered the planning assumptions and practices inherited from the military regime, responding to such shocks as the financial crisis of the 1980s, the post-1985 transition to democracy, and hyperinflation through the 1990s. The reorganization of national planning since the 1990s shaped the idea of using concessions and partnerships in infrastructure, though still a relatively recent development near full institutionalization.

To organize a more transparent process, the Constitution of 1988 (Article 16) mandated four-year plans known as Plano Plurianual (PPA). Each new administration is to elaborate a plan in its first year in office and thus each plan runs through the first year of the subsequent government. But economic and political turbulence prevented serious planning until the mid-1990s.

What should have been the first four-year plan (1992–1995) did not come to life due to the political instability that culminated in the presidential impeachment of December 1992. Hence, PPA 1996–1999 (*Brasil em Ação*) was the first complete plan of the post-1985 democratic era and set the stage for subsequent plans. Prepared by then planning minister José Serra, it called for collaboration between federal and subnational governments and the private sector. This plan's thin discussion of infrastructure owed to a focus on stabilization and structural adjustment as much as to the absence of a well-defined new national approach.[1]

Avança Brasil (PPA 2000–2003) is more complete and ambitious. After identifying nine development corridors or axles, it lists priority infrastructure projects to develop them and integrate Brazil regionally, nationally, and internationally.[2] National planners first identified public-private partnerships as such during the elaboration of this plan under planning minister Martus Tavares, a close associate of Serra. The basic framework articulated in PPA 2000–2003, together with related planning studies, shaped subsequent planning efforts. The approach based on corridors that promote trade as well as national and international integration has been retained in all of them. Of Brazil's five main regions (south, southeast, central-west, north, and northeast), the south and southeast are treated as whole units in *Avança Brasil*. The other three received detailed attention. The central-west region was divided into southwest, west, and north. The latter had three corridors (Araguaia-Tocantins, Madeira-Amazon, and Arco Norte), while the northeast had two (São Francisco and Transnordeste). National planners then focused on specific projects in each of these corridors to promote development and integration within and between the country's five traditional regions, as well as between Brazil and the rest of South America.

The echoes of the acute crisis of public finances of the 1980s and the 1990s drove policymakers to deemphasize traditional dirigisme and retain the macroeconomic and liberalized policies to engage the private sector. They combined traditional public procurement with concessions and public-private partnerships, retaining infrastructure as the main focus.

Planning minister Guido Mantega prepared PPA 2004–2007 (*Brasil de Todos*). While social development stood out as priority, this document built on previous planning efforts and ideas to formulate major infrastructure goals. Throughout the Lula years, planners appeared receptive to concessions and public-private partnerships, but little progress took place. The Growth Acceleration Program of 2007 finally presented a blueprint for Lula's second terms and PPA 2008–2011. The latter, Development with Social Inclusion and Quality Education, sharpened the focus on infrastructure provision and growth.

The plan focused on infrastructure projects in the central-west, northeast, and north regions and adjacent areas. But progress was slow. While some plans were approved, others waited for congressional approval or faced unexpected complications. For example, the BR-319 highway connecting Porto Velho with Manaus was suspended due to environmental concerns. A large number of infrastructure projects experienced delay.[3]

The growth program reformulated and repackaged older plans into a program promising the use of concessions and public-private partnerships to upgrade the railroad system and related infrastructure. In early May 2008, Medida Provisória 427 sketched a railroad expansion

Table C.1 Brazil's national plans since 1992

	Title of plan	*Planning minister*	*Presidency*	*Significant*
1992–1995	–	Several	Collor de Mello	First planning effort mandated by 1988 Constitution; little impact
PPA 1996–1999	Brasil em Ação	José Serra	F. H. Cardoso	First formal PPA, new public administration
PPA 2000–2003	Avança Brasil	Martus Tavares	F. H. Cardoso	New planning model: development axles, project evaluation
PPA 2004–2007	Brasil de Todos	Guido Mantega	Lula da Silva	Continuity on fiscal and monetary policy; social initiatives
PPA 2008–2011	Desenvolvimento com Inclusão	Paulo Bernardo Silva	Lula da Silva	Economic growth with social inclusion and reduction in regional disparities
PAC1 2007–2010	Plano de Aceleração do Crescimento	Paulo Bernardo Silva	Lula da Silva	PAC focuses on infrastructure development (transportation, social inclusion and education)
PAC2 2011–2014	Plano de Aceleração do Crescimento	Miriam Belchior	Dilma Rouseff	Continuity to PAC1 infrastructure investment.

Source: Brazil, Ministério do Planejamento, Orçamento e Gestão. 2011. *Plano Plurianual 2012–2015*. Brasília, DF: Secretaria de Planejamento e Investimentos Estratégicos.

plan defining the emerging approach. However, investments in infrastructure remained considerably below the amount stipulated by PAC, reaching a gap of R$115 billion.[4] The Lula da Silva administration's debates over the design of concessions, public-private partnerships, and the relative roles of government and businesses continued through much of 2008 and 2009. However, in the electoral year of 2010, pre-candidate Dilma Rousseff, a prominent member of the Lula cabinet, played a key role in launching PAC2—a R$1.59 trillion package to build infrastructure and promote growth.[5] It promised nearly a trillion reais of infrastructure by 2014. In terms of railroads, the goal was to increase the existent network of 29,000 kilometers to 40,000 kilometers by 2020. Criticism surfaced regarding the timing of the program during election years and various delays in planning and execution. But Brazilians hoped that the focus would be sustained after the elections.[6]

Short on funds and unable to enact PPP programs without a new national legal foundation, states pressed the Union for such laws. Sensitized to the constraints on new investment, officials in the planning ministry and other high-level agencies in the Lula government have debated this issue at length, even if the federal government had technically endorsed the idea of relying on public-private partnerships for infrastructure projects in 2004 (PPA 2004–2007). It was moved in part by a supportive international context, including China's declared interest in railroad and port projects to enhance Brazil's ability to export soy and other products. As noted, the collapse of negotiations with the Chinese contributed to the abandonment of the idea to construct Ferrovia Norte-Sul as a public-private partnership.

Plans for the implementation of full-fledged public-private programs faced significant delays and alterations in 2006. The federal partnership program had not gone into full effect in the first half of that year, as had been promised. The federal government took a great deal of time to complete an organizational and regulatory framework to implement the public-private partnerships program. Several early projects listed as priorities in 2004 and 2005 were dropped from the list, for example, Ferronorte and FNS. But delays and other changes continued, affecting a number of projects.

The national plan for infrastructure development and export incentives had been fully in place with PPA 2004–2007 and PPA 2008–2011, but relatively little had actually taken place through 2009 in terms of coordinating different national actors as well as better relations between federal and subnational programs. By March 2010, less than half of the projected public works were on schedule. The São Paulo rail beltway remained uncertain, having yet to be fully assessed by the federal bureaucracy. The federal government did not provide clear explanations for the delays and the appearance of improvisation. Though the federal government had very little to show in terms of actual concessions, PAC did refocus policy on infrastructure investment and public-private business models.

The broader policy domain governing design and implementation—mobilized actors, issues, and relationships, including civil society and transnational organizations concerned with social and sustainable development—did not seem fully in place.

Excursus: Shifting Ownership of the Santos Rail Corridor

As an extension of the railroad system of the state of São Paulo, Ferronorte had to wait for the consolidation of this geographically pivotal network, a process that went through several phases. In the 1970s, this system had been converted into FEPASA, a public network controlled by the state of São Paulo. However, the reforms of 1996–1998 first federalized the national railroad system, to then reorganize it in terms of regions before ceding them to private operators as concessions. São Paulo's rail network went through several changes in ownership before eventually merging into Latin American Logistics (ALL).

First, in 1998 Ferroban (Ferrrovias Bandeirantes) won the concession to run the main rail network in São Paulo but continued to run deficits, as did Brasil Ferrovias, the holding company that had acquired the concessions to Ferronorte and Novoeste. As the nation's economy began to improve in 2002, Brasil Ferrovias bought Ferroban and its portfolio, thus now controlling Ferroban, Ferrovia Novoeste, and the fledgling Ferronorte. São Paulo's rail network seemed to have become integrated into one at last, this time under private management, with financing from BNDES.

The vicissitudes of Ferroban and Brasil Ferrovias had been due in large part to uncertain public support, as the federal authorities took considerable time to debate projects and business models for public-private collaboration. In the case of Ferronorte, federal support remained unsettled even as construction approached the state of Mato Grosso in 1998 and early 1999, fanning the dream of railway service into this rising state. But the rapidly expanding soy frontier in Mato Grosso demanded easier access to export corridors.

Ferronorte needed financial infusions to be able to expand. BNDES, pension funds such as Previ and Funcef, as well as other sources bought shares in the company as a way to finance Brasil Ferrovias' march toward Mato Grosso and its capital of Cuiabá and beyond. However, Ferronorte's R$1.5 billion debt with BNDES provided grounds for delays through 2003. Decisive political support would have expedited the request for federal support. Instead, the Ferronorte project advanced at a crawling pace. BNDES specialists and at least two pension funds endorsed Ferronorte's expansion, though they worried about continuing deficits in Brasil Ferrovias.

In mid-2005, BNDES announced a package of R$2.3 billion to refinance Brasil Ferrovias and restructure it as a holding company under the name of Nova Brasil Ferrovias. A more decisive turning point came in mid-2006, when ALL acquired Brasil Ferrovias, Novoeste, and Ferronorte. The original Ferronorte investors, government pension funds Previ (administered by Banco do Brasil), Funcef (Caixa Econômica Federal), and BNDES remained as ALL shareholders.

ALL had come to life in 1997 under a different name to operate in southern Brazil. Later expanding into Argentina, ALL's goal was to become South America's premier railroad company—a network of more than 20,000 kilometers, a 1,000 locomotives, and nearly 30,000 wagons, also involved in logistics, intermodal movement, and storage. It focused mainly on grains, sugar, ethanol, and other agricultural commodities. The consolidated operator came to process half of the soy reaching Santos and a growing share of Mato Grosso's soy. In 2006 alone, ALLMN was responsible for transporting 14.8 million tons of soy. When it announced plans to accelerate work on the stretch to Rondonópolis, and from there to Mato Grosso's capital of Cuiabá, it argued that it could triple the amount of cargo. While stakeholders pleaded for expeditious financial support, the federal government continued to debate its own priorities and questions about business models. The extension of deadlines also came about because of the time to obtain environmental licenses. Still, Ferronorte was gaining momentum after nearly a decade of delays.

APPENDIX D

About Transantiago

Table D.1 Transantiago: institutional and other actors

Created by presidential decree in 2003, the Committee of Ministers for Transport in Santiago headed the design and implementation phase of Transantiago. The members of this Committee were:

- Minister of Public Works, Transportation and Telecommunications
- Minister of Housing and Urbanization
- Director of Government Office for Greater Santiago
- President of Metro, S. A.
- Executive Director of CONAMA (National Commision for the Environment)
- MOPTT's General Coordinator of Concessions (Ministry of Public Works, Transport & Telecommunications)
- Executive Secretary of SECTRA (Inter-Ministerial Secretariat for Transport Planning)
- Transantiago Coordinator, acts as Executive Secretary of Committee

Other Actors:

- Bus drivers
- Private bus owners
- Transportation companies
- Unions ("gremios") and associations
- Nonregulated (and "illegal") buses

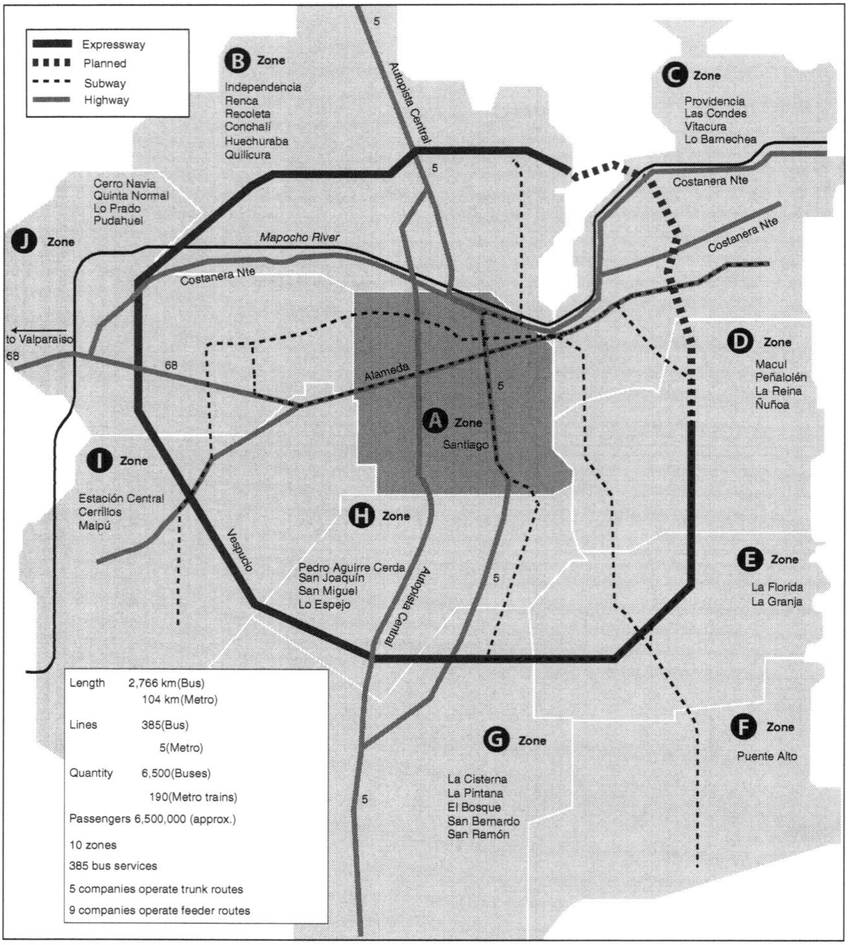

Figure D.1 Transantiago and metro.

Source: The Metro de Santiago website.

Table D.2 Transantiago timeline, 2004–2010

Date	*Event*
March 31, 2004	Extension of subway Line 5 westward to Quinta Normal completed.
September 8, 2004	Extension of subway Line 2 north to Cerro Blanco (including tunnel under Rio Mapocho) completed.
December 22, 2004	Extension of subway Line 2 south to La Cisterna completed.
December 31, 2004	Removal of 800 old buses not meeting PPDA emissions standards.
September 6, 2005	Exclusive bus lane (7.7 km) on Avenue Pajaritos, from Alameda to Plaza Maipú.
October 22, 2005 and after	Transantiago Phase I:
	Ten Concessionaires take control of system. Introduction of 1,181 new buses meeting EURO III standards (replaced 461 old buses) to operate alongside over 7,000 old yellow buses. Old buses upgraded (advanced filters, automatic fare collection devices, and repainting for standardized look).
November 25, 2005	Extension of subway Line 2 north to Ave. Cementerios completed.
November 30, 2005	Extension of subway Line 4 south from Tobalaba to Puente Alto completed.
January 21, 2006	Incorporation of 302 new buses to the system, and 551 old buses taken out of service.
March 11, 2006	Michelle Bachelet assumes office as new Chilean President.
March, 2006	New subway Line 4 (excluding L4A) completed.
July 2006 (Postponed)	Transantiago Phase II:
	Implementation of card payment method, single card for bus-subway integration, addition of advanced filters to Euro I/EPA 91 and Euro II/EPA94 buses.
August 16, 2006	Extension of subway Line 4 (links Vicuña Mackena and Americo Vespucio) completed.
September 14, 2006	Tunnel (1,763 km) connecting Blanco Encalada and Arica streets completed.
September 15, 2006	200 buses to test card payment method integrating bus and subway.
October 16, 2006	Public campaign to educate users.
November 11, 2006	Upgrades of main avenues and streets (trunk lines) begin.
January 1, 2007	Smart card fare system initiated in several locations.

Continued

Table D.2 Continued

Date	*Event*
February 10, 2007	Transantiago Phase II:
	Official inauguration (upgraded buses, removal of 2,900 old buses, inauguration of feeding lines, introduction of electronic information to users).
	Inauguration: debacle and crisis.
(Postponed)	Transantiago Phase III: 800 additional Euro III buses. Additional upgrading of older buses.
March 11, 2007	Presidential announcement of new short term measures, estimated at $27.8 million: 75 additional bus routes to be built; 300 additional buses; integration of taxis; amplification of nocturnal services and schedules.
March 26, 2007	Minister of Transport Sergio Espejo is replaced by René Cortázar.
April 3, 2007	Cortázar orders five new measures: increase fleet of buses by 1000 vehicles (to a total of 6,400); correct the problematic routes; support the operators during their period of fleet service; construction of new bus stops; assignment of exclusive bus lanes.
June 2007	Congress approves $290 million of extra funds.
December 17, 2007	Six new routes and twelve new transport services announced, to affect 600 million users.
April 25, 2008	$400 million loan approved by Inter-American Development Bank (IDB) for funding.
May 2008	$160 million loan approved by BancoEstado for funding.
August 13, 2008	Permanent monthly subsidy bill for Transantiago and Regional Public Transportation passed by the lower Congressional house.
September 2, 2008	Constitutional Tribunal (TC) rejects loans obtained from IDB and BancoEstado.
September 4, 2008	President Bachelet establishes "Consejo Extraordinario" for Transantiago finances.
September 5, 2008	Emergency funds of 2% of national budget to cover Transantiago deficit.
September 9, 2008	Vote for permanent monthly subsidy bill for Transantiago and Regional Public Transportation suspended in the Senate.
September 15, 2008	Members of la Alianza and Parlamentarios Independientes proposed senatorial measure to "terminar de manera definitiva con el Plan Transantiago" (terminate the Transantiago Plan once and for all).
September 17, 2008	Government evaluations determine Transantiago System to be a 4.5 (on a scale of 1 to 7). Measure for additional increase in number of buses to be specified in October, 2008.

Table D.2 Continued

Date	*Event*
January 12, 2009	Minister Cortázar announces new round of modifications to the metro and bus lines, including: 216 new cars to be added to the most-used Metro lines; 1,000 new buses to be added while 30 percent of the old buses are eliminated; expansion of the smart card system by 20 percent; additional technology upgrades to be introduced and a second reform of operator contracts to be initiated to tighten scheduling and frequency of bus patterns.
March 9, 2009	Minister Cortázar submits a proposal for financing, following the IDB loan rejection. Proposal fails to reach a consensus.
May 11, 2009	Coalición por el Cambio submits its own counter proposal for funding of the system. Proposal fails to reach a consensus.
July 14, 2009	Financing agreement reached between Coalición and Concertación for permanent subsidy of Transantiago, providing $3.460 billion between 2009 and 2014.
August 12, 2009	The agreement for Transantiago's permanent subsidy for the 2009–2014 period passes into law, with the Senate voting 68 in favor, 12 against, and 1 abstention.
November 10, 2009	Minister Cortázar announces an initiative to reduce wait time by at least 20 percent. Plans will increase bus frequency for over 146 routes, create 4 new nocturnal routes, and improve the nighttime coverage of over 32 other services in the Metropolitan area.
December 1, 2009	Last round of modifications to complete operational and technological goals: remove 1,400 old yellow buses still running (only 300 will remain by January 2010), to be replaced with 1,130 Mercedes Benz buses equipped with protective driver cabins, Euro III technology, and antismog filtering systems.
December 22, 2009	President Bachelet enacts Law 20.410, that modifies the Concessions and Public Works law.
January 7, 2010	Extension of subway Line 1 to Los Dominicos is completed.
January 17, 2010	Sebastián Piñera, representative of the Coalición por el Cambio, wins the presidential election. He takes office on March 11, 2010.
February 22, 2010	Eight new routes and modifications to seven other routes are initiated to increase coverage in the most inhabited areas of the capital.
March 11, 2010	Sebastián Piñera is inaugurated president of Chile.
March 11, 2010	Felipe Morandé takes office as the new minister of Transportation and Telecommunications.
	Ana Luisa Covarrubias is established as the coordinator of Transantiago.

Continued

Table D.2 Continued

Date	*Event*
April 15, 2010	Minister of Transport Felipe Morandé announces the Anti-Evasion Plan, which called for: fines of $73,300–$184,300 pesos for those caught evading fares; punishment of community service for those who refuse to pay the government fines; increased supervisory agents and authorities to enforce the Plan; and a series of fare increases ($10 pesos and $20 pesos, consecutively) for bus and metro ticket prices, reaching $430 pesos and $490 pesos for peak fares respectively.
May 17, 2010	Bus and metro fares increase by $20 pesos, reaching $450 pesos and $510 pesos for peak fares respectively.
February 3, 2011	Extension of subway Line 5 to Maipú is completed.
August 29, 2011	New Master Plan of Public Transportation infrastructure designed in 2010 for the period 2011–2015 is approved by the Committee of Ministers for Transport in Santiago. It seeks to solve bus circulation problems by utilizing a greater investment in maintenance and quality, the use of more advanced technology for enforcing the system's regulations, and other traffic measures.
September 1, 2012	Seven bus concessionares operating under new contracts with the following market share: Alsacia 12%, Express 20%, Metbus 17%, Vule 18%, Redbus 10%, STP 6%, and Subus 19%.
November, 2012	Contract between state and AFT (Financial Administrator of Transantiago) is restructured after months of negotiations.
April 16, 2013	The Metropolitan Public Transportation Board (Directorio de Transporte Público Metropolitano—DTPM) is created to substitute the original Committee of Ministers for Transport in Santiago created in 2003. In addition to the original tasks, the DTPM is charged with the task of analyzing the city's integral public transportation system and the task of coordinating different forms of transportation in Santiago derived from the actions of the various public and private sectors.
Spetember 27, 2013	New law of Public Transpportation subsidy is approved to improve Santiago's public transportation.
January, 2014	New revised contracts are negotiated with the existing seven bus operators.
May 29, 2014	President Bachelet announces a 2014–2018 Improvement Plan for Transantiago at a cost of $548 million pesos. It focuses on quality of service and information; infrastructure; regulatory supervision and integration; and evasion control.

Source: "Las 8 medidas..." and "Revise en detalle..." *La Nación*, May 29, 2014; Quijada et al., 2007. "Informe Final," Segunda Auditoria Internacional, March 2006, DPT, and author.

NOTES

One State and Market in Global Development

1. The global financial crisis of 2008 brought contrasting movements on the state. To some, it was clear evidence of market failure and the need for a larger role for government (Tanzi, 2009). Others saw it as a failure of national financial supervision, pointing to the need for market coordination or creating supranational institutions to supervise fiscal policy (Sapir, 2012). The first suggested the "comeback" of the nation-state model and the decreasing influence of global forces—a notion seemingly supported by the fact that public spending as share of GDP increased between 2007 and 2012 in many OECD and Latin American countries (IMF, 2014). International trade and global capital flows also fell after the crisis, from new protectionist measures and banking regulations, while trade liberalization shifted to regional and bilateral pacts (The Economist, 2013b).
2. As applied to public-private partnerships, the public goods literature is discussed in Ojha (2010), Ramesh et al. (2010), and Savas (2000: 41–107). Though Savas frames the discussion in terms of the theory and practice of privatization, others do not. In contrast to public goods, "private" goods and services can be denied selectively, with consumption by someone diminishing the supply to others—excludable and subject to competitive consumption, it should normally be left to private firms to supply them.
3. "A Special Report on the Future of the State," *The Economist*, March 12, 2011, diagnosed it as "big, inefficient, and broke."
4. Based on 2004 data from the World Bank (Delmon, 2009). The private sector was responsible for 20 percent and multilateral banks for 10 percent of infrastructure investments.
5. Fisher et al., "America's transport infrastructure: Life in the slow lane," *The Economist*, April 30, 2011. For Latin America, see CAF (2010).
6. For example, Whitfield (2010: 22–31). To promote growth, China invested 49 percent of GDP in 2010, up from 42 percent three years earlier, while India's investment rate fluctuated around 36–37 percent of GDP.

7. See, for instance, *Global Competitiveness Yearbook 2010* (Institute for Management Development) and the WEF's Global Competitiveness Index—both found online. Also useful are various indices of globalization—such as those from European Science Foundation, The Economist Intelligence Unit, A. T. Kearney & Foreign Policy magazine, KOF, and yet others. Social infrastructure for human capital—education, health, housing, and the like—is a high priority in emerging and developing countries, often with the explicit aim of increasing productivity and competitiveness. Gramlich (1994) explores the role of infrastructure on economic growth.
8. China is spending between $300 and $750 billion to expand its rail lines—nearly 10,000 miles of new high-speed trains and 11,000 miles of standard rail lines. The fast-speed network is schedule for completion in 2020. Inaugurated on July 1, 2011, the $33 billion, 820-mile Beijing-Shanghai line augmented the business corridor between China's two largest cities. Ninety daily bullet trains taking 5 hours are to run in each direction. The full north-south trunk line features 12 connections with east-west trains, integrating much of the nation's territory. Keith Bradsher, "High-Speed Rail Poised to Alter China," *New York Times*, June 23, 2011, p. B1 and Ian Johnson, "High-Speed Trains in China to Run Slower, Ministry Says," *New York Times*, June 14, 2011, p. A6. Brian Spegele and Bob Davis, "High-Speed Train Links Beijing, Shanghai," *Wall Street Journal*, June 29, 2011. Supporters point to this network as a way to spread economic development, increase trade and the flow of people and ideas, and integrating the country. Critics, on the other hand, highlight corruption, safety issues, high use price and elite-focus, environmental impact, high cost, and the need for massive subsidies.
9. For example, the total passenger number in Beijing Capital International Airport almost tripled between 2003 and 2010 (from 27 million to 74 million) while air cargo traffic rose from 660,000 total cargo to 1.5 million. Airports Council International. 2012 "World's Top 30 Airports: 2000–2010," online.
10. Of the world's top 10 container ports, eight are in Asia (six of them in China). With 121 million TEU containers in 2011, these six Chinese ports manage nearly one fourth (23 percent) of the world total container traffic. "The JOC TOP 50 World Container Ports," *Journal of Commerce*, 13(29) (August 20–27, 2012): 24–30.
11. The 10 countries are Brazil, Mexico, Chile, Peru, Colombia, Argentina, Uruguay, Paraguay, Ecuador and Bolivia.
12. The seven-point scale Global Competitiveness Index published by the WEF is telling in this regard. In 2012, the aggregated score of the quality of overall infrastructure for eight Latin American countries (Brazil, Chile, Mexico, Argentina, Ecuador, Peru, Bolivia, and Venezuela) was 3.7, while the combined score for four East Asian countries (China, Japan, South Korea, and Taiwan) was significantly higher: 5.4. East Asia and Latin America differ on the quality of road and port infrastructure. The infrastructure gap between these two regions is even more striking in the quality of railroad infrastructure: whereas Asia generally received a 5.6 score, that for Latin America was only 2.1.

13. John Price, "Latin America's Downside: Competitiveness," *Latin American Business Chronicle*, October 11, 2007. Productivity grew less than 4 percent between 2003 and 2005, probably due to annual investments of less than 2 percent of GDP in infrastructure.
14. See The Louis Berger Group's "Linking Argentina and Chile," April 2009, (online) for an IDB-commissioned feasibility study of the Andean Highway Passes Program to expand and modernize the transportation network between Chile and Argentina.
15. Edwards (1995), Glade (1991), Haggard and Kaufman (1992, 1995), Williamson (1990, 1994). My own approximation of the Brazilian case is found in Font (2003).
16. Several international conferences held after 2006 have explored and compared individual Latin American countries and public-private processes, seeking to derive lessons and a comparative paradigm for Latin American partnerships applicable throughout the region. The publication *ProjectFinance* and Euromoney Seminars organized the "Latin American PPP and Infrastructure: Finance Summit" in Miami, March 22–23, 2007, which was repeated in 2008 as the second Finance Summit on Latin American PPP and Infrastructure. Another business group organized a similar conference, "Infrastructure Investment World LatAm 2008" in Miami, September 23–25, 2008.
17. See also Chong and López-de-Salines (2005).
18. "China's Economy and the WTO: All Change," *The Economist*, December 10, 2011. "Ten Years of China in the WTO: Shades of Grey," *The Economist*, December 10, 2011. Bettina Wassener, "For China, a Shift from Exports to Consumption," *New York Times*, January 20, 2014.
19. See also Strange (1988 and 1996).
20. Critics have pointed out that the ISI approach mischaracterized the relationship between exports-led growth and development; said little about the production of capital goods; failed to anticipate that transnational corporations rather than domestic industrialists would benefit from tariff protection; and was too optimistic about larger governments or the prospects for democracy.
21. See also Gereffi and Wyman (1990).
22. World Bank (1993) argued that market-friendly policies played the main role in the success of the Asian tigers.
23. Evans (1995). Gereffi and Wyman (1990) and Gereffi and Korzeniewicz (1994) focused on global commodity chains to account for the dynamism of Asia relative to Latin America. Both strands of analysis agree on the significance of state policies in directing economic behavior. "Late late" development posed challenges for world systemic approaches, the starting point of Gereffi and others. See also Gereffi (2009).
24. Introduced by Pollit and Bouckaert (2004) as a public administration paradigm, the "neo-Weberian state" approach insists that bureaucracy is still the best alternative to organize the operations of state institutions. This model emphasizes the importance of division of labor, as well as rules, procedures, and top-down authority (hierarchy) as crucial coordination instruments (Bouckaert et al., 2010: 34–35; see also Kostakis, 2011). Drechsler (2009), Kostakis (2011), and others

see this approach as superior to the market-oriented New Public Management, using Evans and Rauch (1999) as empirical support for this assertion. The neo-Weberian state concept differs somewhat from the classical bureaucracy model in positing direct external links to citizen need and wishes (Drechsler, 2009; Lynn, 2008; Pollit and Bouckaert, 2004: 99–100). That is, it seeks to supplement the role of representative democracy by new forms of consultation and direct citizen representation. Aspects of European Union administration are seen as successful combinations of modernization, efficiency, and focus on citizens.

25. The need for innovation to enhance competitiveness are also reinforcing the formation of knowledge or innovation system.

Two State and Liberalization in Latin America

1. As stated by a Latin American development bank, "*sin infraestructura no hay desarrollo*" ("there is no development without infrastructure") (CAF, 2010). For more on Latin American infrastructure, see Calderón and Servén (2009).
2. Hirschman (1968) provides an influential early assessment of ISI (Baer, 1972). Edwards (1995) discusses the 1970s, reviews the critical literature, and presents a positive view of post-1982 reforms.
3. The succession of crises had a major impact on South American societies. As oil prices plunged, international financiers stopped investing in many parts of the emerging and developing worlds. Antiglobalization sentiment increased in Argentina and Brazil, contributing to the collapse of multilateral tariff reduction negotiations. Meanwhile, some countries in the region increased their hard currency reserves or dollarized their currency.
4. China's increased demand came from the use of soymeal to feed pork, poultry, and fish—as well as soybeans for direct human consumption.
5. Exports to China as percent of total exports varied a great deal in 2013: Chile 23 percent, Brazil 17 percent, Peru 15 percent, Uruguay 9 percent, Argentina 6 percent, Colombia 5 percent, and Mexico 2 percent. China consumes 42 percent of Peru's copper and 40 percent of Chilean copper.
6. My account of Mexican political and economic change through 2000 draws from Teichman (1988, 1995, 2001), Camp (1999), Cornelius (1996), Babb (2001), Centeno (1994, 1997), Schneider, Ross, and Heredia (2003), Cornelius (1996).
7. According to Chong and López-de-Silanes (2004b), new federal law for state-owned enterprises clarified the relationship and obligations between state-owned enterprises (SOEs) and the state, leading to a large reduction in unprofitable enterprises. See also Aspe (1993).
8. The Library of Congress Country Studies and CIA World Factbook (June 1996) "Mexico Privatization." See also Kapur et al. (1997); Chong and López-de-Silanes (2004b).
9. Calderón and Servén (2004b: 30). Public investment for this period fell to just 5 percent of its level for 1980–1985—from 1.54 to 0.08 percent of GDP.

10. Fideicomiso de Apoyo al Rescate Carretero. Overall, there were three sets of acquisitions: FARAC I, II, and III. The World Bank puts the bailout at $8 billion (Engel et al., 2003; World Bank, 2003). The 2003 World Bank report highlights fours reasons for the failure of the first concessions program: low financial feasibility and poorly made feasibility studies, high toll levels due to short concession periods, underbidding, and ability of contractors to increase costs.
11. Camp (2010) contrasts the two PAN presidencies after 2000, while highlighting differences between this party, the PRI and the PRD. According to Camp, after 2000 technocrats began to lose ground to a new generation of political leaders with more diverse training and background. Pastor and Wise (2005) discuss why the Fox government could not make a major dent in the reform process, pointing to political rivalries, infighting, and other challenges of divided government. Calderón was more adept at negotiation and alliance-building than Fox, but had to face major issues of internal unity and security from drug crime.
12. Within the new PPS scheme, the government authorizes projects through the finance minister (Secretaría de Hacienda y Crédito Público), while sectoral ministries help evaluate them (e.g., SCT or Secretaría de Comunicaciones y Transportes handles new road projects). The "Reglas para la realización de Proyectos para Prestación de Servicios" of April 2004 is the main regulatory law. Partnerships UK advised the Mexican authorities in designing its PPS program, which was inspired by the British PFI model. See Secretaría de Hacienda y Crédito Público "Proyectos para Prestación de Servicios," February 2007.
13. In addition, the program known as Fibras (Fideicomisos de Infraestructura y Bienes Raíces) began to sell bonds linked to the income from some of the above concessions.
14. Mexico also developed a local transit system. In 2007, Mexico City partnered with the World Resources Institute's Center for Sustainable Transport (EMBARQ) to implement a new bus rapid transit called Metrobús. This new transit system with dedicated lanes claimed to transport passengers for less than one-tenth of the cost of an equivalent light rail metro system and in one-half the time of a conventional bus (www.metrobus.df.gob.mx).
15. Mexico's National Infrastructure Program 2007–2012 called for $226 billion investments from public and private sources—with transportation and telecommunications to receive 30 percent, oil and gas 47 percent, electricity 15 percent, and water 8 percent. Government would provide more than half of the budgeted figures for highways, railways, ports, and airports, as well as for water services. In turn, telecom would be mostly private. The plan aimed at increasing competitiveness, building a world-class logistics platform, and promoting the tourist sector (www.infrastructure.gob.mx). In 2008, government created the National Infrastructure Fund (Fonadin) initially financed from the 1990's FARAC highways bailout and later expanded.
16. FARAC I brought in $4.8 billion from a consortium led by Goldman Sachs (Niven et al., 2009: 12).
17. See "Programa para impulsar el crecimiento y el empleo," México, Secretaría de Hacienda y Crédito Público, October 2008.

18. Grey Brosnan, "A Bridge Too Far?" *LatinFinance*, December 2008: 43–45.
19. Derek M. Woodhouse, "Marco Regulatorio para el Desarrollo de Asociaciones Público-Privadas en Estados Mexicanos," Primer Encuentro Técnico sobre la Estructuración de Proyectos de Asociación Público-Privada, Mexico DF, February 19–20, 2009. See also Dirección General de Desarrollo de la Infraestructura Física (DGDIF), PPS.
20. One of the most influential is the Program to Promote Public-Private Partnerships in Mexican States (PIAPPEM), launched with the support of the World Bank and the Inter-American Development Bank. Woodhouse (2009) reviews progress in public-private collaboration by Mexican states. The Instituto Tecnológico de Monterrey developed a program on public-private partnerships in infrastructure and services.
21. The Pact for Mexico listed over 100 agreements on key reforms deemed essential. The mid-2013 subnational elections threatened the reform momentum, though many members of the two opposition parties (PAN and PRD) continued to support it. Pressure to liberalize the energy sector posed the main obstacle: with factions in the PRD and the PRI opposed to break the oil and gas monopoly of the state-owned PEMEX—the inefficient hydrocarbon giant that provided a third of federal government finances and employed a large number of Mexicans. Private companies could already partner with PEMEX on various service contracts, but the existing legal framework did not allow for agreements on profit-sharing and production-sharing. Pressure built for allowing foreign entities to participate in the exploration and production of oil and gas as partners of PEMEX. Tim Johnson, "Mexican President might Push Oil-Sector Revisions Past Skeptical Public," *The State* (South Carolina), July 23, 2013.
22. "Report: Mexico Cheaper than China for Manufacturing Appliances," The Boston Consulting Group. Online. Trucking is the primary mode of transport for the goods, moving approximately 85 percent of the value of goods traded "Supply Chain Bottlenecks: Border Crossing Inefficiencies Between Mexico and the United States," *International Journal of Trasport Economics* 31(2). Connectivity with US interstate highways was partly responsible. In rail, the merging of Canadian Pacific Railway and DM&E (Dakota, Minnesota and Eastern Railroad) and IC&E (Iowa, Chicago and Eastern Railroad) makes the network "the first truly North American continental railroad, positioned not only for NAFTA trade but for a large market share of the millions of containers" ("Deal Creates Path for NAFTA Railway," WND).
23. The circumstances leading to the Peronist return to power in 1989, the political system in the 1990s, and the 2001 economic collapse are discussed in Manzetti (2009: chapter 4), Silva (2009a).
24. A public sector reform bill (Law 23,696) set the framework for the privatization program, while an economic emergency bill (Law 23,697) authorized broad power to contract private enterprises to perform public services and increase productivity. In 2001, Law 1299 and Decree 678 of 2001 refined this framework.
25. Frank Sader, *Attracting Foreign Direct Investment into Infrastructure: Why Is It So Difficult?, World Bank*, November 1999: 86.

26. Silva (2009a) draws from Auyero (2007) and his own research to discuss the anti-Menem ("anti-neoliberal") contentious movement, presenting it as key factor in the victory of populists Peronists Néstor Kirchner (2003–2007) and Cristina Fernández de Kirchner (2008). For a somewhat different account, see Cohen (2012).
27. Santarcángelo and Perrone (2012). Guillermo O'Donnell and other social scientists repeatedly commented on impasse or instability of policymaking in Argentina (e.g., Tommasi, 2010; Corradi, 1985; Lewis, 1992).
28. Belgrano Cargas, a rail network of 10,841 kilometer consolidated as a state enterprise in 1948, was converted to a concession controlled by the rail workers union and an industrial cooperative, after which it was largely privatized (79 percent of shares) in 1999.
29. Pablo González and Matt Craze, "Argentina Banks on Railroads to Prolong Soybean Booms: Freight," *Bloomberg News*, June 18, 2013. See also "The Decadence of Argentina's Rail System," *Buenos Aires Herald*, June 5, 2013
30. Financial losses had provided the main justification for privatizing the rail network between 1992 and 1995. Under increasing competition from trucks and road construction—the 35,000 kilometer national network then run by Ferrocarriles Argentinos was losing more than a billion dollars a year. Privatization of the six components of the network would improve service and force the railways to be financially sound under free market rules, it was hoped. ALL and other operators under this plan won concessions for 30 years, with 10-year extensions. In 1999, ALL acquired a freight railway network of 8,000 kilometer that covered a large part of the country and serviced Bunge, Cargill, and other grains trading companies. The economic contractions and crises of 1994, 1998, and 2001 had a negative impact on concessions. As ALL tended to accumulate debts and service failed to improve, trucks continued to handle much of the freight.
31. "The Tragedy of Argentina: A Century of Decline," *The Economist*, February 25, 2014. Wylde (2011).
32. "Brazil Infrastructure: Paving the Way," *Morgan Stanley Blue Paper*, May 5, 2010.
33. In New York City alone, for instance, the Brazilian-American Chamber of Commerce's Brazil Summit of 2005 had PPP as a main theme—as was also the case in separate visits to that city by the governors of São Paulo and Bahia. In addition, consultants and investors organized various meetings. The IDB, World Bank, and others organized frequent meetings on Brazil. Besides São Paulo and Minas Gerais, the states of Bahia, Ceará, Goiás, Espírito Santo, Rio Grande do Sul, Santa Catarina announced their own programs and legislation (Chapter Five).
34. A federal high-speed authority, Atav, was being formalized in mid-2012 (BNAmericas, June 6, 2012), with ANTT to launch the first tender later in the year.
35. "Copa do Mundo vai custar R$3.5 bi a mais ao governo," *Folha de S. Paulo*, June 16, 2014. This figure would probably grow after accounting for all expenses. According to *Folha*, R$6 billion of World Cup expenses were transferred to the PAC.

36. *Folha de S. Paulo*: 97 percent public sector. Originally, authorities conveyed the impression that the private sector would play a major role.
37. The list of major construction and concession operators includes Odebrecht, Arteris (OHL), Queiroz Galvão, UTC Participações, Eco-Rodovia, CCR, TPI (Triunfo Participacões e Investimentos), Investimentos e Participacões em Infraestrutura. National sources of funding include BNDES, Caixa, Banco do Brasil, and large pension funds as well as the federal government directly. Dozens of firms provide legal, financial, and technical advice. Brazil also had a specialized business press that encompasses large newspapers *Folha de S. Paulo, O Estado de S. Paulo, O Globo, Valor Econõmico*, and several other publications.
38. During much of the nineteenth century and into the 1920s, Chile's relatively small state was guided by economic liberalism, though conflicts and wars within the country and with neighboring Peru and Bolivia had led to a centralized and unitary state, a professional military, and a lasting legacy in state-making (Góngora, 1981; Marcel, 1999; see also Saylor, 2012). After the 1920s, various governments organized a modern welfare state, development agencies, and state companies. Vellinga (1998) discusses the post-1930s changing role of state in Latin American development.
39. Max Weber's (1958) account of the rise of modern capitalist practices in Europe gave prominence to Puritan ethical norms, but only because such ideas and the interest-driven behavior of a market economy proved favorable to each other at a critical juncture and opportunity for social change (Weber, 1968). As the story goes, Pinochet's embrace of the Chicago approach came about when one of his associates, learning of the military government's urgent search for an economic recovery program, brought him into contact with a network of Chilean economists trained at the University of Chicago (see Commanding Heights website). Valdés' (1995) account emphasizes the deliberate transfer of ideas from the United States to Chile. Góngora (1981) provides a distinctive defense of the state against threats posed by the neoliberalism of the Pinochet regime.
40. By 2005, this program was responsible for 44 projects valued at \$5.7 billion (about 6¼ percent of the 2004 GDP). These include: 8 projects to upgrade the Route 5 highway extending the length of Chile, financed through tolls (\$2 billion); additional highway projects for connecting roads to Route 5 (\$1.3 billion); 10 airport projects (\$240 million); 6 urban road projects (\$1.8 billion); and 9 projects too include prisons, public buildings, and a reservoir (\$360 million). See Engel et al. (1997, 2002, 2003, 2006, 2009) for assessment of concessions awarded in Chile between 1993 and 2006.
41. The new concessions law updated previous legislation on the construction, rehabilitation, maintenance, and operation of public works and infrastructure. It aimed at a transparent system of competitive bidding, establishing mutual rights and obligations, and setting up conflict resolution procedures.
42. Interview with Guillermo Díaz (July 2006). As per a July 2006 interview with Germán Correa (former minister of transportation), in the late 1980s he gathered information on Mexico's concessions program to help draft Chile's Concessions Law of 1991.

43. In 1995, after Congress passed unanimous support for legislation and plans, the Ministry of Public Works finally initiated the first wave of concessions (Tune Melón, segments of Highway 5 [Chile's north-south highway], Autopista Santiago-San Antonio, shortly followed by east-west urban highways, and airports).
44. In 1997, Law 19,542 ended state monopoly of ports and authorized concessions and partnerships to improve and operate them. The first wave was in 1999, the second took place during the Lagos presidency, while the third started after the 2010 election of Sebastián Piñera. By then, Chilean firms had gained experience operating ports and were eager to participate in projects linked to the 2010 earthquake (*El Mercurio*).
45. By the early 1990s, fast growth in the second half of the 1980s and 1990s exposed sizeable infrastructure bottlenecks, but adjustment and stabilization programs in the 1980s constrained public investment infrastructure maintenance. Infrastructure deficiencies for the second half of the 1990s were over 20 percent of Chile's 1993 GDP (IMF, April 1, 2005).
46. Hemming, Richard. 2006. "Public-private partnerships, government guarantees, and fiscal risk." Washington, DC: International Monetary Fund.
47. These payments are activated if revenue from tolls falls from a mutually accepted level or if user fees falls below a mutually acceptable level or the exchange rate depreciates by more than 10 percent (as shown by the inflation-adjusted UF unit widely used in Chilean contracts).
48. In a 2006 interview with Gibrán Harcha, he described Transantiago as a system of interconnected concessionaires between companies given exclusive rights over specific routes in exchange for investing in low contamination buses and the obligation to sign contracts with other private operators in charge of finances (the AFT, Financial Administrator of Transantiago) and system administration as well as with private companies in charge of providing information and services to users (SIAUT). In turn, both AFT and SIAUT had to sign contracts with operators. That is, this was not a simple concession between government and a private operators but an advanced form with contractual relations with other companies in the system.
49. Uziel Gómez, "El MOP reactiva los proyectos de concesiones para este año: Aumentan en 136 por ciento," *El Mercurio*, January10, 2009.

Three Liberalization/Anti-Liberalization

1. For example, the August 2004 issue of *Latin American Research Review* includes diverse views on liberalizing reforms (Weyland, Walton, Huber, 2004).
2. Macdonald and Ruckert (2009); Rovira (2011); Boschi and Santana (2012); Costoya (2011); Grugel and Riggirozzi (2012); Kennemore and Weeks (2011); Leiva (2008). Hershberg and Rosen (2006) also present the idea of a postliberal Latin America. For public dissatisfaction with privatization, see, for example, Bonnet et al. (2012).

3. For broad interpretations of left turns in Latin America, see Castañeda (2006); Panizza (2005, 2009); Roberts (1998, 2009); Kaufman (2011); Murillo et al. (2011); Fishlow (2006).
4. See "The Season of El Niño," *The Economist*, June 7, 1998; Suplee (1999); Broad and Orlove (2007). El Niño also had significant impacts in Central America and Mexico, as well as Northeastern Brazil ($4 billion), Guyana, Argentina ($3 billion), and other countries. Weather turbulence resulted in a death toll estimated at 2,100 people and damages of $13–33 billion. According to Suplee, El Niño 1997–1998 had the energy of a million Hiroshima bombs.
5. See Appendix A for inflation, external debt, and macroeconomic indicators. Theoretical formulations on strong state-making includes its impact on democracy (Tilly, 2007).
6. Manzano and Monaldi (2008). Silva (1999) emphasized the role of social movements opposing neoliberalism. Flores-Macías (2010) sees them as more likely in leftist turns with weak party systems, contrasting the above (Bolivia, Ecuador, and Venezuela) with Brazil, Chile, and Uruguay, where a uniform market approach has prevailed. Kennemore and Weeks (2011) see an elusive or frustrated search for alternative socialism due to poor implementation of reforms, economic volatility, and opposition. For a review of the literature on post-neoliberalism, see also Rovira (2011).
7. Huntington (1968) provides an influential account of political instability based on the weaknesses of institutions relative to various sources of social mobilization.
8. The proposal to construct a pipeline to Chile to export gas to the United States fueled the perception that natural resource extraction benefited foreign companies but not the Bolivian people. Opposition to privatization thus had a nationalist as well as antielitist character, in addition to anti-Chile sentiment, a neighbor deeply resented for the loss of land and access to the sea in the War of the Pacific (Sinnott et al., 2010: 34). According to a World Bank report, the Bolivian privatization drive of the 1990s was seen as contributing to inequality as the government share of gas revenue diminished.
9. "Nationalizing Utilities in Bolivia: From Tap to Socket," *The Economist*, January 19, 2013.
10. Emily Achtenberg, "From Water Wars to Water Scarcity: Bolivia's Cautionary Tale," *Rebel Currents*, June 6, 2013.
11. Marcelo Ballvé, "Despite Nationalizations, Bolivia's Resource Sector Attracts Asian Investors," *World Politics Review*, August 9, 2012.
12. Eastern Bolivia consists of fertile lowlands suitable for agriculture and endowed with the country's main gas deposits and other minerals. In differs markedly from the high Andes to the west in terms of ethnic composition, values, lifestyle, and political orientation. It has been influenced by Brazil, with which Bolivia has a great deal of economic exchange, including main destination of its exports).
13. Financed by BNDES, the Brazilian development bank, and built by the Brazilian construction company OAS. Under pressure from various stakeholders, in mid-2012 Morales announced support for a national referendum.

14. The Galápagos Islands would be fourth, but its remoteness and small size of 25,000 make it largely irrelevant to the processes discussed here.
15. "The Ecuadorian currency crisis [of 1998–2000] originated from a series of external shocks. While agriculture products and crude oil were the major exports of Ecuador, El Niño floods in the late 1997 and 1998 destroyed vast agricultural areas in the coastal region and reduced Ecuador's agricultural productions. Oil prices in the world market also sank to its historically low—less than $10 per barrel—significantly reducing the total revenue of the debt-ridden Ecuadorian government. As a result, the fiscal deficit was 6.2 percent of GDP, while the total debt/GDP ratio reached 66.3 percent. Worse still, as the effects of the Asian financial crisis spilled over to Latin America, the foreign loanable funds available to the Ecuadorian government and private banks were further reduced" (Cubas et al., 2010: 3).
16. For the economic and social impact of natural disasters in Ecuador in 1997–1998, see Calero et al. (2009) and Vos (2003). According to Vos, the number of events tripled and agricultural losses equaled an estimated 1.1 percent of GDP for those years. The climate anomalies related to El Niño included droughts, flood, fires, frosts, and infectious diseases. Thirteen of Ecuador's 32 volcanoes are considered active and there were 2 mid-sized eruptions in 1999 (Guagua and Tungurahua regions). Mudslides alone could also wreak havoc (with that of 1993 in the Azuay province causing 50 deaths and losses of over $140 million). El Niño's effects in 1997–1998 included nearly 300 deaths and 30,000 displaced persons who lost their houses. Flooding, brought, economic damages, unemployment, and health consequences to a fourth of the population. To top it all, a large earthquake hit Manati province in 1998. The World Bank's Ecuador Dashboard (online) provides information on climate adversities.
17. Remittances from Ecuadorian migrants to the United States, Spain, and other countries reached $1.3 billion in 2000 (Banco Central del Ecuador).
18. The port city of Guayaquil, by far the largest and most industrialized urban area, has also been the site of powerful political factions often tied to modern business interests. As cultural and political center of the coastal region, Guayaquil often clashes with the more traditional capital city of Quito and the Andean highlands of which it is a part.
19. To that effect, it engaged in political action, including the ousting of the governments of Abdalá Bucaram in 1996 and of Jamil Mahuad in 2000, to then support the election of retired Coronel Lucio Gutiérrez, in whose government they briefly held some cabinet positions, and whose overthrow they also implicitly endorsed. After helping elect Rafael Correa, CONAIE and its political arm have been actively opposing a number of his policies.
20. See also "Ecuador's Economy Grew by 4.5% in 2013," *Wall Street Journal*, April 21, 2014.
21. The policy of economic openness was introduced at the end of the presidency of Virgilio Barco (1986–1990) with the explicit purpose of ending protectionism and import substitution industrialization. For a background to the new approach, known as *apertura*, see "Programa de Modernización de la Economía Colombiana."

22. For Colombia's economic history, see Ocampo (1984), McGreevy (2008), and Palacios (2002).
23. A slowdown of GDP growth did take place between 1981 and 1983, with rates of growth of 2.3 percent, 0.9 percent, and 1.6 percent in these three years, but this downturn was less severe than in most Andean countries.
24. For the development plans of these presidents, visit the Departamento Nacional de Planeación (DNP) website.
25. In addition to the 1997–1999 shocks affecting the entire region, the push for free trade agreement with the United States came to a halt after the latter "decertified" Colombia as a country cooperative with US antinarcotics policies, thus creating a disincentive for US companies to further invest in Colombia.
26. Other exports included gold, chemicals, coffee, machinery, and flowers.
27. Telecommunications' $13.4 billion makes this the top sector in terms of total investment, though it had come about in bursts—1994, 1997–1998, and 2006. Of the $2.9 billion invested in 2011, $2 billion went toward telecommunications. Water-related services have attracted $940 million through 2010.
28. The 2011 transformation of INCO into ANI resulted from restructuring under the newly elected Juan Manuel Santos government.
29. Concessions were governed by a mixture of specific sector laws, such as Law No. 105 and decrees such as No. 4533 of 2008, which modified the concessions laws.
30. For arguments about the pressing need for more investments in infrastructure, see "Los cinco costos del rezago en infraestructura vial," *El Tiempo.com*, June 8, 2012. See also online publications by Cámara Colombiana de la Infraestructura.
31. "Colombia triplicará inversión en infraestructura hasta 2014," *Revista Portafolio*, February 20, 2012. Juan Abarca, "Colombia's ANI Receives 38 Expressions of Interest for Two Highways Worth U.S$1,21Bn," *BNamericas*, May 30, 2013. "Concesiones de Autopistas para la prosperidad despiertan enorme interés de firmas nacionales y extranjeras" May 31, 2013.
32. Sheahan (1999) reviews the frustrated search for development since 1950: political and institutional instability and missed opportunities resulting from mismanagement, inadequate institutions, and rivalries. Various reformist movements unable to form coalitions to bring about agrarian reform, ineffective program of import substituting industrialization, erratic populist interventionism, and the harsh swing toward neoliberalism under Fujimori.
33. Accounts of the Fujimori years can be found in Stokes (2001a), Levitsky (1999), Kay (1996), Roberts (1995), Arce (2010), and Silva (2009b: chapter 8).
34. For Peru's response to the weather, see also Broad and Orlove (2007). Before the late 1990s, weather disturbances associated with El Niño had wreaked havoc in Peru in 1982–1983, causing major flooding as well as droughts in various parts of the country, while also bringing major losses to fishing industry.
35. Victor Bulmer-Thomas (2003). For Peru's current mining boom, see James McKeigue, "This Peru Boom Will Run and Run," *InvestorIdeas.com*, June 11, 2013.

36. In 2000, the nationalist Humala led an unsuccessful military uprising against the Fujimori government and had come second to Alan García in the presidential elections of 2005. In 2011, Ollanta defeated Keiko Fujimori (daughter of the now imprisoned former president Alberto Fujimori) in the runoff elections, with former president Alejandro Toledo, famous writer Mario Vargas Llosa, and other figures representing new or emergent political movements having lost in the first round. Traditional parties failed to run competitive candidates in the highly polarized contest. For an assessment of the Humala government after two years in government, see Robert Kozak, "Peru Leader Surprises Critics with Free-Market Policies," *Wall Street Journal*, June 10, 2013. Economy had doubled since 2002 and was growing at 6.3 percent. Meanwhile, Ollanta Humala' own parents and several siblings continued to advocate a mixture of Peruvian nationalism and Marxism, including active opposition to foreign investment in domestic natural resource extraction.
37. James McKeigue, "Feeling Adventurous? You Should Invest in Peru," *InvestorIdeas.com*, June 10, 2013.
38. The Regional and Local Public Investment with Private Participation Law is taken to have made it easier to attract public investment.
39. The legal framework includes the Law of Concessions in Public Infrastructure and Public Services and the Certificate of the Right to Collect Annual Construction Payments (CRPAO).
40. The Huascacocha sanitation project is a 30-year concession for the construction, operation, and maintenance of a system that dams and diverts river flow. Fourteen firms presented bids for the $75 million project. Another water sanitation and irrigation project in the Olmos region north of Lima was approved as a 20-year BOT (build-operate-transfer) concession. The government approved $77 million to be used as guarantee and absorb some of the private sector risk.
41. The above number was nearly 45 percent of the investments already implemented, according to a 2010 report.
42. Robert Kozak, "Peru Protests Slow Mine Plan, Growth," *Wall Street Journal*, August 25, 2012: A9.
43. Alex Emery, "Newmont's Minas Conga Project could Restart in 2014, Government Says," *Business News Americas*, December 30, 2013. The top partners were Newmont, Buenaventura, and World Bank's International Finance Corporation.
44. "Brecha de infraestructura en Peru es de $88,000 millones," *RPP Notícias*, October 25, 2012. Alex Emery, "Peru to Award $10bn in 2013 Infrastructure Contracts," *Bloomberg News*, July 29, 2012. "Hay proyectos de inversión por más de US$13.5 millones en cartera," *ElComercio.pe*, May 20, 2013. For a brief overview of PPP projects and program in Peru, see Ronceros and Fernandez-Davila (n/d).
45. For example, CEPLAN, "Eje estratégico 5: desarrollo regional e infraestructura," Plan Bicentenario, www.ceplan.gob.pe; Darwin Cruz, "El Ceplan redefinirá objetivos estratégicos del Peru," *ElComercio.pe*, October 31, 2012. Authored by the National Center for Strategic Planning (CEPLAN, Centro Nacional de

Planeación Estratégica), the Bicentennial Plan (Plan Bicentenario: Peru Hacia el 2021) groups objectives related to economic growth and infrastructure, but also modernization of the state, poverty eradication, education improvements, and related measures to improve the quality of life. This report includes productive investments focused in the internal and external market, as well as investments for decentralization, regional development, and the promotion of public-private partnerships.

46. Brazil's four southern states (São Paulo, Paraná, Santa Catarina, and Rio Grande do Sul) share the Southern Cone's mix of prosperity and cultural distinctiveness based on a strong presence of immigrants from Italy and other countries.
47. Pereyra (2009) describes the new concessionaire, CVA, as a private firm owned by the Corporación Nacional para el Desarrollo, an agency under the ministry of transportation and public works, elsewhere defined as an effective megaconcession.
48. "Paraguay mejoró en el ranking de alianzas público-privadas," *La Nación* (Paraguay), March 10, 2013.
49. Journalists argued for public-private alliance to solve problems of the Paraguay River ("Alianza público-privada puede recuperar el río Paraguay," *Ultimahora.com*, July 6, 2013). With 80 percent of goods arriving in local market through the river, but the recently constructed private ports not making the expected contribution, they argued that public-private collaboration as the preferred way to address the problem.
50. "Plan Nacional de Logística, Paraguay: Avances y Plan de Trabajo 2012–2013," September 2012.
51. "Magnate Becomes Paraguay's President, Wooing Foreign Investment and Denying Past Accusations," *Washington Post*, August 15, 2013.
52. Though not discussed in depth in this volume, Venezuela is an important case. Geographically part of the Andean region, its oil wealth and other factors make it a unique case. This country subscribed $15.5 billion public-private investment in infrastructure before 2010, but the presidency of Hugo Chávez brought public-private collaboration to a virtual stop in and after 2004, with the exception of telecommunications.

Four Commodities and Rail in Globalizing Brazil

1. Also in the *Cerrado* ecosystem are the savannas in parts of adjacent states: Bahia, Maranhão, Piauí, and Ceará in the northeast; Tocantins, Pará, and Rondônia in the north or Amazon region; Minas Gerais and the D. F. These states are themselves quite diverse. Rainforest and wetlands occupy major parts of western and northern Mato Grosso as well as Mato Grosso do Sul's floodplain and marshes known as Pantanal—which have warmer and more humid climate than the *Cerrado* of the higher elevations.
2. See Oliveira and Marquis (2002). Larry Rohter, "Scientists Are Making Brazil's Savannah Bloom," *New York Times*, October 2, 2007. EMBRAPA's website

contains considerable information about the *Cerrado* (www.embrapa.br). See also "America's Transport Infrastructure: The Miracle of the Cerrado," *The Economist*, August 26, 2010. Lime and phosphorous are part of the soil treatment.

3. CONAB (Companhia Nacional de Abastecimento) 2014, *Indicadores da Agropecuária* 22 (July 7): 16. See also CONAB's *Séries Históricas*; IBGE; Silva and Marujo, 2012.
4. The greater Amazon Basin covers 7 million square km in several countries. In Brazil, soy in the Amazon or north region has grown from very low levels of 177 thousand tons in 2000 to over 3.25 million tons in 2014. Tocantins, Pará, Rondonia, and other states are poised for expansion, as trading companies install terminals and transhipment centers along the Madeira and Amazons rivers and a system of barges to move grains to shipping ports nearer the mouth of the Amazon river.
5. "China's Interest in Farmland Makes Brazil Uneasy," *New York Times*, May 26, 2011. Agricultural expansion faces opposition over several other issues: encroachment into lands claimed by Amerindian groups, environmental impact, land distribution, and the use of genetically modified soy.
6. Andre Soliani and Humberto Medina, "Safra pára no gargalo da infra-estrutura," *Folha de S. Paulo*, February 1, 2004. This UNESP report is also available online. A report by the US Department of Commerce argues that in 1995 the cost of shipping a ton of soy from Santos or Paranaguá was $14 but it costs only $3 in New Orleans, while average transportation from the point of production to port was more than $80 in Brazil but only $16 in New Orleans (US Department of Commerce, 2005) "Brazilian Infrastructure: Highways, Railways, and Airports," CS Brazil Market Research. In one study, moving one ton of soybeans to shipping port costs $5.50 in the United States, $16 in Argentina, and $23.50 in Brazil. Another estimate for 2013 pointed that while producers in North America paid $25 (R$56) per ton to transport soy to the port of New Orleans, the cost to Brazilian counterparts from Mato Grosso was $144 (R$326) per ton to transport soy by truck to the port of Santos. Brazil's port costs of up to 5 percent of value compared unfavorably to 1–1.5 percent in the United States and Argentina.
7. Rudy Ruitenberg, "Brazil Soybeans Need Heavy Infrastructure Spend to Catch Up U.S.," *Bloomberg Businessweek*, May 13, 2013.
8. World Economic Forum (2012) ranks Brazil in 48th place in competitiveness. Infrastructure has ranked high as impediment to doing business in Brazil, third only to tax rates and regulations according to the WEF's Global Competitiveness Report 2011.
9. Vale owns or controls 10,000 km of railroads and at least 9 ports, together with a fleet of large ships. "Valuable Vale," *The Economist*, September 23, 2010.
10. The other large Brazilian producers of ethanol are Biosev and San Martinho. São Paulo had approximately 380 sugar mills.
11. "Xi Brings Brazil Chinese Deals for Jets, Energy, Cars," *Bloomberg News*, July 17, 2014. Lisandra Paraguassu and Tánia Montenegro, "Brasil e China assinam 32 acordos," *Estadao*, July 18, 2014.

12. "China's Interest in Farmland Makes Brazil Uneasy," *New York Times*, May 26, 2011.
13. After the merger, RFFSA covered 22,000 km. In 1969, this federal network was organized in terms of four broad regions (south, south-central, central, and northeast), increased to ten divisions in 1976. In 1998, São Paulo's FEPASA was briefly incorporated into RFFSA before its conversion to concessions.
14. At the same time, complementary plans sought to create concessions for multimodal networks joining roads and rail to navigable rivers and waterways, such as the Amazon-Madeira, Araguaia, Tapajós, Tocantins, São Francisco, and Tietê-Paraná.
15. Meanwhile, states and subnational units retained authority over state highways and other policy domains. São Paulo, a leader in the use of public-private collaboration, created ARTESP in 2002 to regulate its highway concessions and related projects.
16. See Fitch Ratings, "Evolução do Setor Ferroviário Brasileiro," March 2005; ANTT; and Institute of Logistics & Supply Chain (ILOS).
17. Márcio Rogério Silveira, "A importância geoeconômica das estradas de ferro no Brasil," Universidade Estadual Paulista, September 2003. Though it argues against privatization, this source shows freight increase from 38 million tons in 1995 to 53 million tons in 2002, suggesting more efficiency under private operation. See also "Óbras ferroviárias tem recursos garantidos," *Ministério dos Transportes*, June 5, 2006.
18. Brasil Ferrovias, the 1998 holding company that acquired Ferronorte, Novoeste, and eventually Ferroban, was a major exception, as its debts pushed it toward restructuring. See Daniel Rittner, "Dobram os investimentos nas ferrovias," *Valor Econômico*, September 29, 2004.
19. The Ministry of Transportation developed plans to invest more than R$10 billion in railroad expansion. At the time, Brazilian authorities reported China's willingness to invest up to $10 billion in railways, ports, and highways in Brazil, particularly on the North-South Railway, soy and other agricultural products. Vale/CVRD, owner of Carajás Railroad and Ferrovía Centro-Atlântico, developed plans to improve its Vitória-Minas Railroad. América Latina Logística (ALL) also studied major upgrades. The early Lula administration agreed to $1.4 billion in upgrades to the railroad system, complementing private investments for $2.5 billion already made or planned for the period 2005–2010, including work on the Transnordestina, the 2,000-kilometer railroad linking northeastern states and the connection between grain-producing areas in Maranhão and Piauí to ports in Pernambuco and Ceará (Accioli and Monteiro, 2012).
20. The 2008 law restructured Valec as a state enterprise headquartered in Brasilia. Created in 1972 with Vale as the main shareholder, Valec was later transferred to the Ministry of Transportation. It owned concessions for FNS; E. F. 246 (also known as Transoceanic, Transcontinental, or Central-West, or E. F. 354), from northern Rio to Peru; E. F. 334 (West-East Integration or FICO), E. F. 267 (Novoeste, from FNS to Murtinho). These railways were confirmed in the 2010 national transportation plan.

21. The first progress report for PAC2 in 2011 estimated that at least 26 percent of the projects would not be finished by 2014 with transportation being one of the most worrisome (Fitzpatrick, 2011).
22. "PF aponta superfaturamento na obra da ferrovia Norte-Sul," *Folha de S. Paulo*, July 15, 2012. Agencia Estado reported that Valec and its directors, together with a private company, were part of a scheme to overbill R$48 million in a 105-kilometer segment in central Goiás. Valec's lawyers blamed faulty figures, but investigators found other instances of corruption in the bidding process for other segments.
23. "Acusado de desvios, ex-presidente da Valec deixa prisão," *Estadão*, July 11, 2012.
24. The implicated political party's temporary withdrawal from the alliance helped defuse the crisis. Though this scandal in the most important infrastructure project fed speculation about other large undertakings, it did not lead to a major assessment of state capabilities in this area. The practice of widespread political appointments and still inadequate mechanisms of transparency and accountability were in tension with meritocratic professional civil service and good governance.
25. The original plan called for Ferronorte to be divided into two lines after reaching Mato Grosso's capital of Cuiabá. One branch would head north for 2,000 kilometers to the Amazon port of Santarém (Pará), while the other would run west-northwest for 1,500 kilometers to reach Porto Velho (capital of Rondônia and trading center at the Madeira river, a main tributary of the Amazon).
26. "Novo terminal da Ferronorte será inaugurado neste sábado," *ExpressoMT*, June 20, 2012.
27. "Malha ferroviária reacende expectativa da melhoria logística em MT," *Midia News*, June 9, 2013; "Ferronorte vai escoar a produção do MT," Sindicato dos Engenheros do Estado de São Paulo, 2013.
28. The smaller TKU and TU levels for FNS reflect lower levels of demand as well as shorter distances.
29. For instance, the West-East Integration Railroad (FICO)'s first stage from Campinorte to Lucas do Rio Verde, part of PAC2, was about to start. A second stage would take it to the western state of Rondonia. Meanwhile, Chinese investors hinted that they might help finance the 1,118 miles from Cuiabá to the port of Santarém (Pará), the point where the Tapajós river meets the mighty Amazon.
30. "Silval vai à China viabilizar ferrovia que liga Mato Grosso," *CenárioMT*, June 20, 2012.
31. Already the largest iron ore mine in the world, the S11D project being built next to it would make Carajás much larger after it starts operation in 2016, together with the duplication of the railroad and the upgrade of Vale's Ponta da Madeira port terminal close to the public port of Itaqui also accessed by the northeastern CFN railroad.
32. "Ferrovia Norte-Sul poderá ser implementada sob a forma de concessão comum," *Ministério do Planejamento, Orçamento e Gestão*, June 12, 2005.
33. In early 2004, President Lula visited China with a large number of his ministers and business leaders, while China's President Hu Jintao visited Brazil in

November of that year. In the context of these high-level meetings, the Chinese promised up to $5 billion to complete the North-South Railway, other railroads, and related port facilities. But these negotiations did not advance and the idea for constructing FNS as a public-private partnership was abandoned.

34. Massive investments would also benefit the northeast. Starting in 2006, $6.72 billion would be spent on upgrading 1,728 kilometers of the Transnordestina railroad, including connections to FNS. Financed by the Northeast Development Fund, the Bank of the Northeast, BNDES, and other federal funds, the improvements were to be completed by 2013. However, major parts of the project were reported as abandoned or with no construction activity in 2014 (e.g., Simon Romero, "Grand Visions Fizzle in Brazil," *New York Times*, April 12, 2014). After 2008, the plan also listed a fast or bullet passenger train between Rio, São Paulo, and possibly other cities in the Southeast.
35. In existence since 1973, the Plano Nacional de Viação (PNV) was renamed as Sistema Nacional de Viação (SNV) in 2011.
36. The sixth project called for the construction phase of the 659-kilometer line to connect FNS (São Paulo's Estrela d'Oeste) to Dourados, Mato Grosso do Sul.
37. André Borges, "TCU apura superfaturamento em trechos da ferrovia Norte-Sul," *Estadão*, July 19, 2014. Auditing by the TCU confirms irregularities in FNS: overbilling, flawed supervision, and poor engineering plan. The TCU identified losses of R$27.3 million in contract signed in 2007 for the segment between Palmas and Aguiarnópolis as well as five other instances of overbilling and payments without invoice or exaggerated prices.
38. Ministério dos Transportes, "Contorno Ferroviário de São Paulo: Ferroanel," Seminário Internacional de Co-Financiamento BNDES/CAF Prospecção de Projetos de Integração Sul-Americana, Rio de Janeiro, August 8, 2003.
39. The extended metropolitan area comprising Campinas, Jundiaí, Santos, and São José dos Campos is home to more than 28 million residents.
40. São Paulo's PPA 2004–2007 listed Ferroanel as part of the infrastructure for São Paulo's metropolitan region and anticipated a budget of R$2 billion ("Transposição da Região Metropolitana de São Paulo–Rodoanel/Ferroanel;" see also "Agora é o Ferroanel," *Istoé Dinheiro*, August 24, 2005). As early as 2003, Governor Geraldo Alckmin thought there was agreement between the federal and state governments ("Ferroanel: O primeiro passo," *Brasilnews*, October 9, 2003).
41. Ferroanel can only hope to make progress via negotiations between both levels of government and railroad operators. The federal government has jurisdiction over the railroad network and is thus the key actor in financing, implementation, and development policy and projects, including the adoption of specific forms of public-private collaboration ("Plano de Revitalização das Ferrovias Modelo de PPP," July 2003).
42. São Paulo's vision of a multimodal approach to expedite access to Santos and enhance overall transportation called for building Ferroanel alongside Rodoanel, a highway beltway around São Paulo's metropolitan area. Rodoanel was designed several years earlier with the goal of alleviating traffic congestion from the ten major highways passing through the city—seven from the state system and the

three federal highways running in a north-south direction. It was on track for completion within a few years, as the government of São Paulo made strides in developing a state-level network (e.g., see the 2011 report from the state's Secretaria Estadual de Logística e Transportes).

43. Ministério dos Transportes. 2003. "Contorno Ferroviário de São Paulo: Ferroanel," 1 Seminário Internacional de Co-Financiamento BNDES/CAF Prospecção de Projetos de Integração Sul-Americana, Rio de Janeiro. Once approved, the 66-kilometer project from the Campo Limpo to Eng. Manoel Feio stations will take up to four years to complete.
44. See "Ferroanel deve sair do papel neste ano," *Gazeta Mercantil*, November 9, 2006; *BNAmericas*, November 8, 2006. See also Roberta Paduan, "Só falta tirar o projeto do papel," *Exame*, May 20, 2006.
45. Miriam Leitão and Alvaro Gribel, "Seis anos depois," *O Globo*, September 4, 2014. For background, see Abreu (2014).
46. For example, Brazil responded to the 2008 financial crisis by announcing a new wave of concessions—close to 8,900 kilometers of highways and investments of more than R$22 billion.
47. USDA's (2014) review of ports and rail projects in Brazil's north and northeast notes delays due to red tape, cost overruns, construction problems, coordination with federal authorities, legal challenges, insufficient organizational capacity, shortfalls in capital, environmental licensing, lack of coordination with neighboring states, while noting their potential role in increasing the competitiveness of agricultural commodities.
48. "Caminhoneiros protestam contra más condições nos pátios da ALL," *Jornal Hora do Povo*, February 5, 2010.
49. In the context of relative economic opening, Brazil welcomed the Initiative for the Integration of Regional Infrastructure in South America (IIRSA), a master plan to build roads and railroads linking Brazil to Andes countries and Pacific ports.
50. The mid-2013 urban protests throughout Brazil were fed by citizen grievances over poor services and the seemingly uncontrolled spending in expensive projects.
51. Raquel Landim and David Friedlander, "Com presidentes reféns, Brasil é 'ingerenciável,' diz Abílio Diniz," *Folha de S. Paulo*, August 24, 2014. According to this well-known entrepreneur and former member of the Lula cabinet, Brazil had become unmanageable from the compromises and agreements with 30 political parties and the high number of 39 ministries, making urgent the need for political reform.

Five Subnational Brazil

1. Ministério do Desenvolvimento, Indústria e Comércio Exterior. 2012. *Balança Comercial* (www.desenvolvimento.gov.br).
2. Economist Andrea Calabi's tenure as secretary of Planning from 2003 to 2005 started this idea, which was maintained by Martus Tavares, formerly the minister of Planning in the federal government, upon assuming that post. State legislation

inspired by the *Plano Plurianual* (2004–2007) and its emphasis on infrastructure for export promotion created the necessary regulatory framework for public-private partnerships, with the planning secretariat as manager of the program.

3. The highway *Rodovia dos Imigrantes* was an early example of a successful project entirely financed by the private sector.
4. Catia Seabra, "Alckmin retoma programa de desestatização," *Folha de S. Paulo*, April 3, 2005. The port of São Sebastião was still run by Dersa, a public company linked to São Paulo's Transportation Secretariat. Located about 200 kilometers from the city of São Paulo, this port shipped 400,000 tons in 2005.
5. Governo de Estado de São Paulo, "Programa Estadual de Parcerias Publico-Privadas (PPP)." See www.planejamento.sp.gov.br/.
6. In the bitter 2002 campaign against the PSDB candidate, the Workers' Party relied on harsh rhetoric against what they viewed as privatization and the "pernicious legacy" of the liberalizing reforms.
7. World Bank, PPIAF database. The precipitous decline came after 2000, reaching $3.4 billion in 2001, $1.2 billion in 2002 and 2003, $1.9 billion in 2004, and $2.5 billion in 2005.
8. The state of São Paulo had an important role in the operation of the Sorocabana Railroad and had direct control after 1919.
9. See AES Brasil website. CESP was created in 1966 out of eleven different companies in São Paulo, five of which had mixed capital. PED also converted CPFL, a company that had originally been created in 1912 by the merger of four small energy firms and underwent nationalization in 1964.
10. Tribunal de Contas da União (TCU), 2010, "Simplified Version of the General Accounts of the Republic—Year 2009: Growth Acceleration Program."
11. São Paulo, Secretaria de Planejamento e Desenvolvimento Regional, "Programa de Investimento do Estado de São Paulo: Parcerias Público-Privadas e Concessões," April 2011.
12. São Paulo's PPA 2012–2015 called for total investment of R$118.6 billion over the four years, with R$85.2 from the state government, R$33.4 from PPPs, and additional resources from state enterprises. Of the total, R$60 billion was allocated to metropolitan transport systems.
13. In August 2006, the federal government announced that the government would assume up to 40 percent of the risk of PPP projects. If the public investment is larger, it would be noted as a public asset of the Union, state, or county, in accordance with Portaria 614 published a few days earlier in "Diário Oficial." This regulation aimed at issues of transparency. Risks can be generated by smaller than anticipated demand. Still, the instrument used would be listed as a SPE (Sociedade de Propósito Específico). The federal PPP Trust Fund was listed as having R$3.4 billion, in the form of stocks in Vale do Rio Doce, Banco do Brasil, and Eletrobrás.
14. "Rio Claro Throws out Legal Injunction in PPP Bidding Process," *BNAmericas*, October 19, 2006. www.bnamericas.com.
15. "Rodoanel norte terá verba extra de R$332.8 milhões da União, *Folha de S. Paulo*, August 22, 2013; Augusto Diniz, "Rodoanel norte pode ser objeto de protestos, avalia consultor," *Yahoo Notícias*, August 12, 2013. Three Spanish and three

Brazilian construction companies are in charge of the complex project which also includes seven tunnels.

16. The *Plano Pluriannual 2004–2007* is available at www.saopaulo.sp.gov.br.
17. For a list of specific projects, see the Secretaria de Planejamento e Desenvolvimento Regional and the Portal do Governo do Estado de São Paulo websites.
18. The port of Santos currently handles most goods traded by the state and adjacent regions. Containerized cargo is the most important category, followed by corn and sugar. For statistics, see the port of Santos website www.portodesantos.com.
19. Operational capacity would be increased by installing new piers (a working surface of 17,515 square meters with an investment of R$2.4 million), paving an area of the port for 1,500 vehicles, improving port infrastructure (an investment of R$4.6 million), and enlarging terminals for large cargo ships (an investment of R$155 million).
20. Brazil's transport costs are already amongst the highest in the world. "Frete continua caro na América do Sul," *Valor/Empresas*, June 12, 2006, B6.
21. Relatively new factories in Campinas and Vale do Paraíba produce engines, parts, electronics, and automobiles that might use the enhanced São Sebastião port to lessen congestion in Santos and the capital and making freight circulate more efficiently. MRS Logística, one of the main regional networks created in the 1990s, provides access to the ports of Sepetiba-Itaguaí (shared with FCA) and Campos to railroad networks in Rio, Minas, and São Paulo.
22. OAS Construtora, Cargill, and other companies were interested in these projects (see "Lula quer 'pressão' para liberar Perimetral," *A Tribuna Porto e Mar*, June 9, 2006.)
23. The port of São Sebastião is also a tourism and vacation destination, as is the nearby island of Ilhabela. Residents protested the damage that the proposed project might do to tourism and the landscape. "Governo de SP quer ampliar capacidade do porto de São Sebastião," *Folha*, August 23, 2009.
24. "Lula quer 'pressão' para liberar Perimetral," *A Tribuna Porto e Mar*, June 9, 2006.
25. Environmentalists have been active in countering the claims of PPP advocates in the development of the area and highway SP-055. See "Conselho Consultivo do Parque Estadual quer garantias sobre Corredor de Exportacão," *A.L.Norte*, August 16, 2005.
26. The government of São Paulo considered the northern export corridor in its PPP program, but its first priority was the expansion of Line 4 of the capital's metro. Governor Serra inaugurated some stations just before resigning the São Paulo governorship to run for president in the 2010 elections.
27. Instituto Brasileiro de Geografia e Estadística (IBGE), "Tabela 2—Participação das Grandes Regiões e Unidades da Federação no Produto Interno Bruto—2005–2009."
28. World Bank, PPIAF. Figures include investments in projects within the geographic scope of a single region, excluding projects that extend across regions.
29. In 2003, the PPP program was developed when the newly elected government of Aécio Neves recruited Luiz Antônio Athayde, a member of the original public-private partnership team from the federal Ministry of Planning.

30. "Concessão da MG-050 completa 5 anos e Passos, dona de 2° maior trecho, recebe pouco investimento," *Folha*, May 10, 2012. MG-050 provides an alternative to the congested Fernão Dias highway as link between Belo Horizonte and São Paulo. Its upgrade will also alleviate traffic congestion between these two extended metropolitan areas as well as lower transportation costs and increase regional economic competitiveness.
31. Paulo Peixoto, "Minas Gerais vai ampliar concessão em regime de PPP," *Folha*, October 18, 2007.
32. "Minas Gerais é favorável a concessão de aeroporto de Confins," *Reuters Brasil*, April 25, 2012.
33. Municipalities have also moved to harness public-private collaboration to meet infrastructure needs. More than a billion dollars of investment during 1990–2010 have been used in urban transportation, water projects, prisons, and other areas. Examples are found in Porto Alegre (RGS), Londrina (Parana), Rio Claro (São Paulo), and others.
34. "Leis ambientais retardam infraestrutura no Brasil," *Exame*, September 30, 2011.

Six Transantiago: Urban Development in Chile

1. According to the 2011 *CIA World Factbook*, 89 percent of Chile's population lived in cities in 2010.
2. Throughout this study, Santiago refers to the 37 *comunas* or boroughs in the Greater Metropolitan Area. This "conurbation" includes the 32 boroughs of the Province of Santiago (of which Santiago Centro is only one of them, plus the five additional municipalities to the south of Santiago Province).
3. See Solimare's opinion poll.
4. From 40 percent in 1990 to 18 percent in 2006, as reported by President Michelle Bachelet at the Foreign Policy Association in New York, September 21, 2006.
5. Eugenio Tironi, *El sueño chileno*. Santiago: Taurus, 2005. While Tironi emphasizes the broad search for a sense of community and national identity after economic and political modernization, his argument implies a search for a full sense of modernity.
6. The completion of Panamericana Norte as a fast access toll expressway also contributed to Santiago's new transportation infrastructure. In addition, the expansion of the airport, new access roads, public housing projects, and toll roads brought a large number of outlying areas in closer contact with Santiago.
7. See Javier Etcheberry's "Transantiago, Modern Public Transport for A World-Class City."
8. According to Andres Gómez-Lobo, Economics professor at the University of Chile, the country would complete ambitious public health goals within two years (Interview by Mauricio A. Font. June 22, 2006).
9. "Los errores de la era Lagos en el Transantiago aprobleman a La Moneda," *El Mercurio*, June 18, 2006.

10. Germán Correa was minister of Transportation and Telecommunications from 1990–1992 and was part of the task force and planning committees involved with PTUS and Transantiago.
11. "We worked for over 16 months so that when we took office, the government could be prepared to sign decrees and to make new laws." Interview with Germán Correa, March 29, 2007. Santiago, Chile.
12. The opposition of the bus drivers began with the 1991 national public transport strikes organized by their union associations in an effort to reject the new licitation system.
13. Guillermo Díaz, Andrés Gómez-Lobo, and Andrés Velasco. 2002. "Micros en Santiago: hacia la licitación del 2003." February. Alexander Galetovic and Pablo Jordán. 2006. "Santiago: ¿Dónde estamos? ¿Hacia dónde vamos?" *Estudios Públicos*, 101(Summer): 87–146.
14. Interview with Germán Correa, March 29, 2007. Santiago, Chile.
15. The task force was organized by then minister Carlos Cruz and involved Germán Correa, Eduardo Abedrapo, Sergio Solís, Sergio González Tagle, and others.
16. According to Etcheverry, Transantiago entailed large new investments in four main areas: road infrastructure and transfer stations ($250 million); new technology in buses and control centers; new vehicles and equipment ($230 million); and administrative facilities.
17. According to Germán Correa, during the government of former president Patricio Aylwin, it was impossible to oversee the operation of the public transportation system, which included more than 14,000 buses with use of 15 years, free to operate any route. Interview on July 27, 2006, with Letizzia Wastavino.
18. The increasing rates of bus robbery are reported in *La Tercera* and *El Mercurio*. The phenomenon is also discussed in Guillermo Díaz, Andrés Gómez-Lobo, and Andrés Velasco. 2004. "Micros en Santiago: De enemigo público a servicio public," *Estudios Públicos*, 96(Spring): 5–48.
19. Sergio Espejo, minister of Transportation and Telecommunications in a public statement. Santiago, April 2006.
20. The debate hinged on the main causes of the failures of Transantiago and what to do about its flaws. Bus fares would need to be raised and a subsidy put in place for several years for the system to be financially stable over a take-off period lasting several years.
21. James M. Lents, PhD. University of Tennessee, Gerhard Leutert, PhD. Swiss Federal Institute of Technology, and Humberto Fuenzalida, PhD. University of Michigan.
22. Particulate matter (PM) is an air pollution term for a mixture of solid particles and liquid droplets found in the air. The pollutant comes in a variety of sizes and can be composed of many types of materials and chemicals. Coarse particles (PM10) are inhalable particles less than 10 micrometers (μm) in diameter used as a nominal surrogate for particles between 2.5 and 10 micrometers in diameter; found near roadways and dusty industries. Fine particles (PM2.5) are inhalable particles less than 2.5 micrometers in diameter, generally found in smoke and

haze, emitted from natural sources like forest fires and industrial combustion sources, or formed when gases react in the air (United States Environmental Protection agency).

23. See James M. Lents, Gerhard Leutert, and Humberto Fuenzalida, "Segunda Auditoría Internacional. Plan de Prevención y Descontaminación Atmosférica de la Región Metropolitana (PPDA). Resumen Ejecutivo," Ministerio del Medio Ambiente, Chile, 2006.
24. "Segunda Auditoría Internacional del Plan de Prevención y Descontaminación Atmosférica (PPDA) de la Región Metropolitana," CONAMA, April 1, 2006.
25. "Analisis y evaluación del impacto del Transantiago aire de la Region Metropolitana," Centro Mario Molina Chile, 2008.
26. Centro Mario Molina Chile. 2008.
27. Alejandro Smythe as quoted in "Corema: Transantiago ha contribuido a descontaminar la capital," *Cooperativa.cl*, September 6, 2008.
28. Ministro del Medio Ambiente, Gobierno de Chile.
29. Victor Zúñiga, "Para la USACh hay contaminación del aire 'preocupante' en Santiago desde el verano," *El Mercurio*, January 10, 2009.
30. "Autoridades destacan disminución de episodios ambientales en 2009," CONAMA, September 2, 2009.
31. Pablo Beltran, Antonio Gschwender, and Carolina Palma. "The Impact of Compliance Measures on the Operation of a Bus System: The Case of Transantiago," Research in Transportation Economics, 2013.
32. "Transantiago: El balance a un año del caos," *El Mercurio*, February 10, 2008.
33. "Transportes investiga falla en red de Tarjeta bip!," *La Tercera*, March 2, 2011.
34. "Transantiago ahorró $8.000 millones tras cambio de contrato." *Nación.cl*, December 21, 2012.
35. "Tarjeta Bip! se podrá cargar desde febrero vía internet," *Nación.cl*, January 14, 2014
36. "Transantiago: El balance a un año del caos," *El Mercurio*, February 10, 2008.
37. "En 2010 habrá sólo 300 micros enchuladas," *La Nación*, December 1, 2009.
38. Francisca Javiera Navarrete, and Juan de Dios Ortúzar. 2013. "Subjective Valuation of the Transfer Transit Experience: The Case of Santiago de Chile." *Transport Policy* 25(January): 138–147.
39. "Encuesta Noviembre-Diciembre 2007" and "Encuesta Junio 2007," Catálogo de Encuestas, *Centro de Estudios Públicos.*
40. "Encuesta Adimark: Fuerte caída en aprobación del Transantiago," *La Tercera*, August 5, 2008; "Encuesta Evaluación de Gestión del Gobierno: Informe Mensual Noviembre 2008," Adimark GfK.
41. Centro de Estudios de la Realidad Contemporánea (CERC), "Informe de Prensa Encuesta Nacional: Septiembre de 2008."
42. "Encuesta Evaluación de Gestión del Gobierno: Informe mensual Noviembre 2009," Adimark GfK.
43. Ipsos Public Affairs, "Estudio de Opinión Pública, Agosto 2009," *Santiago de Chile*, August 19, 2009.

44. According to government sources, evasion rates reached 20 percent, while other estimates had it at lower. In September 2008, inspectors were sent out to check the smart cards in 21 different parts of the city, showing 9.1 percent evasion in one morning—that is, nearly one out of every ten riders. Since many passengers sought to avoid inspection by getting off the vehicles before their smart cards were collected, inspectors concluded that the evasion rate was higher. The Bernardo O'Higgins University's Engineering Department issued its own study in September 2008, and concluded that the evasion rate of Transantiago was 11 percent, fluctuating in different areas of the city. Zones H and G showed rates as high as 34 percent and 27 percent, respectively, while zones C and D showed negligible user evasion. Apparently, an evasion rate of 10 percent appeared to be normal in public bus system (9 percent), in contrast to subway or metro systems (2 percent).
45. The Alianza por Chile political party dissolved in May 2009. It was replaced by a new electoral coalition called Coalición por el Cambio, which formed under presidential candidate, and winner, Sebastián Piñera.
46. *La Nación*, July 16, 2009.
47. Sebastián Piñera, as quoted in "Piñera anuncia acuerdo entre Alianza y gobierno sobre Transantiago," *La Tercera*, July 14, 2009.
48. September approval ratings for the government remained very low at 26.4 percent, suggesting that Chileans were separating assessments of the government with those of the president. Transantiago and Transportation Minister René Cortázar continued to receive low but improved marks in the September polls.
49. As argued by Eduardo Engel, Ronald Fischer, and Alexander Galetovic, each of the 50 concessions had been renegotiated an average of three times, with 25 percent of the investment was the result of these renegotiations rather than competitive bids. "Reforma a la Ley de Concesiones," *El Mercurio*, August 24, 2008. See also Carlos Huneeus, "¿Quién manda en las concesiones de infraestructura?," *El Mostrador.cl*, September 8, 2008. The conservative think tank Libertad y Desarrollo endorsed the idea of the reform of the concessions and partnerships law, (see "Concesiones: La importancia de avanzar," *Libertad y Desarrollo*, August 22, 2008), claiming that it was needed for investments of $20.5 billion in infrastructure to be made in the period 2008–2012.
50. Uziel Gómez, "El MOP reactiva los proyectos de concesiones para este ano: Aumentan en 136 por ciento," *El Mercurio*, January 10, 2009

Seven Conclusion: Changing States

1. PwC (2014) projects increase in annual expenditures on infrastructure in Latin America, to reach $557 bn in 2025 (focus on Latin America as a whole, Brazil, Colombia, and Mexico). ECLAC (2011) estimates needs and expenditures from 2012 through 2020.
2. Author's calculation based on the World Bank's PPI Database.

3. In Latin America, 41 percent of infrastructure concessions and partnerships had to be renegotiated at some point between 1985 and 2000 (Guasch and Straub, 2006).
4. Latin American and world leaders also formalized a commitment to aid emerging markets suffering from lack of capital, including the search for new funds and expanding the role of multilateral organizations. Late 2008 even witnessed renewed activity in regard to trade agreements and the further opening of national economies between East Asia and Latin America. With a trade agreement already in place with Chile, China has expanded its economic and trade ties to many countries in the region. For an alternative view, see "The Gated Globe," *The Economist*, October 12, 2013.
5. The national agenda included a transportation funding bill as well as the creation of a national infrastructure bank. "Infrastructure Jobs to Explode Under Obama," *A.E. Feldman*, November 5, 2008. A bill to create a National Infrastructure Bank Act was sent to Congress in August 2007. The proposed act called for a PPP agency responsible for expanding the role of federal government and the private sector in creating massive public works (see "Presidential Candidates Endorse Toll Road Bank," *theNewspaper.com*, March 26, 2008). But the Barack Obama government was unable to obtain congressional approval for roads and highways, alternative-energy initiatives, health and education facilities, and other infrastructure endeavors.

Appendix B Framework

1. A BOT variant is Build-Own-Operate-Transfer (BOOT).
2. Bräutigam and Segarra (2007) discuss the World Bank's role in promoting learning processes in regard to broad forms of partnerships to include nongovernmental organizations.
3. The growing list of specialized websites proving information about PPPs includes WBResearch, ABCON, various firms (Orrick, Hogan, and Hartson, and many others), and Institute of the Americas.
4. As stated by the executive director of the The National Council for Public-Private Partnerships, "strong leadership makes all the other factors come together." Rick Norment (May 2008) "Fundamentals of PPPs," National Council for Public-Private Partnerships: Partnerships for Growth in Infrastructure Workshop, Charlotte, North Carolina.
5. For example, Renda and Schrefler (2006a).

Appendix C Brazil: Planning for New Infrastructure

1. See Pedro Antonio Bertone Ataide, "Avaliação do Plano Plurianual: Análise das restrições à sua integração ao ciclo de gestão pública federal," MA. thesis, Programa de Pós-graduação em Administração, Universidade de Brasilia. 2005. Additionally see the Ministry of Planning's website for a list of all PPPs since PPA 1996–1999.

2. The study and report were prepared by an international consortium that included Booz, Allen, and Hamilton, Bechtel International, and ABN Amro Bank.
3. PAC also entails projects to help the poor and address the problems of inequality—a personal priority of President Lula de Silva. An extensive and already successful plan to improve Brazilian favelas outlines infrastructural improvements in housing, sanitation, sewage, and electricity. See "Environment Minister Suspends US$379 Million Amazon Highway Project, Brazil," *Business News America*, September 26, 2008, and Susan Schaller, "Lula's Growth Acceleration Program: The Best that Brazilian Government Funding Can Buy?" Council of Hemispheric Affairs Report, June 5, 2008.
4. "Estudo critica infraestrutura logística do Brasil," *O Estado de SP*, September 14, 2009.
5. Dilma Rousseff, Lula's hand-picked candidate to replace him as president, took the leadership over the PAC program, which heavily relies on concessions and PPPs.
6. PAC2 projects focus on the urban communities in the periphery of large cities such as São Paulo. Many of the areas of action concentrate on social development and income distribution. Infrastructure remains an area of uncertainty in terms of political continuity and leadership.

BIBLIOGRAPHY

Abreu, Marcelo de Paiva, ed. 2014. *A Ordem do Progresso: Dois Séculos da Política Econômica no Brasil*. Rio: Elsevier/Campus.

Accioli, Claudio, and Solange Monteiro. 2012. "Will the Public-Private Partnership Work?" *The Brazilian Economy* 4(10) (October): 11–16.

"Actas del Transantiago: La historia oficial." Centro de Investigación Periodística, December 6, 2007.

Akintoye, Akintola, and Matthias Beck, eds. 2009. *Policy, Management and Finance for Public-Private Partnerships*. Edison, NJ: John Wiley.

Akintoye, Akintola, Matthias Beck, and Cliff Hardcastle, eds. 2003. *Public-Private Partnerships Managing Risks and Opportunities*. Malden, MA: Blackwell Science.

Amsden, Alice H. 1989. *Asia's Next Giant: South Korea and Late Industrialization*. New York, NY: Oxford University Press.

Amsden, Alice H., and Wan-wen Chu. 2003. *Beyond Late Development: Taiwan's Upgrading Policies*. Cambridge, MA: MIT Press.

Andrés, Luis A., Makthar Diop, and José Luis Guasch. 2008. *Achievements and Challenges of Private Participation in Infrastructure in Latin America: Evaluation and Future Prospects*. New York, NY: Oxford University Press.

Andrés, Luis A., José Luis Guasch, Thomas Haven, and Vivien Foster. 2008. *The Impact of Private Sector Participation in Infrastructure: Lights, Shadows, and the Road Ahead*. Washington, DC: World Bank.

Annuatti-Neto, Francisco, M. Barossi, A. G de Carvalho, and R. Macedo. 2005. "Os efeitos da privatização sobre o desempenho econômico e financeiro das empresas privatizadas." *Revista Brasileira de Economia* 59(2) (April–June): 151–175.

Anós-Casero, Paloma, and Valentina Rollo. 2010. "Argentina: Trade Patterns and Challenges Ahead." *The World Bank: Latin America and the Caribbean*, 1(1) (February): 1–22.

Antico, Claudia. 2005. "Deslocamentos pendulares na região metropolitana de São Paulo." *São Paulo em Perspectiva* 19(4) (December): 110–120.

Aranha, Valmir. 2005. "Mobilidade pendular na metrópole Paulista." *São Paulo em Perspectiva* 19(4) (December): 106–109.

Arce, Moisés. 2008. "The Repoliticization of Collective Action After Neoliberalism in Peru." *Latin American Politics and Society* 50(3) (Fall): 37–62.

Arce, Moisés, and Roberta Rice. 2009. "Societal Protest in Post-Stabilization Bolivia." *Latin American Research Review* 44(1): 88–101.

Arce, Moisés. 2010. *El Fujimorismo y la Reforma del Mercado en la Sociedad Peruana*. Lima, Perú: Instituto de Estudios Peruanos.

Arditi, Benjamin. 2008. "Arguments about the Left Turns in Latin America: A Post-Liberal Politics?" *Latin American Research Review* 43(3): 59–81.

Arellano, Alberto. 2014. "Alsacia al límite: Futuro del mayor operador del Transantiago está en manos del gobierno." Santiago, Chile: Centro de Investigación Periodística.

Aschauer, David A. 1989. "Is Public Expenditure Productive?" *Journal of Monetary Economics* 23(2) (March): 177–200.

Aspe, Pedro. 1993. *Economic Transformation the Mexican Way*. Cambridge, MA: MIT Press.

"Aprobado financiamiento para Transantiago...y hasta el 2014." *United Press International*, August 19, 2009.

Auyero, Javier. 2001. *Poor People's Politics: Peronist Survival Networks and the Legacy of Evita*. Durham, NC: Duke University Press.

Auyero, Javier. 2007. *Routine Politics and Violence in Argentina: The Gray Zone of State Power*. New York, NY: Cambridge University Press.

Ayres, Ian, and John Braithwaite. 1992. *Responsive Regulation: Transcending the Deregulation Debate*. New York, NY: Oxford University Press.

Babb, Sarah. 2001. *Managing Mexico: Economists from Nationalism to Neoliberalism*. Princeton, NJ: Princeton University Press.

Baccaro, Lucio, and Chris Howell. 2011. "A Common Neoliberal Trajectory: The Transformation of Industrial Relations in Advanced Capitalism." *Politics & Society* 39(4) (December): 521–563.

Badie, Bertrand. 2000. *The Imported State: The Westernization of the Political Order*. Stanford, CA: Stanford University Press.

Baer, Werner. 1972. "Import Substitution and Industrialization in Latin America: Experiences and Interpretations," *Latin American Research Review* 7(1) (Spring): 95–122.

Baer, Werner. 2008. *The Brazilian Economy: Growth and Development*. Boulder, CO: Lynne Reinner.

Baer, Werner, and Melissa Birch. 1994. *Privatization in Latin America: New Roles for the Public and Private Sectors*. Westport, CT: Praeger.

Balbachevsky, Elizabeth, and Denilde Oliveira Holzhacker. 2006. "Determinantes dasatitudes do eleitorado brasileiro com relação à privatização e aos serviços públicos." *Opinião Pública* (Campinas) 12(1) (April/May): 38–56.

Baldwin, Robert, and Martin Cave. 1999. *Understanding Regulation: Theory, Strategy and Practice*. New York, NY: Oxford University Press.

Banco Interamericano de Desarrollo (BID). 2003. "Chile, Costanera Norte (CH-0179): Reporte de Impacto Ambiental y Social." June.

Barbosa, Eunice. 2001. "Evolução do uso do solo residencial na área central do muncípio de São Paulo." Dissertation. Escola Politécnica da Universidade de São Paulo, São Paulo.

Barrera-Osorio, Felipe, et al. 2009. "Does Society Win or Lose as a Result of Privatization? The Case of Water Sector Privatization in Colombia." *Economica* 76(304) (October): 649–674.

Basañes, Federico C., and Robert Willig. 2002. *Second-Generation Reforms in Infrastructure Services.* Washington, DC: Johns Hopkins University Press, Inter-American Development Bank.

Batarce, Marco, and Patricia Galilea. 2013. "Power of Incentive Schemes, Provision of Quality and Monitoring: The Case of the Public Transit System in Santiago de Chile." Department of Transport Engineering Logistics, Pontificia Universidad Católica de Chile.

Bekerman, Marta, and Federico Dulcich. 2013. "The International Trade Position of Argentina: Towards a Process of Export Diversification." *Cepal Review* 110 (August): 151–174.

Belini, Claudio. 2012. "Industrial Exports and Peronist Economic Policies in Post-War Argentina." *Journal of Latin American Studies* 44(2) (May): 285–317.

Beltrán, Pablo, Antonio Gschwender, and Carolina Palma. 2013. "The Impact of Compliance Measures on the Operation of a Bus System: The Case of Transantiago." *Research in Transportation Economics* 39(1) (March): 79–89.

Bennett, Elizabeth, Peter Grohmann, and Brad Gentry. 1999. "Public Private Partnerships for the Urban Environment: Options and Issues." Working Paper Series. PPPUE.

Benvenuto, Pedro, and Jorge Mariano. 1997. *Lessons from São Paulo's Metropolitan Busway Concessions Program.* Washington, DC: World Bank.

Berry, Frances Stokes, and William D. Berry. 1999. "Innovation and Diffusion Models in Policy Research." In Paul Sabatier, ed. *Theories of the Policy Process.* Boulder, CO: Westview Press, 223–260.

Bertone Ataide, Pedro Antonio. 2005. "Avaliação do Plano Plurianual: Análise das restrições à sua integração ao ciclo de gestão pública federal." Master Thesis, Programa de Pós-graduação em Administração, Universidade de Brasília.

Bexell, Magdalena, and Ulrika Mörth, eds. 2010. *Democracy and Public-Private Partnerships in Global Governance.* New York, NY: Palgrave Macmillan.

Bhatia, Bhavna. 2010. "Public-Private Partnerships for Infrastructure Development in Developing Countries." In Vishnuprasad Nagadevara G. Ramesh, Gopal Naik, and Anil B. Suraj, eds. *Public Private Partnerships.* Indian Institute Management of Bangalore. New Delhi, India: Routledge, 123–136.

Bickel, Ulrike. 2003. "Will the Soybean Boom in Brazil Never End? Conflicts and Alternatives." www.wervel.be.

Birch, Melissa H., and Jerry Haar, eds. 2000. *The Impact of Privatization in the Americas.* Miami: University of Miami/North-South Center.

Blake, Charles H. 1998. "Economic Reform and Democratization in Argentina and Uruguay: the Tortoise and the Hare Revisited?" *Journal of Interamerican Studies and World Affairs* 40(3) (Fall): 1–26.

Blanco, Fernando, and Santiago Herrera. 2006. "The Quality of Fiscal Adjustment and the Long-Rung Growth Impact of Fiscal Policy in Brazil." World Bank Policy Research Working Paper 4004.

Blanco, Luisa, and Robin Grier. 2013. "Explaining the Rise of the Left in Latin America." *Latin American Research Review* 48(1) (Spring): 68–90.

Bland, Daniel. 2012. "São Paulo Qualifies 18 Offers for US$3.21bn Rodoanel Norte Highway Tender." *BNAmericas*, August 27.

Blom-Hansen, Jens. 1997. "A 'New Institutional' Perspective on Policy Networks." *Public Administration* 75(4) (December): 669–693.

Bloomfield, Pamela. 2006. "The Challenging Business of Long-Term Public-Private Partnerships: Reflections on Local Experience." *Public Administration Review* 66(3) (May/June): 400–412.

Bloomgarden, David. 2009. "Alianzas público-privadas (APP) para la infraestructura: Los proyectos FOMIN." Mexico: PIAPPEM, February.

Bloomgarden, David R. and Asako Maruyama. 2008. "Infrastructure and Public-Private Partnerships in Latin America and the Caribbean." The Multilateral Investment Fund, MIF Retrospectives, September 19.

Boix, Carles. 2005. "Privatization and Public Discontent in Latin America." Washington, DC: Inter-American Development Bank.

Bonnet, Céline, Pierre Dubois, David Martimort, and Stéphane Straub. 2012. "Empirical Evidence on Satisfaction with Privatization in Latin America." *The World Bank Economic Review* 26(1) (January): 1–33.

Boschi, Renato, and Carlos Henrique Santana, eds. 2012. *Development and Semi-Periphery: Post-neoliberal Trajectories in South America and Central Eastern Europe*. New York, NY: Anthem Press.

Bouckaert, Geert, B. Guy Peters, and Koen Verhoest. 2010. *The Coordination of Public Sector Organizations: Shifting Patterns of Public Management*. Basingstoke, NH: Palgrave Macmillan.

Bowman, Louise. 2000. "P3-Problem, Problem, Problem." *Project Finance* (June): 25–27.

Brandão, Luiz E. T., and Eduardo C. G. Saraiva. 2007. "Risco privado em infraestrutura pública: uma análise quantitativa de risco como ferramenta de modelagem de contratos." *Revista de Administração Pública* 41(6) (November–December): 1035–1067.

Bräutigam, Deborah A., and Monique Segarra. 2007. "Difficult Partnerships: The World Bank, States, and NGOs." *Latin American Politics and Society* 49(4) (Winter): 149–181.

Brazil, Ministério do Planejamento, Orçamento e Gestão. 2003. *Plano Plurianual 2004–2007*. Brasília, DF: Secretaria de Planejamento e Investimentos Estratégicos.

Brazil, Ministério dos Transportes. 2003. "Contorno Ferroviário de São Paulo: Ferroanel." 1er Seminário Internacional de Co-Financiamento BNDES/CAF, Rio de Janeiro, August 8.

Brazil, Ministry of Finance/SEAE. 2013. "The Federal Logistic Investment Program (PIL)." December.

Brenck, Andreas, Torsten Beckers, Maria Heinrich, and Christian von Hirschhausen. 2005. "Public-Private Partnerships in the New EU Member Countries of Central and Eastern Europe: An Economic Analysis with Case Studies from the Highway Sector." *EIB Papers* 10(2): 82–111.

Brenner, Neil, and Nik Theodore. 2002. *Spaces of Neoliberalism, Urban Restructuring in North America and Western Europe*. Malden, MA: Blackwell.

Bresser-Pereira, Luiz Carlos, ed. 1996. *Economic Crisis and State Reform in Brazil: Toward a New Interpretation of Latin America*. Boulder, CO: Lynne Reinner.

Bresser-Pereira, Luiz Carlos. 2011. "From the National-Bourgeoisie to the Dependency Interpretation of Latin America." *Latin American Perspectives* 38(3) (May): 40–58.

Broad, Kenneth, and Ben Orlove. 2007. "Channeling Globality: The 1997–98 El Niño Climate Event in Peru." *American Ethnologist* 34(2) (May): 285–302.

Brooks, Sarah M., and Marcus J. Kurtz. 2012. "Paths to Financial Policy Diffusion: Statist Legacies in Latin America's Globalization." *International Organization* 66(1) (January): 95–128.

Broomby, Rob. "China's Controversial Polish Contract." *BBC News*, September 16, 2009.

Brosnan, Greg. 2008. "Mexican Infrastructure Financing: A Bridge Too Far?" *Latin Finance* (203) (December): 43–45.

Budds, Jessica. 2013. "Water, Power, and the Production of Neoliberalism in Chile, 1973–2005." *Environment and Planning D: Society and Space* 31(2): 301–318.

Bulmer-Thomas, Victor. 2003. *The Economic History of Latin America since Independence*. New York, NY: Cambridge University Press.

Bult-Spiering, Mirjam, and Geert Dewulf. 2007. *Strategic Issues in Public-Private Partnerships: An International Perspective*. Oxford, UK: Wiley-Blackwell.

Burdick, John, Philip Oxhorn, and Kenneth M. Roberts, eds. 2009. *Beyond Neoliberalism in Latin America? Societies and Politics and the Crossroads*. New York, NY: Palgrave Macmillan.

Bureau of Economic and Business Affairs. 2012. "2012 Investment Climate Statement—Brazil." US Department of State, June.

CAF (Corporación Andina de Fomento). 2010. "Infraestructura pública y participación privada: conceptos y experiencias en América y España." Caracas.

Calabrese, Daniele, ed. 2008. *Strategic Communication for Privatization, Public-Private Partnerships, and Private Participation in Infrastructure Projects*. Washington, DC: World Bank Publications.

Calderón, Cesar, and Luis Servén. 2002. "The Output Cost of Latin America's Infrastructure Gap." Working Paper 186, Central Bank of Chile.

Calderón, Cesar, and Luis Servén. 2004a. "The Effects of Infrastructure Development on Growth and Income Distribution." Working Paper 270, Central Bank of Chile.

Calderón, César, and Luis Servén. 2004b. "Trends in Infrastructure in Latin America, 1980–2001." Working Paper 269, Central Bank of Chile.

Calderón, César, and Luis Servén. 2009. "Infrastructure in Latin America: An Update, 1980–2006." Unpublished manuscript, Washington, DC: World Bank.

Calderón, César, and Luis Servén. 2010a. "Infrastructure and Economic Development in Sub-Saharan Africa." *Journal of African Economies* 19 (AERC Supplement 1): i13–i87.

Calderón, César, and Luis Servén. 2010b. "Infrastructure in Latin America." In José Antonio Ocampo and Jaime Ros, eds. *The Oxford Handbook of Latin American Economics*. Oxford, UK: Oxford University Press, 659–690.

Calero, Carla, Rosario Maldonado, and Andrea Molina. 2009. "Risk, Natural Disasters and Poverty in Latin America: Case Study, Ecuador." Research for Public Policy, MDGSs and Poverty, MDG-10–2009, Regional Bureau for Latin America and the Caribbean-United Nations Development Programme, New York, NY.

Camp, Roderic A. 1999. *Politics in Mexico*. New York, NY: Oxford University Press.

Camp, Roderic A. 2010. *The Metamorphosis of Leadership in a Democratic Mexico*. New York, NY: Oxford University Press.

Campos, Javier. 2004. "Private Participation and Regulation in Infrastructures: Lessons from Recent Experiences in Latin America." *International Journal of Applied Economics and Econometrics* 12(3): 337–358.

Campos, Javier, Antonio Estache, Noelia Martin, and Lourdes Trujillo. 2003. *Macroeconomic Effects of Private Sector Participation in Infrastructure*. Stanford, CA: Stanford University Press.

Cao, Xun. 2009. "Networks of Intergovernmental Organizations and Convergence in Domestic Economic Policies." *International Studies Quarterly* 53(4) (December): 1095–1130.

Cardoso, Fernando Henrique, and Enzo Faletto. 1979. *Dependency and Development in Latin America*. Berkeley and Los Angeles, CA: University of California Press.

Carpintero, Samuel, and Raphael Barcham. 2012. "Private Toll Roads: Lessons from Latin America." *International Conference on Traffic and Transportation Engineering* 26: 98–102.

Carranza, Luis, Christian Daude, and Ángel Melguizo. 2011. "Public Infrastructure Investment and Fiscal Sustainability in Latin America: Incompatible Goals?" Working Paper 301, OECD Development Center.

Carvajal, Fernando. 2011. "Ecuador: la evolución de su economía 1950–2008." In Alfredo Astorga, Betty Espinosa, Fernando Carvajal, et al., eds. *Estado del País: Informe Cero. Ecuador 1950–2010*. Quito, Ecuador: Estado del País, 95–104.

Castañeda, Jorge G. 2006. "Latin America's Left Turn." *Foreign Affairs* 85(3) (May–June): 28–43.

Castelar, Armando. 2013. "Novo Modelo para as Ferrovias." *Valor Económico*, October 4.

Castelar Pinheiro, Armando, and Kiichiro Fukusaku, eds. 2000. *A privatização no Brasil: O Caso dos Serviços de Utilidade Pública*. Rio de Janeiro, Brazil: BNDES.

Centeno, Miguel A. 1994. *Democracy within Reason: Technocratic Revolution in Mexico*. Philadelphia, PA: Pennsylvania State University Press.

Centeno, Miguel A. 1997. *Democracy within Reason: Technocratic Revolution in Mexico*. Pennsylvania, PA: The Pennsylvania State University. 2nd ed.

Centeno, Miguel A., and Joseph N. Cohen. 2012. "The Arc of Neoliberalism." *Annual Review of Sociology* 38 (August): 317–340.

Centro de Estudios Públicos. 2007a. "Encuesta Noviembre-Diciembre 2007." Chile.

Centro de Estudios Públicos. 2007b. "Encuesta Junio 2007." Chile.

Centro Mario Molina. 2008. "Análisis y evaluación del impacto del Transantiago aire de la Región Metropolitana." Chile.

CEPAL. (Comisión Económica para América Latina y el Caribe). 2008. "La Transformación productiva de 20 años después: viejos problemas, nuevas oportunidades." Estudio presentado en el trigésimo segundo período de sesiones de la CEPAL. Santo Domingo, Dominican Republic, June 9–13.

CEPAL. 2010. "Diagnóstico sobre las restricciones al desarrollo y a una integración económica más profunda." *Boletín FAL* 287(7) (July): 1–7.

Cheibub, José Antonio. 2002. "Minority Governments, Deadlock Situations, and the Survival of Presidential Democracies." *Comparative Political Studies* 35(3) (April): 284–312.

Chibber, Vivek. 2003. *Locked in Place: State-Building and Late Industrialization in India.* Princeton, NJ: Princeton University Press.

Chibber, Vivek, 2007. "Response to Clemens, Paige and Panitch." *Comparative and Historical Sociology* 18(2) (Spring): 9–13.

"Chile." The World Factbook. 2014.

"Chinese Road Building Firm Boycotted." *Warsaw Business Journal*, February 21, 2011.

Chong, Alberto, and Florencio López-de-Silanes. 2004a. "Privatization in Latin America: What Does the Evidence Say?" *Economia* 4(2) (Spring): 37–111.

Chong, Alberto, and Florencio López-de-Silanes. 2004b. "Privatization in Mexico." Working Paper 513, Washington, DC: Inter-American Development Bank, Research Department.

Chong, Alberto, and Florencio Lopez-de-Salines. 2005. *Privatization in Latin America: Myths and Reality.* Latin American Development Forum Series. Stanford, CA: Stanford University Press.

Chong, Alberto, and Juan Benavides. 2007. *Privatization and Regulation in Latin America.* Washington, DC: Stanford University Press, World Bank Press.

Cipoletta Tomassian, Georgina, Patricio Rozas Balbontín, Ricardo Sánchez, and Varinia Tromben. 2010. "Políticas de Infraestructura y Transporte en América Latina: Restricciones al Desarrollo y a la Integración." *Mundo Nuevo* 2(4) (July–December): 165–213.

Coates, David. 2000. *Models of Capitalism: Growth and Stagnation in the Modern Era.* Oxford, UK: Polity Press.

Cohen, Michael A. 2012. *Argentina's Economic Growth and Recovery: The Economy in a Time of Default.* London, UK and New York, NY: Routledge.

Coleman, James. 1990. *The Foundations of Social Theory.* Cambridge, MA and London, UK: Belknap Press of Harvard University Press.

CONAMA (Comisión Nacional del Medio Ambiente). 2003. "Evolución de la calidad del aire en Santiago." Ministerio del Medio Ambiente, Chile.

CONAMA. 2009. "Resultados Plan Operacional para la Gestión de Epsiodios Críticos de Contaminación Atmosférica por Material Particulado Respirable (PM10) en la Región Metropolitana: Período 2009." Ministerio del Medio Ambiente, Chile.

Cornelius, Wayne A. 1996. *Mexican Politics in Transition: The Breakdown of a One-Party-Dominant Regime.* San Diego, CA: University of California Press.

Corradi, Juan E. 1985. *The Fitful Republic: Economy, Society and Politics in Argentina.* Boulder, CO: Westview Press.

Corrales, Javier. 2002. *Presidents without Parties: The Politics of Economic Reform in Argentina and Venezuela in the 1990s.* University Park, PA: Pennsylvania State University Press.

Correa, Eugenia. 2012. "Fiscal Policies and the World Financial Crisis: Understanding the Experience of Three Major Latin American Countries." *International Journal of Political Economy* 41(2) (Summer): 82–97.

Correa, Germán and Patricio Rozas. 2006. *Desarrollo urbano e inversiones en infraestructura: elementos para la toma de decisiones.* Santiago, Chile: Publicación de las Naciones Unidas.

Correa, Germán. 2008. "Off to a Chilly Start: The Case of TranSantiago, Chile or What Went Wrong?" Paper presented at 85th Annual Meeting: Transforming Transport by the Transportation Research Board, World Bank and World Resources Institute, Washington, DC, January 17.

Correa, Germán. 2010. "Transporte y Ciudad." *EURE* 36(107) (April): 133–137.

Correa, Germán and Patricio Rozas. 2006. "Desarrollo Urbano e Inversiones en Infraestructura: Elementos para la Toma de Decisiones." ECLAC Serie Recursos Naturales e Infraestructura 108, May.

Coutinho, Luciano. 2013. "The Brazilian Economy and Financing Its Infrastructure Projects." Presentation by president of BNDES, BNP Paribas, Paris, May.

Cruz, Carlos. 2002. "Transporte urbano para un nuevo Santiago." Ministerio de Obras Públicas, Transportes y Telecomunicaciones, Santiago, Chile.

Cruz, Carlos, and Maria Elena Barrientos. 2001. "Toll Road Concessions: The Chilean Experience." PFG Discussion Paper Series 124, the World Bank's Project Finance and Guarantees Group.

Cruz, Luis Edgar. 2010. "La Constitución Política de 1991 y la Apertura Económica." *Revista Facultad de Ciencias Económicas: Investigación y Reflexión* 18(1) (January–June): 269–280.

Cruz, Sebastião. 1995. *Empresário e Estado na Transição Brasileira: Um Estudo sobre a Economia Política do Autoritarismo, 1974–1977.* Campinas, Brazil: Editora da Unicamp, Sao Paulo, Brazil: FAPESP.

Cubas, German, Anson Ho, Kim P. Huynh, and David T. Jacho-Chávez. 2010. "Reallocation, Productivity, and the Ecuadorian Economic Crisis: Evidence from Firm-Level Data." Discussion paper, MIT Sloan School of Management. www.mitsloab.mit.edu.

D'Alembert, Jaccoud, Priscilla Stephan, Rosa Lemos de Sá, and Sarah Richardson. 2003 "Sustainability Assessment of Export-Led Growth in Soy Production in Brazil." Brasília (Brazil), Gland (Switzerland): WWF-Brazil and WWF-International.

Dar, Vandita. 2010. "Governance Issues in Public-Private Partnership in Infrastructure: India vis-à-vis Brazil." In G Ramesh, Vishnuprasad Nagadevara, Gopal Naik, and Anil B. Suraj, eds. *Public Private Partnerships.* Indian Institute Management of Bangalore. New Delhi, India: Routledge, 51–82.

Davis, Diane E. 2004. *Discipline and Development: Middle Classes and Prosperity in East Asia and Latin America*. New York: Cambridge University Press.

De Bettignies, Jean-Etienne, and Thomas W. Ross. 2004. "The Economics of Public-Private Partnerships." *Canadian Public Policy* 30(2) (June): 135–154.

de la Torre, Carlos. 2000. *Populist Seduction in Latin America: The Ecuadorian Experience*. Athens, OH: Ohio University Press.

de la Torre, Carlos. 2013. "El Tecnopopulismo de Rafael Correa: ¿Es compatible el carisma con la tecnocracia?" *Latin American Research Review* 48(1) (Spring): 24–43.

Delmon, Jeffrey. 2009. *Private Sector Investment in Infrastructure: Project Finance, PPP Projects and Risks*. New York, NY and The Netherlands: Wolters Kluwer.

Delmon, Jeffrey. 2011. *Public-Private Partnership Projects in Infrastructure: An Essential Guide for Policy Makers*. Cambridge, UK, and New York, NY: Cambridge University Press.

Departamento Nacional de Planeación. "Plan Nacional de Desarrollo: 2002–2006." www.dnp.gov.co.

Departamento Nacional de Planeación. 2007. "Plan Nacional de Desarrollo 2006–2010, Estado Comunitario: Desarrollo Para Todos." Bogotá: Imprenta Nacional de Colombia.

Departamento Nacional de Planeación. 2010. "Programa de modernización de la economía colombiana." Documento Conpes No. 35 and 36, *Publicaciones Icesi*, 87–156.

Desantis, Daniela. 2010. "Paraguay Banks on Mega Infrastructure Projects." *Reuters*. www.reuters.com.

Díaz, Guillermo, Andrés Gómez-Lobo, and Andrés Velasco. 2004. "Micros en Santiago: De enemigo público a servicio público." *Estudios Públicos* (96) (Spring): 5–48.

Díaz, Guillermo, Andrés Gómez-Lobo, and Andrés Velasco. 2002. *Micros en Santiago: hacia la licitación del 2003*. Kennedy School of Government, Harvard University, Mimeo.

DiMaggio, Paul J., and Walter W. Powell. 1983. "The Iron Cage Revisited: Institutional Isomorphism and Collective Rationality in Organizational Fields." *American Sociological Review* 48(2) (April): 147–160.

Diniz, Eli. 2011. "Democracy, State, and Industry: Continuity and Change between the Cardoso and Lula Administrations." *Latin American Perspectives* 38(3) (May): 59–77.

Directorio de Transporte Público (DTP). "Evaluación de los Usuarios al Sistema de Transporte Público Metropolitano." July 2014.

DTP. "Transantiago: Estado actual, líneas de acción y equipo de gestió." March 26, 2014.

DTP. "Infraestructura Metro." No date available.

Dobbin, Frank, Beth Simmons, and Geoffrey Garrett. 2007. "The Global Diffusion of Public Policies: Social Construction, Coercion, Competition, or Learning?" *Annual Review of Sociology* (33) (August): 449–472.

Dolowitz, David, and David Marsh. 2000. "Learning from Abroad: The Role of Policy Transfer in Contemporary Policy Making." *Governance: An International Journal of Policy and Administration* 13(1) (January): 5–24.

Domínguez, Jorge I., ed. 1997. *Technopols: Freeing Politics and Markets in Latin America in the 1990s*. University Park, PA: Pennsylvania State University Press.

Domínguez, Jorge I. 1998. "Free Politics and Free Markets in Latin America." *Journal of Democracy* 9(4) (October): 70–84.

Domper, María Luz, and Pablo Allard. 2009. *Concesiones: agenda para el 2020*. Santiago, Chile: Libertad y Desarrollo.

Draibe, Sonia. 1985. *Rumos e Metamorfoses: um Estudo sobre a Constituição do Estado e as Alternativas da Industrialização no Brasil, 1930–1960*. Rio de Janeiro, Brazil: Paz e Terra.

Drechsler, Wolfgang. 2009. "The Rise and Demise of the New Public Management: Lessons and Opportunities for South East Europe." *Uprava/Administration* 7(3): 7–27.

Dresser, Denise. 1991. *Neopopulist Solutions to Neoliberal Problems: Mexico's National Solidarity Program*. San Diego, CA: University of California Center for U.S.-Mexican Studies.

Dudkin, Gerti, and Timo Válilá. 2005. "Transaction Costs in Public-Private Partnership: A First Look at the Evidence." *Economic and Financial Reports* 3, European Investment Bank, March.

Easterly, William, and Luis Servén, eds. 2003. *The Limits of Stabilization: Infrastructure, Public Deficits and Growth in Latin America*. Palo Alto, CA: Stanford University Press, and Washington, DC: World Bank.

Easterly, William, César Calderón, and Luis Servén. 2003a. "Infrastructure Compression and Public Sector Solvency in Latin America." In William Easterly and Luis Servén, eds. *The Limits of Stabilization: Infrastructure, Public Deficits, and Growth in Latin America*. Stanford, CA: Stanford University Press and Washington, DC: World Bank, 119–138.

Easterly, William, César Calderón, and Luis Servén. 2003b. "Latin America's Infrastructure in the Era of Macroeconomic Crises." In William Easterly and Luis Servén, eds. *The Limits of Stabilization: Infrastructure, Public Deficits, and Growth in Latin America*. Stanford, CA: Stanford University Press, and Washington, DC: World Bank, 21–94.

Easterly, William, Norman Loayza, and Peter Montiel. 1997. "Has Latin America's Post-Reform Growth Been Disappointing?" Policy Research Working Paper 1708. Washington, DC: World Bank.

Easterly, William, Timothy Irwin, and Luis Servén. 2008. "Walking up the Down Escalator: Public Investment and Fiscal Stability." *World Bank Research Observer* 23(1) (Spring): 37–56.

ECLAC (Economic Commission for Latin America and the Caribbean). 2010a. "Thirty Years of Contributing to Transport Infrastructure Institution-Building in Latin America and the Caribbean." *Bulletin FAL* 292(12) (December): 1–6.

ECLAC. 2010b. "Estudio Económico de América Latina y el Caribe, 2009–2010: Impacto Distributivo de las Políticas Públicas." División de Desarrollo Económico.

ECLAC. 2011. "The Economic Infrastructure Gap in Latin America and the Caribbean." *Bulletin FAL* 293(1): 1–7.
Economist Intelligence Unit. 2010. "Evaluating the Environment for Public-Private Partnerships in Latin America and the Caribbean: The 2010 Infrascope. A Guide to the Index and Methodology." www.fomin.org.
Economist Intelligence Unit. 2013. "Evaluating the Environment for Public-Private Partnerships in Latin America and the Caribbean: The 2012 Infrascope." www.fomin.org.
Edwards, Sebastian. 1995. *Crisis and Reform in Latin America: From Despair to Hope.* New York, NY: Oxford University Press.
Eggers, William. D., and Stephen Goldsmith. 2004. *Governing by Network: The New Shape of the Public Sector.* Washington, DC: Brookings Institution Press.
Eggers, William D., and Tom Startup. 2006. *Closing the Infrastructure Gap: The Role of Public-Private Partnerships.* New York, NY: The Deloitte Group.
Elkins, Zachary, and Beth Simmons. 2005. "On Waves, Clusters, and Diffusion: a Conceptual Framework." *Annals of the American Academy of Political and Social Science* 598(1) (March): 33–51.
Engel, Eduardo, Ronald Fischer, and Alexander Galetovic. 1997. "Highway Franchising: Pitfalls and Opportunities." *American Economic Review* 87(2) (May): 68–72.
Engel, Eduardo, Ronald Fischer, and Alexander Galetovic. 2002. *A New Approach to Private Roads.* Washington, DC: Cato Institute.
Engel, Eduardo, Ronald Fischer, and Alexander Galetovic. 2003. "Privatizing Highways in Latin America: Fixing What Went Wrong." *Economía* 4(1) (Fall): 129–164.
Engel, Eduardo, Ronald Fischer, and Alexander Galetovic. 2006. "Renegotiation without Holdup: Anticipating Spending and Infrastructure Concessions." Working Paper Series 12399, National Bureau of Economic Research, Cambridge, MA.
Engel, Eduardo, Ronald Fischer, and Alexander Galetovic. 2007. "The Basic Public Finance of Public-Private Partnerships: The Case of Toll Roads." NBER Working Paper 13284.
Engel, Eduardo, Ronald Fischer, and Alexander Galetovic. 2009. "Soft Budgets, Renegotiations and Public-Private Partnerships." Unpublished manuscript, May.
Engler, Mário. 2001. "O programa estadual de desestatização (PED) do Estado de São Paulo." *Cadernos Fundap* (22): 68–73.
Estache, Antonio. 2003. "On Latin America's Infrastructure Privatization and its Distributional Effects." Unpublished manuscript. Washington, DC: World Bank.
Estache, Antonio. 2006. "Infrastructure: A Survey of Recent and Upcoming Issues." Unpublished manuscript. Washington, DC: World Bank.
Etcheberry, Javier. 2007. "Transantiago, Modern Public Transport for a World-Class City." Unpublished manuscript, February 10.
Etchemendy, Sebastián. 2011. *Models of Economic Liberalization: Business, workers, and compensation in Latin America, Spain, and Portugal.* New York, NY: Cambridge University Press.
European Commission. 2004. "Public-Private Partnerships and Community Law on Public Contracts and Concessions." Green Paper, Communication COM, 327.

European Parliament. 2000. "Presidency Conclusions." Lisbon European Council, March 23–24.

European Parliament and Council of European Union. 2004. "Directive 2004/18/EC of the European Parliament and of the Council of 31 March 2004 on the Coordination of Procedures for the Award of Public Works Contracts, Public Supply Contracts and Public Service Contracts." *Official Journal of the European Union* 47 (April 30): 114–240.

Evans, Peter. 1995. *Embedded Autonomy: States and Industrial Transformation.* Princeton, NJ: Princeton University Press.

Evans, Peter, and James E. Rauch. 1999. "Bureaucracy and Growth: A Cross-National Analysis of the Effects of 'Weberian' State." *American Sociological Review* 64(5) (October): 748–765.

Evans, Peter, Dietrich Rueschemeyer, and Theda Skocpol, eds. 1985. *Bringing the State Back In.* Cambridge, UK: Cambridge University Press.

Farkas, Andrew. 1998. *State Learning and International Change.* Ann Arbor, MI: University of Michigan Press.

Farquharson, Edward, Clemencia Torres de Mästle, and E. R. Yescombe, eds. 2011. *How to Engage with the Private Sector in Public-private Partnerships in Emerging Markets.* Washington, DC: World Bank, and IBRD.

Fay, Marianne, and May Morrison. 2005. "Infrastructure in Latin America and the Caribbean: Recent Developments and Key Challenges." Report 32640, the World Bank Finance, Private Sector and Management Unit, August 31.

Féliz, Mariano. 2012. "Neo-Developmentalism: Beyond Neoliberalism? Capitalist Crisis and Argentina's Development since the 1990s." *Historical Materialism* 20(2) (January): 105–123.

Ferreira, Pedro, and Carlos Hamilton. 2005. "On the Economic and Fiscal Effects of Infrastructure Investment in Brazil." Getúlio Vargas Foundation Economic Essay No. 613, Rio de Janeiro, Brazil.

Ferreira, Pedro, and Carlos Hamilton. 2008. "Growth and Fiscal Effects of Infrastructure Investment in Brazil." In Guillermo Perry, Luis Servén, and Rodrigo Suescún, eds. *Fiscal Policy, Stabilization, and Growth: Prudence or Abstinence?.* Washington, DC: World Bank, 297–318.

Ffrench-Davis, Ricardo. 2005. *Reformas para América Latina: Después del fundamentalismo neoliberal.* Buenos Aires: Siglo XXI.

Ffrench-Davis, Ricardo. 2006. *Seeking Growth under Financial Volatility.* New York, NY: Palgrave Macmillan.

Ffrench-Davis, Ricardo. 2010. *Economic Reforms in Chile: From Dictatorship to Democracy.* 2nd ed. Great Britain: Palgrave Macmillan.

Figueroa, Oscar, and Arturo Orellana. 2007. "Transantiago: gobernabilidad e institucionalidad." *EURE (Santiago)* 33(100) (December): 165–171.

Finlayson, Jock, and Ken Peacock. 2002. "The What and Why of Public-Private Partnerships." Policy Perspectives. *Business Council of British Columbia* 9(1) (February): 1–6.

Finnemore, Martha. 1996. *National Interests in International Society.* Ithaca, NY: Cornell University Press.

Fischer Montt, Daniel Andrés. 2010. "Obtención de información para la gestión del Transantiago a través datos operacionales." Santiago, Chile: Departamento de Ingeniería, Universidad de Chile.

Fisher, Daniel, Naazneen Karmali, and Gady Epsein. 2011. "Urban Outfitter." *Forbes* 187(8)(May): 80–98.

Fishlow, Albert. 1980. "Brazilian Development in Long-Term Perspective." *American Economic Review* 70(2) (May): 102–108.

Fishlow, Albert. 1986. "A Economia Política do Ajustamento Brasileiro aos Choques do Petróleo: uma Nota sobre o Período 1974/84." *Pesquisa e Planejamento Econômico* 16(3) (December): 507–550.

Fishlow, Albert. 1990. "The Latin American State." *Journal of Economic Perspectives* 4(3) (Summer): 61–74.

Fishlow, Albert. 2006. "Latin America Jogs Left." *Milken Institute Review* 8(3) (September.): 8–15.

Fitch Ratings. 2005. "Evolução do Setor Ferroviário Brasileiro." Sector Report, March.

Fitzpatrick, Anna. 2011. "PAC Progress in São Paulo." *The Rio Times*. www.riotime sonline.com.

Flinders, Mathew. 2005. "The Politics of Public-Private Partnerships." *British Journal of Politics and International Relations* 7(2) (May): 215–239.

Flores-Macías, Gustavo A. 2010. "Statist vs. Pro-Market: Explaining Leftist Governments' Economic Policies in Latin America." *Comparative Politics* 42(4) (July): 413–433.

Font, Mauricio A. 2003. *Transforming Brazil: A Reform Era in Perspective*. Lanham, MD: Rowman & Littlefield.

Font, Mauricio A. 2010. *Coffee and Transformation in São Paulo, Brazil*. Lanham, MD: Rowman & Littlefield.

Font, Mauricio A., and Laura Randall, eds. 2011. *The Brazilian State: Debate and Agenda*. Landam, MD: Lexington Books.

Forrer, John, James Edwin Kee, Kathryn E. Newcomer, and Eric Boyer. 2010. "Public-Private Partnerships and the Public Accountability Question." *Public Administration Review* (May–June): 475–484.

Foster, Vivien, and Caridad Araujo. 2004. *Does Infrastructure Reform Work for the Poor?* Washington, DC: World Bank.

Foxley, Alejandro. 2010. "Market versus State: Postcrisis Economics in Latin America." Working Paper, Carnegie Endowment for International Peace.

Frank Hartwich, et al. 2008. *Building Public-Private Partnerships for Agricultural Innovation*. Washington, DC: International Food Policy Research Institute.

Frechette, Darren L. 1997. "The Dynamics of Convenience and the Brazilian Soybean Boom." *American Journal of Agricultural Economics* 79(4) (November): 1108–1118.

Frederico, Samuel. 2010. *O novo tempo do cerrado*. São Paulo: Annablume Editora.

Frederico, Samuel. 2013. "Agricultura científica globalizada e fronteira agrícola moderna no Brasil." *Confins* 17. www.confins.revues.org.

Friend, John. 2006. "Partnership Meets Politics: Managing within the Maze." *International Journal of Public Sector Management* 19(3): 261–277.

Fritz, Verena, and A. Rocha Menocal. 2006. "(Re)building Development States: From Theory to Practice." Working Paper 274, Overseas Development Institute, London.

Galiani, Sebastian, and Paulo Somaini. 2010. "Path-Dependent Import-Substitution Policies: The Case of Argentina in the 20th Century." Paper, Social Science Research Network. September.

Galetovic, Alexander, and Pablo Jordán. 2006. "Santiago: ¿Dónde estamos? ¿Hacia dónde vamos?" *Estudios Públicos* 101 (Summer): 87–146.

Gallo, Andres. 2012. "Trade Policy and Protectionism in Argentina." *Economic Affairs* 32(1) (February): 55–59.

Gamarra, Eduardo A. 2003. "Political Parties since 1964: The Construction of Bolivia's Multiparty System." In Merilee S. Grindle and Pilar Domingo, eds. *Proclaiming Revolution: Bolivia in Comparative Perspective*. London/Cambridge, MA: ILAS and David Rockefeller Center, 289–317.

Gary, Jorge Luis. 2004. "Colombia: Estructura Industrial e Internacionalización 1967–1996." Biblioteca Virtual de Banco de la República. www.banrepcultural .org.

Geddes, Barbara. 1995. "The Politics of Economic Liberalization." *Latin American Research Review* 30(2) (June): 195–214.

Gereffi, G. 2009. "Development Models and Industrial Upgrading in China and Mexico." *European Sociological Review* 25(1) (February): 37–51.

Gereffi, Gary, and Donald L. Wyman, eds. 1990. *Manufacturing Miracles: Paths of Industrialization in Latin America and East Asia*. Princeton, NJ: Princeton University Press.

Gereffi, Gary, and Miguel Korzeniewicz, eds. 1994. *Commodity Chains and Global Capitalism*. Westport, CT: Praeger.

Gerschenkron, Alexander. 1943. *Bread and Democracy in Germany*. Ithaca, NY: Cornell University Press.

Gerschenkron, Alexander. 1962. *Economic Backwardness in Historical Perspective: A Book of Essays*. Cambridge, MA: Belknap/Harvard University Press.

Ghobadian, Abby, David Gallear, Nicholas O'Regan, and Howard Viney. 2004. *Public-Private Partnerships: Policy and Experience*. New York, NY: Palgrave Macmillan.

Giambiagi, Fabio, José G. Reis, and André Urani, eds. 2004. *Reformas no Brasil: Balanço e Agenda*. Rio de Janeiro, Brazil: Editora Nova Fronteira.

Giddens, Anthony. 1998. *The Third Way, the Renewal of Social Democracy*. Cambridge, UK: Polity Press.

Giugale, Marcelo M., Vicente Fretes-Cibils, and John L. Newman. 2007. *Infrastructure Concessions: Moving Forward*. Washington, DC: World Bank Press.

Glade, William, ed. 1991. *Privatization of Public Enterprises in Latin America*. La Jolla: Center for U.S.-Mexican Studies.

Glantz, Michael H. 1996. *Currents of Change: El Niño's Impact on Climate and Society*. New York: Cambridge University Press.

Gobierno de Chile. 2013. "Plan de Prevención y Descontaminación Atmosférica R.M." Santiago, Chile: Ministro del Medio Ambiente.

Góngora, Mario. 1981. *Ensayo Histórico sobre la Noción del Estado en Chile en los Siglos XIX y XX*. Santiago: La Ciudad.

Governo de Estado de São Paulo. 2004. "Programa Estadual de Parcerias Publico-Privadas." Secretaria de Planejamento e Desenvolvimento Regional.

Governo do Estado de São Paulo. 2011a. "Plano Plurianual 2012–2015: Diagnósticos, Fundamentos e Visão Estratégica." Secretaria de Planejamento e Desenvolvimento Regional.

Governo do Estado de São Paulo. 2011b. "Programa Estadual de Parcerias Público-Privadas." Legislação de Referência, Secretaria Executiva.

Governo do Estado de São Paulo. 2014. "Mapa do Transporte Metropolitano." metro.sp.gov.br.

Graham, Carol, and Cheikh Kane. 1998. *Private Markets for Public Goods: Raising the Stakes in Economic Reform*. Washington, DC: Brookings Institution.

Graham, Carol, and Moisés Naím. 1998. "The Political Economy of Institutional Reform in Latin America." In Nancy Birdsall and Carol Graham, eds. *Beyond Tradeoffs: Market Reforms and Equitable Growth in Latin America*. Washington, DC: Brookings Institution Press: 321–359.

Graham, Michael, and Jean Woo, eds. 2009. *Fuelling Economic Growth: The Role of Public-Private Sector Research in Development*. Warwickshire, UK and Ottawa, Ontario, Canada: Practical Action Publishing and International Development Research Centre.

Gramlich, Edward M. 1994. "Infrastructure Investment: A Review Essay." *Journal of Economic Literature* 32(3) (September): 1176–1196.

Gramsch, Ernesto, G. Le Nir, M. Araya, Maria Angélica Rubio, Francisco Moreno, and Pedro Oyola. 2013. "Influence of Large Changes in Public Transportation (Transantiago) on the Black Carbon Pollution near Streets." *Atmospheric Environment* 65 (February): 153–163.

Gray Molina, George. "El reto posneoliberal de Bolivia." *Nueva Sociedad* 209 (May–June): 119–129.

Grimsey, Darrin, and Mervyn Lewis. 2005. *The Economics of Public Private Partnerships*. Cheltenham, UK and Northampton, MA: Edward Elgar.

Grindle, Merilee. 1996. *Challenging the State: Crisis and Innovation in Latin America and Africa*. Cambridge, UK: Cambridge University Press.

Grindle, Merilee S. 2000. *Audacious Reforms: Institutional Invention and Democracy in Latin America*. Baltimore, MD: Johns Hopkins University Press.

Gruening, Gernod. 2001. "Origin and Theoretical Basis of New Public Management." *International Public Management Journal* 4 (Spring):1–25.

Grugel, Jean. 2009. "'Basta de Realidades, Queremos Promesas': Democracy after the Washington Consensus." In Jean Grugel and Pía Riggirozzi, eds. *Governance after Neoliberalism in Latin America*. New York, NY: Palgrave Macmillan: 22–48.

Grugel, Jean, and Ben Thirkell White. 2008. "Beyond the Washington Consensus? Asia and Latin America in Search of more Autonomous Development." *International Affairs* 84(3) (May): 499–517.

Grugel, Jean, and Maria Pia Riggirozzi. 2007. "The Return of the State in Argentina." *International Affairs* 83(1) (January): 87–107.

Grugel, Jean, and Pía Riggirozzi. 2009. "The End of the Embrace? Neoliberalism and Alternatives to Neoliberalism in Latin America." In Jean Grugel and Pía

Riggirozzi, eds. *Governance after Neoliberalism in Latin America.* New York, NY: Palgrave Macmillan.: 1–24.

Grugel, Jean, and Pía Riggirozzi, eds. 2009. *Governance after Neoliberalism in Latin America.* New York, NY: Palgrave Macmillan.

Grugel, Jean, and Pía Riggirozzi, eds. 2012. "Post-Neoliberalism in Latin America: Rebuilding and Reclaiming the State after Crisis." *Development and Change* 43 (1) (January): 1–21.

Guaipatín, Carlos. 2007. "La Cooperación público-privada como instrumento de desarrollo: Lecciones de seis aglomeraciones agroindustriales en América Latina." *European Review of Latin American and Caribbean Studies* 82 (April): 51–68.

Guasch, José Luis. 2008. "Granting and Renegotiating Infrastructure Concessions: Doing it Right." Washington, DC: World Bank, Development Studies.

Guasch, José Luis, and Stéphane Straub. 2006. "Renegotiation of Infrastructure Concession: An Overview." *Annals of Public and Cooperative Economics* 77(4) (December): 479–493.

Guasch, José Luis, Jean-Jacques Laffont, and Stéphane Straub. 2008. "Renegotiation of Concession Contracts in Latin America: Evidence from the Water and Transport Sectors." *International Journal of Industrial Organization* 26(2) (March): 421–442.

Gutiérrez, Francisco and Gerd Schönwälder, eds. *Economic Liberalization and Political Violence: Utopia or Dystopia?* Ottawa: Pluto Press and International Development Research Center.

Haas, Peter M. 1992. "Introduction: Epistemic Communities and International Policy Coordination." *International Organization* 46(1) (Winter): 1–36.

Haber, Stephen. 2006. "The Political Economy of Industrialization." In Victor Bulmer-Thomas, John H. Coatsworth, and Roberto Cortés Conde, eds. *The Cambridge Economic History of Latin America*, vol. 2. New York, NY: Cambridge University Press.

Haggard, Stephan, and Robert R. Kaufman, eds. 1992. *The Politics of Economic Adjustment: International Constraints, Distributive Conflicts, and the State.* Princeton, NJ: Princeton University Press.

Haggard, Stephan, and Steven B. Webb, eds. 1994. *Voting for Reform: Democracy, Political Liberalization, and Economic Adjustment.* New York, NY: Oxford University Press and Washington, DC: World Bank.

Haggard, Stephan, Sylvia Maxfield, and Ben Ross Schneider. 1997. "Theories of Business and Business-State Relations." In Sylvia Maxfield and Ben Ross Schneider, eds. *Business and the State in Developing Countries.* Ithaca, NY: Cornell University Press: 36–60.

Haggard, Stephen, and Robert R. Kaufman. 1995. *The Political Economy of Democratic Transitions.* Princeton, NJ: Princeton University Press.

Hall, Peter A. 1989. *The Political Power of Economic Ideas: Keynesianism across Nations.* Princeton, NJ: Princeton University Press.

Hall, Peter A., and David Soskice, eds. 2001. *Varieties of Capitalism: The Institutional Foundations of Comparative Advantage.* New York, NY: Oxford University Press.

Hardcastle, Cliff, Matthias Beck, and Akintola Akintoye. 2003. *Public-Private Partnerships: Managing Risks and Opportunities.* Oxford, UK: Blackwell.

Heclo, Hugh. 1978. "Issue Networks and the Executive Establishment." In Anthony King, ed. *The New American Political System*. Washington, DC: The AEI Press.

Held, David, and Anthony McGrew. 2007. *Globalization/Anti-Globalization: Beyond the Great Divide*. Malden, MA: Polity Press.

Hellman, Joel S. 1998. "Winners Take All: The Politics of Partial Reforms in Postcommunist Transitions." *World Politics* 50(2) (February): 203–234.

Hellman, Judith Adler. 1988. *Mexico in Crisis*. New York, NY: Holmes and Meier.

Hemming, Richard. 2006. "Public-Private Partnerships, Government Guarantees, and Fiscal Risk." Washington, DC: International Monetary Fund.

Herrera, Germán, and Andrés Tavosnanska. 2011. "Argentine Industry in the Early Twenty-first Century (2003–2008)." *CEPAL Review* 104 (August): 99–116.

Hershberg, Eric, and Fred Rosen, eds. 2006. *Latin America after Neoliberalism*. New York: New Press/NACLA.

Hinojosa, Sergio, and Andrés Gómez-Lobo. 2000. "Broad Roads in a Thin Country: Infrastructure Concessions in Chile." Working Paper 2279. Washington, DC: World Bank's Institute Policy Research.

Hirschman, Albert O. 1968. "The Political Economy of Import-Substituting Industrialization in Latin America." *The Quarterly Journal of Economics* 82(1) (February): 1–32.

Hirschman, Albert O. 1971. *A Bias for Hope: Essays on Development and Latin America*. New Haven, CT: Yale University Press.

Hirschman, Albert O. 1981. *Essays in Trespassing: Economics to Politics and Beyond*. New York, NY: Cambridge University Press.

Hirschman, Albert O. 1985. *Rival Views of Market Society and Other Recent Essays*. Cambridge, MA: Harvard University Press.

Ho, S. Ping. 2006. "Model for Financial Renegotiation in Public-Private Partnership Projects and Its Policy Implications: Game Theoretic View." *Journal of Construction Engineering & Management* 132(7) (July): 678–688.

Hodge, Graeme A., and Carsten Greve. 2007. "Public-Private Partnerships: An International Performance Review." *Public Administration Review* 67(3) (May–June): 545–558.

Hodge, Graeme A., and Carsten Greve. 2008. "The PPP Debate: Taking Stock of the Issues and Renewing the Research Agenda." Paper presented at the Public Management Annual Conference for the International Research Society, Brisbane, Australia, March 26–28.

Hodge, Graeme A., Carsten Greve, and Anthony E. Boardman, eds. 2010. *International Handbook on Public Private Partnerships*. Cheltenham, UK and Northampton, MA: Edward Elgar.

Hollingsworth, J. Rogers, and Robert Boyer, eds. 1997. *Contemporary Capitalism: The Embeddedness of Institutions*. New York, NY: Cambridge University Press.

Hood, Christopher. 1991. "A Public Management for all Seasons?" *Public Administration* 69(1) (Spring): 3–19.

Hood, Christopher, Henry Rothstein, and Robert Baldwin. 2001. *The Government of Risk: Understanding Risk Regulation Regimes*. New York, NY: Oxford University Press.

Huber, Evelyn, and Fred Solt. 2004. "Successes and Failures of Neoliberalism." *Latin American Research Review* 39(3) (October): 150–164.

Hufbauer, Gary Clyde, and Jeffrey J. Schott. 2005. *NAFTA Revisited: Achievements and Challenges*. Washington, DC: Institute for International Economics.

Huntington, Samuel P. 1968. *Political Order in Changing Societies*. New Haven, CT: Yale University Press.

IBGE (Instituto Brasileiro de Geografia e Estatística). 2003. "Municipal Agricultural Production (PAM 1990–2007)." Levantamento Sistemático da Produção Agrícola (LSPA). December.

IBGE. 2011. "Tabela 2—Participação das Grandes Regiões e Unidades da Federação no Produto Interno Bruto—2005–2009." In Contas Nacionais No. 35. *Contas Regionais Do Brasil 2005–2009*. Rio de Janairo, Brazil, 55.

IDB (Inter-American Development Bank). 1997. *América Latina tras una década de reformas: Progreso económico y social en América Latina*. Washington, DC: IDB.

IDB. 2003. *Modernizing the State*. Washington, DC: IDB.

IDB. 2007. "Privatization and Social Exclusion in Latin America." In IDB 2008 Report. *Outsiders? The Changing Patterns of Exclusion in Latin America and the Caribbean*. Washington, DC, 149–157.

IDB. 2010. "The Political Economy of Fiscal Reform: The Case of Colombia, 1986–2006." Working Paper Series No. IDB-WP-181, May.

IDB. 2012. *The World of Forking Paths: Latin America and the Caribbean Facing Global Economic Risks*. 2012 Latin America and Caribbean Macroeconomic Report. Washington, DC.

Ikenberry, John G. 1990. "The International Spread of Privatization Polices: Inducements, Learning, and Policy Bandwagoning." In Ezra Suleiman and John Waterbury, eds. *The Political Economy of Public Sector Reform and Privatization*. Boulder, CO: Westview Press, 88–110.

IMF (International Monetary Fund). 2005. "Public Investment and Fiscal Policy: Summaries of the Pilot Country Studies." Fiscal Affairs Department, April 1.

IMF. 2014. World Economic Outlook Database. www.img.org.

"Informe alternativo a la Comisión Investigadora de Transantiago." Centro de Investigación Periodística, December 6, 2007.

Ipsos Public Affairs. 2009. "Estudio de Opinión Pública, Agosto 2009." Santiago, Chile.

Javiera Navarrete, Francisca, and Juan de Dios Ortúzar. 2013. "Subjective Valuation of the Transit Transfer Experience: The Case of Santiago de Chile." *Transport Policy* 25 (January): 138–147.

Jenkins, Rhys 2012. "China and Brazil: Economic Impacts of a Growing Relationship." *Journal of Current Chinese Affairs* 41(1) (March): 21–47.

Jimeno, Pamela. "Subsidio al Transantiago entre 2012 y 2022 costará al país US$16.000 millones." *La Tercera Edición Impresa* July 8, 2012.

Johnson, Chalmers. 1982. *MITI and the Japanese Miracle*. Stanford, CA: Stanford University Press.

Johnson, Chalmers. 1995. *Japan: Who Governs? The Rise of the Developmental State*. New York, NY: Norton.

Jong, Martin de. 2008. "The Effectiveness of Public-Private Partnerships in China's Transport Infrastructure." *Network Industries Quarterly* 10(2): 12–14.

Jong, Martin de, Mu Rui, Dominic Stead, Ma Yongchi, and Xi Bao. 2010. "Introducing Public-Private Partnerships for Metropolitan Subways in China: What is the Evidence?" *Journal of Transport Geography* 18(2) (March): 301–313.

Kalmanovitz, Salomón, ed. 2010. *Nueva historia económica de Colombia*. Bogota: Taurus.

Kantor, Paul, and H. V. Savitch. 2005. "How to Study Comparative Urban Development Politics: A Research Note." *International Journal of Urban and Regional Research* 29(1) (March): 135–151.

Kapur, Devesh, John P. Lewis, and Richard Charles Webb. 1997. *The World Bank: Its First Half Century*. Washington, DC: Brookings Institution Press.

Kaufman, Robert R. 2011. "The Political Left, the Export Boom, and the Populist Temptation." In Steven Levitsky and Kenneth Roberts, eds. *The Resurgence of the Latin American Left*. Baltimore, MD: Johns Hopkins University Press, 93–116.

Kay, Bruce H. 1996. "'Fujipopulism' and the Liberal State in Peru, 1990–1995." *Journal of Interamerican Studies and World Affairs* 38(4) (Winter): 55–98.

Kehoe, Timothy J., and Felipe Meza. 2012. "Catch-Up Growth Followed by Stagnation: Mexico, 1950–2010." Working Paper 693, Federal Reserve Bank of Minneapolis, Research Department, revised November.

Kennemore, Amy, and Gregory Weeks. 2011. "Twenty-First Century Socialism? The Elusive Search for a Post-Neoliberal Development Model in Bolivia and Ecuador." *Bulletin of Latin American Research* 30(3) (July): 267–281

Keynes, John Maynard. 1936. *The General Theory of Employment, Interest, and Money*. New York, NY: Harcourt Brace.

Kingstone, Peter R. 1999. *Crafting Coalitions for Reform Business Preferences, Political Institutions, and Neoliberal Reform in Brazil*. University Park, PA: University of Pennsylvania Press.

Klein, Herbert S. 2003. *A Concise History of Bolivia*. New York, NY: Cambridge University Press.

Klijn, Erick-Hans, and Joop F. M. Koppenjan. 2000. "Public Management and Policy Networks: Foundations of a Network Approach to Governance." *Public Management* 2(2):135–158.

Knopf, Jeffrey W. 2003. "The Importance of International Learning." *Review of International Studies* 29(2) (April): 185–207.

Kohli, Atul. 2004. *State-Directed Development: Political Power and Industrialization in the Global Periphery*. Cambridge, UK: Cambridge University Press.

Kornai, Janos. 1992. *The Socialist System: The Political Economy of Socialism*. Princeton, NJ: Princeton University Press.

Korol, Juan Carlos, and Hilda Sabato. 1990. "Incomplete Industrialization: An Argentine Obsession." *Latin American Research Review* 25(1) (February): 7–30.

Kostakis, Vasilis. 2011. "Commons-Based Peer Production and the Neo-Weberian State: Synergies and Interdependencies." *Halduskultuur-Administrative Culture* 12(2) (October): 146–161.

Krueger, Anne O. 1974. "The Political Economy of the Rent-Seeking Society." *American Economic Review* 64(3) (January): 291–303.

Kuczynski, Pedro-Pablo, and John Williamson, eds. 2003. *After the Washington Consensus: Restarting Growth and Reform in Latin America.* Washington, DC: Institute for International Economics.

Kurtz, Marcus J. 2004. "The Dilemmas of Democracy in the Open Economy: Lessons from Latin America." *World Politics* 56(2) (January): 262–302.

Lange, Matthew, and Dietrich Rueschemeyer. 2005. *States and Development: Historical Antecedents of Stagnation and Advance.* New York, NY: Palgrave Macmillan.

"Las 8 medidas que en 7 años han intentado mejorar el Transantiago." *La Nación*, May 29, 2014.

Lascano Kezic, M., and Pablo Durango-Cohen. 2012. "The Transportation Systems of Buenos Aires, Chicago and São Paulo: City Centers, Infrastructure and Policy Analysis." *Transportation Research Part A* 46(1) (January): 102–122.

Lationobarómetro. 2010. *Informe 2010.* Santiago, Chile, December.

Latour, Bruno. 1987. *Science in Action: How to Follow Scientists and Engineers thorough Society.* Cambridge, MA: Harvard University Press.

Le Clech, Nestor Adrian. 2007. "Reformas Estructurales y Desempeño Económico en Argentina: 1976–2000." *Problemas Del Desarrollo* 38(151) (October–December): 151–175.

Leahy, Patricia. 2005. "Lessons from the Private Finance Initiative in the United Kingdom." *EIB Papers* 10(2) (June): 58–71.

Lee, Chang Kil, and David Strang. 2006. "The International Diffusion of Public Sector Downsizing: Network Emulation and Theory-Driven Learning." *International Organization* 60(4) (October): 883–909.

Lehman, Glen, and Ian Tregoning. 2004. "Public-Private Partnerships, Taxation and a Civil Society." *Journal of Corporate Citizenship* 15 (Autumn): 77–89.

Leiva, Fernando Ignacio. 2008. *Latin American Neostructuralism: The Contradictions of Post-Neoliberal Development.* Minneapolis, MN: University of Minnesota Press.

Lents, James M., Gerhard Leutert, and Humberto Fuenzalida. 2006. "Segunda auditoria internacional: Plan de prevención y descontaminación atmosférica de la región metropolitana (PPDA)." Comisión Nacional del medio ambiente región metropolitana.

Levi-Faur, David. 1998. "The Competition State as a Neo-Mercantilist State." *The Journal of Socio-Economics* 27(6) (November–December): 665–685.

Levinson, Marc. 2006. *The Box: How the Shipping Container Made the World Small and the World Economy Bigger.* Princeton, NJ: Princeton University Press.

Levitsky, Steven, and María Victoria Murillo. 2008. "Argentina: From Kirchner to Kirchner." *Journal of Democracy* 19 (2) (April): 16–30.

Levitsky, Steven. 1999. "Fujimori and Post-Party Politics in Peru." *Journal of Democracy* 10(3) (July): 78–92.

Levitt, Barbara, and James G. March. 1988. "Organizational Learning." *Annual Review of Sociology* 14 (August): 319–340.

Levy, Jonah. 2006. "The State after Statism: From Market Direction to Market Support." In Jonah Levy, ed. *The State after Statism: New State Activities in the Age of Liberalization.* Cambridge, MA: Harvard University Press, 367–394.

Lewis, Paul. 1992. *The Crisis of Argentine Capitalism*. Chapel Hill, NC: University of North Carolina Press.

Link, Albert N. 2006. *Public/Private Partnerships: Innovation Strategies and Policy Alternatives*. New York, NY: Springer.

López-Carlos, Augusto, Michael E. Porter, Klaus Schwab, and Xavier Sala-i-Martin. 2006. "The Global Competitiveness Report 2006–2007." World Economic Forum.

Lora, Eduardo, ed. 2007. *The State of State Reform in Latin America*. Palo Alto, CA: Stanford University Press and Washington, DC: World Bank.

Loureiro, Maria Rita, Fábio Pereira dos Santos, and Alexandre de Ávila Gomide. 2011. "Entre O Mercado E O Povo: Desafios Para A Política Econômica Do Governo Lula." In Lourdes E. Loureiro Sola and Maria Rita, eds. *Democracia, Mercado E Estado—O B De Brics*. Rio De Janeiro, Brazil: Fgv, 284–314.

Love, Joseph. 1980. "Raúl Prebisch and the Origins of the Doctrine of Unequal Exchange." *Latin American Research Review* 15(3) (October): 45–72.

Lucero, José Antonio. 2009. "Decades Lost and Won: Indigenous Movements and Multicultural Neoliberalism in the Andes." In John Burdick, Philip Oxhorn, and Kenneth M. Roberts, eds. *Beyond Neoliberalism in Latin America? Societies and Politics and the Crossroads*. New York, NY: Palgrave Macmillan, 63–82.

Lucioni, Luis. 2009. "La Provisión de Infraestructura en América Latina: Tendencias, Inversiones y Financiamiento." ECLAC, Macroeconomía del Desarrollo Series 72, January.

Lynn, Laurence. 2008. "What is a Neo-Weberian State? Reflections on a Concept and its Implications." *NISPAcee Journal of Public Administration and Policy* 1(2) (Winter): 17–30.

Macdonald, Laura, and Arne Ruckert, eds. 2009. *Post-Neoliberalism in the Americas*. New York, NY: Palgrave Macmillan.

MacLeod, Dag. 2004. *Downsizing the State: Privatization and the Limits of Neoliberal Reform in Mexico*. University Park, PA: Pennsylvania State University Press.

Madrid, Raúl L. 2002. "The Politics and Economics of Pension Privatization in Latin America." *Latin American Research Review* 37(2) (June): 159–182.

Madrid, Raúl L. 2008. "The Rise of Ethnopopulism in Latin America." *World Politics* 60 (3) (April): 475–508.

Mahoney, James. 2000. "Path Dependence in Historical Sociology." *Theory and Society* 29 (4) (August): 507–548.

Mahoney, James. 2001. *The Legacies of Liberalism: Path Dependence and Political Regimes in Central America*. Baltimore, MD: Johns Hopkins University Press.

Mahoney, James. 2010. *Colonialism and Postcolonial Development: Spanish America in Comparative Perspective*. New York, NY: Cambridge University Press.

Maman, Daniel, and Zeev Rosenhek. 2011. "The Institutional Dynamics of a Developmental State: Change and Continuity in State-Economy Relations in Israel." Research Institute for Policy, Political Economy and Society/The Open University of Israel Working Paper 5–2011.

Manzanelli, Pablo, and Schorr Martin. 2011. "Extranjerización y Poder Económico Industrial en Argentina." *Revista Problemas del Desarrollo* 170(43) (July–September): 39–67.

Manzano, Osmel, and Francisco Monaldi. 2008. "The Political Economy of Oil Production in Latin America." *Economía* 9(1) (Fall), 59–103.

Manzetti, Luigi. 1999. *Privatization South American Style.* Oxford, UK: Oxford University Press.

Manzetti, Luigi, ed. 2000. *Regulatory Policy in Latin America: Post-Privatization Realities.* Miami, FL: North-South Center Press, University of Miami.

Manzetti, Luigi. 2003. "Political Manipulations and Market Reforms Failures." *World Politics* 55(3) (April): 315–360.

Manzetti, Luigi. 2009. *Neoliberalism, Accountability, and Reform Failures in Emergent Markets.* University Park, PA: Pennsylvania State University Press.

Marcel, Mario C. 1999. "Effectiveness of the State and Development: Lessons from the Chilean Experience." In Guillermo Perry, and Danny M. Leipziger, eds. *Chile: Recent Policy Lessons and Emerging Challenges.* Washington, DC: World Bank Institute, 265–325.

Marcel, Mario C. 2006. "Reflexiones acerca del proceso de modernización del Estado en Chile y desafíos futuros." *Revista del Clad, Reforma y Democracia* 34 (February): 217–232.

Mardones, Rodrigo. 2008. "Chile: Transantiago Recargado." *Revista de Ciencia Política* 28(1): 103–119.

Margheritis, Ana, and Anthony W. Pereira (2007) "The Neoliberal Turn in Latin America: The Cycle of Ideas and the Search for an Alternative." *Latin American Perspectives* 34(3) (May), 25–48.

Marin, Philippe. 2009. "Public-Private Partnerships for Urban Water Utilities: A Review of Experiences in Developing Countries." Trends and Policy Options No. 8. Washington, DC: World Bank, PPIAF (Public-Private Infrastructure Advisory Facility).

Martimort, David, and Jerome Pouyet. 2008. "To Build or not to Build: Normative and Positive Theories of Public-Private Partnerships." *International Journal of Industrial Organization* 26(2) (March): 393–411.

Maskin, Eric, and Jean Tirole. 2008. "Public-Private Partnerships and Government Spending Limits." *International Journal of Industrial Organization* 26(2) (March): 412–420.

Mayda, Anna Maria, and Dani Rodrik. 2005. "Why are Some People (and Countries) More Protectionist than Others?" *European Economic Review* 49(6) (August): 1393–1430.

McAdam, Doug, Sidney Tarrow, and Charles Tilly. 2001. *Dynamics of Contention.* New York, NY: Cambridge University Press.

McGreevy, William P. 2008. *An Economic History of Colombia, 1845–1930.* New York: Cambridge University Press.

McKeigue, James. 2013. "This Peru Boom Will Run and Run." *Money Week*, October 6. www.moneyweek.com.

Mejía, Abel. 2011. "Responding to Global Changes: Water in an Urbanizing World, Challenges for Urban Water Provision in Latin America and the Caribbean." Presentation at World Water Week, Stockholm, Sweden, August 24.

Mejido Costoya, Manuel. 2011. "Politics of Trade in Post-neoliberal Latin America: The Case of Bolivia." *Bulletin of Latin American Research* 30(1) (January): 80–95.

Melo, Marcus A. 2003. "When Institutions Matter: A Comparison of the Politics of Administrative, Social Security, and Tax Reforms in Brazil." In Ben Ross Schneider and Blanca Heredia, eds. *The Politics of Administrative Reform in Developing Countries.* Miami, FL: North-South Center Press, 211–249.

Mendes, Sérgio Magno, Erly Cardoso Teixeira, and Márcio Antônio Salvato. 2009. "Investimentos em infra-estrutura e produtividade total dos fatores na agricultura brasileira: 1985–2004." *Revista Brasileira de Economia* 63(2) (April): 91–102.

Mery, Valentina, and Benjamían Blanco. "Transantiago: Las preocupaciones de los operadores del sistema de transporte." *La Tercera*, August 28, 2014.

Messeguer, Covadonga. 2005. "Policy Learning, Policy Diffusion, and the Making of a New Order." *Annals of the American Academy of Political and Social Science* 598(1) (March): 67–82.

México, Secretaría de Hacienda y Crédito Público. 2008. "Programa para impulsar el crecimiento y el empleo." Press Release, October 8.

Meyer W. John, John Boli, George M. Thomas, and Francisco O. Ramírez. 1997. "World Society and the Nation-State." *American Journal of Sociology* 103(1) (July): 144–181.

Meyer, Peter J. 2010. "Uruguay: Political and Economic Conditions and U.S. Relations." Congressional Research Service.

Mia, Irene, Julio Estrada, and Thierry Geiger. 2007. "Benchmarking National Attractiveness for Private Investment in Latin American Infrastructure." Paper, World Economic Forum, Global Competitiveness Network.

Miguez, Eduardo. 2006. "The Argentinean Failure: An Interpretation of Economic Evolution in the 'Short 20th Century.'" *Desarrollo Económico* 44(176) (January–March): 483–514.

Milner, Helen V., and Bumba Mukherjee. 2009. "Democratization and Economic Globalization." *Annual Review of Political Science* 12: 163–181.

Milner, Helen V., and Keiko Kubota. 2005. "Why the Move to Free Trade? Democracy and Trade Policy in the Developing Countries." *International Organization* 59(1) (January): 107–143.

Minogue, Martin. 2004. "Public Management and Regulatory Governance: Problems of Policy Transfer to Developing Countries." In Paul Crook, Colin Kirkpatrick, Martin Minogue, and Ledivina Carino, eds. *Leading Issues in Regulation, Competition and Development.* Cheltenham, UK and Northampton, MA: Edward Elgar, 165–181.

Molano, Walter. 1997. *The Logic of Privatization: The Case of Telecommunications in the Southern Cone of Latin America.* Westport, CT and London, UK: Greenwood Press.

Molero Simarro, Ricardo, and María José Antolín. 2012. "Development Strategy of the MAS in Bolivia: Characterization and Early Assessment." *Development and Change* 43(2) (March): 531–556.

Montecinos, Veronica, and John Markoff, eds. 2010. *Economists in the Americas.* Cheltenham, UK and Northampton, MA: Edward Elgar.

Mora, Monica. 2002. "Federalismo e Dívida Estadual no Brasil." Rio de Janeiro, Brazil: *IPEA*, Research Paper No. 866.

Morgenstern, Richard. 2004. "Policy Studies on Greenhouse Gas Mitigation and Economic Development: Synergies and Challenges." Working Paper, Inter-American Development Bank.

Morrison, Wayne M. 2014. "China's Economic Rise: History, Trends, Challenges, and Implications for the United States." Congressional Research Service. No. 7–5700.

Müller, Jan Marco. 2004. "El impacto de la apertura económica sobre el sistema de transporte y el desarrollo regional en Colombia." *Territorios* 10–11 (January): 145–172.

Muñoz Gomá, Oscar. 2001. *Estrategias de desarrollo en economías emergentes: Lecciones de la experiencia latinoamericana*. Santiago: Libros FLACSO.

Muñoz, Juan Carlos, and Louis de Grange. 2010. "On the Development of Public Transit in Large Cities." *Research in Transportation Economics* 29(1): 379–386.

Murillo, María Victoria. 2001. *Labor Unions, Partisan Coalitions, and Market Reforms in Latin America*. New York, NY: Cambridge University Press.

Murillo, María Victoria. 2002. "Political Bias in Policy Convergence: Privatization Choices in Latin America." *World Politics* 54(4) (July): 462–493.

Murillo, María Victoria, Virginia Oliveros, and Milan Vaishnav. 2011. "Economic Constraints and Presidential Agency." In Steven Levitsky and Kenneth Roberts, eds. *The Resurgence of the Latin American Left*. Baltimore, MD: The Johns Hopkins University Press, 52–70.

Murphy, Peter. 2012. "The Long, Brutal Haul from Farm to Port in Brazil." *Reuters*. www.reuters.com.

Murray, Warwick E., and John D. Overton. 2011. "Neoliberalism is Dead, Long Live Neoliberalism? Neostructuralism and the International Aid Regime of the 2000s." *Progress in Development Studies* 11(4) (July): 307–319.

NAO (National Audit Office). 2003. "PFI Construction Performance." Report HC371 2002–2003. London, February 5.

NAO. 2010. "The Performance and Management of Hospital PFI Contracts." June.

Naranjo S., Montserrat. "Transantiago: Una historia de retrasos y críticas." *Cooperativa.cl*, February 10, 2007.

Navarrete, Francisca Javiera, and Juan de Dios Ortúzar. 2013. "Subjective Valuation of the Transit Transfer Experience: The Case of Santiago de Chile." *Transport Policy* 25 (January): 138–157.

Neto, Carlos Alvares, Bolívar Pêgo Filho, Alfredo Eric Romminger, Iansã Melo Ferreira, and Leonardo Fernandes Soares Vasconcelos. 2010. "Gargalos e demandas da infraestrutura ferroviária e os investimentos do PAC: mapeamento IPEA de obras ferroviárias." Rio de Janeiro, Brazil: IPEA, Research Paper No. 1465.

Norment, Richard. 2008. "Fundamentals of PPPs." Partnerships for Growth in Infrastructure Workshop, National Council for Public-Private Partnerships, Charlotte, NC, May 21.

North, Liisa L. 2004. "State Building, State Dismantling, and Financial Crises in Ecuador." In Jo-Marie Burt and Philip Mauceri, eds. *Politics in the Andes: Identity, Conflict, Reform*. Pittsburgh, PA: University of Pittsburgh Press, 187–206.

Noulton, John. 1999. "Lessons from the Channel Tunnel Experience." Seminar on PPPs in Transport Infrastructure Financing, European Conference of Ministers of Transport, Paris, France, January 12.

Noumba-Um, Paul. 2010. "Empirical Evidence of Infrastructure Public-Private Partnerships: Lessons from the World Bank Experience." In Graeme A. Hodge, Carsten Greve, and Anthony E. Boardman, eds. *International Handbook on Public-Private Partnerships.* Cheltenham, UK and Northampton, MA: Edward Elgar, 456–478.

O Riain, Sean. 2004. *The Politics of High-Tech Growth: Developmental Network States in the Global Economy.* New York, NY: Cambridge University Press.

O'Donnell, Guillermo A. 1973. *Modernization and Bureaucratic-Authoritarianism: Studies in South American Politics.* Politics of Modernization Series No. 9. Berkeley, CA: Institute of International Studies.

O'Donnell, Guillermo A. 1977. "Estado y Alianzas en la Argentina, 1956–1976." *Desarrollo Económico* 16(64) (January–March): 523–554.

O'Donnell, Guillermo A. 1986. *Bureaucratic Authoritarianism: Argentina 1966–1973 in Comparative Perspective.* Berkeley, CA: University of California Press.

O'Donnell, Guillermo. 1993. "On the State, Democratization and Some Conceptual Problems: A Latin American View with Glances at Some Post-communist Countries." *World Development* 21(8): 1355–1369.

O'Donnell, Guillermo A. 1994. "Delegative Democracy." *Journal of Democracy* 5(1) (January): 55–69.

Ocampo, José Antonio. 1984. *Colombia y la economía mundial, 1830–1910.* Bogotá: Siglo Veintiuno.

Ocampo, José Antonio. 2007. "The Macroeconomics of the Latin American Economic Boom." *Cepal Review* 93 (December): 7–28.

Ocampo, José Antonio, and Joseph Stiglitz, eds. 2008. *Capital Market Liberalization and Development.* New York, NY: Oxford University Press.

OECD (Organization for Economic Co-operation and Development). 2008. *Public-Private Partnerships: In Pursuit of Risk Sharing and Value for Money.* Paris: OECD.

OECD. 2009. *Contracting Out Government Functions and Services: Emerging Lessons from Post-conflict and Fragile Situations.* Paris: OECD.

OECD. 2010. *Handbook on contracting out government functions and services in post-conflict and fragile situations.* Paris: PDG (Partnership for Democratic Governance).

Ojha, Abhoy K. 2010. "Public-Private Partnerships: Analyzing the Network Form of Organization." In G. Ramesh, V. Nagadevara, G. Naik, and A. B. Suraj, eds. *Public Private Partnerships.* Indian Institute Management of Bangalore. New Delhi, India: Routledge, 1–19.

Nunes, Edson. 1997. *A Gramática Política do Brasil: Clientelismo e Insulamento Burocrático.* Rio de Janeiro, Brazil: Jorge Zahar.

Nunes, Edson. 2010. *A Pragmática Política Do Brasil*: Clientelismo, Corporativismo E Insulamento Burocrático. Rio de Janeiro, Brazil: Garamond.

Nunes, Edson, André Magalhães Nogueira, Cátia Couto da Costa, Helenice Vieira de Andrade, and Leandro Molhano Ribeiro. 2007. *Agências Reguladoras E Reforma*

Do Estado No Brasil–Inovação E Continuidade No Sistema Político-Institucional. Rio de Janeiro, Brazil: Garamond Universitária.

Oliveira, Paulo, and Robert J. Marquis, eds. 2002. *The Cerrados of Brazil: Ecology and Natural History of a Neotropical Savanna*. New York, NY: Columbia University Press.

Olivera, Mauricio, Mónica Pachón, and Guillermo Perry. 2010. "The Political Economy of Fiscal Reform: The Case of Colombia, 1986–2006." Working Paper, Inter-American Development Bank, Research Department, Washington, DC.

Olivos Marín, Oriana. "Costanera Norte: El túnel gigante del río Mapocho." *Ediciones especiales* April 21, 2005.

Oncala, Andréa Arean. 2004. "Brazil Turns to PPP for Infrastructure Investment." *International Financial Law Review* 23(11) (November): 26–28.

Osborne, Stephen P. 2000. *Public-Private Partnerships: Theory and Practice in International Perspective*. Routledge Advances in Management and Business Studies. New York, NY: Routledge, Taylor and Francis.

Oviedo, Eduardo Daniel. 2013. "Argentina Facing China: Modernization, Interests and Economic Relations Model." *East Asia: An International Quarterly* 30 (1) (November): 7–34.

Owen, John Malloy. 2002. "The Foreign Imposition of Domestic Institutions." *International Organization* 56(2) (Spring): 375–409.

Oxhorn, Philip. 2009. "Beyond Neoliberalism? Latin America's New Crossroads." In John Burdick, Philip Oxhorn, and Kenneth M. Roberts, eds. *Beyond Neoliberalism in Latin America? Societies and Politics and the Crossroads*. New York, NY: Palgrave Macmillan, 217–234.

Oxhorn, Philip, and Pamela K. Starr, eds. 1999. *Market and Democracy in Latin America: Conflict or Convergence?* Boulder, CO: Lynne Rienner.

Paige, Jeffery. 2007. "India and the Myth of the Anti-Developmental State." *Comparative and Historical Sociology* 18(2) (Spring): 2–4.

Palacios, Marco. 2002. *Coffee in Colombia, 1850–1970: An Economic, Social and Political History*. New York, NY: Cambridge University Press.

Pang, Eul-Soo. 2000. "The Financial Crisis of 1998–98 and the End of the Asian Developmental State." *Contemporary Southeast Asia* 22(3) (December): 570–593

Panizza, Francisco. 2005. "Unarmed Utopia Revisited: The Resurgence of Left-of-Centre Politics in Latin America." *Political Studies* 53(4) (December): 716–734.

Panizza, Francisco. 2009. *Contemporary Latin America: Development and Democracy beyond the Washington Consensus*. London: Zed Books.

"Paraguay to Improve Urban Infrastructure, Public Transportation with IDB Assistance." *IDB (Inter-American Development Bank)*, September 30, 2010.

Paredes, Ricardo M. 2001. "Redistributive Impact of Privatization and the Regulation of Utilities in Chile." Discussion Paper 2001/19, The United Nations University, World Institute for Development, June.

Paredes, Ricardo D., and José Miguel Sanchez. 2004. "Government Concession Contracts in Chile: The Role of Competition in the Bidding Process." *Economic Development and Cultural Change* 53(1) (October): 215–234.

Parker, David, and Catarina Figueira. 2010. "PPPs in Developed and Developing Economies: What Lessons Can Be Learned?" In Graeme A. Hodge, Carsten Greve, and Anthony. E. Boardman, eds. *International Handbook on Public-Private Partnerships*. Cheltenham, UK and Northampton, MA: Edward Elgar, 526–547.

Pastor, Manuel Jr., and Carol Wise. 2005. "The Lost Sexenio: Vicente Fox and the New Politics of Economic Reform in Mexico." *Latin American Politics and Society* 47(4) (Winter): 135–160.

Payne, Michael. 2007. "A Gold-Medal Partnership." *Strategy+Business Management Magazine*. February 28.

Pempel, T. J. 1999. "The Developmental Regime in a Changing World Economy." In Meredith Woo-Cumings, ed. *The Developmental State*. Ithaca, NY: Cornell University, 137–181.

Pereira, Ricardo A. de Castro, and Pedro Cavalcanti Ferreira. 2008. "Efeitos de Crescimento e Bem-estar da Lei de Parceria Público-Privada no Brasil." *Revista Brasileira de Economia* 62(2) (April–June): 207–219.

Pereyra, Andrés. 2009. "Articulacion público-privada en el financiamiento de la infraestructura de carreteras en Uruguay." *Cuadernos de Economía* 28(50) (January–June): 95–115.

Pérez Guerra, Arnaldo. "Chile: Las mentiras del Transantiago." *La insignia*, July 3, 2007.

Pérez Salas, Gabriel, Georgina Cipoletta Tomassian, and Ricardo Sánchez. 2009. "Infraestructura y Servicios de Transporte y su Relación con los Objetivos de Desarrollo del Milenio." Santiago, Chile: CEPAL.

Perrotti, Daniel. 2011. "The Economic Infrastructure Gap in Latin America and the Caribbean." *FAL Bulletin* [ECLAC] 293(1) (January): 1–7.

Pinaud, Nicolas. 2007. *Public-Private Dialogue in Developing Countries: Opportunities and Risks*. Paris: OECD.

Plant, Raymond, ed. 2009. *The Neoliberal State*. Oxford, UK: Oxford University Press.

Polanyi, Karl. 1944. *The Great Transformation*. New York, NY: Rinehart

Pollitt, Christopher, and Geert Bouckaert. 2004. *Public Management Reform: A Comparative Analysis*. New York, NY: Oxford University Press. 2nd ed.

Portes, Alejandro. 2005. "Sociology in the Hemisphere: Past Convergencies and a New Middle-Range Agenda." In Charles H. Wood and Bryan R. Roberts, eds. *Rethinking Development in Latin America*. University Park, PA: Pennsylvania State University Press, 27–52.

Portes, Alejandro. 2010. *Economic Sociology: A Systematic Inquiry*. Princeton, NJ and Oxford, UK: Princeton University Press.

Powell, Walter W. 1990. "Neither Market nor Hierarchy: Network Forms of Organization." *Research in Organizational Behavior* 12: 295–336.

Prebisch, Raúl. 1950. *The Economic Development of Latin America and Its Principal Problems*. New York, NY: United Nations.

Przeworski, Adam. 1993. "The Neoliberal Fallacy." In Larry Diamond and Marc F. Plattner, eds. *Capitalism, Socialism, and Democracy Revisited*. Baltimore, MD: John Hopkins University Press, 39–53.

Puryear, Jeffrey M. 1994. *Thinking Politics: Intellectuals and Democracy in Chile.* Baltimore, MD: Johns Hopkins University Press.

PwC (PriceWaterhouseCoopers). 2005. "Delivering the PPP promise: A Review of PPP Issues and Activity." www.pwc.com.

PwC. 2014. "Capital Project and Infrastructure Spending: Outlook to 2025. www.pwc.com.

Quijada, Rodrigo. "Los misteriosos cambios a los contratos de Transantiago." *el quinto poder*, February 9, 2014.

Quijada, Rodrigo, Alejandro Tirachini, Rodrigo Henríquez, and Ricardo Hurtubia. "Investigación al Transantiago: Sistematización de Declaraciones hechas ante la Comisión Investigadora, Resumen de Contenidos de los Principales Informes Técnicos, Información de Documentos Públicos Adicionales y Comentarios Críticos." Cipercile.cl, November 30, 2007.

Ramanayya, Tammana V., and Vishnuprasad Nagadevara. 2010. "Bus Rapid Transit Systems through Public-Private Participation for Improving Urban Mobility." In G. Ramesh, Vishnuprasad Nagadevara, Gopal Naik, and Anil B. Suraj, eds. *Public Private Partnerships.* Indian Institute Management of Bangalore. New Delhi, India: Routledge, 204–225.

Ramesh, G., Vishnuprasad Nagadevara, Gopal Naik, and Anil B. Suraj, eds. 2010. *Public Private Partnerships.* Indian Institute Management of Bangalore. New Delhi, India: Routledge.

Reeves, Eoin, and James Ryan. 2007. "Piloting Public-Private Partnerships: Expensive Lessons from Ireland's Schools' Sector." *Public Money & Management* 27(5) (November): 331–338.

Remmer, Karen L. 1991. "The Political Impact of Economic Crisis in Latin America in the 1980s." *American Political Science Review* 85(3) (September):777–800.

Remmer, Karen L. 1998. "The Politics of Neoliberal Economic Reform in South America., 1980–1994." *Studies in Comparative International Development* 33(2) (Summer): 3–29.

Remmer, Karen L., and Erik Wibbels. 2000. "The Subnational Politics of Economic Development: Provincial Politics and Fiscal Performance in Argentina." *Comparative Political Studies* 33(4) (May): 419–451.

Renda, Andrea, and Lorna Schrefler. 2006. "Public-Private Partnerships: Models and Trends in the European Union." Economic and Scientific Policy, Directorate A, European Parliament.

República de Chile. "Revisa, Reformula y Actualiza Plan de Prevención y Descontaminación Atmosférica para la Región." Ds. No. 66, Santiago, Ministerio Secretaría General de la Presidencia de la República.

Resende, Paulo. 2009. "Infrastructure: Will PAC Really Accelerate Growth?" *The Brazil Competitiveness Report 2009.* Geneva: World Economic Forum.

"Revise en detalle el plan de mejoramiento del Transantiago." *La Nación*, May 29, 2014.

Rhodes, R. A. W. 1991. "Interorganisational Networks and the Policy Process." In F. X. Kaufman, ed. *The Public Sector: Challenge for Co-ordination and Learning.* Berlin and New York: de Gruyter, 525–534.

Richardson Jeremy J., and Grant Jordan. 1979. *Governing Under Pressure: The Policy Process in a Post-Parliamentary Democracy*. Oxford Road, UK: Manchester University Press.

Riggirozzi, Pía and Jean Grugel. 2009. "Conclusion Governance after Neoliberalism." In Jean Grugel and Pía Riggirozzi, eds. *Governance after Neoliberalism in Latin America*. New York, NY: Palgrave Macmillan, 217–230.

Roberts, Kenneth M. 1995. "Neoliberalism and the Transformation of Populism in Latin America: The Peruvian Case." *World Politics* 48(1) (October): 82–116.

Roberts, Kenneth M. 1998. *Deepening Democracy? The Modern Left and Social Movements in Chile and Peru*. Stanford, CA: Stanford University Press.

Roberts, Kenneth M. 2009. "Beyond Neoliberalism: Popular Responses to Social Change in Latin America." In John Burdick, Philip Oxhorn, and Kenneth M. Robert, eds. *Beyond Neoliberalism in Latin America? Societies and Politics and the Crossroads*. New York, NY: Palgrave Macmillan, 1–16.

Rocha Menocal, Alina. 2004. "And If There Was No State? Critical Reflections on Bates, Polanyi and Evans on the Role of the States in Promoting Development." *Third World Quarterly* 25(4): 765–77.

Rodal, Alti. 1993. "Managing Partnerships." *Optimum* 24(3) (Winter):49–63.

Rodrigue, Jean-Paul. 2013. *The Geography of Transport Systems*. London, UK: Taylor & Francis. 3rd ed.

Rodríguez, Octavio. 2010. "The Emergence and Entrenchment of a New Political Regime in Mexico." *Latin American Perspectives* 37(1) (January): 35–61.

Rodrik, Dani. 2006. "Goodbye Washington Consensus, Hello Washington Confusion? A Review of the World Bank's Economic Growth in the 1990s: Learning from a Decade of Reform." *Journal of Economic Literature* 44(4) (December): 973–987.

Rodrik, Dani. 2007. *One Economics, Many Recipes: Globalization, Institutions, and Economic Growth*. Princeton, NJ: Princeton University Press.

Ronceros, Miguel, and Ronald Fernandez-Davila. n/d. "An Overview of Public-Private Partnerships in Peru: The Past, Present, and Future." Rosello Abogados. www.rossellolaw.com/files.

Rosa, Taina. 2008. "Growing in Slow Motion." *Latin Finance* 203 (December): 33–34.

Rostow, Walt W. 1960. *The Stages of Economic Growth: A Non-Communist Manifesto*. Cambridge, MA: Cambridge University Press.

Rovira Kaltwasser, Cristóbal. 2011. "Toward Post-Neoliberalism in Latin America?" *Latin American Research Review* 46(2) (June): 225–234.

Rozas, Patricio. 2010. "América Latina: Problemas y desafíos del financiamiento de la infraestructura." *Revista CEPAL* (101) (August): 59–82.

Rozas, Patricio and Ricardo Sánchez. 2004. "Desarrollo de Infraestructura y Crecimiento Económico: Revisión Conceptual." *ECLAC* Serie Recursos Naturales e Infraestructura Series 75 (October).

Ruiz, Jorge Ernesto Sánchez. 1993. "Privatização de estradas no Brasil: comentário sobre a viabilidade financeira." *Revista de Economia Política* 13(3) (July–September): 41–53.

Ruster, Jeff. 1997. "A Retrospective on the Mexican Tool Road Program (1989–94)." Public Policy for the Private Sector; Note no. 125. Washington, DC: World Bank.

Saad, Mohammed, and Girma Zawdie, eds. 2011. *Theory and Practice of the Triple Helix System in Developing Countries: Issues and Challenges.* New York, NY: Routledge.

Sant Ana, Paulo Henrique de Mello, Gilberto De Martino Jannuzzi, and Sergio Valdir Bajay. 2011. "Natural Gas Regulation in Brazil: a Framework to Stimulate Competition in the State of São Paulo from 2011." www.fem.unicamp.br.

Santarcángelo, Juan E., and Guido Perrone. 2012. "La Cúpula Empresaria Argentina y su Rol en el Desarrollo Económico." *Problemas del Desarrollo* 43(168) (January–March): 37–62.

Santiso, Javier. 2006. *Latin America's Political Economy of the Possible. Beyond Good Revolutionaries and Free Marketeers.* Cambridge, MA: MIT Press.

Santiso, Javier, and Jeff Dayton-Johnson. 2012. *The Oxford Handbook of Latin American Political Economy.* New York, NY: Oxford University Press.

"Sao Paulo-Santos: Logistics Corridor Program." *DuisPort*, June 3, 2012.

Sapir, André. 2012. "Europe after the Crisis: Less or More Role for Nation States in Money and Finance? *Oxford Review of Economic Policy* 27(4) (December): 608–619.

Sassen, Saskia. 2006. *Territory, Authority, Rights: From Medieval to Global Assemblages.* Princeton, NJ: Princeton University Press.

Savas, Emanuel S. 2000. *Privatization and Public-Private Partnerships.* New York, NY: Chatham House.

Saxton, Jim. 2003. "Argentina's Economic Crisis: Causes and Cures." Presented at Joint Economic Committee, US Senate, June.

Saylor, Ryan. 2012. "Sources of State Capacity in Latin America: Commodity Booms and State Building Motives in Chile." *Theory and Society* 41(3) (May): 301–324.

Scartascini, Carlos, and Mariano Tommasi. 2012. "The Making of Policy: Institutionalized or Not?" *American Journal of Political Science* 56(4) (October): 787–801.

Schamis, Hector E. 1999. "Distributional Coalitions and the Politics of Economic Reform in Latin America." *World Politics* 51(2) (January): 236–268.

Schamis, Hector E. 2002. *Re-Forming the State: The Politics of Privatization in Latin America and Europe.* Ann Arbor, MI: University of Michigan Press.

Scharpf, Fritz. 1997. *Games Real Actors Play: Actor-Centered Institutionalism in Policy Research.* Boulder, CO: Westview Press.

Schneider, Ben Ross. 1991. *Politics within the State: Elite Bureaucrats and Industrial Policy in Authoritarian Brazil.* Pittsburgh, PA: University of Pittsburgh Press.

Schneider, Ben Ross. 1998. "Elusive Synergy: Business-Government Relations and Development." *Comparative Politics* 31(1) (October): 101–122.

Schneider, Ben Ross. 2010. "Business Politics and Policy Making in Contemporary Latin America." In Carlos Scartascini, Ernesto Stein, and Mariano Tommasi, eds. *How Democracy Works: Political Institutions, Actors and Arenas in Latin American Policymaking.* Washington, DC: Inter-American Development Bank and David Rockefeller Center for Latin American Studies, Harvard University, 217–246.

Schneider, Ben Ross, and Blanca Heredia, eds. 2003. *Reinventing Leviathan: The Politics of Administrative Reform in Developing Countries.* Miami, FL: North-South Center Press of the University of Miami.

Schneider, Ronald. 2008. *Caribbean Crusader: Leonel Fernandez and the Transformation of the Dominican Republic.* Pittsburgh, PA: Dorrance.

Scott, Colin. 2008. "Privatization and Regulatory Regimes." In *The Oxford Handbook of Public Policy.* Oxford, UK: Oxford University Press, 659–669.

Sheahan, John. 1999. *Searching for a Better Society: The Peruvian Economy from 1950.* University Park, PA: The Pennsylvania State University.

Shirley, Mary M. 2008. *Institutions and Development.* Northampton, MA: Edward Elgar.

Siemens Financial Services. 2007. "Public Infrastructure and Private Funding." Brochure.

Sikkink, Kathryn. 1991. *Ideas and Institutions: Developmentalism in Brazil and Argentina.* Ithaca, NY: Cornell University Press.

Silva, Eduardo 1996a. *The State and Capital in Chile: Business Elites, Technocrats and Market Economics.* Boulder, CO: Westview Press.

Silva, Eduardo. 1996b. "From Dictatorship to Democracy: The Business-State Nexus in Chile's Economic Transformation, 1975–1994. *Comparative Politics* 28(3) (April): 299–320.

Silvia, Eduardo. 1999, "Organized Business, Neo-Liberal Restructuring and Redemocratization in Chile." In Francisco Durand and Eduardo Silva, eds. *Organized Business, Economic Change, and Democracy in Latin America.* Miami, FL: North-South Center Press, 217–252.

Silva, Eduardo. 2009a. *Challenging Neoliberalism in Latin America.* New York, NY: Cambridge University Press.

Silva, Eduardo. 2009b. *In the Name of Reason: Technocrats and Politics in Chile.* University Park, PA: Pennsylvania State University.

Silva, Michael Pinheiro, and Lino Guimarães Marujo. 2012. "Análise de modelo intermodal para escoamento da produção da soja no centro oeste brasileiro." *Journal of Transport Literature* 6(3): 90–106.

Silveira, Márcio Rogério. 2003. "A importância geoeconômica das estradas de ferro no Brasil." Doctoral Thesis, Universidade Estadual Paulista, São Paulo.

Simmons, Beth A., and Zachary Elkins. 2004. "The Globalization of Liberalization: Policy Diffusion in the International Political Economy." *American Political Science Review* 98(1) (February): 171–189.

Simmons, Beth, Frank Dobbin, and Geoffrey Garrett, eds. 2007. *The Global Diffusion of Markets and Democracy.* Cambridge, UK: Cambridge University Press.

Sims, Brian G., and Josef Kienzle. 2009. "Farm Equipment Supply Chains: Guidelines for Policy-Makers and Service Providers: Experiences from Kenya, Pakistan, and Brazil." Report 7, Food and Agriculture Organization of the United Nations, Rome.

Sinnott, Emily, John Nash, and Augusto de la Torre. 2010. *Natural Resources in Latin America and the Caribbean: Beyond Booms and Busts.* World Bank, Commodities Report.

Sirtaine, Sophie, Maria Elena Pinglo, José Luis Guasch, and Vivien Foster. 2005. "How Profitable are Private Infrastructure Concessions in Latin America? Empirical Evidence and Regulatory Implications." *Quarterly Review of Economics and Finance* 45(2–3) (May): 380–402.

Smith, Peter H., ed. 1995. *Latin America in Comparative Perspective: New Approaches to Methods and Analysis.* Latin American Global Perspective Series. Boulder, CO: Westview Press.

Smith, William C. 1989. *Authoritarianism and the Crisis of the Argentine Political Economy.* Palo Alto, CA: Stanford University Press.

Smith, William C., Carlos H. Acuña, and Eduardo A. Gamarra, eds. 1994. *Latin American Political Economy in the Age of Neoliberal Reform: Theoretical and Comparative Perspective for the 1990s.* Miami, FL: North-South Center Press.

Solimano, Andrés. 2012. *Chile and the Neoliberal Trap: The Post-Pinochet Era.* New York, NY: Cambridge University Press.

Sorensen, Eva, and Jacob Torfing. 2005. "The Democratic Anchorage of Governance Networks." *Scandinavian Political Studies* 28(3) (September):195–218.

Spiller, Pablo T., and Mariano Tommasi. 2007. *The Institutional Foundations of Public Policy in Argentina: A Transactions Cost Approach.* New York, NY: Cambridge University Press.

Stallings, Barbara. 1978. *Class Conflict and Economic Development in Chile, 1958–1973.* Palo Alto, CA: Stanford University Press.

Stallings, Barbara, and William Peres. 2000. *Growth, Employment, and Equity: The Impact of the Economic Reforms in Latin America and the Caribbean.* Washington, DC: Brookings Institution Press.

Stallings, Barbara. 2003. "Globalization and Liberalization: The Impact on Developing Countries." In Atul Kohli et al., eds. *States, Markets, and Just Growth: Development in the Twenty-first Century.* Tokyo: United Nations University Press.

Stallings, Barbara, and William Peres. 2011. "Is Economic Reform Dead in Latin America? Rhetoric and Reality since 2000." *Journal of Latin American Studies* 43(4) (November): 755–786.

Standard and Poor's. 2005. "Public-Private Partnerships." Global Credit Survey, Infrastructure & Public Finance Ratings, May.

Steiner, Roberto, and Hernán Vallejo. 2010. "Mining and Energy." In Rex A. Hudson, ed. *Colombia: A Country Study.* 5th ed. Washington, DC: Library of Congress, 160–186.

Stephan, Alfred. 1978. *The State and Society: Peru in Comparative Perspective.* Princeton, NJ: Princeton University Press.

Stiglitz, Joseph. 2002. *Globalization and its Discontents.* New York, NY: W. W. Norton.

Stokes, Susan C. .2001a. "Economic Reform and Public Opinion in Fujimori's Peru." In Susan C. Stokes, ed. *Public Support for Market Reforms in New Democracies.* Cambridge, UK: Cambridge University Press.

Stokes, Susan C., ed. 2001b. *Public Support for Market Reforms in New Democracies.* Cambridge, UK: Cambridge University Press.

Stone, Diane. 2002. "Introduction: Global Knowledge and Advocacy Networks." *Global Networks* 2(1) (January): 1–12.

Strange, Susan. 1988. *States and Markets*. London, UK: Continuum.

Strange, Susan. 1996. *The Retreat of the State: The Diffusion of Power in the World Economy*. Cambridge, UK: Cambridge University Press.

Straub, Stephane. 2008. "Infrastructure and Development: A Critical Appraisal of the Macro Level Literature." Policy Research Working Paper 4460. Washington, DC: World Bank.

Suplee, Curt. 1999. "El Niño/La Niña: Nature's Vicious Cycle." *National Geographic Magazine*, March.

"Taming Leviathan" A Special Report on the Future of the State. *The Economist*, March 17, 2011.

Tankha, Sunil. 2009. "Lost in Translation: Interpreting the Failure of Privatisation in the Brazilian Electric Power Industry." *Journal of Latin American Studies* 41(1) (February): 59–90.

Tanzi, Vito. 2009. "The Economic Role of the State before and after the Current Crisis." Paper presented at the 65th Congress of the International Institute of Public Finance, August 13.

Tanzi, Vito, and Ludger Schuknecht. 2000. *Public Spending in the 20th Century: A Global Perspective*. Cambridge, UK and New York: Cambridge University Press.

"Tarjetas bip! se podrá cargar desde febrero vía internet." *La Nación*, January 14, 2014.

Tavares, Maria da Conceição. 1972. "Auge e Declínio do Processo de Substituição de Importações no Brasil." In *Da Substituição de Importações ao Capitalismo Financeiro*. Rio de Janeiro, Brazil: Zahar, 27–124.

Tavener, Ben. "R$400B Investment Awaiting Approval." *The Rio Times*, June 12, 2012. www.riotimesonline.com.

Teichman, Judith A. 1988. *Policymaking in Mexico: From Boom to Crisis*. Boston, MA: Unwin Hyman.

Teichman, Judith A. 1995. *Privatization and Political Change in Mexico*. Pittsburgh, PA: University of Pittsburgh Press.

Teichman, Judith A. 2001. *The Politics of Freeing Markets in Latin America: Chile, Argentina, and Mexico*. Chapel Hill, NC: University of North Carolina Press.

Teichman, Judith A. 2004. "The World Bank and Policy Reform in Mexico and Argentina." *Latin American Politics and Society* 46(1) (Spring): 39–74.

Tenbensel, Tim. 2005. "Multiple Modes of Governance." *Public Management Review* 7(2) (June): 267–288.

Tendler, Judith. 2001. "Public-Private Collaborations: Influence, Politics, and Upgrading." Working Paper, Massachusetts Institute of Technology, Cambridge.

Thatcher, Mark. 1998. "The Development of Policy Network Analyses: From Modest Origins to Overarching Frameworks." *Journal of Theoretical Politics* 10(4) (October): 389–416.

The Economist. 2009a. "Partnerships for Progress? Evaluating the Environment for Public-Private Partnerships in Latin America and the Caribbean." Study by the Economist Intelligence Unit, Commissioned by the World Bank's Multilateral Investment Fund, June.

The Economist. 2009b. "Uruguay's elections: The mystery behind Mujica's mask." October 22. www.economist.com.

The Economist. 2010. "Brazilian Agriculture: The Miracle of the Cerrado." August 26.

The Economist. 2011. "America's Transport Infrastructure: Life in the Slow Lane." April 28.

The Economist. 2013a. "Evaluating the Environment for Public-Private Partnership in Latin America and the Caribbean: The 2012 Infrascope." Report of the Economist Intelligence Unit, Commissioned by the IDB, February.

The Economist. 2013b. "The Gated Globe." October 12.

The World Bank Group. 2010. "Private Participation in Infrastructure Database." www.ppi.worldbank.org.

Thelen, Kathlen. 2012. "Varieties of Capitalism: Trajectories of Liberalization and the New Politics of Social Solidarity." *Annual Review of Political Science* 15 (June): 137–159.

Thorps, Rosemary, and Francisco Durand. 1997. "A Historical View of Business-State Relations: Colombia, Peru and Venezuela Compared." In Sylvia Maxfield and Ben Ross Schneider, eds. *Business and the State in Developing Countries*. Ithaca, NY: Cornell University Press, 216–236.

Tilly, Charles. 2006. "Why And How History Matters." In Robert E. Goodin and Charles Tilly, eds. *The Oxford Handbook Of Contextual Political Analysis*. Nova Iorque: Oxford University Press, 417, 437, 102.

Tilly, Charles. 2007. *Democracy*. New York, NY: Cambridge University Press.

Tironi, Eugenio. 2005. *El sueño chileno*. Santiago, Chile: Taurus Editorial.

Tommasi, Mariano. 2010. "Un País Sin Rumbo: Política, Políticas Públicas y el Desarrollo en la Argentina (con una breve comparación al caso chileno." *Desarrollo Económico* 50(199) (October–December): 391–421.

Tommasi, Mariano. 2011. "Latin America: How State Capacity Determines Policy Success." *Governance* 24(2) (April): 199–203.

UN Comtrade (United Nations Commodity Trade Statistics Database). Department of Economic and Social Affairs/Statistics Division. http://comtrade.un.org/db/.

UNDP (United Nations Development Programme). 2009. *Human Development Report 2009: Overcoming Barriers, Human Mobility and Development*. New York, NY: Palgrave Macmillan.

UNECE (United Nations Economic Commission for Europe). 2008. *Guidebook on Promoting Good Governance in Public-Private Partnerships*. Geneva: United Nations.

United Nations. 1998. *Public-Private Partnerships: A New Concept for Infrastructure Development*. New York, NY: BOT Expert Group.

US Department of Commerce. 2005. "Brazilian Infrastructure: Highways, Railways, and Airports." CS Brazil Market Research.

USDA (US Department of Agriculture). 2012. "Bolivia: Oilseeds and Products." Annual report, prepared by Gaspar E. Nolte.

USDA. 2014. "North and Northeast Brazil Port Infrastructure Report." GAIN Report January 10.

Vagliasindi, Maria. 2012. *Implementing Energy Subsidy Reforms: Evidence from Developing Countries (Directions in Development)*. Washington, DC: International Bank for Reconstruction and Development/ World Bank.

Valdés, Juan Gabriel. 1995. *Pinochet's Economists: The Chicago School in Chile*. Cambridge, UK: Cambridge University Press.

Vásquez, Carla. "¿Cómo se distribuyen los fondos del Transantiago?" *La Tercera*, August 2, 2014.

Vellinga, Menno. 1998. "The Changing Role of the State in Latin America." In Menno Vellinga, ed. *The Changing Role of the State in Latin America*. Boulder, CO: Westview Press, 1–25.

Vilaça, Rodrigo. 2008. "Desafios do crescimento ferroviario." Associação Nacional dos Transportadores Ferroviarios (ANTF), October 21.

Vivallos, Leonel. 2003. "La experiencia de Chile en el otorgamiento de concesiones de obras viales: Lecciones y desafíos." ECLAC, Coordinación General de Concesiones, Ministerio de Obras Públicas, República de Chile.

Vos, Rob, Margarita Velasco, and Edgar Labastida. 1999. "Economic and Social Effects of El Niño in Ecuador, 1997–1998." Sustainable Development Department Technical Paper Series, Inter-American Development Bank, Washington, DC.

Vos, Rob, ed. 2003. *¿Quién se beneficia del gasto social en el Ecuador?: desafíos para mejorar la calidad y eficiencia del gasto social*. Quito, Ecuador: Unidad de Información y Análisis (SIISE) de la Secretaría Técnica del Frente Social.

Wade, Jeffry S. 2012. "The Future of Urban Water Services in Latin America." *Bulletin of Latin American Research* 31(2) (April): 207–221.

Wade, Robert. 2003. "What Strategies are Viable for Developing Countries Today? The World Trade Organization and the Shrinking of 'Development Space.'" *Review of International Political Economy* 10(4) (November): 621–644.

Wade, Robert. 2004. *Governing the Market: Economic Theory and the role of the government in East Asian Industrialization*. Princeton, NJ: Princeton University Press.

Waissbluth, Mario. 2006. "La Reforma del Estado en Chile, 1990–2005: De la Confrontación al Consenso." *Boletín Electrónico de Esade*, Barcelona.

Waldner, David. 1999. *State Building and Late Development*. Ithaca, NY: Cornell University Press.

Walter, Powell W., and Paul J. DiMaggio. 1991. *The New Institutionalism in Organizational Analysis*. Chicago, IL: Chicago University Press.

Way, Christopher R. 2005. "Political Insecurity and the Diffusion of Financial Market Regulation." *Annals of the American Academy of Political and Social Science* 598(1) (March): 125–144.

Weber, Max. 1958. *The Protestant Ethic and the Spirit of Capitalism*. Trans. Talcott Parsons. New York, NY: Scribners.

Weber, Max. 1968. *Economy and Society*. New York: Bedminster

Weihe, Guri. 2005. "Public-Private Partnerships: Addressing a Nebulous Concept." Working Paper 16, Copenhagen Business School, International Center for Business and Politics, Denmark.

Weiss, Linda. 1998. *The Myth of the Powerless State*. Ithaca, NY: Cornell University Press.

Weiss, Linda. 2003. "Guiding globalisation in East Asia: new roles for old developmental states." In Linda Weiss, ed. *States in the Global Economy: Bringing Domestic Institutions Back In*. Cambridge, UK: Cambridge University Press, 245–270.

Wettenhall, Roger. 2008. "Public-Private Mixes and Partnerships: A Search for Understanding." *The Asia Pacific Journal of Public Administration* 30(2) (December): 119–138.

Weyland, Kurt. 1996. "Neopopulism and Neoliberalism in Latin America: Unexpected Affinities." *Studies in Comparative International Development* 31(3) (Fall): 3–31

Weyland, Kurt. 2002. *The Politics of Market Reform in Fragile Democracies: Argentina, Brazil, Peru, and Venezuela*. Princeton, NJ: Princeton University Press.

Weyland, Kurt. 2004. "Assessing Latin American Neoliberalism: Introduction to a Debate." *Latin American Research Review* 39(3) (October): 143–149.

Weyland, Kurt. 2008. "Toward a New Theory of Institutional Change." *World Politics* 60(2) (January): 281–314.

Wheatley, Jonathan. 2010. "Brazil to Spend R$958.9bn on Infrastructure." *Financial Times*, March 29, 2010. São Paulo, Brazil

Whitfield, Dexter. 2010. *Global Auction of Public Assets: Public Sector Alternatives to the Infrastructure Market and Public Private Partnerships*. Nottingham, UK: Spokesman.

Williamson, John, ed. 1990. *Latin American Adjustment: How Much Has Happened*. Washington, DC: Institute for International Economics.

Williamson, John, ed. 1994. *The Political Economy of Policy Reform*. Washington, DC: Institute for International Economics.

Wise, Carol. 2003. *Reinventing the State: Economic Strategy and Institutional Change in Peru*. Ann Arbor, MI: University of Michigan Press.

Wise, Carol. 2006. "Learning from Foreign Models: Latin America Policy Reform (review)." *Latin American Politics & Society* 48(3) (Fall): 203–208.

Wise, Carol, and Manuel Pastor Jr. 2005. "The Lost Sexenio: Vicente Fox and the New Politics of Economic Reform in Mexico." *Latin American Politics and Society* 47(4) (Winter): 135–160.

Wong, Joseph. 2004. "The Adaptive Developmental State in East Asia." *Journal of East Asian Studies* 4(3) (September–December):345–362.

Wood, Charles H., and Bryan R. Roberts, eds. 2005. *Rethinking Development In Latin America*. University Park, PA: Pennsylvania State University Press.

Woodhouse, Derek M. 2009. "Regulatory Framework for the Development of Public-Private Partnerships in Mexican States." First Technical Gathering for Training Regarding the Structuring of Public-Private Partnership Projects organized by the IADB under the PIAPPEM in Mexico City, February 19–20.

World Bank. 1993. *The East Asian Miracle: Economic Growth and Public Policy*. Washington, DC: World Bank.

World Bank. 1994. *World Development Report: Infrastructure for Development*. Washington, DC: World Bank.

World Bank. 2003. *Private Solutions for Infrastructure in Mexico*. A Country Framework Report. Washington, DC: Public-Private Infrastructure Advisory Facility (PPIAF) and World Bank.

World Bank. 2004. *World Development Report 2005: A Better Investment Climate for Everyone*. Washington, DC: World Bank.

World Bank. 2005. *Infrastructure in Latin America: Recent Developments and Key Challenges*. Washington, DC: World Bank.

World Bank. 2006. "Peru: Rethinking Private Sector Participation in Infrastructure." Report No. 32674-PE, World Bank, June 30.

World Bank. 2014a. Private Participation in Infrastructure Project Database (PPI). www.ppi.worldbank.org, accessed November 2014.

World Bank. 2014b. World Development Indicators. Data.worldbank.org, accessed November 14, 2014.

World Economic Forum. 2012. *The Global Competitiveness Report 2012–2013*. Geneva, Switzerland: World Economic Forum.

World Trade Organization. 2013. Statistics Database.

Wylde, Christopher. 2011. "State, Society and Markets in Argentina: The Political Economy of 'Neodesarrollismo' under Néstor Kirchner, 2003–2007." *Bulletin of Latin American Research* 30(4) (October): 436–452.

Yáñez, María Francisca, Patricio Manzilla, and Juan de Dios Ortúzar. 2010. "The Santiago Panel: Measuring the Effects of Implementing Transantiago." *Transportation* 39(1) (January): 125–149.

Yashar, Deborah J. 2005. *Contesting Citizenship in Latin America: The Rise of Indigenous Movements and the Postliberal Challenge*. New York, NY: Cambridge University Press.

Yepes, Tito. 2008. "New Estimates of Infrastructure Expenditure Requirements." Washington, DC: World Bank.

Yescombe, E. R. 2007. *Public-Private Partnerships: Principles of Policy and Finance*. New York, NY: Elsevier.

Zamosc, Leon. 2007. "The Indian Movement and Political Democracy in Ecuador." *Latin American Politics and Society* 49 (3) (Fall): 1–34.

INDEX

Page numbers in italics denote Figures and Tables

Printed and bound in the United States of America